Marxism and Anarchism

Including selections by Frederick Engels, V. I. Lenin, Leon Trotsky, Alan Woods, and others

wellred
•books

London

Marxism and Anarchism

Marxism and Anarchism second edition published in April 2015.
Copyright © Wellred Books. All rights reserved.

Editing for this edition by Wellred Books, based on the 2012 edition layout by Steve Iverson, Josh Lucker and the editorial board of Socialist Appeal (www.socialistappeal.org). Copyright © Wellred USA, 2012.

Layout by Guy Howie based on US edition.

Printed by Lightning Source, England.

Cover photo: 1000 Words / Shutterstock.com

ISBN — 978 1 900 007 53 5

United Kingdom Distribution:
Wellred Books
PO Box 50525
London
E14 6WG
books@wellredbooks.net
www.wellredbooks.net

United States Distribution:
Wellred Books
PO Box 1575
New York
NY 10013
sales@wellredusa.com
www.marxistbooks.com

Contents

Introduction

Alan Woods

The present period is the most stormy and convulsive period in history. Globalisation now manifests itself as a global crisis of capitalism. Given the depth of the crisis and the worsening conditions, things are developing very quickly. The stage is set for a general revival of the class struggle, and in fact, this process has already begun.

The most striking manifestation of the changed situation is the emergence of a worldwide protest movement that is rejecting capitalism and all of its works. A growing number of people are reacting against the crying injustice of the existing order: the unemployment that condemns millions to enforced inactivity; the gross inequality, which concentrates obscene wealth and impoverishment for the vast majority of the world's population; and the endless wars, racism, and restrictions on "life, liberty, and the pursuit of happiness."

The top one percent of the USA owns 34.6% of the wealth in total net worth; the next 19% owns 50.5%; the bottom 80% owns only 15%. In financial wealth, the figures are even more startling: 42.7%, 50.3%, and 7.0% respectively. These statistics are from 2007, but the most recent complete data show that the recession has meant a massive drop of 36.1% in median household wealth as compared to 11.1% for the top one percent, further widening the gulf between the obscenely rich and the rest of us—the 99%.

The 2008–09 recession has meant an even greater increase in inequality: further enrichment for the super-rich and more poverty for the poorest. The revolting spectacle of wealthy bankers walking away from the crisis with billions of dollars of public money while over 10 million mortgages are set to default and the unemployed stand in line for food handouts is stoking the fires of mass indignation.

In "normal" circumstances most people do not protest. They remain passive spectators of a historic drama that is played out before their eyes, in which they play no part but which determines their lives and fate. But every once in a while, people are shaken out of their apparent apathy by great events—such as a war or an economic crisis. They begin to take action, to take an interest in politics and to try to regain control over their lives.

Such moments in history have a name: they are called revolutions. Such was the American Revolution of 1776; the French Revolution of 1789–93; the revolutionary movements in Europe in 1848; the Paris Commune of 1871; the Russian Revolutions of 1905 and 1917; the Spanish Revolution of 1931–37; and more recently, the Egyptian and Tunisian Revolutions.

The events that are unfolding before our eyes have many of the features of the early stages of a revolutionary situation. Many people who hitherto took little or no interest in politics now find themselves in the streets protesting and demonstrating against a social and political order that has become intolerable.

There is an old saying: "life teaches." This is very true. The workers and students in Tahrir Square learned more in 24 hours of struggle than in twenty years of "normal" existence. Similarly, the experience of the participants of the Occupy movement in the USA and other countries is being compressed time-wise. It will not take 20 years for them to absorb the lessons. People are learning fast.

Under these conditions, the ideas of libertarianism, anarchism, and socialism are all making a revival, as the youth and workers search for an explanation of the crisis and a road forward. The heroic "glory days" of the Industrial Workers of the World are being revived in the minds of many young people as they fight to form unions in their minimum-wage workplaces. Anarchist writers such as Proudhon, Kropotkin, Bakunin and Durruti are being rediscovered by new layers of youth. Authors such as Howard Zinn, Michael Albert, and Noam Chomsky, who expose the evils of imperialism and capitalism, are being eagerly read by a new generation.

Insofar as they open peoples' eyes as to the undemocratic and exploitative nature of capitalist society, the growing interest in these ideas is extremely positive. Anarchism is appealing to many young people due to its simplicity: to reject anything and everything to do with the status quo. But upon deeper examination, there is a pervasive lack of real substance and depth of analysis in these ideas. Above all, there is very little in the way of an actually viable *solution* to the crisis of capitalism. After reading their material, one is inevitably left asking: "but what is to replace capitalism, and how can we make this a reality, starting from the conditions actually existing today?"

It is this author's contention that only the ideas of Marxism can provide a theoretical guide to action that can actually harness the movement's energy into the revolutionary transformation of society. Not Stalinism—that bureaucratic, undemocratic, totalitarian caricature of socialism; and not the lifeless, mechanical, deterministic "Marxism" of the academic world—but genuine Marxism: the most modern, dynamic, and all-encompassing tools of social analysis yet developed by humanity. Only these ideas can provide not only an analysis, but a revolutionary socialist solution to the crisis facing the world working class.

The publication of this volume marks an important step forward in the theoretical arming of a new generation of class fighters in the US The question of Marxism vs Anarchism has long been discussed. It is no accident that as the class struggle again boils to the surface, the old debates are being revived. Many people newly awakening to political life imagine that they are involved in something entirely new and original; but as the Bible says, there is nothing new under the sun. And although they do not know it, many of these debates have already taken place in the past.

There are many misconceptions about the history, genesis, and real content of both Marxism and anarchism. We can and should learn from the collective experience of our class; from what has worked and what has not worked. This collection of writings will go a long way towards clarifying the Marxist perspective on the limitations of anarchism, and the need for a party, theory, programme, perspectives, organisation, internal democracy, and accountability.

Limits of spontaneity

The millions of people who have come out onto the streets and squares of Spain and Greece to oppose the policy of cuts and austerity do not trust the politicians and trade union leaders. And who can blame them? In both Greece and Spain the governments that carried out these attacks were supposed to be "socialist." The masses deposited their confidence in them, and found themselves betrayed. They conclude that in order to defend their interests they must not leave things to the politicians but take action themselves.

This shows a correct revolutionary instinct. Those who sneer at the movement as "merely spontaneous" display their ignorance of the essence of a revolution, which is precisely the direct intervention of the masses in politics. This spontaneity is an enormous strength—but at a certain point it will become a fatal weakness of the movement.

Those who criticise the protest movement because it lacks a clear programme show their ignorance of what a revolution is. This kind of approach is worthy of a pedant and a snob, but never a revolutionary. A revolution, by its very essence, stirs society up to the depths, arousing even the most backward and "apolitical" layers into direct action. To demand of the masses a perfect understanding of what is required is to demand the impossible.

Of course, the mass movement will necessarily suffer from confusion in its initial stages. The masses can only overcome these shortcomings through their direct experience of the struggle. But if we are to succeed, it is absolutely necessary to pass beyond the initial confusion and naïveté, to grow and mature, and to draw the correct conclusions.

Those "anarchist" leaders—yes, the anarchists also have leaders, or people who aspire to lead—who believe that confusion, organisational amorphousness, and the absence of ideological definition and are both positive and necessary, play a pernicious role. It is like trying to maintain a child in a state of childishness, so that it is forever unable to talk, walk, and think for itself.

Many times in the history of warfare, a big army composed of brave but untrained soldiers has been defeated by a smaller force of disciplined and well-trained professional troops led by skilled and experienced officers. To occupy the squares is a means of mobilising the masses in action. But in itself it is not enough. The ruling class may not be able to evict the protesters initially by force, but they can afford to wait until the movement begins to die down, and then act decisively to put an end to the "disturbances."

It goes without saying that the Marxists will always be in the first line of any battle to improve the conditions of the working class. We will fight for any conquest, no matter how small, because the fight for socialism would be unthinkable without the day-to-day struggle for advances under capitalism. Only through a series of partial struggles, of a defensive and offensive character, can the masses discover their own strength and acquire the confidence necessary to fight to the end. There are certain circumstances in which strikes and mass demonstrations can force the ruling class to make concessions. But in the conditions prevailing today, this is not one of them.

In order to succeed it is necessary to take the movement to a higher level. This can only be done by linking it firmly to the movement of the workers in the factories and the trade unions. The slogan of the general strike has already come to the fore in an embryonic form. But even a general strike in and of itself cannot solve the problems of society. It must eventually be linked to the need for an indefinite general strike, which directly poses the question of state power.

Confused and vacillating leaders are capable of producing only defeats and demoralisation. The struggle of the workers and youth would be infinitely easier if they were led by courageous and farsighted people. But such leaders do not fall from the skies. In the course of struggle, the masses will put to the test every tendency and leader. They will soon discover the deficiencies of those accidental figures that appear in the early stages of the revolutionary movement, like the foam that appears on the crest of the wave, and who will vanish as the waves crash into the shore, just like that foam.

These spontaneous movements are the consequence of decades of bureaucratic and reformist degeneration of the traditional parties and unions. In part, this represents a healthy reaction, as Lenin wrote in *The State and Revolution*, when he referred to the anarchists. Movements like the *indignados* in Spain arise because most workers and youth feel they are not represented by anybody. They are not anarchists. They display confusion and lack a clear programme. But then, where would they get clear ideas from?

The new movements are an expression of the deep crisis of the capitalist system. On the other hand, the new movements themselves have not understood the seriousness of the situation. For all their energy and élan, these movements have limitations that will quickly be exposed. The occupation of squares and parks, though it can be a potent statement, ultimately leads nowhere. More radical measures are necessary to bring about a root-and-branch transformation of society.

Unless the movement is taken to a higher level, at a certain stage, it will subside, leaving the people disappointed and demoralised. Upon reflection of their experience, an increasing number of activists will come to see the need for a consistent revolutionary programme. It is the contention of this writer that this can only be provided by Marxism.

Do we need a leadership?

The argument that we don't need parties and leaders is false to the core. As a matter of fact it is not even logical. It is not enough to reject something you don't like. You must say what is to be put in its place.

If my shoe pinches my foot, the answer is not to go barefoot, but to get a shoe that fits. If our food is bad, the conclusion is not that we must go without food altogether, but that we need decent, tasty, wholesome food. If I am not satisfied with my doctor, I look for a better one. Why should it be any different with a party or leadership?

The present leadership of the working class is very bad. We agree with the anarchists on this. But the conclusion is not that we do not need any leadership. It is that we must fight to replace the present leadership with one that really represents the interests and aspirations of the working class. We stand for the revolutionary transformation of society. The objective conditions for such a transformation are more than ripe. We firmly believe that the working class is equipped for such a task. How then can we doubt that the workers will be able to transform their own organisations into fighting vehicles to change society? If they cannot accomplish even that, how will they possibly overthrow the whole of capitalism itself?

Many young people, when they look at the existing organisations of the working class, the trade unions and especially the mass workers parties, are repelled by their bureaucratic structures and the conduct of their leaders, who are constantly hobnobbing with the bankers and capitalists. They appear to be just another part of the Establishment. In the US there is not yet even a mass party of labour. So it is no wonder that many people reject all parties and even claim to reject politics entirely.

However, this is a contradiction in terms. The Occupy movement itself is profoundly political. In rejecting the *existing* political parties, they immediately put themselves forward as an alternative. But what sort of an alternative? It is not enough to say: "we are against the present system because it is unjust, oppressive and inhuman." It is necessary to propose an alternative system that would be just, egalitarian and humane.

Although they are still very weak, anarchist trends have been growing recently as a result of the bankruptcy of the reformist leaders of the mass workers organisations. The monstrous opportunism of the workers' leaders gives rise to ultra-left and anarchist moods among a layer of the youth. As Lenin once said, ultra-leftism is the price the movement has to pay for opportunism.

At first sight the idea seems attractive: "Just look at the labour leaders! They are just a lot of bureaucrats and careerists who always sell us out. We don't need leaders! We don't need organisation!" Unfortunately, without organisation we can accomplish nothing. The trade unions may be far from perfect, but they are all that the workers have to prevent the capitalists from trampling them underfoot.

The bosses understand the danger posed to them by the unions. That is why they are always trying to undermine the unions, restrict their rights, and smash them altogether. We can see that with anti-union laws such as Taft-Hartley which have severely restricted the workers' right to strike. Scott Walker, the Republican governor of Wisconsin, introduced anti-union legislation to disarm the workers in the face of savage cuts. In Ohio, a similar attempt was defeated in a referendum by the people, who understood the need to defend the unions.

"But the union leaders are bureaucrats! They are always striving to do deals with the bosses!" Maybe so, but what alternative do you propose? Can we do without the unions? That would reduce the working class to a collection of isolated atoms at the mercy of the bosses. Marx pointed out long ago that without organisation the working class is just raw material for exploitation. The task is not to throw out the baby with the bathwater, but to transform the unions into militant, fighting, class-struggle organisations.

More than at any other period in history, the leadership of the workers' organisations has come under the pressure of the bourgeoisie. They have abandoned the ideas upon which the movement was founded and become divorced from the class they are supposed to represent. They represent the past, not the present or the future. The masses will push them to the left or sweep them aside in the stormy period that now opens up.

Without the aid of the reformists, Stalinists, and the class-collaborationist trade union leaders, it would not be possible to maintain the capitalist system for any length of time. This is an important idea which we have to stress continually. The leaders of the trade unions and reformist parties in all countries have colossal power in their hands—far greater than at any other time in history.

In the final analysis, the labour bureaucracy is the most conservative force in society. They use their authority to support the capitalist system. That is why Trotsky said that the crisis of humanity was reduced to a crisis of leadership of the proletariat. The fate of humanity depends on the resolution of this problem. But anarchism is not capable of resolving this problem, since it does not even accept that the problem exists.

It is necessary to fight to drive the bureaucrats and careerists from their positions, to purge the labour organisations of bourgeois elements, and replace them with men and women who are really prepared to fight for the working class. To advocate abstentionism, to refuse to fight for a change of leadership, is to advocate the perpetuation of the rule of the bureaucracy; that is, for the perpetuation of capitalist slavery. As Trotsky explained, to refuse to struggle for political or trade union power means to leave that power in the hands of those who now hold it.

"One big union"?

The IWW (Industrial Workers of the World) did outstanding work before the First World War organising the unorganised sections of the working class— the farm hands and unskilled workers, the dock workers, lumberjacks and the immigrants. The slogan "One Big Union" served as an inspiring rallying point in opposition to the conservative craft unionism of the old AFL.

The "Wobblies," as they were known, led important strikes, starting with Goldfield, Nevada in 1906 and the Pressed Steel Car Strike of 1909 at McKees Rocks, Pennsylvania; the Lawrence textile strike in 1912; and the Paterson silk strike in 1913. They often faced ferocious repression, beatings and lynching. Joe Hill (Joel Hägglund), the "Wobbly bard" who wrote inspiring verses and songs, was accused of murder and was executed by the state of Utah in 1915 on the flimsiest of evidence.

At the founding convention of the IWW, Bill Haywood, then the General Secretary of the Western Federation of Miners, said: "This is the Continental Congress of the working class. We are here to confederate the workers of this country into a working class movement that shall have for its purpose the emancipation of the working class from the slave bondage of capitalism." (*Proceedings of the First Convention of the Industrial Workers of the World*)

The IWW was consistently revolutionary and based itself on the most intransigent class struggle doctrines. It was never an anarchist organisation, but it lacked a coherent and consistent ideology. One might say that its ideology was a strange mixture of anarcho-syndicalism and Marxism. This contradiction was soon exposed in an early debate. Daniel De Leon, the pioneering American Marxist, was a founding member of the IWW in 1905. But he disagreed with the leaders of the IWW over their opposition to political action.

Whereas De Leon argued for support of political action via the Socialist Labour Party, other leaders, including Big Bill Haywood, argued instead for direct action. Haywood's faction prevailed, and as a result the Preamble was altered to preclude "affiliation with any political party." De Leon's followers left the IWW in protest. That was a mistake, because life itself made people like Big Bill Haywood change his mind.

In fact, the IWW borrowed heavily from Marxism. The two main planks in its platform, the doctrine of the class struggle and the idea that the emancipation of the workers must be the task of the workers themselves, came straight from Marx. The truth is that the IWW was more than just a union. It was at the same time a militant industrial union and a revolutionary organisation—an embryonic revolutionary party. This was soon demonstrated by the stormy events surrounding the First World War and the Russian Revolution.

The IWW was internationalist to the core. They opposed the First World War, as did the Russian Bolsheviks. An IWW newspaper, the *Industrial Worker*, wrote just before the US declaration of war: "Capitalists of America, we will fight against you, not for you! There is not a power in the world that can make the working class fight if they refuse." The organisation passed a resolution against the war at its convention in November 1916. Lenin took a lively interest in the IWW mainly for this reason.

The war and the Russian Revolution demonstrated that political action was not merely a question of parliament and votes, but the highest expression of the class struggle. The IWW could not ignore politics. America's entry into the war in 1917, which unleashed a ferocious wave of state repression against the IWW and everyone who opposed the war, proved the need to fight the centalised power of the ruling class. And the Bolshevik Revolution showed how the old state power could be overthrown and replaced with the democratic rule of the workers themselves.

When the Russian workers took the state power into their own hands and used that power to expropriate the capitalists, it had a profound effect in the ranks of the Wobblies. Some of their most outstanding leaders, like Big Bill Haywood, James Cannon, and John Reed began to question many of their old assumptions. Understanding the need for a revolutionary political organisation, they went over to the side of Bolshevism.

The best elements in the IWW joined the young American Communist Party. In April 1921 Haywood said in an interview with Max Eastman, published in *The Liberator*: "'I feel as if I'd always been there,' he said to me. 'You remember I used to say that all we needed was fifty thousand real IWWs, and then about a million members to back them up? Well, isn't that a similar idea? At least I always realised that the essential thing was to have an organisation of *those* who *know*.'"

The fact that the Stalinist degeneration of the Russian Revolution later distorted the development of the Communist Party takes nothing away from the courageous pioneers who began the task of organising the revolutionary vanguard in the USA in the teeth of the most terrible repression.

Those who refused to make the transition to Marxism led the IWW into a blind alley from which it never recovered. The sterile anti-political dogma doomed it to isolation from the great historical events that were taking place on a world scale. By the time of its fifteenth anniversary in 1920 the IWW had already entered into an irreversible decline. In 2005, the 100th anniversary of its founding, the IWW had about 5,000 members, compared to 13 million members in the AFL-CIO.

The idea of "One Big Union" still resonates with many. Young workers in particular are understandably frustrated with the endless divisions and infighting in the mainstream unions today, or they do not have a union at all. However, despite the heroic efforts of the Wobblies to organise a handful of coffee shops and fast food restaurants, building such a union one member at a time will never reach its goals. For this, the vast resources of the major unions are required. To change the policy of the current labour leadership will require a political struggle within the AFL-CIO and Change to Win unions, not on the fringes. Furthermore, the only way to really achieve this is through the coming to political power of the working class, the expropriation of the capitalists, and the passing of laws that guarantee every worker union rights, wages, and benefits. This would lay the basis for the realisation of "One Big Union," as hundreds of millions of workers would be organised in a mass, united trade union federation.

Even in its decline, the IWW played a key role in inspiring the development of the modern industrial unionism, which resulted in the creation of the CIO in the 1930s. That was a tremendous achievement. But although in its ranks there are some very militant workers, nowadays the IWW is only a shadow of its former self.

The history of the IWW is an endless source of inspiration to the youth of today. We fully recognise the pioneering role played by the IWW in the early years and embrace wholeheartedly its militant class-consciousness and its revolutionary traditions. We recognise that its "anarcho-syndicalist" tendencies were only a superficial manifestation—the outer shell of an embryonic Bolshevism. We are proud to claim the IWW as an important part of our historical heritage.

No leaders?

At first sight, it seems an attractive idea. If all leaders sell out, why do we need leaders at all? Yet this notion does not bear the slightest critical analysis. Even in a strike of half an hour in a factory there is leadership. Somebody has to go into the boss's office to put the workers' demands. Who will the workers chose for this role? Will they leave it to chance, or maybe pull a name out of a hat?

No, it is too serious a business to be left to chance. The workers will elect the person who they know will defend their interests: a man or woman who has the necessary experience, intelligence, and courage to represent the people who elected him or her. These are the natural leaders of the working class, and they are present in every workplace. To deny this is to deny the facts of life, known to every worker.

While there have not been many successful, large-scale strikes in the recent period in the US, nonetheless, many workers have at the very least participated in a strike. But how many workers have lived through the experience of a revolutionary general strike or a mass insurrection? Very few have this experience, and are therefore unable to draw any conclusions or learn the lessons. This is only possible from the standpoint of theory and the past experience of our class.

In the animal world, the accumulated experience of past generations is passed on through the mechanism of genetic transmission. The animal knows instinctively how to react in a given situation. But human society is different from any other animal collective. Here culture and education play a more important role than genetics. How are the lessons of past generations passed on to the new generations? There is no automatic mechanism for this. The transmission must be performed through the mechanism of learning. And this takes time.

What is true of society in general is also true of the working class and the struggle for socialism. The revolutionary party is the mechanism whereby the lessons of the past are transmitted to the new generation in a generalised form (theory). This is the equivalent of genetic information. If the genetic information is correct and complete, it will lead to the formation of a healthy human being. If it is distorted, it will be stillborn.

It is the same with theory. A theory that correctly sums up the experience of the past can be of great help in allowing the new generation to avoid the mistakes of the past. But an erroneous theory will only cause confusion, disorientation, or worse. If we are serious about revolution, we must approach it seriously, not in a superficial and amateur fashion. Questions of strategy and tactics must occupy a central place in the considerations of the Marxists. Without tactics, all talk of the building of the revolutionary movement is idle chatter: it is like a knife without a blade.

The conception of revolutionary strategy flows from the influence of military terminology. There are many parallels between the class struggle and a war between nations. In order to overthrow the bourgeoisie, the working class and its vanguard must possess a powerful, centalised, and disciplined organisation. Its leading cadres must possess the necessary knowledge of when to advance and when to retreat, when to give battle and when to avoid it.

Such knowledge presupposes, in addition to experience, a careful and detailed study of past battles, victories, and defeats. In other words, it presupposes a knowledge of theory. A slipshod or dismissive attitude to theory is impermissible, because theory is, in part, the generalisation of the historical experience of the working class of all countries.

But is it not possible to improvise and make up new ideas on the basis of our living experience of the class struggle? Yes, of course it is possible. But there will be a price to pay. In a revolution, events move very swiftly. There is no time to improvise and blunder about like a blind man in a dark room. Every mistake we make will be paid for, and can cost us very dearly.

In denying the importance of organisation and leadership, the anarchists wish to keep the movement in an embryonic state, unorganised and amateurish. But the class struggle is not a child's game and it must not be treated childishly. The American philosopher George Santayana once said, very wisely: "Those who do not learn from history are doomed to repeat it." The history of revolutionary movements provides us with a rich treasury of examples, which deserve careful study if we do not wish to repeat the tragic mistakes and defeats of the past.

The need for theory

The movement is still only at the beginning of the beginning. And in the beginning there is naturally a great deal of confusion, vacillation, and indecision. The Occupy movement, however, contains many contradictory elements within it. There are those who wish to abolish capitalism, and others who only seek to reform it by such things as tinkering with the tax system and regulation of the banks.

By contrast, the rulers of society are implacable and determined. They can rely on decades of experience in handling protests and opposition movements. They combine media distortions and increasingly militarised police violence with more subtle methods: blackmail, bribery, deceit, and police provocateurs. The state has at its disposal the services of an army of hardened bureaucrats, cynical politicians, smart lawyers, lying journalists, learned academics, and cunning priests: all united to defend the status quo in which they all have a vested interest.

Marxists wholeheartedly support the Occupy movement and the collective search for solutions to the crisis of capitalism. It represents a new social awakening and is reflected in a renewed interest in ideas and theory. Yet there are some who deride the very notion of theory. "We do not need outmoded political theories!" they say. "We are engaged in a great experiment and we will improvise and evolve our ideas as we go along." These words, superficially appealing, conceal a profound contradiction.

In real life, no serious person would ever adopt such an attitude in their daily affairs. Just imagine going to the dentist with a toothache, and the dentist says: "Actually, I have never studied dentistry, but open your mouth anyway and I'll give it a shot." You would run out the door! Or a plumber knocks at the door and says: "I know nothing about plumbing, but let me get my hands on your septic system." You would throw him out of your house.

But while we insist (quite rightly!) on a serious and professional attitude to everything in our daily life, when it comes to the revolutionary struggle against capitalism, we are asked to abandon all our critical faculties. Suddenly, anything goes. One idea is as good as any other idea, no matter how irrelevant or crazy. Everything is reduced to a permanent assembly of a hardened core of activists, which is thus debased to the level of an impotent talking shop.

Such a thing represents no threat to the capitalist system. It is no more than a minor inconvenience. It has even been seriously suggested that the bankers and capitalists, instead of violently dispersing the protests, ought to go along and participate in the debates, thus establishing a friendly dialogue with the young dissenters, and show them that the exploiters are really not so bad after all.

In this way the protest movement would lose its revolutionary character. It would be gradually integrated into the system it is supposed to be challenging. The most militant spokespersons of the protests can be taken to one side and enticed with flattery, jobs, and careers: "What an intelligent young person! Why, you almost convince me! You know, we need capable youngsters like you in business..." We have seen this happen many times before.

In order to avoid these pitfalls, an understanding of theory and the lessons of the past is an essential precondition for success. While most people will have to go through a painful process of learning by trial and error, Marxists base themselves on the lessons of the past. We can say what has worked and what hasn't and apply this knowledge to the present situation. We will still make some mistakes, and it is not as simple as looking up the answer in a revolutionary cookbook, but we really have no need to reinvent the wheel; it was invented a very long time ago!

Reformism or revolution?

In the past, the reformists were actually able to negotiate a few extra crumbs for the workers from the capitalists' table. However, the crisis of capitalism necessarily means the crisis of reformism. The way forward demands a serious struggle against reformism, a struggle to regenerate the mass organisations of the working class, beginning with the unions. They must be transformed into fighting organisations of the working class.

Marxists are not opposed to reforms. On the contrary, we will fight stubbornly for each and every reform that can help make life better for the majority. But under present conditions, no meaningful reforms can be won without an all-out struggle. The days when workers could get serious wage increases by merely threatening strike action are long gone. The bosses say they cannot afford even to maintain the present level of wages, let alone give additional concessions. The days when the right-wing trade union leaders could reach a cosy agreement with the employers and the state have passed into history.

In criticising the present policies of the labour leaders, it is necessary to advance other, better policies. But the protest movement has not yet come up with a clear alternative to reformism. Attempts to limit speculation by imposing a tax on financial transactions is not an alternative to the capitalist system, only a half-hearted attempt to reform a system that cannot be reformed. This is merely another type of reformism. It is significant that even some capitalist politicians support such taxes. That is sufficient to show that such a measure poses no threat whatsoever to capitalism. It will solve precisely nothing in the long run.

Those who dream of solving the crisis through reforms are living in the past, in a phase of capitalism that has ceased to exist. It is they, not the Marxists, who are utopians! What we need is a full-blooded militancy and a revival of the class struggle. But in the last analysis, militancy is not enough. Under conditions of capitalist crisis, even the gains of the working class cannot be long-lasting.

What the bosses concede with the left hand they will take back with the right, and vice versa. Wage increases are cancelled out by inflation or tax increases. Factories are closed and unemployment increases. The only way to ensure that reforms are not rolled back is by fighting for a radical change in society. Moreover, even the struggle for reforms can only succeed to the degree that it acquires the widest and most revolutionary scope. All history shows that the ruling class will only make serious concessions when it fears that it will lose everything.

It is not enough simply to say "no." We must offer an alternative. Just as we need a viable alternative to capitalism, so we need a viable alternative to the old reformist leadership. We must fight against the right-wing bureaucratic leadership of the labour organisations. We must fight for a break with the Democrats and the Republicans and the formation of a labour party based on the unions. But in order to do this, it is absolutely necessary to organise, educate, and train revolutionary cadres who have drawn the correct conclusions from the whole history of the class struggle nationally and internationally.

The theory and practice of anarchism

It is true that in the ranks of the anarchists there have been many courageous fighters. This was especially true of Spain in the 1920s and 30s. But taken as a whole, the history of anarchism over the last hundred years shows clearly that it is a blind alley. The most striking fact is the stark contrast between theory and practice. Trotsky said that the theories of anarchism are like an umbrella full of holes: useless precisely when it rains. This can be shown time and time again.

As a theory, anarchism is confused and superficial. The ideas of Bakunin were cobbled together and plagiarised from the nineteenth century utopian socialists, particularly Proudhon. Moreover, they were immediately contradicted by Bakunin's practice. While preaching "freedom," within his own organisation he introduced a ruthless centralism. Bakunin (or "Citizen B" as he was known) exercised a tyrannical personal dictatorship over his organisation. In his polemics against Marx, he did not hesitate to use the vilest methods, including anti-Semitism. This is further explored in the article *Marx versus Bakunin*, included in this volume.[1]

Of far greater interest are the writings of Peter Kropotkin, a man of ideas who wrote one of the best histories of the French Revolution, which was greatly admired by Trotsky. Nevertheless, it must be pointed out that Kropotkin forgot all about his anarchist ideals in 1914, when he supported the Allies in World War I. He was not the only one.

In France, before World War I, the anarcho-syndicalists succeeded in dominating the main trade union confederation. Their main slogan was for the general strike, which they regarded as a panacea. This was a mistake. Although the general strike is one of the most powerful weapons in the arsenal of the class struggle, it cannot solve the central question: the question of state power.

An all-out general strike—as opposed to a one-day general strike, which is in effect only a demonstration—*poses the question of power*. It raises the issue: who runs society; you or us? Therefore, it logically must lead to the assumption of power by the working class, or else end in defeat. If the working class does not take state power, then the entire coercive apparatus of the army, police, courts, laws, etc., remains in the hands of the capitalists. This is something the anarchists could never understand, since for most of them, the question of state power is either irrelevant, or can simply be abolished from one day to the next. The anarchists may well "ignore" the state, but the state certainly does not ignore the workers struggling to change society!

Unfortunately, the question of the state, of who rules society, cannot be so easily disposed of. It cannot be ignored. Let us pose the question concretely. If the workers all go on strike, what will happen? All industry, transport, and communications will come to a halt. The factories, shops and banks will be shut. And then what? The capitalists can afford to wait. They are in no danger of starving. But the working class cannot wait indefinitely. They can be starved back to work. And if waiting the movement out does not suffice, the state has many reserves of repression that can be called on to complete the job. This has happened more than once in history. It is happening now with the Occupy movement.

In other words, if it is not linked to the perspective of the working class taking power, the question of the general strike is mere empty demagogy.

So how did matters with the anarcho-syndicalists in France turn out in practice? In 1914, as soon as France entered World War I, the anarcho-syndicalist trade union leaders immediately dropped their fine words about a general strike and entered a coalition government with the bourgeois parties,

1 See this volume, 81-133.

the Sacred Union (*L'Union Sacrée*), where they pursued a strike-breaking role for the duration of the war.

This contrast between theory and practice, between words and deeds, was absolutely typical of the history of anarchism from the very beginning. It had its most tragic consequences in Spain in the revolutionary period of the 1930s.

Anarchism in Spain

In Spain, the anarchists had behind them the flower of the working class. In their ranks there were many courageous and dedicated class fighters. The anarchist union, the CNT, was by far the biggest workers' organisation in Spain. The anarchist workers were outstanding for their courage and militancy. Yet the Spanish Revolution of 1931–37 demonstrated the complete bankruptcy of anarchism as a guide for the workers on the road to a socialist society.

In the summer of 1936, when Franco declared a fascist military uprising against the Republic, the workers of Barcelona, mostly organised in the CNT, stormed the army barracks. Armed only with improvised weapons, they smashed the fascists before they could join Franco's coup. By this courageous action, they prevented the victory of the fascists in 1936.

As a result of this insurrection, the anarchist workers had complete control of Barcelona. They elected workers' committees to run the factories under workers' control and established the workers' militias. The old bourgeois state had ceased to exist. The sole power was the working class.

It would have been very easy to elect delegates from the factories and militias to a central committee, which could have proclaimed a workers' government in Catalonia, appealing to the workers and peasants in the rest of Spain to follow their example.

But the leadership of the anarchists did not do this; they refused to form a workers' government in Catalonia when they had the chance. Even when Lluís Companys, the President of the old bourgeois government of Catalonia (the *Generalitat*), invited them to take the power, they refused to do so. This was fatal to the revolution. Gradually, the bourgeoisie and the Stalinists rebuilt the old state power in Catalonia, and used it to disarm the popular militias and crush the elements of workers' power.

Then what did the anarchist leaders do? The same ladies and gentlemen who had earlier refused to form a workers' government later joined a bourgeois government and helped to shipwreck the revolution. There were actually anarchist ministers in the national bourgeois government in Valencia and the regional government in Catalonia. In practice, the CNT leadership served as a "red front" for the bourgeois government. These actions powerfully contributed to the defeat of the Spanish Revolution, and the people of Spain paid the price with four decades of fascist barbarism.

This was not the result of a "few bad apples" in the anarchist leadership, but flows from the weaknesses inherent in anarchist theory and practice. Without a firm theoretical compass to guide you through the storm and stress of a revolution, decisions are improvised on the fly. "Pragmatism" and empty demagogy rule the day. And without a strong, centalised, democratic, and accountable organisational structure, the leaders are not under the control of the membership and the organisation cannot act as a united, and thereby more powerful whole.

There was one notable exception to the rule, and that was José Buenaventura Durruti, an extraordinary revolutionary fighter who organised an army based on the workers' militia. This army entered Aragon and waged a revolutionary war against the fascists, turning every village into a bastion of the revolution. But Durruti could only achieve these things to the degree that he broke from the old anarchist dogmas and in practice moved closer to revolutionary Marxism—to Bolshevism.

Although the rank-and-file anarchist workers were undoubtedly sincere and courageous, the balance sheet of the whole historical experience of anarchism was completely negative. That is why today, anarchism has been almost totally eradicated as a trend in the workers' movement, and survives only in the margins of the student and protest movement, where it simply serves to sow confusion, as we shall see.

Anarchism in the anti-capitalist movement

What effect does the theory and practice of anarchism have in the anti-capitalist movement?

The first problem was the refusal to accept majority decisions. It is an elementary proposition of democracy that the minority must accept the decision of the majority. The anarchists object to this, since, for them, it represents the "tyranny" of the majority over the minority.

Unfortunately, since it is rarely possible in any collective to achieve 100% satisfaction for everybody, someone is bound to be displeased if their particular viewpoint is not accepted by the majority. But what is the alternative? The only alternative is *the politics of consensus*. What does this mean in practice?

If there are, say, a hundred people in an assembly, and 99 vote in favour of a proposition, and just one person votes against, what should happen? According to the democratic principle, the view of the 99 carries the day and the one dissenting individual accepts the decision. He or she is not required to change his or her views, and may reserve the right to continue to argue their case and attempt to get the majority to change its mind. But in the meantime, the decision of the majority stands.

Apart from making good sense from a strictly democratic point of view, this procedure has the advantage of allowing us to proceed from talking to action. This is at bottom a class question. The democratic procedure is well-known to workers and trade unionists. It can be seen in every strike. The discipline that is imposed on the worker through the capitalist system—through the division of labour and regimentation of production—is the very same discipline that the workers turn against the bosses through organisation into trade unions and political parties of labour.

In contrast to the workers, the middle classes are used to individualistic methods and have an individualistic mentality. An assembly of students can debate for hours, days, and weeks without ever coming to a conclusion. They have plenty of time and are accustomed to that kind of thing. But a factory mass meeting is an entirely different affair. Before a strike, the workers discuss, debate, and listen to different opinions. But at the end of the day, the issue must be decided. It is put to the vote and the majority decides.

This is clear and obvious to any worker. And nine times out of ten, the minority will voluntarily accept the decision of the majority. Once the decision to strike has been made, all the workers will abide by it. In most cases, even those who argued against a strike will support it and even play an active role on the picket line.

What about the anarchist method of consensus? It means, in practice, that if even one person disagrees, no decision can be reached. This signifies the *tyranny of the minority over the majority*, whose rights are being denied. It can even signify the dictatorship of a single individual—the very opposite of democracy from any point of view. This has absolutely nothing to do with democracy or socialism, but is a clear expression of petty-bourgeois individualism and egotism.

To see where this can lead, let us return to the example of a strike. There are always a few individuals who will try to go to work although their workmates have decided to drop tools. They complain that their individual rights have been violated by the "tyranny of the majority." This is the same logic behind so-called "right to work" legislation. These people are always presented by the bourgeois press as "fighters for freedom and the rights of the individual." The workers, however, have another name for such great individualists: they are called class traitors and *scabs*.

Here, in a nutshell, we have the difference between the proletarian-revolutionary standpoint, based on the collective will of the workers, and the standpoint of petty-bourgeois individualism.

A recipe for impotence

The recent experience of the protest movement provides many examples of the negative role of anarchist methods. To help illustrate this concretely, I have taken a random sample of comments written by participants in the Occupy movement, all of which I found on the Reddit website.

One participant wrote:

> "So I went to our local Occupy Wall Street meeting called "Occupy Victoria." There I discovered that anarchists couldn't organise their way out of a box if their lives depended on it."

Another person had this to say:

> "Despite being led by a self-appointed committee, the local Occupy Wall Street group functions on what they refer to as 'consensus based decision making', which is where if *one single person* disagrees then they can derail the entire conversation and continue to debate, debate, debate until *everybody agrees*."

In other words: The dictatorship of the lowest common denominator.

> "It took an hour and a half before anybody was informed of what we were even *thinking of doing* this Saturday. Up until we were haphazardly/accidentally told what was going on, we had an endless parade of ultra-leftist fluff speeches, "moments of silence to reflect upon our feelings," debating on whether or not we should allow photographs to be taken, arguing over the role of the police, whether or not we should officially endorse a declaration in solidarity with the first nations peoples, etc...it was a complete debacle and waste of time and in the 2 hours we were there, essentially nothing got done except we handed out a few posters for people to put up.

> "The only conclusive decision that we came to was that we "would continue the discussion on the website.""

This is a very typical example of how "consensus politics" serves to paralyse the protest movement, to reduce it to a mere talking shop and prevent it from taking a single step forward. Just because a small group is not satisfied, the meeting is condemned to go round and round in circles: "We must discuss more! We must discuss more!" And as a result we never actually do anything. This is like a man who tries to quench his thirst by drinking salt water.

Another person had this observation:

> "One problem with consensus is that dissenting views actually get papered over. Because everyone has to agree, or at least pretend to agree, dissenting views cannot continue to be clearly expressed, for fear of upsetting the "consensus." It ends up becoming a war of attrition—who's willing to hold out the longest to

their position—and necessarily drives away larger numbers of people, since most people don't have the time or inclination to put up with this type of process.

"In practice, consensus ends up being the dictatorship of the minority—sometimes a minority of one—over the majority. It's completely undemocratic and holds back organising and political development.

"It allows for a couple people to derail the process. All voices can be heard under democracy, but that a small minority disagrees strongly is not an argument for why they should be able to stall further decision making.

"Also, if one or two people have a strong ethical objection to a proposal, it suggests a principled difference with the broader group, which raises the question of whether the group is a logical one for them to be part of in the first place."

Frustration

This kind of thing naturally generates frustration among those for whom the protest movement should be more than a talking shop. Sadly, the experience will be only too familiar to many participants in the protest movement. Here is another account, this time from Florida:

"It's exactly the same thing with Occupy Florida. The self-appointed administrator/volunteer who runs the Facebook group of the local chapter of this *leaderless* movement speaks for the entire group, and the ideology of this dictator is that the problem comes down to *corporatism* (how it's misused in the vernacular). Capitalism isn't even discussed as possibly being the culprit.

"I interjected with: 'It's the system, stupid. I'm sorry but I don't think that fighting corporatism is enough when...'

The dictator replies with: 'Don't call me stupid! And then don't go on to apologise for it...'"

These crying contradictions are recognised by honest anarchists, as the following comment shows:

"I'm an anarchist and I absolutely agree with you. I had exactly the same experience at a local protest. We spent over two hours discussing the formation of work groups, and the majority of that discussion was a meta-discussion about how we should discuss the formation of work groups. I ultimately ran out of time and had to leave, and I was kind of happy about it because that organisation process was like pulling teeth."

Another Reddit user gave vent to the sense of frustration felt by many:

"Are *all* anarchist groups this *completely* f***ing *useless?* Has anybody else had a similar experience?"

The whole point of democracy is majority rule. As someone wittily observed: "If everyone has to agree about everything, maybe we should change the slogan to: 'We are the 100%'!" With all its limitations, the democratic system is the only one that allows a genuine participation of the masses. There must be a full and free debate, with every viewpoint freely expressed. But if it is not to degenerate into a mere talking shop, debate must end in a vote in which the majority must decide, and the minority must accept the decision of the majority.

The imposition of consensus leads inevitably to inaction, frustration, time-wasting and, eventually, to a falling-off of participation. Many people who took part in the initial Occupy meetings drift away and leave the organising committees because they are frustrated with the endless debates and discussions that are going nowhere.

The methods that seemed so democratic, that were supposed to encourage the maximum of participation, in the end only succeed in alienating people and undermining the movement. A different method is needed, a genuinely democratic method which allows everyone to speak their mind freely, but which at the end of the day leads to clear-cut decisions and positive action.

Self-appointed cliques

The Russian Bolshevik Bukharin once joked that anarchism has two rules: the first rule is that you must not form a party; the second rule is that nobody must obey the first rule! Although in theory these anarchist methods are ultra-democratic, in practice they produce the worst kind of bureaucracy: the rule of self-appointed cliques. The contradictory nature of this position is clear to the more thinking elements among the anarchists:

"I'm an anarchist and I agree with the critique of consensus decision-making. Allowing everyone in a large group to have a veto is paralysing. Mass assemblies, especially without a well-set agenda, tend to veer far off-topic.

"I've been to activist meetings that have been made up of mostly anarchists where consensus decision-making was used. There were problems, but the group tried very hard to be aware of these issues and they did manage to get things done. I learned a number of different things from this experience.

"Though there were obviously no official leaders in the group, a de facto leadership of 3 people emerged, who dominated the discourse and decision-making by simply being older, more experienced, and more confident. There was even one person (a white guy, surprise surprise) who was particularly leading the group. There was a lot of drama over this, and I was actually happy that people were pointing out discussing the effects of race, class, and gender on decision-making and leadership, but nevertheless the group collapsed due to all of the discontent.

"This was a group of like 9 people, and even that low number of people had a tough time getting their sh*t together through consensus decision-making. It seemed like a lot of things passed simply because the younger, less confident members were too nervous to object or to stall a decision. Again, I applaud them for trying to be aware of these problems but the problems still persisted, often unspoken of except for in small groups of members."

The anarchist methods of organisation invariably turns into their opposite. The "anti-leader," "anti-centralist," and "anti-bureaucratic" tendency turns out to be the most bureaucratic and undemocratic system of all. We have seen this many times. Behind the apparently democratic anarchy of a formless assembly with no rules, no structure, and (theoretically) no leaders, someone always makes decisions. But this "someone" is *not elected by anybody—* "Elections? By majority vote? God forbid!"—and is therefore *not responsible to anybody.*

Behind the scenes, these "non-bureaucratic" setups are run by self-appointed cliques of individuals (very often anarchists). This, in practice, is the worst form of bureaucracy—*an irresponsible bureaucracy that can do just what it likes because there is no formal democratic method of control.*

The state

The question of the state is one of the points that have traditionally divided Marxism and anarchism. So just what is the state? Marxism explains that the state is a product and a manifestation of the irreconcilability of class antagonisms in society. It arises where, when, and insofar as class antagonisms cannot be reconciled. Conversely, the very existence of the state proves that the class antagonisms are irreconcilable.

Summing up his historical analysis of the state, Frederick Engels says:

"The state is, therefore, by no means a power forced on society from without; just as little is it "the reality of the ethical idea," "the image and reality of reason," as Hegel maintains. Rather, it is a product of society at a certain stage of development; it is the admission that this society has become entangled in an insoluble contradiction with itself, that it has split into irreconcilable antagonisms which it is powerless to dispel. But in order that these antagonisms, these classes with conflicting economic interests, might not consume themselves and society in fruitless struggle, it became necessary to have a power, seemingly standing above society, that would alleviate the conflict and keep it within the bounds of "order"; and this power, arisen out of society but placing itself above it, and alienating itself more and more from it, is the state."[2]

The modern state is a bureaucratic behemoth that devours a colossal amount of the wealth produced by the working class. Marxists and anarchists agree that the state is a monstrous instrument of oppression that must be eliminated. The question is: How? By whom? And what will replace it? This is a fundamental question for any revolution. In a speech on anarchism during the Russian Civil War, Trotsky summarized very well the Marxist position on the state:

> "The bourgeoisie says: don't touch the state power; it is the sacred hereditary privilege of the educated classes. But the Anarchists say: don't touch it; it is an infernal invention, a diabolical device, don't have anything to do with it. The bourgeoisie says don't touch it because it's sacred. The Anarchists say: don't touch it, because it's sinful. Both say: don't touch it. But we say: don't just touch it, take it in your hands, and set it to work in your own interests, for the abolition of private ownership and the emancipation of the working class."[3]

Marxism explains that that the state consists ultimately of armed bodies of men: of the army, police, courts, and jails. It is an instrument of the ruling class for the oppression of other classes. Against the confused ideas of the anarchists, Marx argued that the workers need a state to overcome the resistance of the exploiting classes. But that argument of Marx has been distorted by both the bourgeois and the anarchists.

The Paris Commune of 1871 was one of the greatest and most inspiring episodes in the history of the working class. In a tremendous revolutionary movement, the working people of Paris replaced the capitalist state with their own organs of government and held political power until their downfall a few months later. The Parisian workers strove, in extremely difficult circumstances, to put an end to exploitation and oppression, and to reorganise society on an entirely new foundation.

The Commune was a glorious episode in the history of the world working class. For the first time, the popular masses, with the workers at their head, overthrew the old state and at least began the task of transforming society. With no clearly-defined plan of action, leadership or organisation, the masses displayed an astonishing degree of courage, initiative and creativity. Yet in the last analysis, the lack of a bold and far-wsighted leadership and a clear programme led to a terrible defeat. Marx and Engels followed the developments in France very closely and based themselves upon the experience to work out

---

2 F. Engels, *The Origin of the Family, Private Property and the State,* in *Marx-Engels Collected Works, Volume 3, 326–27.*

3 Leon Trotsky, *How The Revolution Armed,* Vol. 1, 1918 (London: New Park, 1979), 400–401.

their theory of the "dictatorship of the proletariat," which is merely a more scientifically precise term for "the political rule of the working class."

Marx and Engels drew a thorough balance sheet of the Commune, pointing out its advances as well as its errors and deficiencies. These can almost all be traced to the failings of the leadership. The leaders of the Commune were a mixed bunch, ranging from a minority of Marxists to elements who stood closer to reformism or anarchism. One of the reasons the Commune failed was that it did not launch a revolutionary offensive against the reactionary government that had installed itself at Versailles. This gave time to the counterrevolutionary forces to rally and attack Paris. Over 30,000 people were butchered by the counterrevolution. The Commune was literally buried under a mound of corpses.

Summing up the experience of the Paris Commune, Marx and Engels explained: "One thing especially was proved by the Commune, *viz.*, that 'the working class cannot simply lay hold of the ready-made state machinery, and wield it for its own purposes'...."[4]

Stalinism or communism?

The bourgeois and its apologists wish to confuse the workers and youth by attempting to identify the idea of communism with the monstrous bureaucratic and totalitarian regime of Stalinist Russia. "Do you want Communism? Here it is! That is Communism! The Berlin Wall is Communism! Hungary 1956 is Communism! The Soviet gulags are Communism!" Unfortunately, the anarchists also echo these arguments.

This is a stupid calumny. The workers' state established by the Bolshevik Revolution was neither bureaucratic nor totalitarian. On the contrary, before the Stalinist bureaucracy usurped control from the masses, *it was the most democratic state that ever existed.* The basic principles of the Soviet power were not invented by Marx or Lenin. They were based on the concrete experience of the Paris Commune, and later elaborated upon by Lenin.

The basic conditions for workers' democracy were set forth in one of Lenin's most important works: *The State and Revolution.*[5] Ted Grant summarized Lenin's ideas in the following four points:

1. Free and democratic elections with the right of recall of all officials

2. No official to receive a higher wage than a skilled worker.

3. No standing army or police force, but the armed people.

---

4 Karl Marx, Preface to the 1872 German edition of *Manifesto of the Communist Party*, in *Marx/Engels Collected Works*, vol. 23 (New York: International, 1976), 175.
5 Lenin, "What is to Replace the Smashed State Machine?" in *The State and Revolution, Four Marxist Classics* (St. Paul: Wellred, 2008), 109–21.

4. Gradually, all the administrative tasks to be done in turn by all. "Every cook should be able to be Prime Minister—When everyone is a 'bureaucrat' in turn, nobody can be a bureaucrat."[6]

These were the conditions which Lenin laid down, not for full-fledged socialism or communism, but for the very first period of a workers' state, *at its inception*—the period of the transition from capitalism to socialism.

The transition to socialism—a higher form of society based on genuine democracy and plenty for all—can only be accomplished by the *active and conscious participation of the working class in the running of society, of industry, and of the state.* It is not something that is kindly handed down to the workers by kindhearted capitalists or bureaucratic mandarins. The whole conception of Marx, Engels, Lenin, and Trotsky was based upon this fact.

Under Lenin and Trotsky, the Soviet state was constructed as to facilitate the drawing of workers into the tasks of control and accounting, to ensure the uninterrupted progress of the reduction of the "special functions" of officialdom and of the power of the state. Strict limitations were placed upon the salaries, power, and privileges of officials in order to prevent the formation of a privileged caste.

The Soviets of Workers' and Soldiers' Deputies were elected assemblies composed not of professional politicians and bureaucrats, but of ordinary workers, peasants, and soldiers. It was not an alien power standing over society, but a power based on the direct initiative of the people from below. Its laws were not like the laws enacted by a capitalist state power.

As Lenin explained:

"It is an entirely different kind of power from the one that generally exists in the parliamentary bourgeois-democratic republics of the usual type still prevailing in the advanced countries of Europe and America....*This* power is of *the same type* as the Paris Commune of 1871.

The fundamental characteristics of this type are: (1) the source of power is not a law previously discussed and enacted by parliament, but the direct initiative of the people from below, in their local areas—direct "seizure," to use a current expression; (2) the replacement of the police and the army, which are institutions divorced from the people and set against the people, by the direct arming of the whole people; order in the state under such a power is maintained by the armed workers and peasants *themselves*, by the armed people *themselves*; (3) officialdom, the bureaucracy, are either similarly replaced by the direct rule of the people themselves or at least placed under special control; they not only become elected officials, but are also *subject to recall* at the people's first demand; they are reduced to the position of simple agents; from a privileged group holding

6 Ted Grant, "Hungary and the Crisis in the Communist Party," in *Ted Grant: Selected Works*, vol. 1 (St. Paul: Wellred, 2009), 150.

xxxii
Marxism and Anarchsim

"jobs" remunerated on a high, bourgeois scale, they become workers of a special "arm of the service" whose remuneration *does not exceed* the ordinary pay of a competent worker.

This, and this *alone*, constitutes the *essence* of the Paris Commune as a special type of state."[7]

Lenin emphasised that the proletariat needs only a state that is "so constituted that it will at once begin to die away and cannot help dying away." A genuine workers' state has nothing in common with the bureaucratic monster that exists today, and even less the one that existed in Stalinist Russia.

The early Soviet Union was in fact not a state at all in the sense we normally understand it, but only the organised expression of the revolutionary power of the working people. To use the phrase of Marx, it was a "semi-state," a state so designed that it would eventually wither away and be dissolved into society, giving way to the collective administration of society for the benefit of all, without force or coercion. That, and only that, is the genuine Marxist conception of a workers' state.

Violence or non-violence?

The question of the state is naturally linked with the question of violence. The ruling class has at its disposal a vast apparatus of coercion: the army, the police, the intelligence services, the courts, the prisons, the lawyers, judges, and prison wardens. Many protesters have recently received a valuable education in the Marxist theory of the state—on the end of a policeman's baton.

This should not really surprise us. All history shows that no ruling class ever gives up its wealth, power and privileges without a fight—and that usually means a fight with no holds barred. Every revolutionary movement will come up against this apparatus of state repression.

What is the Marxists' attitude towards violence? The bourgeoisie and its defenders always accuse Marxists of advocating violence. This is highly ironic, considering the vast arsenals of weaponry that the ruling class has piled up, the armies of heavily armed troops, cops, prisons, and so on and so forth. The ruling class is not at all opposed to violence *per se*. In fact, its rule is based on violence in many different forms. The only violence that the ruling class abhors is when the poor, downtrodden, and exploited masses attempt to defend themselves against the organised violence of the bourgeois state. That is, it is against any violence directed at its class rule, power, and property.

It goes without saying that we do not advocate violence. We are prepared to make use of each and every opening allowed to us by bourgeois democracy.

7 V.I. Lenin, *The Dual Power in Collected Works*, vol. 24 (Moscow: Progress, 1980), 38–39.

But we should be under no illusions. Beneath the thin veneer of democracy there is the reality of the dictatorship of the banks and big corporations.

While the people are told that they can democratically decide the direction of the country through elections, in reality, all the real decisions are taken by the boards of directors. The interests of a tiny handful of bankers and capitalists carry much more weight than the votes of millions of ordinary citizens. The real meaning of formal bourgeois democracy is this: anyone can say (more or less) what they like, as long as big business decides what really happens.

This dictatorship of big business is normally concealed behind a smiling mask. But at critical moments, the smiling mask of "democracy" slips to reveal the ugly face of the dictatorship of capital. The question is whether "We, the People" have the right to fight against this dictatorship and strive to overthrow it.

The answer was given long ago when the American people rose up, arms in hand, to defend their rights against the tyranny of the English Crown. It is enshrined in the Second Amendment of the American Constitution, which defends the people's right to bear arms as a guarantee of freedom. The "founding fathers" upheld the rights of the people to armed insurrection against a tyrannical government. The New Hampshire Constitution of 1784 tells us that "non-resistance against arbitrary power, and oppression, is absurd, slavish, and destructive of the good and happiness of mankind."

Every revolution in history—including the American Revolution—shows the correctness of Marx's words when he wrote that "force is the midwife of every old society pregnant with a new one." Nonetheless, in the very first programmatic statement of Marxism, *The Principles of Communism*, Engels wrote the following:

> *"Question 16*: Will it be possible to bring about the abolition of private property by peaceful means?
>
> *"Answer*: It is to be desired that this could happen, and Communists certainly would be the last to resist it. The Communists know only too well that all conspiracies are not only futile but even harmful. They know only too well that revolutions are not made deliberately and arbitrarily, but that everywhere and at all times they were the essential outcome of circumstances quite independent of the will and the leadership of particular parties and entire classes. But they likewise perceive that the development of the proletariat is in nearly every civilised country forcibly suppressed, and that thereby the opponents of the Communists

are tending in every way to promote revolution. Should the oppressed proletariat in the end be goaded into a revolution, we Communists will then defend the cause of the proletarians by deed as well as we do now by word."[8]

The fact is that once the working class is organised and mobilised to change society, no state, army, or police can stop it. Nine times out of ten, any violence arising during a revolutionary situation is initiated by the ruling class, which is desperate to hold on to power. Therefore, the danger of violence is in inverse proportion to the willingness of the working class to fight to change society. As the ancient Romans used to say: *Si pacem vis para bellum*—if you want peace, prepare for war.

However, that does not mean that we advocate sporadic acts of violence by groups or individuals: senseless rioting, breaking windows, arson, etc. Such things sometimes reflect the genuine anger and frustration felt by people, especially the unemployed and dispossessed youth, at the sheer injustice of class society. But these kinds of actions achieve nothing positive. They merely alienate the broader layers of the working class and give the ruling class an excuse to unleash the full force of the state, in order to crack down on the protest movement in general.

There is a force in society that is far stronger than even the most powerful state or army: that is the power of the working class, once it is organised and mobilised to change society. Not a wheel turns, not a phone rings, not a light bulb shines without the permission of the working class! Once this enormous power is mobilised, no force on earth can stop it.

Powerful union organisations exist that would be more than capable of overthrowing capitalism if the millions of workers they represent were mobilised to this end. The problem once again reduces itself to a problem of leadership of the working class and its organisations.

What is to be done?

The leadership of the mass organisations, beginning with the trade unions, is in a lamentable state everywhere. A panorama opens up not only of great battles, but also of defeats of the working class as a result of bad leadership. It is understandable that some young people, disgusted with the role of the current leaderships, look to anarchist ideas as a solution.

In most cases, however, those who describe themselves as anarchists have no knowledge either of the theories or history of anarchism. Their anarchism is not really anarchism at all, but it is a healthy reaction against bureaucracy and reformism. When they say: "we are against politics!" what they mean is: "we are against the existing politics, which do not represent the views

8 Engels, *Principles of Communism,* in *Marx and Engels Selected Works,* vol. 1 (Moscow: Progress, 1969), 89.

of ordinary people!" When they say: "we do not need parties and leaders!" they mean: "we do not need the present political parties and leaders who are remote from society and only defend their own interests and the rich people who back them."

This "anarchism" is in reality only the outer shell of an immature Bolshevism, of revolutionary Marxism. These are sincere young people who desire to transform society with all their heart. Many of them will come to understand the limitations of anarchist ideas and methods and will seek a more effective revolutionary alternative. The lack of an adequate leadership and a clear programme for action is already being felt by an increasing number of activists in the Occupy movement.

Through painful experience, the new generation of workers and youth are beginning to understand the nature of the problems that lie before them and are gradually beginning to grasp the need for radical solutions. The best elements are beginning to realise that the only way out of the impasse is through the revolutionary reconstruction of society from top to bottom.

It will not be easy to achieve this; but then, nothing worthwhile in life is ever easy. The first and most important step is to say *no* to the existing society, its institutions, values and morality. In many ways this is the easiest step. It is not difficult to protest and reject. But what is also necessary is to say positively *what is to be done*.

This underlines the need for clarity in ideas, programmes and tactics. Mistakes in theory inevitably lead to mistakes in practice. This is not an academic exercise. The class struggle is not a game, and history is full of examples where the lack of political clarity led to the most tragic consequences. Spain in the 1930s is a case in point.

The first stages of the revolution are inevitably accompanied by naïveté and all kinds of illusions. But such illusions will be destroyed by events. The movement is proceeding by trial and error. It needs time to learn. If a Marxist party already existed, with roots in the masses and political authority, the learning process would undoubtedly be much shorter, and there would be fewer defeats and setbacks. But such a party does not yet exist. It has to be built in the heat of events.

Confusion, the lack of a programme, and never-ending debate is no substitute for positive action. If the Occupy movement is to succeed, it must be armed with clear ideas and a consistent revolutionary programme. That can only be provided by Marxism. The workers and students have shown the most tremendous resourcefulness and initiative. All now depends on the ability of the most revolutionary elements of the workers and youth to draw all the necessary conclusions. Armed with a genuine socialist revolutionary programme, they would be invincible.

Fight for socialism!

Is it really true that there is no alternative to capitalism? No, it is not true! The alternative is a system based on production for the needs of the many and not the profits of the few; a system that replaces economic chaos and anarchy with harmonious planning; that replaces the rule of a minority of wealthy parasites with the rule of the majority who produce all the wealth of society. The name of this alternative is socialism.

Genuine socialism has nothing in common with the bureaucratic and totalitarian caricature that existed in Stalinist Russia. It is a genuine democracy based on the ownership, control and management of the key levers of the productive forces by the working class.

Some think it is utopian to suggest that the human race can take hold of its own fate and run society on the basis of a democratic plan of production. However, the need for a socialist planned economy is not an invention of Marx or any other thinker. It flows from objective necessity. The potential for world socialism flows from the present conditions of capitalism itself. All that is necessary is for the working class, which constitutes the majority, to take over the running of society, expropriate the banks and giant monopolies, and mobilise the vast unused and untapped productive potential to begin solving the problems we face.

In order that humanity can be free to realise its full potential, it is necessary to free industry, agriculture, science, and technology from the suffocating restraints of capitalism. Once the productive forces are free from these suffocating limitations, society would be capable of immediately satisfying all human wants and preparing the way for a gigantic advance for humanity.

We invite all those who are interested in fighting to change society to join with us, to discuss, debate our differences, and to test the viability of ideas and programmes in the practice of the class struggle. Only in this way can we put an end to the prevailing confusion and attain the ideological clarity and organisational cohesion that are necessary to achieve our final victory.

London, 6th December 2011

Section One

Marxist and Anarchist Theory

Marxist and Anarchist Theory
Daniel Morley

What distinguishes Marxism from anarchism? Why two theories? By what are they distinguished from each other? What are their relative merits, and which of the two theories—or which combination of their ideas—is the best tool for fighting capitalism and the bourgeois state? Such a process of questioning is necessary for any revolutionary, as an attempt to grasp and conquer revolutionary theory.

Most anarchist theory expresses the same goal as Marxism—the establishment of a classless and stateless society. Marxism and anarchism are united insofar as they participate in the movement against oppression and inequality in all forms. And it is very often the case that those becoming radicalised are sympathetic to both theories for this reason.

We believe that, although Marxist and anarchist theory are united in their struggle to liberate humanity, whereas anarchism paradoxically rejects theory as an accomplice of intellectual elitism or armchair inaction, Marxism is distinguished by utilizing all the developments of scientific method and historical analysis so that the working class may understand society in order to change it.

Marxist theory is chiefly concerned with understanding inequality and oppression, why they exist, where they come from, what role they play, and under what conditions they may be overcome. And to understand them means not only to describe them, or to assert that the division of society into classes is unjust, and that the state apparatus is fundamentally repressive, but to explain them materially and historically.

Origins of class and the state

Everywhere we look we see examples of extreme inequality, suffering and state oppression, so much so that we take them for granted, seeming like a natural state of affairs. Even the most ordinary individual lives under the yoke of the humiliating and endless power of money, and finds themselves compelled to organise their whole life around the task of making money for someone else, following their boss's timetable and instructions.

As Rousseau said, everywhere man is in chains, and yet we are all born free, that is to say, the bonds we suffer are man-made, and what is more, they are the constructions of people fundamentally equal to ourselves—the capitalist class has no magic powers or superhuman strengths. So why do we suffer at all? Why do (and when did) the vast majority of people allow themselves to become powerless in the face of the apparently artificial power of a minority of people? There must be some condition we have to thank for being exploited by only a few. What is it?

As Marxists and materialists, we understand that the class struggle does not arise of itself, but is conditioned by the more general struggle for existence; it is an expression of the unavoidable struggle with nature, to use a rather crude expression. For before we are enslaved by our fellow man, we are at the whim of the all powerful laws of nature. Yes, each person is born into the world free, i.e., not with some rank preordained by God, but at the same time each person is born very much a prisoner of nature. As Marx said, mankind is a suffering, limited being; we feel our dependence on nature every second that we breathe, every time the involuntary muscles in our stomach compel us to look for a meal, every time our puny composition makes our bodies shudder with cold. If we did not have such pressing material needs, we would not need to go to the capitalist begging for work. So before we can understand the lack of freedom in our society, we must recognise this most fundamental of social laws—material conditions determine consciousness.

History knows all kind of strange transformations. For much of our history there was no oppressive state authority or class exploitation to speak of, and yet somehow out of such a situation exploitation and coercion have arisen. Furthermore, the forms of exploitation and state authority have transformed themselves many times, and with them the relative level of culture has changed also. What underlying mechanism or process ties all this together, what is the common thread that allows us to put them all under one and the same category, "society"? For Marxists, it is the struggle for the economisation of labour, the development of the forces of production (or useful technology) to be wielded by one or another class as part of the struggle with nature. For when we develop useful technology, the immediate aim is always that someone may live better, may secure themselves in the struggle with nature. But such technology, developed and used socially, has unplanned social consequences, changing the structure of society, giving some power over others. Those who control the productive forces control society.

As we have said, the first forms of society lacked a system of exploitation and a state apparatus, having arisen immediately out of "nature," which knows nothing of formal rank and chains of command. Productivity would have been so low that society could not have afforded any privileged stratum. Although life in these conditions was undoubtedly tough, there must have been relative harmony within the community, since everyone would have had to "pull their weight" in roughly equal measure. But this harmony finished at the geographical threshold of the tribe, outside of which we find other tribes. And, as the geographically dispersed communities developed their productive forces, so would they have expanded, and, ultimately, come into contact with other similar communities. Trade between them would have developed based on the different goods they were able to produce, such trade being used by each community to enrich themselves. Although within each community there may have been enormous unity and cooperation in production, between the communities there must have been little or none. The respective communities would not be interested in producing for the sake of the other, but to get something in return. And so not only would competition and antagonism develop between the communities, but more and more the internal life of each community would be determined by the need to produce more for exchange outside the community. We may surmise that those with more involvement in the process, e.g., elders who led production and were in contact with other communities, had an advantageous position. In addition, the struggle for resources and control of land must emerge from such a situation of geographical dispersion and antagonisms. War between communities for conquest of land and the use of a rival community's labour power flows from such a situation. In this way, the communal struggle to develop the productive forces led to the dissolution of the community in favour of class divisions.

This is the material, economic basis for class and the state. There is a debate between Marxists and anarchists as to whether class division arises first, followed by a coercive state apparatus tasked with protecting the ruling class (the Marxist position), or whether state power with its instruments of oppression developed first and gave rise to class division, which some anarchists argue. But the question is not so much a chronological one, i.e., whether class or the state arose first, as one of form and content, i.e., whether state power is fundamental and class inequalities are merely the formal expression of the former, whose aim is simply the maintenance of state power (an anarchist position), or alternatively whether the real content and basis for all political power, state authority and coercion is economic class relations, as Engels points out in polemic with Dühring (who was not an anarchist):

> "...even if we assume for a moment that Herr Dühring is right in saying that all past history can be traced back to the enslavement of man by man, we are still

very far from having got to the bottom of the matter. For the question then arises: how did Crusoe come to enslave Friday? Just for the fun of it? By no means. On the contrary, we see that Friday "is compelled to render *economic* service as a slave or as a mere tool and is maintained also only as a tool" {D. C. 9}. Crusoe enslaved Friday only in order that Friday should work for Crusoe's benefit. And how can he derive any benefit for himself from Friday's labour? Only through Friday producing by his labour more of the necessaries of life than Crusoe has to give him to keep him fit to work... The childish example specially selected by Herr Dühring in order to prove that force is "historically the fundamental thing," therefore, proves that force is only the means, and that the aim, on the contrary, is economic advantage. And "the more fundamental" the aim is than the means used to secure it, the more fundamental in history is the economic side of the relationship than the political side... Subjugation has always been—to use Herr Dühring's elegant expression—a "stomach-filling agency" (taking stomach-filling in a very wide sense), but never and nowhere a political grouping established "for its own sake"... Crusoe, "sword in hand" {D. C. 23}, makes Friday his slave. But in order to manage this, Crusoe needs something else besides his sword. Not everyone can make use of a slave. In order to be able to make use of a slave, one must possess two kinds of things: first, the instruments and material for his slave's labour; and secondly, the means of bare subsistence for him. Therefore, before slavery becomes possible, a certain level of production must already have been reached and a certain inequality of distribution must already have appeared." (Engels, *Anti-Dühring*)

State authority, then, is not some arbitrary evil, existing for its own sake, and it does not gain its negative properties of oppression and inequality purely from itself; rather, it arises out of developing economic inequality and plays a role dependent upon the latter. And the state does not oppress all in society equally; indeed, in our society there are many capitalists who have no direct involvement with the state, and yet feel themselves very well represented by it. This is because, in the final analysis, the state gets its power from the ruling economic class, whom it serves by protecting its property and generally maintaining the social order.

Two things of interest to us follow from this. If a class can wield economic power, then it can in principle control its own state apparatus, rather than being the victim of it, since the state power is, in the final analysis, dependent on economic relations. If the state apparatus is a tool with which to repress other classes, and if Marxists and anarchists can agree that a working-class–led revolution will face active, organised opposition from the bourgeoisie (a fact many anarchists recognise), then the working class can and must wield this state power, i.e., organise their own coercive apparatus to defend their revolution from counterrevolution. So long as the working class can collectively, democratically, run and develop the economy in its own interests, through democratic workers' committees, then it can maintain control of its state apparatus so long as it needs it. For many anarchists, representation itself as a political form contains the seeds of, or is, the problem. They say one cannot be genuinely represented, and that the representative will always abuse their position. But it is not the form that is the problem. As we said, if that were the case, the bourgeoisie would always be oppressed by its own state representatives. A bourgeois parliament always fails to represent "the people" not because representation per se is a sham, but because parliament is controlled by that class which controls the economy, the media, etc., and that class's interests do not coincide with "the people's".

The same applies to the workers' own organisations. If the leadership of the unions and of workers' parties sells out the working class, it is not so much because it is a leadership, but because it comes under the enormous social pressure of the ruling class, whose ideology dominates society. The solution to such a problem is never to abandon the concept of leadership in the workers' movement, but to wage a struggle against a leadership which has sold out to the bourgeois class. Ironically, despite professing a burning hatred of bureaucracy and leadership, the anarchist movement has often displayed a tendency to make a fetish out of right-wing leadership and an ignorance of the working-class rank and file—they tend to blame only the existence of a bureaucracy or participation in parliament for the degeneration of workers' parties, ignoring the fact that the precondition for the rightward shift of the bureaucracy is always a lack of open class struggle, lack of pressure from below. But there is no remedy for this other than the mass movement of the working class and the struggle for revolutionary ideas within these organisations. That is how we remove a betraying leadership and replace it with a revolutionary one. If such a struggle in workers' mass organisations does not take place, then it is inevitable that the top layers of such organisations become distant from the rank and file and will attempt to collaborate with the capitalists.

But a workers' state, and genuine revolutionary working class leadership, is not the end goal for Marxists; we, too, see the need for a stateless society. That can exist only when the objective conditions that require a state apparatus (class struggle) have disappeared. In other words, when the working class has dissolved itself as a class by dissolving all classes, by uniting humanity in a global plan of production that leaves no lasting material antagonisms between classes or nations, and when production has attained such a level that the working week is sufficiently shortened so that all may participate in education and running society, then coercion and subjugation will have no objective role, and become worthless.

Objective role of leadership

Kropotkin, a famous Russian anarchist, feared that should a socialist society be established through political leadership, and be organised centrally, on a large national or international scale, then the intellectual elite who led the revolution would install themselves as a new ruling group above the rest of society. In turn, the complexity of production for such a society would mean that "technocrats" would be needed to guide and plan the process (the assumption being that it would be too complex for workers to get their head around), and they, too, would lord it over the workers:

> "...collectivism necessitated some authority within the workers' association to measure individual performance and to supervise the distribution of goods and services accordingly. Consequently... a collectivist order contained the seeds of inequality and domination." (Avrich, *The Russian Anarchists*, p. 29)

But it is not "collectivism" on a large and complex scale that contains the seeds of inequality and domination, but already existing material inequality and exploitation that give rise to the division between mental and manual labour in class society, where some have the luxury to study and others are told what to do. It is class exploitation and long hours of work that mean that in our society, workers cannot plan and direct production themselves, firstly because the capitalist class produces for their own private profit, and so cannot permit workers a say in controlling that profit, and secondly because workers do not have the time to democratically plan society. Kropotkin has the whole thing on its head, and so his solution—localism, federalism, and a "simple" economy—would only reintroduce the problem on a small scale. Only a globalised economy, a global division of labour, which capitalism has made a fact, harmoniously planned on a global scale (whereas the globalised capitalist economy is not planned at all but full of regional imbalances and antagonisms), can liberate the working class and put ordinary people in control. Only the high productivity this economy creates, and the technological sophistication involved, can shorten the working week to allow for mass participation, and do away with the miserable struggle between people and nations for jobs, control of resources, etc. Kropotkin actually ends up patronising workers by implying that the mass of people are incapable of planning the economy, when in reality it is only as exploited workers that they are prevented from doing so. "Technocrats" are only able to fulfil their role above workers because, in a society based on exploiting the working class, workers are barred access to higher education—do away with that exploitation by nationalising the economy, and this problem can be overcome; in fact, it is the only way to overcome it.

"Localisation," so to speak, did occur in the Russian Revolution directly after 1917, and it was precisely part of the problem that led to Stalinism.

"The workingmen, the report [from a British trade union delegation to the USSR in 1924] said, had been transformed overnight into "a new body of shareholders." A similar observation was made by a Bolshevik commentator early in 1918: the workers [in factories now under their control], he wrote, considered tools and equipment "their own property." Cases of pillage and theft were not uncommon... Individual factory committees sent "pushers" into the provinces to purchase fuel and raw materials, sometimes for outrageous prices. Often they refused to share available supplies with other factories in direst need." (Avrich, *The Russian Anarchists*, pp. 162–63)

What is the explanation for this? Is workers' control in each local factory not possible? No, that is not the explanation. Instead it is the extreme economic chaos and poverty following the revolution in 1917, where German imperialism took the majority of Russian industry, already decimated by the war. The problem precisely was "localism." The apparent autonomy of these sets of workers (in reality not autonomous at all, but under the firm control of the market, money and their empty stomachs) arose in response to the inability of the revolution (which was also "local" in that it was isolated to Russia and thus starved of resources) to solve dire material problems overnight. The crushing weight of Stalinism is explained not by centralism and the complexity of the economy, but by the disintegration of the economy into regional antagonisms, between town and country, out of which the old tsarist bureaucracy reasserted its control and privileges, precisely because the same conditions of poverty persisted. The working class revolutionaries were too busy struggling for immediate survival, or fighting and dying in the Civil War, to collectively and harmoniously plan the economy. Makhno's anarchist movement in the Ukraine during the Russian Civil War was an expression of antagonisms between countryside and town—where the countryside could not afford to feed the town—and not a solution to it:

"Makhno led a peasant movement, and so never had a strong base of support in any of the cities. Most of the workers who lived in areas of the Ukraine under Makhno's control sided either with the Bolsheviks or the Mensheviks. The following examples illustrate the attitude that Makhno had towards the working class. When railway and telegraph workers from the Ekaterinoslav-Sinelnikovo line were still suffering after a long period of starvation under Denikin's occupation, they asked Makhno to pay them for their work. He responded with, "We are not like the Bolsheviks to feed you, we don't need the railways; if you need money, take the bread from those who need your railways and telegraphs." In a separate incident, he told the workers of Briansk, "Because the workers do not want to support Makhno's movement and demand pay for the repairs of the armored car, I will take this armored car for free and pay nothing." (A Kramer, *The Makhno Anarchists, Kronstadt and the Position of the Russian Peasants in Post-Revolutionary Russia*)

The lack of class and state in primitive communities is not a result of "autonomy," "localism," or economic simplicity, but actually thanks to their internal "centralism" or unity demanded by the material conditions. Everyone must work together to survive. Likewise, the way to do away with Kropotkin's technocrats, who will despotically tell the workers how much to produce and consume, is to develop production to such an extent that the need for such guidance disappears:

> The material premise of communism should be so high a development of the economic powers of man that productive labour, having ceased to be a burden, will not require any goad, and the distribution of life's goods, existing in continual abundance, will not demand—as it does not now in any well-off family or "decent" boarding-house—any control except that of education, habit and social opinion. (Trotsky, *The Revolution Betrayed*)

Contrary to anarchist hopes, political leadership in our society is necessary for the working class. It could only be discarded, made superfluous, if the working class had the time and inclination to collectively develop revolutionary theory, collectively grasp the need for a revolution, and therefore organise it at once. The very existence of famous theorists such as Marx and Bakunin, who do play a leading role (whether they like it or not) by developing theory with which to educate the movement, is proof that in capitalist society this is not the case. Some anarchists propose that, instead of a leadership of people, we have a leadership of ideas. Actually, this shows how the objective necessity for political leadership forces its way into anarchist theory all the time. Only they give it another name instead. Anarchist theorists, themselves acting as leaders by developing theory to influence society, have variously made use of concepts such as "helpers" of the working class, working class "spokesmen," revolutionary "pathfinders," the need for a "conscious minority in the trade unions," or Bakunin's concept of a disciplined Blanquist "directorate" for the revolution. They use these terms but do not explain why they are necessary and how they really differ from political leadership. Why does the working class need helpers, pathfinders, a directorate, spokesmen, or a conscious minority? And what role would such people play? And if we merely have a leadership of ideas, then what of the people who developed those ideas (for they weren't developed by the whole working class in a collective, uniform way), who presumably can explain them best, who can be most trusted to put the ideas forward in trade union negotiations, which, after all, cannot involve the whole working class at once? To change the name of something is not to change its essence.

Whenever anarchists have found themselves with some influence in a real revolutionary movement, they have always had to reintroduce leadership or the state in some form. Makhno's movement, in order to defend itself from the White counterrevolution, "voted in favour of 'voluntary mobilisation,' which in reality meant outright conscription, as all able bodied men were required to serve when called up." With such military authority, they "allotted each commune livestock and farm implements confiscated from the neighbouring estates of the nobility." In other words, under Makhno's leadership they organised a state which repressed the counterrevolution and nobility, only one that was localised. Yes, they were autonomous from the Bolshevik government, but within their territory no one was autonomous. In addition, the movement had an extremely political character:

> "...the new council stimulated [i.e., led] the election of "free" soviets in the towns and villages, that is, soviets from which members of political parties were excluded [in other words, it was a dictatorship of Makhno's *de facto* party!]... the reigns of authority rested firmly with Makhno and his staff of commanders... Makhno appointed key officers." (Avrich, *The Russian Anarchists*, 214–15)

We do not say this in an attempt to besmirch his regime, rather to point out the way in which the crushing necessity of objective circumstances in a violent class struggle and civil war forced the role of political and personal leadership onto Makhno.

Syndicalist anarchists propose that a general strike, involving the vast majority of the working class, can be sufficient to overthrow capitalism, and moreover has the advantage of doing so without a party leadership. But the history of general strikes teaches otherwise—both in that on their own they are insufficient to overthrow capitalism (for we have had many general strikes, but still have capitalism) and in that trade unions do have political leadership in them. Unfortunately, this leadership rarely has a determined revolutionary mission, and tends to sell out general strikes. So, the demand for a general strike must also be accompanied by a political struggle against the ideas of the reformist trade union leadership. But history has shown that such a struggle does not emerge, and certainly does not succeed, in a purely automatic fashion. In a general strike some organised political grouping must raise the idea of the need to use the strike as a launch pad to overthrow capitalism so that the working class can build socialism. And such an organisation would therefore be playing a leading role. Its task must be to win the struggle, to defeat the reformists by convincing the mass of the working class that its ideas are correct and necessary; in other words, its task is to *lead the working class to take power and overthrow capitalism.*

Rejection of theory

As has been suggested above, there is a strong tendency in anarchism to reject theory as a scientific study of society, as they associate this with the intellectual elite and inaction. For this reason they tend to see all talk of "historical laws" in society, and of the objective roles of various classes, as intellectual charlatanism, as an idealist (meaning putting ideas or theory before or above society) invention with which to confuse the masses into accepting our leadership:

> Only feeling, passion, and desire have moved and will move men to acts of heroism and self-sacrifice; only in the realm of passionate life, the life of feeling, do heroes and martyrs draw their strength... we do not recognise the inevitability of social phenomena; we regard with scepticism the scientific value of many so-called laws of sociology. (Unknown author, from article in Russian anarchist journal *Burevestnik*, quoted in Avrich, *The Russian Anarchists*, p. 92)

As materialists we must ask—which passions, whose passions, under what circumstances, in aid of what? Do they speak of the passion of a Russian aristocrat with his mistress, the frustrated Russian intellectual who passionately threw a bomb into a crowded cafe, or a striking worker? And how is the passion to be used to aid the revolution rather than be wasted? Marxist theory is idealist only if its social laws are arbitrarily invented, and that is something the anarchists must themselves prove, and the only way to prove it is in society, by comparing Marxist theory with actual history. It is not sufficient to simply declare Marx's theories as bad for the movement because he thought them up in a library and not in the street, passions blazing. Unfortunately, twentieth-century history, with its industrialisation and mass workers parties, and general sidelining of all anarchist tendencies, would suggest that Marx's laws are not so arbitrary.

Because of their rejection of theory, many anarchists have resorted to simply describing the problems of capitalist society, and proposing antidotes as superficial as the act of simply inverting the names they give to capitalist oppression:

> The Gordins [a prominent Russian anarchist tendency in the early twentieth century] worked out a philosophy which they called "Pan-Anarchism" and which prescribed five remedies for the five baneful institutions that tormented the five oppressed elements of modern society. The remedies for the state and capitalism were, simply enough, statelessness and communism; for the remaining three oppressors, however, the antidotes were rather more novel:

"cosmism" (the universal elimination of national persecution), "gyneantropism" (the emancipation and humanization of women), and "pedism" (the liberation of the young from "the vice of slave education"). (Avrich, *The Russian Anarchists*, 177)

Visionary utopians, the anarchists paid scant attention to the practical needs of a rapidly changing world; they generally avoided careful analysis of social and economic conditions... in place of complex ideologies, they offered simple action-slogans. (Avrich, *The Russian Anarchists*, 253)

Rather than study the causes for all these social problems, the anarchists would treat them as arbitrary, and all that is needed to overcome them is for society to somehow collectively realise that it is suffering under some arbitrary injustice, and then collectively liberate itself. Political ideas, if they are complex (we actually hold that Marxism is not so complex or difficult to grasp), are complex because society itself is extremely complex, has a long history, and demands that serious attention be paid to it if it is to be changed in accordance with our wishes.

Anarchists mistakenly claim that Bakunin predicted Stalinism when he argued that, should the revolution be led by Marxists, it would inevitably degenerate into a dictatorship over the working class. But because of his lack of theory and of materialist, historical analysis, Bakunin actually failed to understand the material basis for the state which he hated so much. He simply registered the fact that for much of human history, state oppression existed, and drew the simple conclusion that it may also exist again in the future, without understanding why. His theory does not explain Stalinism. In the same way, I may witness stormy weather and expect it to come around again in the future, without having the slightest idea of what causes stormy weather. A stopped clock is "right" twice a day, but it cannot be used to tell the time.

As these lines are written, insurgents in Libya are waging a war with a counterrevolutionary state. But despite the obvious international implications and origins of this movement, they are struggling in isolation. Imperialism has now intervened, exploiting the lack of an international revolutionary organisation capable of intervening and offering revolutionary assistance. But the "West" has only intervened to secure its own interests, and not those of the Libyan masses. Thus, the international, revolutionary proletariat has a duty to offer their own assistance, which *would* be in the interests of the Libyan people. That, ultimately, means overthrowing imperialism in its heartland, so that the Libyans may never again feel its oppression. But to do that, a coordinated, worldwide struggle must be launched and fought to the finish. Only an international revolutionary leadership, drawing together the workers of the world, can live up to this task.

Bakunin said, "for as long as political power exists, there will always be rulers and ruled, masters and slaves, exploiters and exploited." We say, "for as long as exploiters and exploited, masters and slaves exist, there will always be political power, rulers, and the ruled."

31ˢᵗ March 2011

Anarchism and Socialism
G V Plekhanov

Preface to the first English edition by Eleanor Marx

The work of my friend Georgi Plekhanov, *Anarchism and Socialism*, was written originally in French. It was then translated into German by Mrs. Bernstein, and issued in pamphlet form by the German Social-Democratic Publishing Office *Vorwaerts*. It was next translated by myself into English, and so much of the translation as exigencies of space would permit, published in the *Weekly Times and Echo*.

As to the book itself. There are those who think that the precious time of so remarkable a writer, and profound a thinker as Georgi Plekhanov is simply wasted in pricking anarchist windbags. But, unfortunately, there are many of the younger, or of the more ignorant sort, who are inclined to take words for deeds, high-sounding phrases for acts, mere sound and fury for revolutionary activity, and who are too young or too ignorant to know that such sound and fury signify nothing. It is for the sake of these younger, or for the sake of the more ignorant, folk, that men like Plekhanov deal seriously with this matter of anarchism, and do not feel their time lost if they can, as this work must, help readers to see the true meaning of what is called "Anarchism."

And a work like this one of Plekhanov's is doubly necessary in England, where the socialist movement is still largely disorganised, where there is still such ignorance and confusion on all economic and political subjects; where, with the exception, among the larger Socialist organisations, of the Social-Democratic Federation (and even among the younger SDF members there is a vague sort of idea that anarchism is something fine and revolutionary), there has been no little coquetting with anarchism under an impression that it was very "advanced," and where the Old Unionist cry of "No politics!" has unconsciously played the reactionary anarchist game. We cannot afford to overlook the fact that the Socialist League became in time—when some of us had left it—an anarchist organisation, and that since then its leaders have been, or still are, more or less avowed anarchists. While quite recently the leader of a new party—and that a would-be political one!—did not hesitate to declare his anarchist sympathies or to state that "The methods of the anarchists might differ from those of the socialists, but that might only prove that the former were more zealous than the latter." It is also necessary to point out once again that anarchism and nihilism have no more in common than anarchism and socialism. As Plekhanov said at the Zurich International Congress: "We (i.e., the Russians) have had to endure every form of persecution, every thinkable misery; but we have been spared one disgrace, one humiliation; we, at least, have no anarchists." A statement endorsed and emphasised by other Russian revolutionists, and notably by the American delegate, Abraham Cahan—himself a Russian refugee. The men and women who are waging their heroic war in Russia and in Poland against tsarism have no more in common with anarchism than had the founders of the modern socialist movement—Karl Marx and Frederick Engels.

This little book of Plekhanov will assuredly convince the youngest even that under any circumstances anarchism is but another word for reaction; and the more honest the men and women who play this reactionist game, the more tragic and dangerous it becomes for the whole working class movement.

Eleanor Marx Aveling
Green Street Green, Orpington, Kent.
August 1895.

I. The point of view of the utopian socialists

The French Materialists of the eighteenth century while waging relentless war against all the "infames" whose yoke weighed upon the French of this period, by no means scorned the search after what they called "perfect legislation," i.e., the best of all possible legislations, such legislation as should secure to "human beings" the greatest sum of happiness, and could be alike applicable to all existing societies, for the simple reason that it was "perfect" and therefore the most "natural." Excursions into this domain of "perfect legislation" occupy no small place in the works of a d'Holbach and a Helvétius. On the other hand, the Socialists of the first half of our century threw themselves with immense zeal, with unequalled perseverance, into the search after the best of possible social organisations, after a perfect social organisation. This is a striking and notable characteristic which they have in common with the French Materialists of the last century, and it is this characteristic which especially demands our attention in the present work.

In order to solve the problem of a perfect social organisation, or what comes to the same thing, of the best of all possible legislation, we must eventually have some criterion by the help of which we may compare the various "legislations" one with the other. And the criterion must have a special attribute. In fact, there is no question of a "legislation" *relatively* the best, i.e., *the best legislation under given conditions*. No, indeed! We have to find a *perfect* legislation, a legislation whose perfection should have nothing relative about it, should be entirely independent of time and place, should be, in a word, absolute. We are therefore driven to make abstraction from history, since everything in history is relative, everything depends upon circumstance, time, and place. But abstraction made of the history of humanity, what is there left to guide us in our "legislative" investigations. Humanity is left us, man in general, human nature—of which history is but the manifestation. Here then we have our criterion definitely settled, a perfect legislation. The best of all possible legislation is that which best harmonises with human nature. It may be, of course, that even when we have such a criterion we may, for want of "light" or of logic, fail to solve this problem of the best legislation. *Errare humanum est,* but it seems incontrovertible that this problem can be solved, that we can, by taking our stand upon an exact knowledge of human nature, find a perfect legislation, a perfect organisation.

Such was, in the domain of social science, the point of view of the French Materialists. Man is a sentient and reasonable being, they said; he avoids painful sensations and seeks pleasurable ones. He has sufficient intelligence to recognise what is useful to him as well as what is harmful to him. Once you admit these axioms, and you can in your investigations into the best legislation, arrive, with the help of reflection and good intentions, at conclusions as well founded, as exact, as incontrovertible as those derived from a mathematical demonstration. Thus Condorcet undertook to construct deductively all precepts of healthy morality by starting from the truth that man is a sentient and reasonable being.

It is hardly necessary to say that in this Condorcet was mistaken. If the "philosophers" in this branch of their investigations arrived at conclusions of incontestable though very relative value, they unconsciously owed this to the fact that they constantly abandoned their abstract standpoint of human nature in general, and took up that of a more or less idealised nature of a man of the Third Estate. This man "felt" and "reasoned," after a fashion very clearly defined by his social environment. It was his "nature" to believe firmly in bourgeois property, representative government, freedom of trade ("laissez faire, laissez passer!" the "nature" of this man was always crying out), and so on. In reality, the French philosophers always kept in view the economic and political requirements of the Third Estate; this was their real criterion. But they applied it unconsciously, and only after much wandering in the field of abstraction, did they arrive at it. Their conscious method always reduced itself to abstract considerations of "human nature," and of the social and political institutions that best harmonise with this nature.

Their method was also that of the socialists. A man of the eighteenth century, Morelly, "to anticipate a mass of empty objections that would be endless," lays down as an incontrovertible principle "that in morals nature is one, constant, invariable ... that its laws never change;" and that "everything that may be advanced as to the variety in the morals of savage and civilised peoples, by no means proves that nature varies;" that at the outside it only shows "that from certain accidental causes which are foreign to it, some nations have fallen away from the laws of nature; others have remained submissive to them, in some respects from mere habit; finally, others are subjected to them by certain reasoned-out laws that are not always in contradiction with nature;" in a word, "man may abandon the true, but the true can never be annihilated!" Fourier relies upon the analysis of the human passions; Robert Owen starts from certain considerations on the formation of human character; Saint-Simon [Claude Henri de Rouvroy, comte de Saint-Simon, often referred to as Henri de Saint-Simon (17th October 1760, Paris – 19th May 1825, Paris)], despite his deep comprehension of the historical evolution of humanity, constantly returns to "human nature" in order to explain the laws of this evolution; the Saint-Simonians declared their philosophy was "based upon a new conception of human nature." The socialists of the various schools may quarrel as to the cause of their different conceptions of human nature; all, without a single exception, are convinced that social science has not and cannot have, any other basis than an adequate concept of this nature. In this they in no wise differ from the materialists of the eighteenth century. Human nature is the one criterion they invariably apply in their criticism of existing society, and in their search after a social organisation as it should be, after a "perfect" legislation.

Morelly, Fourier, Saint-Simon, Owen—we look upon all of them today as utopian socialists. Since we know the general point of view that is common to them all, we can determine exactly what the utopian point of view is. This will be the more useful, seeing that the opponents of socialism use the word "utopian" without attaching to it any, even approximately, definite meaning.

The utopian is one who, starting from an abstract principle, seeks for a perfect social organisation. The abstract principle which served as starting point of the utopians was that of human nature. Of course there have been utopians who applied the principle indirectly through the intermediary of concepts derived from it. Thus, e.g., in seeking for "perfect legislation," for an ideal organisation of society, one may start from the concept of the rights of man. But it is evident that in its ultimate analysis this concept derives from that of human nature.

It is equally evident that one may be a utopian without being a socialist. The bourgeois tendencies of the French Materialists of the last century are most noticeable in their investigations of a perfect legislation. But this in no wise destroys the utopian character of these enquiries. We have seen that the method of the utopian socialist does not in the least differ from that of d'Holbach or Helvétius, those champions of the revolutionary French bourgeoisie.

Nay, more. One may have the profoundest contempt for all "music of the future," one may be convinced that the social world in which one has the good fortune to live is the best possible of all social worlds, and yet in spite of this one may look at the structure and life of the body social from the same point of view as that from which the utopians regarded it.

This seems a paradox, and yet nothing could be more true. Take but one example.

In 1753 there appeared Morelly's work, *Les Isles Flottantes on la Basiliade du célébre Pelpai, traduit de l'Indien*. Now, note the arguments with which a review, *La Bibliotheque Impartiale*, combated the communistic ideas of the author: "One knows well enough that a distance separates the finest speculations of this kind and the possibility of their realisation. For in theory one takes imaginary men who lend themselves obediently to every arrangement, and who second with equal zeal the views of the legislator; but as soon as one attempts to put these things into practice one has to deal with men as they are, that is to say, unsubmissive, lazy, or else in the thralldom of some violent passion. The scheme of equality especially is one that seems most repugnant to the nature of man; they are born to command or to serve, a middle term is a burden to them."

Men are born to command or to serve. We cannot wonder, therefore, if in society we see masters and servants, since human nature wills it so. It was all very well for *La Bibliotheque Impartiale* to repudiate these communist speculations. The point of view from which it itself looked upon social phenomena, the point of view of human nature, it had in common with the utopian Morelly.

And it cannot be urged that this review was probably not sincere in its arguments, and that it appealed to human nature with the single object of saying something in favour of the exploiters, in favour of those who "command." But sincere or hypocritical in its criticism of Morelly, the *Bibliotheque Impartiale* adopted the standpoint common to all the writers of this period. They all of them appeal to human nature conceived of in one form or another, with the sole exception of the retrograde, who, living shadows of passed times, continued to appeal to the will of God.

As we know, this concept of human nature has been inherited by the nineteenth century from its predecessor. The utopian socialists had no other. But here again it is easy to prove that it is not peculiar to the utopians.

Even at the period of the Restoration, the eminent French historian, Guizot, in his historical studies, arrived at the remarkable conclusion that the political constitution of any given country depended upon the "condition of property" in that country. This was an immense advance upon the ideas of the last century which had almost exclusively considered the action of the "legislator." But what in its turn did these "conditions of property" depend on? Guizot is unable to answer this question, and after long, vain efforts to find a solution of the enigma in historical circumstances, he returns, falls back *nolens volens*, upon the theory of human nature. Augustin Thierry, another eminent historian of the Restoration, found himself in almost the same case, or rather he would have done so if only he had tried to investigate this question of the "condition of property" and its historical vicissitudes. In his concept of social life, Thierry was never able to go beyond his master Saint-Simon, who, as we have seen above, held firmly to the point of view of human nature.

The example of the brilliant Saint-Simon, a man of encyclopedic learning, demonstrates more clearly perhaps than any other, how narrow and insufficient was this point of view, in what confusion worse confounded of contradictions it landed those who applied it. Says Saint-Simon, with the profoundest conviction: "The future is made up of the last terms of a series, the first of which consist of the past. When one has thoroughly mastered the first terms of any series it is easy to put down their successors; thus from the past carefully observed one can easily deduce the future." This is so true that one asks oneself at the first blush why a man who had so clear a conception of the connection between the various phases of historical evolution, should be classed among the utopians. And yet, look more closely at the historical ideas of Saint-Simon, and you will find that we are not wrong in calling him a utopian. The future is deducible from the past, the historical evolution of humanity is a process governed by law. But what is the impetus, the motive power that sets in motion the human species, that makes it pass from one phase of evolution to another? Of what does this impetus consist? Where are we to seek it? It is here that Saint-Simon comes back to the point of view of all the utopians, to the point of view of human nature. Thus, according to him, the essential fundamental cause of the French Revolution was a change in the temporal and spiritual forces, and, in order to direct it wisely and conclude it rightly, it "was necessary to put into direct political activity the forces which had become preponderant." In other words, the manufacturers and the savants ought to have been called upon to formulate a political system corresponding to the new social conditions. This was not done, and the Revolution which had begun so well was almost immediately directed into a false path. The lawyers and metaphysicians became the masters of the situation. How to explain this historical fact? "It is in the nature of man," replies Saint-Simon, "to be unable to pass without some intermediate phase from any one doctrine to another. This law applies most stringently to the various political systems, through which the natural advance of civilisation compels the human species to pass. Thus the same necessity which in industry has created the element of a new temporal power, destined to replace military power, and which in the positive sciences, has created the element of a new spiritual power called upon to take the place of theological power, must have developed and set in activity (before the change in the conditions of society had begun to be very perceptible) a temporal or spiritual power of an intermediary, bastard, and transitory nature, whose only mission was to bring about the transition from one social system to another."

So we see that the "historical series" of Saint-Simon really explained nothing at all; they themselves need explanation, and for this we have again to fall back upon this inevitable human nature. The French Revolution was directed along a certain line, because human nature was so and so.

One of two things. Either human nature is, as Morelly thought, invariable, and then it explains nothing in history, which shows us constant variations in the relations of man to society; or it does vary according to the circumstances in which men live, and then, far from being the *cause*, it is itself the *effect* of historical evolution. The French Materialists knew well enough that man is the product of his social surroundings. "Man is all education," said Helvétius. This would lead one to suppose that Helvétius must have abandoned the human nature point of view in order to study the laws of the evolution of the environment that fashion human nature, giving to socialised man such or such an "education." And indeed Helvétius did make some efforts in this direction. But not he, nor his contemporaries, nor the socialists of the first half of our century, nor any representatives of science of the same period, succeeded in discovering a new point of view that should permit the study of the evolution of the social environment; the cause of the historical "education" of man, the cause of the changes which occur in his "nature." They were thus forced back upon the human nature point of view as the only one that seemed to supply them with a fairly solid basis for their scientific investigations. But since human nature in its turn varied, it became indispensable to make abstraction from its variations, and to seek in nature only stable properties, fundamental properties preserved in spite of all changes of its secondary properties. And in the end all that these speculations resulted in was a meagre abstraction, like that of the philosophers, e.g., "man is a sentient and reasonable being," which seemed all the more precious a discovery in that it left plenty of room for every gratuitous hypothesis, and every fantastical conclusion.

Guizot had no need to seek for the best of social organisations for a perfect legislation. He was perfectly satisfied with the existing ones. And assuredly the most powerful argument he could have advanced to defend them from the attacks of the malcontents would still have been human nature, which he would have said renders every serious change in the social and political constitution of France impossible. The malcontents condemned this same constitution, making use of the same abstraction. And since this abstraction, being completely empty, left, as we have said, full room for every gratuitous hypothesis and the logical consequences resulting therefrom, the "scientific" mission of these reformers assumed the appearance of a geometrical problem; given a certain nature, find what structure of society best corresponds with it. So Morelly complains bitterly because "our old teachers" failed to attempt the solution of "this excellent problem"—"to find the condition in which it should be almost impossible for men to be depraved, or wicked, or at any rate, *minima de malis.*" We have already seen that for Morelly human nature was "one, constant, invariable."

We now know what was the "scientific" method of the utopians. Before we leave them let us remind the reader that in human nature, an extremely thin and therefore not very satisfying abstraction, the utopians really appealed, not to human nature in general, but to the idealised nature of the men of their own day, belonging to the class whose social tendencies they represented. The social reality, therefore, inevitably appears in the words of the utopians, but the utopians were unconscious of this. They saw this reality only across an abstraction which, thin as it was, was by no means translucent.

II. The point of view of scientific socialism

The great idealist philosophers of Germany, Schelling and Hegel, understood the insufficiency of the human nature point of view. Hegel, in his *Philosophy of History*, makes fun of the utopian bourgeoisie in search of the best of constitutions. German Idealism conceived history as a process subject to law, and sought the motive-power of the historical movement *outside the nature of man*. This was a great step towards the truth. But the Idealists saw this motive-power in the absolute idea, in the "Weltgeist"; and as their absolute idea was only an abstraction of "our process of thinking," in their philosophical speculation upon history, they reintroduced the old love of the Materialist philosophers—human nature—but dressed in robes worthy of the respectable and austere society of German thinkers. Drive nature out of the door, she flies in at the window! Despite the great services rendered to social science by the German Idealists, the great problem of that science, its essential problem, was no more solved in the time of the German Idealists than in the time of the French Materialists. What is this hidden force that causes the historic movement of humanity? No one knew anything about it. In this field there was nothing to go upon save a few isolated observations, more or less accurate, more or less ingenious—sometimes indeed, very accurate and ingenious—but always disjointed and always incomplete.

That social science at last emerged from this dead end, it owes to Karl Marx.

According to Marx, "legal relations, like forms of state, can neither be understood in themselves nor from the so-called general development of the human mind, but are rather rooted in those material conditions of life, whose totality Hegel, following the English and the French of the eighteenth century, summed up under the name of 'bourgeois society'." This is almost the same as Guizot meant when he said that political constitutions had their roots in "the condition of property." But while for Guizot "the condition of property" remained a mystery which he vainly sought to elucidate with the help of reflections upon human nature, for Marx this "condition" had nothing mysterious; it is determined by the condition of the productive forces at the disposal of a given society. "The anatomy of bourgeois society is to be sought in political economy." But Marx himself shall formulate his own conception of history.

"In the social production of their lives, men enter upon certain definite, necessary relations, relations independent of their will, relations of production that correspond with definite degrees of development of their material productive forces. The totality of these relations of production constitute the economic structure of society, the true basis from which arises a juridical and political superstructure to which definite social forms of consciousness correspond. The mode of production of material life determines the social, political, and intellectual processes of life. It is not the consciousness of mankind that determines their being, but, on the contrary, their social being that determines their consciousness. In a certain stage of their development, the material forces of production of society come into contradiction with the existing relations of production, or, which is only a juridical expression for the same thing, with the relations of property within which they had hitherto moved. From forms for the development of these forces of production, they are transformed into their fetters. We then enter upon an epoch of social revolution."[1]

This completely materialist conception of history is one of the greatest discoveries of our century, so rich in scientific discoveries. Thanks to it alone sociology has at last, and forever, escaped from the vicious circle in which it had, until then, turned; thanks to it alone this science now possesses a foundation as solid as natural science. The revolution made by Marx in social science may be compared with that made by Copernicus in astronomy. In fact, before Copernicus, it was believed that the earth remained stationary, while the sun turned round it. The Polish genius demonstrated that what occurred was the exact contrary. And so, up to the time of Marx, the

1 1859 Preface to *A Contribution to the Critique of Political Economy* in *Marx/Engels Collected Works*, vol. 29 (New York: International, 1987), 263

point of view taken by social science, was that of "human nature"; and it was from this point of view that men attempted to explain the historical movement of humanity. To this the point of view of the German genius is diametrically opposed. While man, in order to maintain his existence, acts upon nature outside himself, he alters his own nature. The action of man upon the nature outside himself, presupposes certain instruments, certain means of production; according to the character of their means of production men enter into certain relations within the process of production (since this process is a social one), and according to their relations in this social process of production, their habits, their sentiments, their desires, their methods of thought and of action, in a word, their nature, vary. Thus it is not human nature which explains the historical movement; it is the historical movement which fashions diversely human nature.

But if this is so, what is the value of all the more or less laborious, more or less ingenious enquiries into "perfect legislation" and the best of possible social organisations! None; literally none! They can but bear witness to the lack of scientific education in those who pursue them. Their day is gone forever. With this old point of view of human nature must disappear the utopias of every shade and colour. The great revolutionary party of our day, the International Social-Democracy, is based not upon some "new conception" of human nature, nor upon any abstract principle, but upon a scientifically demonstrable economic necessity. And herein lies the real strength of this party, making it as invincible as the economic necessity itself.

> "The means of production and exchange on whose foundation the bourgeoisie built itself up, were generated in feudal society. At a certain stage in the development of these means of production and exchange, the conditions under which feudal society produced and exchanged, the feudal organisation of agriculture and manufacturing industry, in one word, the feudal relations of property become no longer compatible with the already developed productive forces, they become so many fetters. They had to be burst asunder; they were burst asunder. Into their place stepped free competition, accompanied by a social and political constitution adapted to it, and by the economic and political sway of the bourgeois class. A similar movement is going on before our own eyes. Modern bourgeois society, with its relations of production, of exchange, and of property, a society that has conjured up such gigantic means of production and of exchange, is like the sorcerer, who is no longer able to control the powers of the nether world whom he has called up by his spells. For many a decade past the history of industry and commerce is but the history of the revolt of modern productive forces against the property relations that are the conditions for the existence of the bourgeoisie and its rule. It is enough to mention the commercial crises that by their periodical return put on its trial, each time more threateningly, the existence of the entire bourgeois society....The weapons with

which the bourgeoisie felled feudalism to the ground are now turned against the bourgeoisie itself."[2]

The bourgeoisie destroyed the feudal conditions of property; the proletariat will put an end to the bourgeois conditions of property. Between the proletariat and the bourgeoisie a struggle, an implacable war, a war to the knife, is as inevitable as was, in its way, the struggle between the bourgeoisie and the privileged estates. *But every class war is a political war.* In order to do away with feudal society the bourgeoisie had to seize upon political power. In order to do away with capitalist society the proletariat must do the same. Its political task is therefore traced out for it beforehand by the force of events themselves, and not by any abstract consideration.

It is a remarkable fact that it is only since Karl Marx that socialism has taken its stand upon the class war. The utopian socialists had no notion—even an inexact one—of it. And in this they lagged behind their contemporary theorists of the bourgeoisie, who understood very well the historical significance at any rate of the struggle of the third estate against the nobles.

If every "new conception" of human nature seemed to supply very definite indications as to the organisation of "the society of the future," scientific socialism is very chary of such speculations. The structure of society depends upon the conditions of its productive forces. What these conditions will be when the proletariat is in power we do not know. We now know but one thing – that the productive forces already at the disposal of civilised humanity imperatively demand the socialisation and systematised organisation of the means of production. This is enough to prevent our being led astray in our struggle against "the reactionary mass." "The Communists, therefore, are practically the most advanced and resolute section of the working class parties of every country ... theoretically they have over the great mass of the proletariat the advantage of clearly understanding the line of march, the conditions, and the ultimate general results of the proletarian movement."[3] These words, written in 1848, are today incorrect only in one sense: they speak of "working class parties" independent of the Communist party; there is today no working class party which does not more or less closely follow the flag of scientific socialism, or, as it was called in the *Manifesto*, "Communism."

Once again, then, the point of view of the utopian socialists, as indeed of all social science of their time, was human nature, or some abstract principle deriving from this idea. The point of view of the social science, of the socialism of our time is that of economic reality, and of the immanent laws of its evolution. It is easy, therefore, to form an idea of the impression made

2 Karl Marx, *The Communist Manifesto* in *Four Marxist Classics* (St. Paul: Wellred, 2008), 8–9
3 Ibid., 15

upon modern socialists by the arguments of the bourgeois theorists who sing ceaselessly the same old song of the incompatibility of human nature and communism. It is as though one would wage war upon the Darwinians with arms drawn from the scientific arsenal of Cuvier's time. And a most noteworthy fact is that the "evolutionists" like Herbert Spencer, themselves are not above piping to the same tune.

And now let us see what relation there may be between modern socialism and what is called anarchism.

III. The historical development of the anarchist doctrine

"I have often been reproached with being the father of anarchism. This is doing me too great an honour. The father of anarchism is the immortal Proudhon, who expounded it for the first time in 1848."

Thus spoke Peter Kropotkin in his defence before the Correctional Tribunal of Lyons at his trial in January, 1883. As is frequently the case with my amiable compatriot, Kropotkin has here made a statement that is incorrect. For "the first time" Proudhon spoke of anarchism was in his celebrated book, *Qu'est-ce que le Proprieté, ou Recherches sur le principe du droit et du Gouvernement*, the first edition of which had already appeared in 1840. It is true that he "expounds" very little of it here; he only devotes a few pages to it. And before he set about expounding the anarchist theory "in 1848," the job had already been done by a German, Max Stirner (the pseudonym of Caspar Schmidt) in 1845, in his book *Der Einzige und sein Eigenthum*. Max Stirner has therefore a well-defined claim to be the father of anarchism. "Immortal" or not, it is by him that the theory was "expounded" *for the first time*.

The anarchist theory of Max Stirner has been called a caricature of the "philosophy of religion" of Ludwig Feuerbach. It is thus, e.g. that Ueberweg in his *Grundzüge der Geschichte der Philosophie*, (3rd part, *Philosophie der Neuen Zeit*) speaks of it. Some have even supposed that the only object Stirner had in writing his book was to poke fun at this philosophy. This supposition is absolutely gratuitous. Stirner in expounding his theory was not joking. He is in deadly earnest about it, though he now and again betrays a tendency, natural enough in the restless times when he wrote, to outdo Feuerbach and the radical character of his conclusions.

For Feuerbach, what men call divinity, is only the product of their fantasy, of a psychological aberration. It is not divinity that has created man, but man who creates divinity in his own image. In God man only adores his own being. God is only a fiction, but a very harmful fiction. The Christian God is supposed to be all love, all pity for poor suffering humanity. But in spite of this, or rather because of it, every Christian really worthy the name, hates, and must hate, the atheists, who appear to him the living negation of all love and all pity. Thus the god of love becomes the god of hate, the god of persecution; the product of the fantasy of man becomes a real cause of his suffering. So we must make an end of this phantasmagoria. Since in divinity man adores only his own being, we must once for all rend and scatter to the winds the mystic veil beneath which this being has been enveloped. The love of humanity must not extend beyond humanity. "*Der Mensch ist dem Menschen das höchste Wesen*" (Man is the highest being for man).

Thus Feuerbach. Max Stirner is quite at one with him, but wishes to deduce what he believes to be the final, the most radical consequences of his theory. He reasons in this fashion. God is only the product of fantasy, is only a *spook*. Agreed. But what is this humanity the love of which you prescribe to me? Is not this also a spook, an abstract thing, a creature of the imagination? Where is this humanity of yours? Where does it exist but in the minds of men, in the minds of individuals? The only reality, therefore, is the *individual*, with his wants, his tendencies, his will. But since this is so, how can the *individual*, the reality, sacrifice himself for the happiness of man, an abstract being? It is all very well for you to revolt against the old God; you still retain the religious point of view, and the emancipation you are trying to help us to is absolutely theological, i.e., "God-inspired." "The highest being is certainly that of man, but because it is his *being* and is not he himself, it is quite indifferent if we see this Being outside of him as God, or find it in him and call it the 'Being of Mankind' or 'Man.' I am neither God nor man, neither the highest being, nor my own being, and therefore it is essentially a matter of indifference if I imagine this being in myself or outside myself. And, indeed, we do always imagine the highest being in the two future states, in the internal and external at once; for the 'Spirit of God' is, according to the Christian conception, also 'our spirit' and 'dwells within us.' It dwells in heaven and dwells in us; but we poor things are but its 'dwelling-place,' and if Feuerbach destroys its heavenly dwelling-place and forces it to come down to us bag and baggage, we, its earthly abode, will find ourselves very over-crowded."

To escape the inconveniences of such over-crowding, to avoid being dominated by any spook, to at last place our foot upon actual ground, there is but one way: to take as our starting point the only real being, our own ego. "Away then with everything that is not wholly and solely my own affair! You think my own concerns must at least be 'good ones'? A fig for good and evil! I am I, and I am neither good nor evil. Neither has any meaning for me. The godly is the affair of God, the human that of humanity. My concern is neither the Godly nor the Human, is not the True, the Good, the Right, the Free, etc., but simply my own self, and it is not general, it is individual, as I myself am individual. For me there is nothing above myself."

Religion, conscience, morality, right, law, family, state, are but so many fetters forced upon me in the name of an abstraction, but so many despotic lords whom "I," the individual conscious of my own "concerns," combat by every means in my power. Your "morality," not merely the morality of the bourgeois philistines, but the most elevated, the most humanitarian morality is only religion which has changed its supreme beings. Your "right," that you believe born with man, is but a ghost, and if you respect it, you are no farther advanced than the heroes of Homer who were afraid when they beheld a god fighting in the ranks of their enemies. Right is might. "Whoever has might, he has right; if you have not the former you have not the latter. Is this wisdom so difficult of attainment?" You would persuade me to sacrifice my interests to those of the state. I, on the contrary, declare war to the knife to all states, even the most democratic. "Every State is a despotism, whether it is the despotism of one or many, or whether, as one might suppose would be the case in a Republic, all are masters, i.e., one tyrannises over the rest. For this is the case whenever a given law, the expressed will perhaps of some assemblage of the people, is immediately to become a law to the individual, which he must obey, and which it is his *duty* to obey. Even if one were to suppose a case in which every individual among the people had expressed the same will, and thus a perfect "will of all" had easily been arrived at, the thing would still be the same. Should I not today and in the future be bound by my will of yesterday? In this event my will would be paralysed. Fatal stagnation! My creation, i.e. a certain expression of will would have become my master. But I, in my will should be constrained, I, the creator should be constrained in my development, my working out. Because I was a fool yesterday, I must remain one all my life. So that in my life in relation to the State I am at best—I might as well say at worst—a slave to my own self. Because yesterday I had a will, I am today without one; yesterday free, today bound."

Here a partisan of the "People's State" might observe to Stirner, that his "I" goes a little too far in his desire to reduce democratic liberty to absurdity; further, that a bad law may be abrogated as soon as a majority of citizens desire it, and that one is not forced to submit to it "all one's life." But this is only an insignificant detail, to which, moreover, Stirner would reply that the very necessity for appealing to a majority proves that "I" am no longer the master of my own conduct. The conclusions of our author are irrefutable, for the simple reason that to say, I recognise nothing above myself, is to say, I feel oppressed by every institution that imposes any duty upon me. It is simply tautology.

It is evident that no "Ego" can exist quite alone. Stirner knows this perfectly, and this is why he advocates "Leagues of Egoists," that is to say, free associations into which every "Ego" enters, and in which he remains when and so long as it suits his interests.

Here let us pause. We are now face to face with an "egoist" system "par excellence." It is, perhaps, the only one that the history of human thought has to chronicle. The French Materialists of the last century have been accused of preaching egoism. The accusation was quite wrong. The French Materialists always preached "Virtue," and preached it with such unlimited zeal that Grimm could, not without reason, make fun of their "capucinades" on the subject. The question of egoism presented to them a double problem. (1) Man is all sensation (this was the basis of all their speculations upon man); by his very nature he is forced to shun suffering and to seek pleasure; how comes it then that we find men capable of enduring the greatest sufferings for the sake of some idea, that is to say, in its final analysis, in order to provide agreeable sensations for their fellow men. (2) Since man is all sensation he will harm his fellow man if he is placed in a social environment where the interests of an individual conflict with those of others. What form of legislation therefore can harmonise public good and that of individuals? Here, in this double problem, lies the whole significance of what is called the materialist ethics of the eighteenth century. Max Stirner pursues an end entirely opposed to this. He laughs at "Virtue," and, far from desiring its triumph, he sees reasonable men only in egoists, for whom there is nothing above their own "Ego." Once again, he is the theorist "par excellence" of egoism.

The good bourgeois whose ears are as chaste and virtuous as their hearts are hard; they who, "drinking wine, publicly preach water," were scandalised to the last degree by the "immorality" of Stirner. "It is the complete ruin of the moral world," they cried. But as usual the virtue of the philistines showed itself very weak in argument. "The real merit of Stirner is that he has spoken the last word of the young atheist school" (i.e., the left wing of the Hegelian school), wrote the Frenchman, Saint-René Taillandier. The philistines of other lands shared this view of the "merits" of the daring publicist. From the point of view of modern socialism this "merit" appears in a very different light.

To begin with, the incontestable merit of Stirner consists in his having openly and energetically combated the sickly sentimentalism of the bourgeois reformers and of many of the utopian socialists, according to which the emancipation of the proletariat would be brought about by the virtuous activity of "devoted" persons of all classes, and especially of those of the possessing class. Stirner knew perfectly what to expect from the "devotion" of the exploiters. The "rich" are harsh, hard-hearted, but the "poor" (the terminology is that of our author) are wrong to complain of it, since it is not the rich who create the poverty of the poor, but the poor who create the wealth of the rich. They ought to blame themselves then if their condition is a hard one. In order to change it they have only to revolt against the rich; as soon as they seriously wish it, they will be the strongest and the reign of wealth will be at an end. Salvation lies in struggle, and not in fruitless appeals to the generosity of the oppressors. Stirner, therefore, preaches the class war. It is true that he represents it in the abstract form of the struggle of a certain number of egoist "Egos" against another smaller number of "Egos" not less egoist. But here we come to another merit of Stirner's.

According to Taillandier, he has spoken the last word of the young atheist school of German philosophers. As a matter of fact he has only spoken the last word of idealist speculation. But that word he has incontestably the merit of having spoken.

In his criticism of religion Feuerbach is but half a materialist. In worshipping God, man only worships his own being idealised. This is true. But religions spring up and die out, like everything else upon earth. Does this not prove that the human being is not immutable, but changes in the process of the historical evolution of societies? Clearly, yes. But, then, what is the cause of the historical transformation of the "human being"? Feuerbach does not know. For him the human being is only an abstract notion, as human nature was for the French Materialists. This is the fundamental fault of his criticism of religion. Stirner said that it had no very robust constitution. He wished to strengthen it by making it breathe the fresh air of reality. He turns his back upon all phantoms, upon all things of the imagination. In reality, he said to himself, these are only individuals. Let us take the individual for our starting-point. But *what* individual does he take for his starting-point? Tom, Dick, or Harry? Neither. He takes the *individual in general*—he takes a new abstraction, the thinnest of them all—he takes the "Ego."

Stirner naïvely imagined that he was finally solving an old philosophical question, which had already divided the Nominalists and the Realists of the Middle Ages. "No Idea has an existence," he says, "for none is capable of becoming corporeal. The scholastic controversy of Realism and Nominalism had the same content." Alas! The first Nominalist he came across could have demonstrated to our author by the completest evidence, that his "Ego" is as much an "Idea" as any other, and that it is as little real as a mathematical unit.

Tom, Dick and Harry have relations with one another that do not depend upon the will of their "Ego," but are imposed upon them by the structure of the society in which they live. To criticise social institutions in the name of the "Ego," is therefore to abandon the only profitable point of view in the case, i.e., that of society, of the laws of its existence and evolution, and to lose oneself in the mists of abstraction. But it is just in these mists that the "Nominalist" Stirner delights. I am I—that is his starting point; not I is not I—that is his result. I + I + I + etc.—is his social utopia. It is subjective idealism, pure and simple applied to social and political criticism. It is the suicide of idealist speculation.

But in the same year (1845) in which *Der Einzige* of Stirner appeared, there appeared also, at Frankfort-on-Maine the work of Marx and Engels, *Die heilige Familie, oder Kritik der Kritischen Kritik, gegen Bruno Bauer und Consorten* [*The Holy Family, or Critique of Critical Criticism: Against Bruno Bauer and Co.—ed.*]. In it idealist speculation was attacked and beaten by materialist dialectic, the theoretical basis of modern socialism. *Der Einzige* came too late.

We have just said that I + I + I + etc. represents the social utopia of Stirner. His League of Egoists is, in fact, nothing but a mass of abstract quantities. What are, what can be the basis of their union? Their interests, answers Stirner. But what will, what can be the true basis of any given combination of their interests? Stirner says nothing about it, and he can say nothing definite, since from the abstract heights on which he stands, one cannot see clearly economic reality, the mother and nurse of all the "Egos," egoistic or altruistic. Nor is it surprising that he is not able to explain clearly even this idea of the class struggle, of which he nevertheless had a happy inkling. The "poor" must combat the "rich." And after, when they have conquered these? Then every one of the former "poor," like every one of the former "rich" will combat every one of the former poor, and against every one of the former rich. There will be the war of all against all. (These are Stirner's own words). And the rules of the "Leagues of Egoists" will be so many partial truces in this colossal and universal warfare. There is plenty of fight in this idea, but of the "realism" Max Stirner dreamed of, nothing.

But enough of the "Leagues of Egoists." A utopian may shut his eyes to economic reality, but it forces itself upon him in spite of himself; it pursues him everywhere with the brutality of a natural force not controlled by force. The elevated regions of the abstract "I" do not save Stirner from the attacks of economic reality. He does not speak to us only of the "Individual"; his theme is "the Individual *and his property.*" Now, what sort of a figure does the property of the "Individual" cut?

It goes without saying, that Stirner is little inclined to respect property as an "acquired right." "Only that property will be legally and lawfully another's which it suits *you* should be his property. When it ceases to suit you, it has lost its legality for you, and any absolute right in it you will laugh at." It is always the same tune: "For me there is nothing above myself." But his scant respect for the property of others does not prevent the "Ego" of Stirner from having the tendencies of a property owner. The strongest argument against communism, is, in his opinion, the consideration that communism by abolishing individual property transforms all members of society into mere beggars. Stirner is indignant at such an iniquity.

"Communists think that the Commune should be the property owner. On the contrary, I am a property owner, and can only agree with others as to my property. If the Commune does not do as I wish I rebel against it, and defend my property, I am the owner of property, but property *is not sacred*. Should I only be the holder of property (an allusion to Proudhon)? No, hitherto one was only a holder of property, assured of possession of a piece of land, because one left others also in possession of a piece of land; but now *everything* belongs to me, I am the owner of *everything I need*, and can get hold of. If the Socialist says, society gives me what I need, the Egoist says, I take what I want. If the Communists behave like beggars, the Egoist behaves like an owner of property." The property of the egoist seems pretty shaky. An "Egoist" retains his property only as long as the other "Egoists" do not care to take it from him, thus transforming him into a "beggar." But the devil is not so black as he is painted. Stirner pictures the mutual relations of the "Egoist" proprietors rather as relations of exchange than of pillage. And force, to which he constantly appeals, is rather the economic force of a producer of commodities freed from the trammels which the state and "Society" in general impose, or seem to impose, upon him.

It is the soul of a producer of commodities that speaks through the mouth of Stirner. If he falls foul of the state, it is because the state does not seem to respect the "property" of the producers of commodities sufficiently. He wants *his* property, his *whole* property. The state makes him pay taxes; it ventures to expropriate him for the public good. He wants a "jus utendi et abutendi;" the state says "agreed"—but adds that there are abuses and abuses. Then Stirner cries "stop thief!" "I am the enemy of the State," says he, "which is always fluctuating between the alternative: He or I.... With the State there is no property, i.e., no individual property, only State property. Only through the State have I what I have, as it is only through the State that I am what I am. My private property is only what the State leaves me of its own, while it deprives other citizens of it: that is State property." So down with the state and long live full and complete individual property!

Stirner translates into German J.B. Say's *Traite D'Economie Politique Pratique* (Leipzig, 1845–46). And although he also translated Adam Smith, he was never able to get beyond the narrow circle of the ordinary bourgeois economic ideas. His "League of Egoists" is only the utopia of a petty-bourgeois in revolt. In this sense one may say he has spoken the last word of bourgeois individualism.

Stirner has also a third merit—that of the courage of his opinions, of having carried through to the very end his individualist theories. He is the most intrepid, the most consequent of the anarchists. By his side Proudhon, whom Kropotkin, like all the present day anarchists, takes for the father of anarchism, is but a straight-laced Philistine.

IV. Proudhon

If Stirner combats Feuerbach, the "immortal" Proudhon imitates Kant. "What Kant did some sixty years ago for religion what he did earlier for certainty of certainties; what others before him had attempted to do for happiness or supreme good, the *Voice of the People* proposes to do for the government," pompously declares "the father of Anarchism." Let us examine his methods and their results.

According to Proudhon, before Kant, the believer and the philosopher moved "by an irresistible impulse," asked themselves, "What is God?" They then asked themselves "Which, of all religions, is the best?" "In fact, if there does exist a being superior to humanity, there must also exist a system of the relations between this being and humanity. What then is this system? The search for the best religion is the second step that the human mind takes in reason and in faith. Kant gave up these insolvable questions. He no longer asked himself what is God, and which is the best religion; he set about explaining the origin and development of the idea of God; he undertook to work out the biography of this idea." And the results he attained were as great as they were unexpected. "What we seek, what we see, in God, as Malebranche said ... is our own ideal, the pure essence of humanity ... The human soul does not become conscious of its ego through premeditated contemplation, as the psychologists put it; the soul perceives something outside itself, as if it were a different being face to face with itself, and it is this inverted image which it calls God. Thus morality, justice, order, law, are no longer things revealed from above, imposed upon our free will by a so-called creator, unknown and ununderstandable; they are things that are proper and essential to us as our faculties and our organs, as our flesh and our blood. In two words religion and society are synonymous terms, man is as sacred to himself as if he were God."

Belief in authority is as primitive, as universal as belief in God. Wherever men are grouped together in societies there is authority, the beginning of a government. From time immemorial men have asked themselves, What is authority? Which is the best form of government? And replies to these questions have been sought for in vain. There are as many governments as there are religions, as many political theories as systems of philosophy. Is there any way of putting an end to this interminable and barren controversy? Any means of escape from this impasse?" Assuredly! We have only to follow the example of Kant. We have only to ask ourselves whence comes this idea of authority, of government? We have only to get all the information we can upon the legitimacy of the political idea. Once safe on this ground and the question solves itself with extraordinary ease.

> "Like religion, government is a manifestation of social spontaneity, a preparation of humanity for a higher condition.

> "What humanity seeks in religion and calls God, is itself….What the citizen seeks in government and calls king, emperor, or president, is again himself, is liberty….Outside humanity there is no God; the theological concept has no meaning—outside liberty no government, the political concept has no value."

So much for the "biography" of the political idea. Once grasped it must enlighten us upon the question as to which is the best form of government.

> "The best form of government, like the most perfect of religions, taken in a literal sense, is a contradictory idea. The problem is not to discover how we shall be best governed, but how we shall be most free. Liberty commensurate and identical with order—this is the only reality of government and politics. How shall this absolute liberty, synonymous with order, be brought about? We shall be taught this by the analysis of the various formulas of authority. For all the rest we no more admit the governing of man by man than the exploitation of man by man."

We have now climbed to the topmost heights of Proudhon's political philosophy. It is from this that the fresh and vivifying stream of his anarchist thought flows. Before we follow the somewhat tortuous course of this stream let us glance back at the way we have climbed.

We fancied we were following Kant. We were mistaken. In his *Critique of Pure Reason* Kant has demonstrated the impossibility of proving the existence of God, because everything outside experience must escape us absolutely. In his *Critique of Practical Reason* Kant admitted the existence of God in the name of morality. But he has never declared that God was a topsy-turvy image of our own soul. What Proudhon attributes to Kant, indubitably belongs to Feuerbach. Thus it is in the footsteps of the latter that we have been treading, while roughly tracing out the "biography" of the political idea. So that Proudhon brings us back to the very starting point of our most unsentimental journey with Stirner. No matter. Let us once more return to the reasoning of Feuerbach.

It is only itself that humanity seeks in religion. Self, it is liberty that the citizen seeks in government ... Then the very essence of the citizen is liberty? Let us assume this is true, but let us also note that our French "Kant" has done nothing, absolutely nothing, to prove the "legitimacy" of such an "Idea." Nor is this all. What is this liberty which we are assuming to be the essence of the citizen? Is it political liberty which ought in the nature of things to be the main object of his attention? Not a bit of it! To assume this would be to make of the "citizen" an "authoritarian" democrat. It is the *absolute liberty of the individual,* which is at the same time *commensurate and identical* with order, that our citizen seeks in government. In other words, it is the anarchism of Proudhon which is the essence of the "citizen." It is impossible to make a more pleasing discovery, but the "biography" of this discovery gives us pause. We have been trying to demolish every argument in favour of the idea of authority, as Kant demolished every proof of the existence of God. To attain this end we have—imitating Feuerbach to some extent, according to whom man adored his own being in God—assumed that it is liberty which the citizen seeks in government. And as to liberty we have in a trice transformed this into "absolute" liberty, into anarchist liberty. *Eins, zwei, drei; Geschwindigkeit ist keine Hexerei!* [One, two, three; speed is not magic!—ed.]

Since the "citizen" only seeks "absolute" liberty in government, the state is nothing but a fiction ("this fiction of a superior person, called the 'State'"), and all those formulas of government for which people and citizens have been cutting one another's throats for the last sixty centuries, are but the phantasmagoria of our brain, which it would be the first duty of free reason to relegate to the museums and libraries. Which is another charming discovery made *en passant.* So that the political history of humanity has, "for sixty centuries," had no other motive power than a phantasmagoria of our brain!

To say that man adores in God his own essence is to indicate the origin of religion, but it is not to work out its "biography." To write the biography of religion is to write its history, explaining the evolution of this essence of man which found expression in it. Feuerbach did not do this—could not do it. Proudhon, trying to imitate Feuerbach, was very far from recognising the insufficiency of his point of view. All Proudhon has done is to take Feuerbach for Kant, and to ape his Kant-Feuerbach in a most pitiful manner. Having heard that divinity was but a fiction, he concluded that the state is also a figment: since God does not exist, how can the state exist? Proudhon wished to combat the state and began by declaring it non-existent. And the readers of the *Voix du Peuple* applauded, and the opponents of M. Proudhon were alarmed at the profundity of his philosophy! Truly a tragi-comedy!

It is hardly necessary for modern readers to add that in taking the state for a fiction we make it altogether impossible to understand its "essence" or to explain its historical evolution. And this was what happened to Proudhon.

"In every society I distinguish two kinds of constitution," says he; "the one which I call *social,* the other which is its *political* constitution; the first innate in humanity, liberal, necessary, its development consisting above all in weakening, and gradually eliminating the second, which is essentially factitious, restrictive, and transitory. The social constitution is nothing but the equilibration of interests based upon free contract and the organisation of the economic forces, which, generally speaking, are labour, division of labour, collective force, competition, commerce, money, machinery, credit, property, equality in transactions, reciprocity of guarantees, etc. The principle of the political constitution is authority. Its forms are: distinction of classes, separation of powers, administrative centalisation, the judicial hierarchy, the representation of sovereignty by elections, etc. The political constitution was conceived and gradually completed in the interest of order, for want of a social constitution, the rules and principles of which could only be discovered as a result of long experience, and are even today the object of socialist controversy. These two constitutions, as it is easy to see, are by nature absolutely different and even incompatible: but as it is the fate of the political constitution to constantly call forth and produce the social constitution something of the latter enters into the former, which, soon becoming inadequate, appears contradictory and odious, is forced from concession to concession to its final abrogation." The social constitution is innate in humanity, necessary. Yet it could only be discovered as the result of long experience, and for want of it humanity had to invent the political constitution. Is not this an entirely utopian conception of human nature, and of the social organisation peculiar to it? Are we not coming back to the standpoint of Morelly who said that humanity in the course of its history has always been "outside nature"? No— there is no need to come back to this standpoint, for with Proudhon we have never, for a single instant, got away from it. While looking down upon the utopians searching after "the best form of government," Proudhon does not by any means censure the utopian point of view. He only scoffs at the small perspicacity of men who did not divine that the best political organisation is the absence of all political organisation, is the social organisation, proper to human nature, necessary, immanent in humanity.

The nature of this social constitution is absolutely different from, and even incompatible with, that of the political constitution. Nevertheless it is the fate of the political constitution to constantly call forth and produce the social constitution. This is tremendously confusing! Yet one might get out of the difficulty by assuming that what Proudhon meant to say was that the political constitution acts upon the evolution of the social constitution. But then we are inevitably met by the question, is not the political constitution in its turn rooted—as even Guizot admitted—in the social constitution of a country? According to our author *no*; the more emphatically *no*, that the social organisation, the true and only one, is only a thing of the future, for want of which poor humanity has "invented" the political constitution.

Moreover, the "Political Constitution" of Proudhon covers an immense domain, embracing even "class distinctions," and therefore "non-organised" property, property as it ought not to be, property as it is today. And since the whole of this political constitution has been invented as a mere stop-gap until the advent of the anarchist organisation of society, it is evident that all human history must have been one huge blunder. The state is no longer exactly a fiction as Proudhon maintained in 1848; "the governmental formulas for which people and citizens have been cutting one another's throats for sixty centuries are no longer a "mere phantasmagoria of our brain," as the same Proudhon believed at this same period; but these formulas, like the state itself, like every political constitution, are but the product of human ignorance, the mother of all fictions and phantasmagorias. At bottom it is always the same. The main point is that anarchist ("social") organisation could only be discovered as the result of "many experiences." The reader will see how much this is to be regretted.

The political constitution has an unquestionable influence upon the social organisation; at any rate it calls it forth, for such is its "fate" as revealed by Proudhon, master of Kantian philosophy and social organisation. The most logical conclusion to be drawn therefrom is that the partisans of social organisation must make use of the political constitution in order to attain their end. But logical as this deduction is, it is not to the taste of our author. For him it is but a phantasmagoria of our brain. To make use of the political constitution is to offer a burnt offering to the terrible god of authority, to take part in the struggle of parties. Proudhon will have none of this. "No more parties," he says; "no more authority, absolute liberty of the man and the citizen—in three words, such is our political and social profession of faith."

Every class struggle is a political struggle. Whosoever repudiates the political struggle, by this very act gives up all part and lot in the class struggle. And so it was with Proudhon. From the beginning of the Revolution of 1848 he preached the reconciliation of classes. Here, e.g., is a passage from the circular which he addressed to his electors in Doubs, which is dated 3rd April of this same year: "The social question is there; you cannot escape from it. To solve it we must have men who combine extreme radicalism of mind with extreme conservatism of mind. Workers, hold out your hands to your employers; and you, employers, do not deliberately repulse the advances of those who were your wage earners."

The man whom Proudhon believed to combine this extreme radicalism of mind with extreme conservatism of mind, was himself— P.J. Proudhon. There was, on the one hand, at the bottom of this belief a "fiction," common to all utopians who imagine they can rise above classes and their struggles, and naïvely think that the whole of the future history of humanity will be confined to the peaceful propagation of their new gospel. On the other hand, this tendency to combine radicalism and conservatism shows conclusively the very "essence" of the "Father of Anarchy."

Proudhon was the most typical representative of petty-bourgeois socialism. Now the "fate" of the petty-bourgeois— in so far as he does not adopt the proletarian standpoint—is to constantly oscillate between radicalism and conservatism. To make more understandable what we have said, we must bear in mind what the plan of social organisation propounded by Proudhon was.

Our author shall tell us himself. It goes without saying that we shall not escape a more or less authentic interpretation of Kant. "Thus the line we propose to follow in dealing with the political question and in preparing the materials for a constitution will be the same as that we have followed hitherto in dealing with the social question." The *Voix du Peuple* while completing the work of its predecessors, the two earlier journals, will follow faithfully in their footsteps. What did we say in these two publications, one after the other of which fell beneath the blows of the reaction and the state of siege? We did not ask, as our precursors and colleagues had done, which is the best system of community? The best organisation of property? Or again: Which is the better, property or the community? The theory of Saint-Simon or that of Fourier? The system of Louis Blanc or that of Cabet? Following the example of Kant we stated the question thus: "How is it that man possesses? How is property acquired? How lost? What is the law of its evolution and transformation? Whither does it tend? What does it want? What, in fine, does it represent?...Then how is it that man labours? How is the comparison of products instituted? By what means is circulation carried out in society? Under what conditions? According to what laws?" And the conclusion arrived at by this monograph of property was this: Property indicates function or attribution; community; reciprocity of action; usury ever decreasing, the identity of labour and capital (sic!). In order to set free and to realise all these terms, until now hidden beneath the old symbols of property, what must be done? The workers must guarantee one another labour and a market; and to this end must accept as money their reciprocal pledges. Good! Today we say that political liberty, like industrial liberty, will result for us from our mutual guarantees. It is by guaranteeing one another liberty that we shall get rid of this government, whose destiny is to symbolize the republican motto: "Liberty, Equality, Fraternity," while leaving it to our intelligence to bring about the realisation of this. Now, what is the formula of this political and liberal guarantee? At present universal suffrage; later on free contract.... Economic and social reform through the mutual guarantee of credit; political reform through the interaction of individual liberties; such is the programme of the *Voix du Peuple.*" We may add to this that it is not very difficult to write the "biography" of this programme.

In a society of producers of commodities, the exchange of commodities is carried out according to the labour socially necessary for their production. Labour is the source and the measure of their exchange value. Nothing could seem more "just" than this to any man imbued with the ideas engendered by a society of producers of commodities. Unfortunately this justice is no more "eternal" than anything else here below. The development of the production of commodities necessarily brings in its train the transformation of the greater part of society into proletarians, possessing nothing but their labour power, and of the other part into capitalists, who, buying this power, the only commodity of the proletarians, turn it into a source of wealth for themselves. In working for the capitalists the proletarian produces the income of his exploiter, at the same time as his own poverty, his own social subjection. Is not this sufficiently unjust? The partisan of the rights of the producer of commodities deplores the lot of the proletarians; he thunders against capital. But at the same time he thunders against the revolutionary tendencies of the proletarians who speak of expropriating the exploiter and of a communistic organisation of production. Communism is unjust, it is the most odious tyranny. What wants organising is not *production* but *exchange*, he assures us. But how organise exchange? That is easy enough, and what is daily going on before our eyes may serve to show us the way. Labour is the source and the measure of the *value* of commodities. But is the price of commodities always determined by their value? Do not prices continually vary according to the rarity or abundance of these commodities? The value of a commodity and its price are two different things; and this is the misfortune, the great misfortune of all of us poor, honest folk, who only want justice, and only ask for our own. To solve the social question, therefore we must put a stop to the *arbitrariness of prices*, and to the anomaly of value (Proudhon's own expressions). And in order to do this we must "constitute" value; i.e., see that every producer shall always, in exchange for his commodity, receive exactly what it costs, private property not only cease to be theft, it will become the most adequate expression of justice. To constitute value is to constitute small private property, and small private property once constituted, everything will be justice and happiness in a world now so full of misery and injustice. And it is no good for proletarians to object, they have no means of production: by guaranteeing themselves *credit gratis*, all who want to work will, as by the touch of a magic wand, have everything necessary for production.

Small property and small parceled-out production, its economic basis, was always the dream of Proudhon. The huge modern mechanical workshop always inspired him with profound aversion. He says that labour, like love, flies from society. No doubt there are some industries—Proudhon instances railways—in which *association* is essential. In these, the isolated producer must make way for "companies of workers." But the exception only proves the rule. Small private property must be the basis of "social organisation."

Small private property is tending to disappear. The desire not merely to preserve it, but to transform it into the basis of a new social organisation is extreme conservatism. The desire at the same time to put an end to "the exploitation of man by man," to the wage system, is assuredly to combine with the most conservative the most radical aspirations.

We have no desire here to criticise this petty-bourgeois utopia. This criticism has already been undertaken by a master hand in the works of Marx: *La Misère de la Philosophie* [*The Poverty of Philosophy—ed.*], and *Zur Kritik der Politischen Oekonomie* [*A Contribution to the Critique of Political Economy—ed.*]. We will only observe the following:

The only bond that unites the producers of commodities upon the domain of economics is exchange. From the juridical point of view, exchange appears as the relation between two wills. The relation of these two wills is expressed in the "contract." The production of commodities duly "constituted" is therefore the reign of "absolute" individual liberty. By finding myself bound through a contract that obliges me to do such and such a thing, I do not renounce my liberty. I simply use it to enter into relations with my neighbours. But at the same time this contract is the regulator of my liberty. In fulfilling a duty that I have freely laid upon myself when signing the contract, I render justice to the rights of others. It is thus that "absolute" liberty becomes "commensurate with order." Apply this conception of the contract to the "political constitution" and you have "Anarchy."

> "The idea of the contract excludes that of government. What characterises the contract, reciprocal convention, is that by virtue of this convention the liberty and well-being of man are increased, while by the institution of authority both are necessarily decreased.

> "... Contract is thus essentially synallagmatic; it lays upon the contracting parties no other obligation than that which results from their personal promise of reciprocal pledges; it is subject to no external authority; it alone lays down a law common to both parties, and it can be carried out only through their own initiative. If the contract is already this in its most general acceptation and in its daily practice, what will the social contract be—that contract which is meant to bind together all the members of a nation by the same interest? The social contract is the supreme act by which every citizen pledges to society his love, his intellect, his labour, his service, his products, his possessions, in exchange for the affection, the ideas, the labour, products, service, and possessions of his fellows; the measure of right for each one being always determined by the extent

of his own contribution, and the amount recoverable being in accordance with what has been given....The social contract must be freely discussed, individually consented to, signed *manu propria*, by all who participate in it. If its discussion were prevented, curtailed or burked; if consent to it were filched; if the signature were given to a blank document in pure confidence, without a reading of the articles and their preliminary explanation; or even if, like the military oath, it were all predetermined and enforced, then the social contract would be nothing but a conspiracy against the liberty and well-being of the most ignorant, the most weak, and most numerous individuals, a systematic spoliation, against which every means of resistance or even of reprisal might become a right and a duty.

"... The social contract is of the essence of the reciprocal contract; not only does it leave the signer the whole of his possessions; it adds to his property; it does not encroach upon his labour; it only affects exchange....Such, according to the definitions of right and universal practice, must be the social contract."

Once it is admitted as an incontestable fundamental principle that the contract is "the only moral bond that can be accepted by free and equal human beings" nothing is easier than a "radical" criticism of the "political constitution." Suppose we have to do with justice and the penal law, for example? Well, Proudhon would ask you by virtue of what contract society arrogates to itself the right to punish criminals. "Where there is no contract, there can be, so far as any external tribunal is concerned, neither crime nor misdemeanor. The law is the expression of the sovereignty of the people; that is, or I am altogether mistaken, the social contract and the personal pledge of the man and the citizen. So long as I did not want this law, so long as I have not consented to it, voted for it, it is not binding upon me, it does not exist. To make it a precedent before I have recognised it, and to use it against me in spite of my protests is to make it retroactive, and to violate this very law itself. Every day you have to reverse a decision because of some formal error. But there is not a single one of your laws that is not tainted with nullity, and the most monstrous nullity of all, the very hypothesis of the law. Soufflard, Lacenaire, all the scoundrels whom you send to the scaffold, turn in their graves and accuse you of judicial forgery. What answer can you make them?"

If we are dealing with the administration and the police Proudhon sings the same song of contract and free consent. "Cannot we administer our goods, keep our accounts, arrange our differences, look after our common interests at least as well as we can look after our salvation and take care of our souls?" What more have we to do with state legislation, with state justice, with state police, and with state administration than with state religion?"

As to the Ministry of Finance, "it is evident that its *raison d'être* is entirely included in that of the other ministries. Get rid of all the political harness and you will have no use for an administration whose sole object is the procuring and distribution of supplies."

This is logical and "radical"; and the more radical, that this formula of Proudhon's—constituted value, free contract—is a universal one, easily, and even necessarily applicable to all peoples. "Political economy is, indeed, like all other sciences; it is of necessity the same all over the world; it does not depend upon the arrangements of men or nations, it is subject to no one's caprice. There is no more a Russian, English, Austrian, Tartar, or Hindu political economy than there is a Hungarian, German, or American physics or geometry. Truth is everywhere equal to itself: Science is the unity of the human race. If science, therefore, and no longer religion or authority is taken in all countries as the rule of society, the sovereign arbiter of all interests, government becomes null and void, the legislators of the whole universe are in harmony."

But enough of this! The "biography" of what Proudhon called his programme is now sufficiently clear to us. Economically it is but the utopia of a petty-bourgeois, who is firmly convinced that the production of commodities is the most "just" of all possible modes of production, and who desires to eliminate its bad sides (hence his "Radicalism") by retaining to all eternity its good sides (hence his "Conservatism"). Politically the programme is only the application to public relations of a concept (the "contract") drawn from the domain of the private right of a society of producers of commodities. "Constituted value" in economics, the "contract" in politics—these are the whole scientific "truth" of Proudhon. It is all very well for him to combat the utopians; he is a utopian himself to his fingertips. What distinguishes him from men like Saint-Simon, Fourier, and Robert Owen is his extreme pettiness and narrowness of mind, his hatred of every really revolutionary movement and idea.

Proudhon criticised the "political constitution" from the point of view of private right. He wished to perpetuate private property, and to destroy that pernicious "fiction," the state, forever.

Guizot had already said that the political constitution of a country has its root in the conditions of property existing there. For Proudhon the political constitution owes its origin only to human ignorance, has only been "imagined" in default of the "social organisation" at last "invented" by him, Proudhon, in the year of our Lord so and so. He judges the political history of mankind like a utopian. But the utopian negation of all reality by no means preserves us from its influence. Denied upon one page of a utopian work it takes its revenge on another, where it often appears in all its nakedness. Thus Proudhon "denies" the state. "The State—no, no—I will none of it, even as servant; I reject all government, even direct government," he cries *ad nauseam*.

But, oh! irony of reality! Do you know how he "invents" the constitution of value? It is very funny.

The constitution of value is the selling at a fair price, at the cost price. If a merchant refuses to supply his merchandise at cost price it is because he is not certain of selling a sufficient quantity to secure a due return, and further he has no guarantee that he will get "quid pro quo" for his purchases. So he must have guarantees. And there may be "various kinds" of these guarantees. Here is one.

"Let us suppose that the Provisional Government or the Constituent Assembly...had seriously wished to help along business, encourage commerce, industry, agriculture, stop the depreciation of property, assure work to the workers—it could have been done by guaranteeing, e.g., to the first 10,000 contractors, factory owners, manufacturers, merchants, etc., in the whole Republic, an interest of 5 percent. on the capital, say, on the average, 100,000 francs, that each of them had embarked in his competitive business. For it is evident that the State"...Enough! It is evident that the state has forced itself upon Proudhon, at least "as servant." And it has done this with such irresistible force that our author ends by surrendering, and solemnly proclaiming:

> "Yes, I say it aloud: the workers' associations of Paris and the departments hold in their hands the salvation of the people, the future of the revolution. They can do everything, if they set about it cleverly. Renewed energy on their part must carry the light into the dullest minds, and at the election of 1852 [he wrote this in the summer of 1851] must place on the order of the day, and at the head of it, the constitution of value."

Thus "No more parties! No politics!" when it is a question of the class struggle—and "Hurrah for politics! Hurrah for electoral agitation! Hurrah for state interference!" when it is a question of realising the vapid and meagre utopia of Proudhon!

"*Destruam et aedificabo*," says Proudhon, with the pompous vanity peculiar to him. But on the other hand—to use the phrase of Figaro—it is the truest truth of all he has ever uttered in his life. He destroys and he builds. Only the mystery of his "destruction" reveals itself completely in his formula, "The contract solves all problems." The mystery of his "*aedificatio*" is in the strength of the social and political bourgeois reality with which he reconciled himself, the more readily in that he never managed to pluck from it any of its "secrets."

Proudhon will not hear of the state at any price. And yet—apart from the political propositions such as the constitution of value, with which he turns to the odious "fiction"—even theoretically he "builds up" the state as fast as he "destroys" it. What he takes from the "State" he bestows upon the "communes" and "departments." In the place of one great state we see built up a number of small states; in the place of one great "fiction" a mass of little ones. To sum up, "anarchy" resolves itself into federalism, which among other advantages has that of making the success of revolutionary movements much more difficult than it is under a centalised state. So endeth Proudhon's *General Idea of the Revolution.*

It is a curious fact that Saint-Simon is the "father" of Proudhon's anarchy. Saint-Simon has said that the end of social organisation is production, and that, therefore, political science must be reduced to economics, the "art of governing men" must give way to the art of the "administration of things." He has compared mankind to the individual, who, obeying his parents in childhood, in his ripe age ends by obeying no one but himself. Proudhon seized upon this idea and this comparison, and with the help of the constitution of value, "built up" anarchy. But Saint-Simon, a man of fertile genius, would have been the very first to be alarmed at what this socialistic petty-bourgeois made of his theory. Modern scientific socialism has worked out the theory of Saint-Simon very differently, and while explaining the historical origin of the state, shows in this very origin, the conditions of the future disappearance of the state.

> "The state was the official representative of society as a whole, the gathering of it together into a visible embodiment. But it was this only in so far as it was the state of that class which itself represented, for the time being, society as a whole; in ancient times the state of slave-owning citizens; in the middle ages, the feudal lords; in our own time, the bourgeoisie. When at last it becomes the real representative of the whole of society, it renders itself unnecessary. As soon as there is no longer any social class to be held in subjection; as soon as class rule and the individual struggle for existence based on our present anarchy in production, with the collisions and excesses arising from these are removed, nothing more remains to be repressed, and a special repressive force, a state, is no longer necessary. The first act by virtue of which the state really constitutes itself the representative of the whole of society, the taking possession of the means of production in the name of society, this is, at the same time, its last independent act as a state. State interference in social relations becomes, in one domain after another, superfluous, and then dies out of itself; the government of persons is replaced by the administration of things, and by the conduct of processes of production. The state is not "abolished." *It dies out.*"

V. Bakunin

We have seen that in their criticism of the "political constitution," the "fathers" of anarchy always based themselves on the utopian point of view. Each one of them based his theories upon an abstract principle. Stirner upon that of the

"Ego," Proudhon upon that of the "Contract." The reader has also seen that these two "fathers" were individualists of the first water.

The influence of Proudhonian individualism was, for a time, very strong in the Romance countries (France, Belgium, Italy, Spain) and in the Slav countries, especially Russia. The internal history of the International Workingmen's Association is the history of this struggle between Proudhonism and the modern socialism of Marx. Not only men like Tolain, Chemalé or Murat, but men very superior to them, such as De Paepe, e.g., were nothing but more or less opinionated, more or less consistent "Mutualists." But the more the working class movement developed, the more evident it became that "Mutualism" could not be its theoretical expression. At the International Congresses the Mutualists were forced by the logic of facts to vote for the Communist resolutions. This was the case, e.g., at Brussels in the discussion on landed property. Little by little the left wing of the Proudhonian army left the domain of individualism to entrench itself upon that of "Collectivism."

The word "Collectivism" was used at this period in a sense altogether opposed to that which it now has in the mouths of the French Marxists, like Jules Guesde and his friends. The most prominent champion of "Collectivism" was at this time Mikhail Bakunin.

In speaking of this we shall pass over in silence his propaganda in favour of the Hegelian philosophy, as far as he understood it, the part he played in the revolutionary movement of 1848, his Panslavist writings in the beginning of the sixties, and his pamphlet, *Romanov, Pougatchev, or Pestel?* (London 1862), in which he proposed to go over to Alexander II, if the latter would become the "Tsar of the Muzhiks." Here we are exclusively concerned with his theory of Anarchist Collectivism.

A member of the "League of Peace and Liberty," Bakunin, at the Congress of this Association at Berne in 1869, called upon the League—an entirely bourgeois body—to declare in favour of "the economical and social equalisation of classes and of individuals." Other delegates, among whom was Chaudey, reproached him with advocating Communism. He indignantly protested against the accusation.

"Because I demand the economic and social equalisation of classes and individuals, because, with the Workers' Congress of Brussels, I have declared myself in favour of collective property, I have been reproached with being a communist. What difference, I have been asked, is there between communism and collectivism. I am really astounded that M. Chaudey does not understand this difference, he who is the testamentary executor of Proudhon! I detest communism, because it is the negation of liberty, and I cannot conceive anything human without liberty. I am not a communist, because communism concentrates and causes all the forces of society to be absorbed by the State, because it necessarily ends in the centalisation of property in the hands of the State, while I desire the abolition of the state—the radical extirpation of this principle of the authority and the tutelage of the State, which, under the pretext of moralising and civilising men, has until now enslaved, oppressed, exploited, and depraved them. I desire the organisation of society and of collective or social property from below upwards, by means of free association and not from above downwards by means of some authority of some sort. Desiring the abolition of the state, I desire the abolition of property individually hereditary, which is nothing but an institution of the State. This is the sense, gentlemen, in which I am a collectivist, and not at all a communist."

In another speech at the same Congress Bakunin reiterates what he had already said of "Statist" communism. "It is not we, gentlemen," he said, "who systematically deny all authority and all tutelary powers, and who in the name of Liberty demand the very abolition of the 'authoritarian' principle of the state; it is not we who will recognise any sort of political and social organisation whatever, that is not founded upon the most complete liberty of everyone....But I am in favour of collective property, because I am convinced that so long as property, individually hereditary, exists, the equality of the first start, the realisation of equality, economical and social, will be impossible." This is not particularly lucid as a statement of principles. But it is sufficiently significant from the "biographical" point of view.

We do not insist upon the ineptitude of the expression "the economic and social equalisation of classes"; the General Council of the International dealt with that long ago. We would only remark that the above quotations show that Bakunin—

1. Combats the state and "Communism" in the name of "the most complete liberty of everybody";

2. Combats property, "individually hereditary", in the name of economic equality;

3. Regards this property as "an institution of the state", as a "consequence of the very principles of the state";

4. Has no objection to individual property, if it is not hereditary; has no objection to the right of inheritance, if it is not individual.

In other words:

1. Bakunin is quite at one with Proudhon so far as concerns the negation of the state and communism;

2. To this negation he adds another, that of property, individually hereditary;

3. His programme is nothing but a total arrived at by the adding up of the two abstract principles—that of "liberty", and that of "equality"; he applies these two principles, one after the other, and independently one of the other, in his criticism of the existing order of things, never asking himself whether the results of these two negations are reconcilable with one another.

4. He understands, just as little as Proudhon, the origin of private property and the causal connection between its evolution and the development of political forms.

5. He has no clear conception of the meaning of the words "individually hereditary".

If Proudhon was a utopian, Bakunin was doubly so, for his programme was nothing but a utopia of "Liberty", reinforced by a utopia of "Equality". If Proudhon, at least to a very large extent, remained faithful to his principle of the contract, Bakunin, divided between liberty and equality, is obliged from the very outset of his argument constantly to throw over the former for the benefit of the latter, and the latter for the benefit of the former. If Proudhon is a Proudhonian *sans reproche*, Bakunin is a Proudhonian adulterated with "detestable" communism, nay even by "Marxism."

In fact, Bakunin has no longer that immutable faith in the genius of the "master" Proudhon, which Tolain seems to have preserved intact. According to Bakunin "Proudhon, in spite of all his efforts to get a foothold upon the firm ground of reality, remained an idealist and metaphysician. His starting point is the abstract side of law; it is from this that he starts in order to arrive at economic facts, while Marx, on the contrary, has enunciated and proved the truth, demonstrated by the whole of the ancient and modern history of human societies, of peoples and of states, that economic facts preceded and precede the facts of political and civil law. The discovery and demonstration of this truth is one of the greatest merits of M. Marx." In another of his writings he says, with entire conviction, "All the religions, and all the systems of morals that govern a given society are always the ideal expression of its real, material condition, that is, especially of its economic organisation, but also of its political organisation, the latter, indeed, being never anything but the juridical and violent consecration of the former." And he again mentions Marx as the man to whom belongs the merit of having discovered and demonstrated this truth. One asks oneself with astonishment how this same Bakunin could declare that private property was only a consequence of the principle of authority. The solution of the riddle lies in the fact that he did not understand the materialist conception of history; he was only "adulterated" by it.

And here is a striking proof of this. In the Russian work, already quoted, *Statism and Anarchy*, he says that in the situation of the Russian people there are two elements which constitute the conditions necessary for the social (he means socialist) revolution. "The Russian people can boast of excessive poverty, and unparalleled slavery. Their sufferings are innumerable, and they bear these, not with patience, but with a profound and passionate despair, that twice already in our history has manifested itself in terrible outbursts: in the revolt of Stephan Razine, and in that of Pougatschew." And that is what Bakunin understood by the material conditions of a socialist revolution! Is it necessary to point out that this "Marxism" is a little too *sui generis*?

While combating Mazzini from the standpoint of the materialist conception of history, Bakunin himself is so far from understanding the true import of this conception, that in the same work in which he refutes the Mazzinian theology, he speaks, like the thorough-faced Proudhonian that he is, of "absolute" human morality, and he bolsters up the idea of this morality—the morality of "solidarity,"—with such arguments as these:

> "Every actual being, so long as he exists, exists only by virtue of a principle which is inherent in himself, and which determines his particular nature; a principle that is not imposed upon him by a divine law-giver of any sort" (this is the "materialism" of our author!), "but is the protracted and constant result of combinations of natural causes and effects; that is not, according to the ludicrous idea of the idealists, shut up in him like a soul within its body, but is, in fact, only the inevitable and constant form of his real existence. The human, like all other species, has inherent principles quite special to itself, and all these principles are summed up in, or are reducible to, a single principle, which we call *solidarity*. This principle may be formulated thus: No human individual can recognise his own humanity, nor, therefore, realise it in his life except by recognising it in others, and by helping to realise it for others. No man can emancipate himself, except by emancipating with him all the men around him. My liberty is the liberty of everyone, for I am not truly free, free not only in thought but in deed, except when my liberty and my rights find their confirmation, their sanction, in the liberty and the rights of all men, my equals."

As a moral precept, solidarity, as interpreted by Bakunin, is a very excellent thing. But to set up this morality, which by the way is not at all "absolute," as a principle "inherent" in humanity and determining human nature, is playing with words, and completely ignoring what materialism is. Humanity only exists "by virtue" of the principle of solidarity. This is coming it a little too strong. How about the "class war, and the cursed state, and property, "individually hereditary"—are these only manifestations of "solidarity," inherent in humanity, determining its special nature, etc., etc.? If this is so, everything is alright, and Bakunin was wasting his time in dreaming of a "social" revolution. If this is not so, this proves that humanity may have existed "by virtue" of other principles than that of solidarity, and that this latter principle is by no means "inherent" in it. Indeed, Bakunin only enunciated his "absolute" principle in order to arrive at the conclusion that "no people could be completely free, free with solidarity, in the human sense of the word, if the whole of humanity is not free also."

This is an allusion to the tactics of the modern proletariat, and it is true in the sense that—as the rules of the International Workingmen's Association put it—the emancipation of the workers is not a merely local or national problem, but, on the contrary, a problem concerning every civilised nation, its solution being necessarily dependent upon their theoretical and practical cooperation. It is easy enough to prove this truth by reference to the actual economic situation of civilised humanity. But nothing is less conclusive, here as elsewhere, than a "demonstration" founded upon a utopian conception of "human nature." The "solidarity" of Bakunin only proves that he remained an incorrigible utopian, although he became acquainted with the historical theory of Marx.

VI. Bakunin (concluded)

We have said that the principal features of Bakunin's programme originated in the simple addition of two abstract principles: that of liberty and that of equality. We now see that the total thus obtained might easily be increased by the addition of a third principle, that of solidarity. Indeed, the programme of the famous "Alliance" adds several others. For example, "The Alliance declares itself atheist; it desires the abolition of religions, the substitution of science for faith, of human for divine justice." In the proclamation with which the Bakuninists placarded the walls of Lyons, during the attempted rising at the end of September, 1870, we read (Article 41) that "the state, fallen into decay, will no longer be able to intervene in the payment of private debts." This is incontestably logical, but it would be difficult to deduce the non-payment of private debts from principles inherent in human nature.

Since Bakunin in tacking his various "absolute" principles together does not ask himself, and does not need to ask himself—thanks to the "absolute" character of his method—whether one of these principles might not somewhat limit the "absolute" power of others, and might not in its turn be limited by them, he finds it an "absolute" impossibility to harmonise the various items of his programme whenever words no longer suffice, and it becomes necessary to replace them by more precise ideas. He "desires" the abolition of religion. But, "the state having fallen into decay," who is to abolish it? He "desires" the abolition of property, individually hereditary. But what is to be done if, "the

State having fallen into decay," it should continue to exist? Bakunin himself feels the thing is not very clear, but he consoles himself very easily.

In a pamphlet written during the Franco-German war, *Lettres à un français sur la crise actuelle*, while demonstrating that France can only be saved by a great revolutionary movement, he comes to the conclusion that the peasants must be incited to lay hands upon the land belonging to the aristocracy and the bourgeoisie. But so far, the French peasants have been in favour of property, "individually hereditary," so this unpleasant institution would be bolstered up by the new Social Revolution?

"Not at all," answers Bakunin, "once the state is abolished they" (i.e., the peasants) *"will no longer have the juridical and political consecration, the guarantee of property by the state. Property will no longer be a right, it will be reduced to the condition of a simple fact."* [The italics are Bakunin's own]

This is very reassuring. "The state having fallen into decay," any fellow that happens to come along, stronger than I, will incontinently possess himself of my field, without having any need to appeal to the principle of "solidarity"; the principle of "liberty" will sufficiently answer his purpose. A very pleasant "equalisation of individuals"!

"It is certain," Bakunin admits, "that at first things won't work in an absolutely peaceful manner; there will be struggles; public order, that arch saint of the bourgeois, will be disturbed, and the just deeds which will result from such a state of things may constitute what one is agreed to call a civil war. But do you prefer to hand over France to the Prussians?...Moreover, do not fear that the peasants will devour one another; even if they tried to do so in the beginning, they would soon be convinced of the material impossibility of persisting in this course, and then we may be sure they would try to arrive at some understanding, to come to terms, to organise among themselves. The necessity of eating, of providing for their families, and the necessity therefore of safeguarding their houses, their families, and their own lives against unforeseen attacks, all this would soon force them individually to enter into mutual arrangements. And do not believe, either, that in these arrangements, *arrived at outside all official tutelage"* (italicised by Bakunin), "by the mere force of events, the strongest, the richest, will exercise a predominant influence. The wealth of the wealthy, no longer guaranteed by juridical institutions, will cease to be a power ... As to the most cunning, the strongest, they will be rendered innocuous by the collective strength of the mass of the small, and very small peasants, as well as by the agricultural proletarians, a mass of men today reduced to silent suffering, but whom the revolutionary movement will arm with an irresistible power. Please note that I do not contend that the agricultural districts which will thus reorganise themselves, from below upwards, will immediately create an ideal organisation, agreeing at all points with the one of which we dream. What I am convinced of is that this will be a living organisation, and as such, one a thousand times superior to what exists now. Moreover, this new organisation being always open to the propaganda of the towns, as it can no longer be held down, so to say petrified by the juridical sanction of the state, it will progress freely, developing and perfecting itself indefinitely, but always living and free, never decreed nor legalised, until it attains as reasonable a condition as we can hope for in our days."

The "idealist" Proudhon was convinced that the political constitution had been invented for want of a social organisation "immanent in humanity." He took the pains to "discover" this latter, and having discovered it, he could not see what further *raison d'être* there was for the political constitution. The "materialist" Bakunin has no "social organisation" of his own make. "The most profound and rational science," he says, "cannot divine the future forms of social life." This science must be content to distinguish the "living" social forms from those that owe their origin to the "petrifying" action of the state, and to condemn these latter. Is not this the old Proudhonian antithesis of the social organisation "immanent in humanity," and of the political constitution "invented" exclusively in the interests of "order"? Is not the only difference that the "materialist" transforms the utopian programme of the "idealist," into something even more utopian, more nebulous, more absurd?

"To believe that the marvellous scheme of the universe is due to chance, is to imagine that by throwing about a sufficient number of printers' characters at hazard, we might write the Iliad." So reasoned the Deists of the eighteenth century in refuting the atheists. The latter replied that in this case everything was a question of time, and that by throwing about the letters an infinite number of times, we must certainly, at some period, make them arrange themselves in the required sequence. Discussions of this kind were to the taste of the eighteenth century, and we should be wrong to make too much fun of them now-a-days. But it would seem that Bakunin took the atheist argument of the good old times quite seriously, and used it in order to make himself a "programme." Destroy what exists; if only you do this often enough you are bound at last to produce a social organisation, approaching at any rate the organisation you "dream" of. All will go well when once the revolution has come to stay. Is not this sufficiently "materialist"? If you think it is not, you are a metaphysician, "dreaming" of the impossible!

The Proudhonian antithesis of the "social organisation" and the "political constitution" reappears "living" and in its entirety in what Bakunin is forever reiterating as to the "social revolution" on the one hand, and the "political revolution" on the other. According to Proudhon the social organisation has unfortunately, up to our own days, never existed, and for want of it humanity was driven to "invent" a political constitution. According to Bakunin the social revolution has never yet been made, because humanity, for want of a good "social" programme had to content itself with political revolutions. Now that this programme has been found, there is no need to bother about the "political" revolution; we have quite enough to do with the "social revolution."

Every class struggle being necessarily a political struggle, it is evident that every political revolution, worthy of the name, is a social revolution; it is evident also that for the proletariat the political struggle is as much a necessity as it has always been for every class struggling to emancipate itself. Bakunin anathematises all political action by the proletariat; he extols the "social" struggle exclusively. Now what is this social struggle?

Here our Proudhonian once again shows himself adulterated by Marxism. He relies as far as possible upon the Rules of the International Workingmen's Association.

In the preamble of these Rules it is laid down that the subjection of the worker to capital lies at the bottom of all servitude, political, moral and material, and that therefore the economic emancipation of the workers is the great end to which all political movements must be subordinated as a means. Bakunin argues from this that "every political movement which has not for its immediate and direct object the final and complete economic emancipation of the workers, and which has not inscribed upon its banner quite definitely and clearly, the principle of *economic equality*, that is, the integral restitution of capital to labour, or else the social liquidation—every such political movement is a bourgeois one, and as such must be excluded from the International." But this same Bakunin has heard it said that the historical movement of humanity is a process in conformity with certain laws, and that a revolution cannot be improvised at a moment's notice. He is therefore forced to ask himself, what is the policy which the International is to adopt during that "more or less prolonged period of time which separates us from the terrible social revolution which everyone foresees today." To this he replies, with the most profound conviction, and as if quoting the Rules of the International:

> "Without mercy the policy of the democratic bourgeois, or bourgeois-socialists, must be excluded, which, when these declare that political freedom is a necessary condition of economic emancipation, can only mean this: political reforms, or political revolutions must precede economic reforms or economic revolutions; the workers must therefore join hands with the more or less radical bourgeois, in order to carry out the former together with them, then, being free, to turn the latter into a reality against them. We protest loudly against this unfortunate theory, which, so far as the workers are concerned, can only result in their again

letting themselves be used as tools against themselves, and handing them over once more to bourgeois exploitation."

The International "commands" us to disregard all national or local politics; it must give the working-class movement in all countries an "essentially economic" character, by setting up as final aim "the shortening of the hours of labour, and the increase of wages," and as a means "the association of the working masses, and the starting of "funds for fighting." It is needless to add that the shortening of the hours of labour must, of course, be obtained without any intervention from the accursed state.

Bakunin cannot understand that the working class in its political action can completely separate itself from all the exploiting parties. According to him, there is no other "role" in the political movement for the workers than that of satellite of the radical bourgeoisie. He glorifies the "essentially economic" tactics of the old English trade unions, and has not the faintest idea that it was these very tactics that made the English workers the tail of the Liberal Party.

Bakunin objects to the working class lending a hand in any movement whose object is the obtaining or the extension of political rights. In condemning such movements as "bourgeois," he fancies himself a tremendous revolutionist. As a matter of fact he thus proves himself essentially conservative, and if the working class were ever to follow this line of inaction the governments could only rejoice.

The true revolutionists of our days have a very different idea of socialist tactics. They "everywhere support every revolutionary movement against the existing social and political order of things; which does not prevent them (but quite the contrary) from forming the proletariat into a party separate from all the exploiter parties, opposed to the whole 'reactionary mass'."

Proudhon, who we know had not an overwhelming sympathy for "politics," nevertheless advised the French workers to vote for the candidates who pledged themselves to "constitute value." Bakunin would not have politics at any price. The worker cannot make use of political liberty: "in order to do so he needs two little things—leisure and material means." So it is all only a bourgeois lie. Those who speak of working-class candidates are but mocking the proletariat. "Working-class candidates, transferred to bourgeois conditions of life, and into an atmosphere of completely bourgeois political ideas, ceasing to be actually workers in order to become statesmen, will become bourgeois, and possibly will become even more bourgeois than the bourgeois themselves. For it is not the men who make positions, but, on the contrary, positions which make the men."

This last argument is about all Bakunin was able to assimilate of the materialist conception of history. It is unquestionably true that man is the product of his social environment. But to apply this incontestable truth with advantage it is necessary to get rid of the old, metaphysical method of thought which considers things *one after the other, and independently one of the other*. Now Bakunin, like his master, Proudhon, in spite of his flirtation with the Hegelian philosophy, all his life remained a metaphysician. He does not understand that the environment which makes man may change, thus changing man, its own product. The environment he has in his mind's eye when speaking of the political action of the proletariat, is the bourgeois parliamentary environment, that environment which must necessarily fatally corrupt labour representatives. But the environment of the *electors*, the environment of a working-class party, conscious of its aim and well-organised, would this have no influence upon the elected of the proletariat? No! Economically enslaved, the working class must always remain in political servitude; in this domain it will always be the weakest; to free itself it must begin by an economic revolution. Bakunin does not see that by this process of reasoning he inevitably arrives at the conclusion that a victory of the proletariat is absolutely impossible, unless the owners of the means of production voluntarily relinquish their possessions to them. In effect the subjection of the worker to capital is the source not only of political but of moral servitude. And how can the workers, morally enslaved, rise against the bourgeoisie? For the working class movement to become possible, according to Bakunin, it must therefore first make an economic revolution. But the economic revolution is only possible as the work of the workers themselves. So we find ourselves in a vicious circle, out of which modern socialism can easily break, but in which Bakunin and the Bakuninists are forever turning with no other hope of deliverance than a logical *salto mortale*.

The corrupting influence of the Parliamentary environment on working-class representatives is what the anarchists have up to the present considered the strongest argument in their criticism of the political activity of Social Democracy. We have seen what its theoretical value amounts to. And even a slight knowledge of the history of the German socialist party will sufficiently show how in practical life the anarchist apprehensions are answered.

In repudiating all "politics" Bakunin was forced to adopt the tactics of the old English trade unions. But even he felt that these tactics were not very revolutionary. He tried to get out of the difficulty by the help of his "Alliance," a kind of international secret society, organised on a basis of frenetic centalisation and grotesque fancifulness. Subjected to the dictatorial rule of the sovereign pontiff of anarchy, the "international" and the "national" brethren were bound to accelerate and direct the "essentially economic" revolutionary movement. At the same time Bakunin approved of "riots," of isolated risings of workers and peasants which, although they must inevitably be crushed out, would, he declared, always have a good influence upon the development of the revolutionary spirit among the oppressed. It goes without saying that with such a "programme" he was able to do much harm to the working class movement, but he was not able to draw nearer, even by a single step, to that "immediate" economic revolution of which he "dreamed." We shall presently see the result of the Bakuninist theory of "riots." For the present let us sum up what we have said of Bakunin. And here, he shall help us himself:

"Upon the Pan-Germanic banner [i.e., also upon the banner of German Social-Democracy, and consequently upon the socialist banner of the whole civilised world] "is inscribed: The conservation and strengthening of the state at all costs; on the socialist-revolutionary banner [read Bakuninist banner] is inscribed in characters of blood, in letters of fire: the abolition of all states, the destruction of bourgeois civilisation; free organisation from the bottom to the top, by the help of free associations; the organisation of the working populace [*sic!*] freed from all trammels, the organisation of the whole of emancipated humanity, the creation of a new human world."

It is with these words that Bakunin concludes his principal work *Statism and Anarchy* (Russian). We leave our readers to appreciate the rhetorical beauties of this passage. For our own part we shall be content with saying that it contains absolutely no human meaning whatsoever.

The absurd, pure and simple—that is what is inscribed upon the Bakuninist "banner." There is no need of letters of fire and of blood to make this evident to anyone who is not hypnotised by a phraseology more or less sonorous, but always void of sense.

The anarchism of Stirner and of Proudhon was completely individualist. Bakunin did not want individualism, or to speak more correctly, one particular phase of individualism. He was the inventor of "Collectivist-Anarchism." And the invention cost him little. He completed the "liberty" utopia, by the "equality" utopia. As these two utopias would not agree, as they cried out at being yoked together, he threw both into the furnace of the "permanent revolution" where they were both at last forced to hold their tongues, for the simple reason that they both evaporated, the one as completely as the other.

Bakunin is the "decadent" of utopianism.

VII. The smaller fry

Among our present-day anarchists some, like John Mackay, the author of *Die Anarchisten, Kulturgemalde aus dem Ende des xix. Jahrhunderts* [*The Anarchists:*

A Picture of Civilisation at the Close of the Nineteenth Century—ed.], declare for individualism, while others—by far the more numerous—call themselves communists. These are the descendants of Bakunin in the anarchist movement. They have produced a fairly considerable literature in various languages, and it is they who are making so much noise with the help of the "propaganda by deed." The prophet of this school is the Russian refugee, P.A. Kropotkin.

I shall not here stop to consider the doctrines of the individualist-anarchists of today, whom even their brethren, the communist-anarchists, look upon as "bourgeois." We will go straight on to the anarchist-"communist."

What is the standpoint of this new species of communism? "As to the method followed by the anarchist thinker, it entirely differs from that of the utopists," Kropotkin assures us.

> "The anarchist thinker does not resort to metaphysical conceptions (like 'natural rights,' the 'duties of the state' and so on) to establish what are, in his opinion, the best conditions for realising the greatest happiness of humanity. He follows, on the contrary, the course traced by the modern philosophy of evolution. He studies human society as it is now, and was in the past; and, without either endowing men altogether, or separate individuals, with superior qualities which they do not possess, he merely considers society as an aggregation of organisms trying to find out the best ways of combining the wants of the individual with those of cooperation for the welfare of the species. He studies society and tries to discover its tendencies, past and present, its growing needs, intellectual and economical, and in this he merely points out in which direction evolution goes."

So the anarchist-communists have nothing in common with the utopians. They do not, in the elaborating of their "ideal," turn to metaphysical conceptions like "natural rights," "duties of the state," etc. Is this really so?

So far as the "duties of the state" are concerned, Kropotkin is quite right; it would be too absurd if the anarchists invited the state to disappear in the name of its own "duties." But as to "natural rights" he is altogether mistaken. A few quotations will suffice to prove this.

Already in the *Bulletin de la Federation Jurasienne* (No. 3, 1877), we find the following very significant declaration: "The sovereignty of the people can only exist through the most complete autonomy of individuals and of groups." This "most completely autonomy," is it not also a "metaphysical conception"?

The *Bulletin de la Fédération Jurasienne* was an organ of collectivist anarchism. At bottom there is no difference between "Collectivist" and "Communist" anarchism. And yet, since it might be that we are making the communists responsible for the collectivists, let us glance at the "Communist" publications, not only according to the spirit but the letter. In the autumn of 1892 a few "companions" appeared before the Assize Court of Versailles in consequence of a theft of dynamite at Soisy-sous-Étiolles. Among others there was one G. Etiévant, who drew up a declaration of anarchist-communist principles. The tribunal would not allow him to read it, whereupon the official organ of the anarchists, *La Révolte*, undertook to publish this declaration, having taken great pains to secure an absolutely correct copy of the original. The *Declaration of G. Etiévant* made a sensation in the anarchist world, and even "cultured" men like Octave Mirbeau quote it with respect along with the works of the "theorists," Bakunin, Kropotkin, the "unequalled Proudhon," and the "aristocratic Spencer" (!). Now this is the line of Etiévant's reasoning:

No idea is innate in us; each idea is born of infinitely diverse and multiple sensations, which we receive by means of our organs. Every act of the individual is the result of one or several ideas. The man is not therefore responsible. In order that responsibility should exist, will would have to determine the sensations, just as these determine the idea, and the idea, the act. But as it is, on the contrary, the sensations which determine the will, all judgment becomes impossible, every reward, every punishment unjust, however great the good or the evil done may be. "Thus one cannot judge men and acts unless one has a sufficient criterion. Now no such criterion exists. At any rate it is not in the laws that it could be found, for true justice is immutable and laws are changeable. It is with laws as with all the rest (!). For if laws are beneficent what is the good of deputies and senators to change them? And if they are bad what is the good of magistrates to apply them?"

Having thus "demonstrated" "liberty," Etiévant passes on to "equality." From the zoophytes to men, all beings are provided with more or less perfect organs destined to serve them. All these beings have therefore the right to make use of their organs according to the evident will of Mother Nature. "So for our legs we have the right to all the space they can traverse; for our lungs to all the air we can breathe; for our stomach to all the food we can digest; for our brain to all we can think, or assimilate of the thoughts of others; for our faculty of elocution to all we can say; for our ears to all we can hear; and we have a right to all this because we have a right to life, and because all this constitutes life. These are the true rights of man! No need to decree them, they exist as the sun exists. They are written in no constitution, in no law, but they are inscribed in ineffaceable letters in the great book of nature and are imprescriptible. From the cheese-mite to the elephant, from the blade of grass to the oak, from the atom to the star, everything proclaims it."

If these are not "metaphysical conceptions," and of the very worst type, a miserable caricature of the metaphysical materialism of the eighteenth century, if this is the "philosophy of evolution," then we must confess that it has nothing in common with the scientific movement of our day.

Let us hear another authority, and quote the now famous book of Jean Grave, *La société mourante et l'Anarchie* [*The Dying Society and Anarchy—ed.*], which was recently condemned by French judges, who thought it dangerous, while it is only supremely ridiculous.

> "Anarchy means the negation of authority. Now, government claims to base the legitimacy of its existence upon the necessity of defending social institutions: the family, religion, property, etc. It has created a vast machinery in order to assure its exercise and its sanction. The chief are: the law, the magistracy, the army, the legislature, executive powers, etc. So that the anarchist idea, forced to reply to everything, was obliged to attack all social prejudices, to become thoroughly penetrated by all human knowledge, in order to demonstrate that its conceptions were in harmony with the physiological and psychological nature of man, and in harmony with the observance of natural laws, while our actual organisation has been established in contravention of all logic and all good sense....Thus, in combating authority, it has been necessary for the anarchists to attack all the institutions which the government defends, the necessity for which it tries to demonstrate in order to legitimate its own existence."

You see what was "the development" of the "Anarchist Idea." This idea "denied" authority. In order to defend itself, authority appealed to the family, religion, property. Then the "Idea" found itself forced to attack institutions, which it had not, apparently, noticed before, and at the same time the "Idea," in order to make the most of its "conceptions," penetrated to the very depths of all human knowledge (it is an ill wind that does not blow some good!) All this is only the result of chance, of the unexpected turn given by "authority" to the discussion that had arisen between itself and the "Idea."

It seems to us that however rich in human knowledge it may be now, the "Anarchist Idea" is not at all communistic; it keeps its knowledge to itself, and leaves the poor "companions" in complete ignorance. It is all very well for Kropotkin to sing the praises of the "Anarchist thinker"; he will never be able to prove that his friend Grave has been able to rise even a little above the feeblest metaphysics.

Kropotkin should read over again the anarchist pamphlets of Elisée Reclus—a great "theorist" this —and then, quite seriously tell us if he finds anything else in them but appeals to "justice," "liberty," and other "metaphysical conceptions."

Finally, Kropotkin himself is not so emancipated from metaphysics as he fancies he is. Far from it! Here, e.g., is what he said at the general meeting of the Federation of the Jura, on 12ᵗʰ October 1879, at Chaux-de-Fonds:

> "There was a time when they denied anarchists even the right to existence. The General Council of the International treated us as factious, the press as

dreamers; almost all treated us as fools; this time is past. The anarchist party has proved its *vitality*; it has surmounted the obstacles of every kind that impeded its development; today it is *accepted*. [By whom?] To attain to this, it has been necessary, above all else, for the party to hold its own in the domain of *theory*, to establish its ideal of the society of the future, to prove that this ideal is the best; to do more than this—to prove that this ideal is not the product of the dreams of the study, but flows directly from the popular aspirations, that it is in accord with the historical progress of culture and ideas. This work has been done, etc. ..."

The hunt after the best ideal of the society of the future, is not this the utopian method *par excellence*? It is true that Kropotkin tries to prove "that this ideal is not the product of dreams of the study, but flows directly from the popular aspirations, that it is in accord with the historical progress of culture and ideas." But what utopian has not tried to prove this equally with himself? Everything depends upon the value of the proofs, and here our amiable compatriot is infinitely weaker than the great utopians whom he treats as metaphysicians, while he himself has not the least notion of the actual methods of modern social science. But before examining the value of these "proofs," let us make the acquaintance of the "ideal" itself. What is Kropotkin's conception of anarchist society?

Preoccupied with the reorganising of the governmental machine, the revolutionist-politicians, the "Jacobins" (Kropotkin detests the Jacobins even more than our amiable Empress, Catherine II, detested them) allowed the people to die of hunger. The anarchists will act differently. They will destroy the state, and will urge on the people to the expropriation of the rich. Once this expropriation accomplished, an "inventory" of the common wealth will be made, and the "distribution" of it organised. Everything will be done by the people themselves. "Just give the people elbow room, and in a week the business of the food supply will proceed with admirable regularity. Only one who has never seen the hard-working people at their labour, only one who has buried himself in documents, could doubt this. Speak of the organising capacity of the Great Misunderstood, the people, to those who have seen them at Paris on the days of the barricades" (which is certainly not the case of Kropotkin) "or in London at the time of the last great strike, when they had to feed half a million starving people, and they will tell you how superior the people is to all the hide-bound officials."

The basis upon which the enjoyment in common of the food supply is to be organised will be very fair, and not at all "Jacobin." There is but one, and only one, which is consistent with sentiments of justice, and is really practical. The taking in heaps from what one possesses abundance of! Rationing out what must be measured, divided! Out of 350 million who inhabit Europe,

200 million still follow this perfectly natural practice—which proves, among other things, that the anarchist ideal "flows from the popular aspirations."

It is the same with regard to housing and clothing. The people will organise everything according to the same rule. There will be an upheaval; that is certain. Only this upheaval must not become mere loss, it must be reduced to a minimum. And it is again—we cannot repeat it too often—by turning to those immediately interested and not to bureaucrats that the least amount of inconvenience will be inflicted upon everybody

Thus from the beginning of the revolution we shall have an "organisation"; the whims of sovereign "individuals" will be kept within reasonable bounds by the wants of society, by the logic of the situation. And, nevertheless, we shall be in the midst of full-blown anarchy; individual liberty will be safe and sound. This seems incredible, but it is true; there is anarchy, and there is organisation, there are obligatory rules for everyone, and yet everyone does what he likes. You do not follow? 'Tis simple enough. This organisation—it is not the "authoritarian" revolutionists who will have created it—these rules, obligatory upon all, and yet anarchical, it is the people, the Great Misunderstood, who will have proclaimed them, and the people are very knowing as anyone who has seen—what Kropotkin never had the opportunity of seeing—days of barricade riots, knows."

But if the Great Misunderstood had the stupidity to create the "bureaus" so detested of Kropotkin? If, as it did in March 1871, it gave itself a revolutionary government? Then we shall say the people is mistaken, and shall try to bring it back to a better state of mind, and if need be we will throw a few bombs at the "hidebound officials." We will call upon the people to organise, and will destroy all the organs it may provide itself with.

This then is the way in which we realise the excellent anarchist ideal—in imagination. In the name of the liberty of individuals all action of the individuals is done away with, and in the name of the people we get rid of the whole class of revolutionists; the individuals are drowned in the mass. If you can only get used to this logical process, you meet with no more difficulties, and you can boast that you are neither "authoritarian" nor "Utopian." What could be easier, what more pleasant?

But in order to consume, it is necessary to produce. Kropotkin knows this so well that he reads the "authoritarian" Marx a lesson on the subject.

> "The evil of the present organisation is not in that the 'surplus value' of production passes over to the capitalist—as Rodbertus and Marx had contended—thus narrowing down the socialist conception, and the general ideas on the capitalist regime. Surplus value itself is only a consequence of more profound causes. The evil is that there can be any kind of 'surplus value,' instead of a surplus not consumed by each generation; for, in order that there may be 'surplus value,'

men, women, and children must be obliged by hunger to sell their labour powers, for a trifling portion of what these powers produce, and, especially of what they are capable of producing. [Poor Marx, who knew nothing of all these profound truths, although so confusedly expounded by the learned Prince!] ... It does not, indeed, suffice to distribute in equal shares the profits realised in one industry, if, at the same time, one has to exploit thousands of other workers. The point is to *produce with the smallest possible expenditure of human labour power the greatest possible amount of products necessary for the well-being of all.*"

Ignorant Marxists that we are! We have never heard that a socialist society presupposes a systematic organisation of production. Since it is Kropotkin who reveals this to us, it is only reasonable that we should turn to him to know what this organisation will be like. On this subject also he has some very interesting things to say.

"Imagine a society comprising several million inhabitants engaged in agriculture, and a great variety of industries—Paris, for example, with the Department of Seine-et-Oise. Imagine that in this society all children learn to work with their hand as well as with their brain. Admit, in fine, that all adults, with the exception of the women occupied with the education of children, undertake to work *five hours a day* from the age of twenty or twenty-two to forty-five or fifty, and that they spend this time in any occupations they choose, in no matter what branch of human labour considered *necessary*. Such a society could, in return, guarantee well-being to all its members, i.e., far greater comfort than that enjoyed by the bourgeoisie today. And every worker in this society would moreover have at his disposal at least five hours a day, which he could devote to science, to art, and to those individual needs that do not come within the category of *necessities*, while later on, when the productive forces of man have augmented, everything may be introduced into this category that is still today looked upon as a luxury or unattainable."

In anarchist society there will be no authority, but there will be the "Contract" (oh! immortal Monsieur Proudhon, here you are again; we see all still goes well with you!) by virtue of which the infinitely free individuals "agree" to work in such or such a "free commune." The contract is justice, liberty, equality; it is Proudhon, Kropotkin, and all the saints. But, at the same time, do not trifle with the contract! It is a thing not so destitute of means to defend itself as would seem. Indeed, suppose the signatory of a contract freely made does not wish to fulfil his duty? He is driven forth from the free commune, and he runs the risk of dying of hunger—which is not a particularly gay outlook.

I suppose a group of a certain number of volunteers combining in some enterprise, to secure the success of which all rival each other in zeal, with the exception of one associate, who frequently absents himself from his post. Should they, on his account, dissolve the group, appoint a president who would inflict fines, or else, like the academy, distribute attendance-counters ? It is evident that we shall do neither the one nor the other, but that one day the comrade who threatens to jeopardize the enterprise will be told: "My friend, we should have been glad to work with you, but as you are often absent from your post, or do your work negligently, we must part. Go and look for other comrades who will put up with your offhand ways." This is pretty strong at bottom; but note how appearances are saved, how very "Anarchist" is his language. Really, we should not be at all surprised if in the "Anarchist-Communist" society people were guillotined by persuasion, or, at any rate, by virtue of a freely-made contract.

But farther, this very anarchist method of dealing with lazy "free individuals" is perfectly "natural," and "is practiced everywhere today in all industries, in competition with every possible system of fines, stoppages from wages, espionage, etc.; the workman may go to his shop at the regular hour, but if he does his work badly, if he interferes with his comrades by his laziness or other faults, if they fall out, it is all over. He is obliged to leave the workshop." Thus is the anarchist "Ideal" in complete harmony with the "tendencies" of capitalist society.

For the rest, such strong measures as these will be extremely rare. Delivered from the yoke of the state and capitalist exploitation, individuals will of their own free motion set themselves to supply the wants of the great all of society. Everything will be done by means of "free arrangement."

> "Well, Citizens, let others preach industrial barracks, and the convent of 'Authoritarian' communism, we declare that the *tendency* of societies is in the opposite direction. We see millions and millions of groups constituting themselves freely in order to satisfy all the varied wants of human beings, groups formed, some by districts, by streets, by houses; others holding out hands across the walls (!) of cities, of frontiers, of oceans. All made up of human beings freely seeking one another, and having done their work as producers, associating themselves, to consume, or to produce articles of luxury, or to turn science into a new direction. This is the tendency of the nineteenth century, and we are following it; we ask only to develop it freely, without let or hindrance on the part of governments. Liberty for the individual! 'Take some pebbles,' said Fourier, 'put them into a box and shake them; they will arrange themselves into a mosaic such as you could never succeed in producing if you told off someone to arrange them harmoniously.'"

A wit has said that the profession of faith of the anarchists reduces itself to two articles of a fantastic law: (1) There shall be nothing. (2) No one is charged with carrying out the above article. This is not correct.

The anarchists say: (1) There shall be everything. (2) No one is held responsible for seeing that there is anything at all.

This is a very seductive "Ideal", but its realisation is unfortunately very improbable.

Let us now ask, what is this "free agreement" which, according to Kropotkin, exists even in capitalist society? He quotes two kinds of examples by way of evidence: (a) those connected with production and the circulation of commodities; (b) those belonging to all kinds of societies of amateurs— learned societies, philanthropic societies, etc.

"Take all the great enterprises: the Suez Canal, e.g., transatlantic navigation, the telegraph that unites the two Americas. Take, in fine, this organisation of commerce, which provides that when you get up in the morning you are sure to find bread at the bakers'...meat at the butchers', and everything you want in the shops. Is this the work of the state? Certainly, today we pay middlemen abominably dearly. Well, all the more reason to suppress them, but not to think it necessary to confide to the government the care of providing our goods and our clothing."

Remarkable fact! We began by snapping our fingers at Marx, who only thought of suppressing surplus value, and had no idea of the organisation of production, and we end by demanding the suppression of the profits of the middleman, while, so far as production is concerned, we preach the most bourgeois *laissez-faire, laissez passer.* Marx might, not without reason, have said, he laughs best who laughs last!

We all know what the "free agreement" of the bourgeois "entrepreneur" is, and we can only admire the "absolute" naïveté of the man who sees in it the precursor of communism. It is exactly this anarchic "arrangement" that must be got rid of in order that the producers may cease to be slaves of their own products.

As to the really free societies of "savants," artists, philanthropists, etc., Kropotkin himself tells us what their example is worth. They are "made up of human beings freely seeking one another after having done their work as producers." Although this is not correct—since in these societies there is often not a single *producer*—this still farther proves that we can only be free after we have settled our account with production. The famous "tendency of the nineteenth century," therefore, tells us nothing on the main question— how the unlimited liberty of the individual can be made to harmonise with the economic requirements of a communistic society. And as this "tendency" constitutes the whole of the scientific equipment of our "Anarchist thinker," we are driven to the conclusion that his appeal to science was merely verbiage, that he is, in spite of his contempt for the utopians, one of the least ingenious of these, a vulgar hunter in search of the "best Ideal."

The "free agreement" works wonders, if not in anarchist society, which unfortunately does not yet exist, at least in anarchist arguments. "Our present society being abolished, individuals no longer needing to hoard in order to make sure of the morrow, this, indeed being made impossible, by the suppression of all money or symbol of value—all their wants being satisfied and provided for in the new society, the stimulus of individuals being now only that ideal of always striving toward the best, the relations of individuals or groups no longer being established with a view to those exchanges in which each contracting party only seeks to 'do' his partner" (the "free agreement" of the bourgeois, of which Kropotkin has just spoken to us) "these relations will now only have for object the rendering of mutual services, with which particular interests have nothing to do, the agreement will be rendered easy, the causes of discord having disappeared."

Question: How will the new society satisfy the needs of its members? How will it make them certain of the morrow?

Answer: By means of free agreements.

Question: Will production be possible if it depends solely upon the free agreement of individuals?

Answer: Of course! And in order to convince yourself of it, you have only to *assume* that your morrow is certain, that all your needs are satisfied, and, in a word, that production, thanks to free agreement, is getting on swimmingly.

What wonderful logicians these "companions" are, and what a beautiful ideal is that which has no other foundation than an illogical assumption!

> "It has been objected that in leaving individuals free to organise as they like, there would arise that competition between groups which today exists between individuals. This is a mistake, for in the society we desire money would be abolished, consequently there would no longer be any exchange of products, but exchange of services. Besides, in order that such a social revolution as we contemplate can have been accomplished we must assume that a certain evolution of ideas will have taken place in the mind of the masses, or, at the least, of a considerable minority among them. But if the workers have been sufficiently intelligent to destroy bourgeois exploitation, it will not be in order to re-establish it among themselves, especially when they are assured all their wants will be supplied."

It is incredible, but it is incontestably true: the only basis for the "Ideal" of the anarchist-communists, is this *petitio principii*, this "assumption" of the very thing that has to be proved. Companion Grave, the "profound thinker," is particularly rich in assumptions. As soon as any difficult problem presents itself, he "assumes" that it is already solved, and then everything is for the best in the best of ideals.

The "profound" Grave is less circumspect than the "learned" Kropotkin. And so it is only he who succeeds in reducing the "ideal" to "absolute" absurdity.

He asks himself what will be done if in "the society of the day after the revolution" there should be a papa who should refuse his child *all education*. The papa is an individual with unlimited rights. He follows the anarchist rule, "Do as thou wouldst." No one has any right, therefore, to bring him to his senses. On the other hand, the child also may do as he likes, and he wants to learn. How to get out of this conflict, how resolve the dilemma without offending the holy laws of anarchy? By an "assumption." "Relations" (between citizens) "being much wider and more imbued with fraternity than in our present society, based as it is upon the antagonism of interests, it follows that the child by means of what he will see passing before his eyes, by what he will daily hear, will escape from the influence of the parent, and will find every facility necessary for acquiring the knowledge his parents refuse to give him. Nay more, if he finds himself too unhappy under the authority they try to force upon him, he would abandon them in order to place himself under the protection of individuals with whom he was in greater sympathy. The parents could not send the gendarmes after him to bring back to their authority the slave whom the law today gives up to them."

It is not the child who is running away from his parents, but the utopian who is running away from an insurmountable logical difficulty. And yet this judgment of Solomon has seemed so profound to the companions that it has been literally quoted by Emile Darnaud in his book *La Société Future* (Foix, 1890, p. 26)—a book especially intended to popularize the lucubrations of Grave.

"Anarchy, the no-government system of socialism, has a double origin. It is an outgrowth of the two great movements of thought in the economical and the political fields which characterise our century, and especially its second part. In common with all socialists, the anarchists hold that the private ownership of land, capital, and machinery has had its time; that it is condemned to disappear; and that all requisites of production must, and will, become the common property of society, and be managed in common by the producers of wealth. And, in common with the most advanced representative of political radicalism, they maintain that the ideal of the political organisation of society is a condition of things where the functions of government are reduced to a minimum, and the individual recovers his full liberty of initiative and action for satisfying, by means of free groups and federations—freely constituted—all the infinitely varied needs of the human being. As regards socialism, most of the anarchists arrive at its ultimate conclusion, that is, at a complete negation of the wage-system, and at communism. And with reference to political organisation, by giving a farther development to the above-mentioned part of the radical programme, they arrive at the conclusion that the ultimate aim of society is the reduction of the functions of governments to "nil"—that is, to a society without government, to anarchy. The anarchists maintain, moreover, that such being the ideal of social and political organisation they must not remit it to future centuries, but that only those changes in our social organisation which are in accordance with the above double ideal, and constitute an approach to it, will have a chance of life and be beneficial for the commonwealth."

Kropotkin here reveals to us, with admirable clearness the origin and nature of his "Ideal." This ideal, like that of Bakunin, is truly "double"; it is really born of the connection between bourgeois radicalism, or rather that of the Manchester school, and communism; just as Jesus was born in connection between the Holy Ghost and the Virgin Mary. The two natures of the anarchist ideal are as difficult to reconcile as the two natures of the Son of God. But one of these natures evidently gets the better of the other. The anarchists "want" to begin by immediately realising what Kropotkin calls "the ultimate aim of society," that is to say, by destroying the "State." Their starting point is always the unlimited liberty of the individual. Manchesterism before everything. Communism only comes in afterwards. But in order to reassure us as to the probable fate of this second nature of their ideal, the anarchists are constantly singing the praises of the wisdom, the goodness, the forethought of the man of the "future." He will be so perfect that he will no doubt be able to organise communist production. He will be so perfect that one asks oneself, while admiring him, why he cannot be trusted with a little "authority."

VII. The so-called anarchist tactics

The anarchists are utopians. Their point of view has nothing in common with that of modern scientific socialism. But there are utopias and utopias. The great utopians of the first half of our century were men of genius; they helped forward social science, which in their time was still entirely utopian. The utopians of today, the anarchists, are the abstractors of quintessence, who can only fully draw forth some poor conclusions from certain mummified principles. They have nothing to do with social science, which, in its onward march, has distanced them by at least half a century. Their "profound thinkers," their "lofty theorists," do not even succeed in making the two ends of their reasoning meet. They are the "decadent" utopians, stricken with incurable intellectual anemia. The great utopians did much for the development of the working class movement. The utopians of our days do nothing but retard its progress. And it is especially their so-called tactics that are harmful to the proletariat.

We already know that Bakunin interpreted the Rules of the International in the sense that the working class must give up all political action, and concentrate its efforts upon the domain of the "immediately economic" struggle for higher wages, a reduction of the hours of labour, and so forth. Bakunin himself felt that such tactics were not very revolutionary. He tried to complete them through the action of his "Alliance"; he preached riots. But the more the class-consciousness of the proletariat develops, the more it inclines towards political action, and gives up the "riots," so common during its infancy. It is more difficult to induce the working men of Western Europe, who have attained to a certain degree of political development, to riot, than, for example, the credulous and ignorant Russian peasants. As the proletariat has shown no taste for the tactics of "riot," the companions have been forced to replace it by "individual action." It was especially after the attempted insurrection at Benevento in Italy in 1877 that the Bakuninists began to glorify the "propaganda of deed." But if we glance back at the period that separates us from the attempt of Benevento, we shall see that this propaganda too assumed a special form: very few "riots," and these quite insignificant, a great many personal attempts against public edifices, against individuals, and even against property—"individually hereditary," of course. It could not be otherwise.

"We have already seen numerous revolts by people who wished to obtain urgent reforms," says Louise Michel, in an interview with a correspondent of the *Matin*, on the occasion of the Vaillant attempt. "What was the result? The people were shot down. Well, we think the people have been sufficiently bled; it is better large-hearted people should sacrifice themselves, and, at their own risk, commit acts of violence whose object is to terrorize the government and the bourgeois."

This is exactly what we have said—only in slightly different words. Louise Michel has forgotten to say that revolts, causing the bloodshed of the people, figured at the head of the anarchists' programme, until the anarchists became convinced, not that these partial risings in no way serve the cause of the workers, but that the workers, for the most part, will not have anything to do with these risings.

Error has its logic as well as truth. Once you reject the political action of the working class, you are fatally driven—provided you do not wish to serve the bourgeois politicians—to accept the tactics of the Vaillants and the Henrys. The so-called "Independent" (*Unabhängige*) members of the German Socialist Party have proved this in their own persons. They began by attacking "Parliamentarism," and to the "reformist" tactics of the "old" members they opposed—on paper, of course—the "revolutionary struggle," the purely "economic" struggle. But this struggle, developing naturally, must inevitably bring about the entry of the proletariat into the arena of political struggles. Not wishing to come back to the very starting point of their negation, the "Independents," for a time, preached what they called "political demonstrations," a new kind of old Bakuninist riots. As riots, by whatever name they are called, always come too late for the fiery "revolutionists" there was only left to the independents to "march forward," to become converts to anarchy, and to propagate—in words—the propaganda of deed. The language of the "young" Landauers and Co. is already as "revolutionary" as that of the "oldest" anarchists.

> "Reason and knowledge only thou despise
>
> The highest strength in man that lies!
>
> Let but the lying spirit bind thee,
>
> With magic works and shows that blind thee,
>
> And I shall have thee fast and sure."

As to the "magic work and shows," they are innumerable in the arguments of the anarchists against the political activity of the proletariat. Here hate becomes veritable witchcraft. Thus Kropotkin turns their own arm—the materialist conception of history—against the Social-Democrats. "To each new economical phase of life corresponds a new political phase," he assures us. "Absolute monarchy—that is Court rule—corresponded to the system of serfdom. Representative government corresponds to capital rule. Both, however, are class rule. But in a society where the distinction between capitalist and labourer has disappeared, there is no need of such a government; it would be an anachronism, a nuisance." If Social-Democrats were to tell him they know this at least as well as he does, Kropotkin would reply that possibly they do, but that then they will not draw a logical conclusion from these premises. He, Kropotkin, is your real logician. Since the political constitution of every country is determined by its economic condition, he argues, the political action of socialists is absolute nonsense. "To seek to attain socialism or even (!) an agrarian revolution by means of a political revolution, is the merest utopia, because the whole of history shows us that political changes flow from the great economic revolutions, and not 'vice versa.'" Could the best geometrician in the world ever produce anything more exact than this demonstration? Basing his argument upon this impregnable foundation, Kropotkin advises the Russian revolutionists to give up their political struggle against tsarism. They must follow an "immediately economic" end. "The emancipation of the Russian peasants from the yoke of serfdom that has until now weighed upon them, is therefore the first task of the Russian revolutionist. In working along these lines he directly and immediately works for the good of the people... and he moreover prepares for the weakening of the centalised power of the State and for its limitation.

Thus the emancipation of the peasants will have prepared the way for the weakening of Russian tsarism. But how to emancipate the peasants before overthrowing tsarism? Absolute mystery! Such an emancipation would be a veritable "witchcraft." Old Liscow was right when he said, "It is easier and more natural to write with the fingers than with the head."

However this may be, the whole political action of the working class must be summed up in these few words: "No politics! Long live the purely economic struggle!" This is Bakuninism, but perfected Bakuninism. Bakunin himself urged the workers to fight for a reduction of the hours of labour, and higher wages. The anarchist-communists of our day seek to "make the workers understand that they have nothing to gain from such child's play as this, and that society can only be transformed by destroying the institutions which govern it." The raising of wages is also useless. "North America and South America, are they not there to prove to us that whenever the worker has succeeded in getting higher wages, the prices of articles of consumption have increased proportionately, and that where he has succeeded in getting 20 francs a day for his wages, he needs 25 to be able to live according to the standard of the better class workman, so that he is always below the average?" The reduction of the hours of labour is at any rate superfluous since capital will always make it up by a "systematic intensification of labour by means of improved machinery. Marx himself has demonstrated this as clearly as possible."

We know, thanks to Kropotkin, that the anarchist ideal has double origin. And all the anarchist "demonstrations" also have a double origin. On the one hand they are drawn from the vulgar handbooks of political economy, written by the most vulgar of bourgeois economists, e.g., Grave's dissertation upon wages, which Bastiat would have applauded enthusiastically. On the other hand, the "companions," remembering the somewhat "Communist" origin of their ideal, turn to Marx and quote, without understanding, him. Even Bakunin has been "sophisticated" by Marxism. The latter-day anarchists, with Kropotkin at their head, have been even more sophisticated.

The ignorance of Grave, "the profound thinker," is very remarkable in general, but it exceeds the bounds of all probability in matters of political economy. Here it is, only equalled by that of the learned geologist Kropotkin, who makes the most monstrous statements whenever he touches upon an economic question. We regret that space will not allow us to amuse the reader with some samples of anarchist economics. They must content themselves with what Kropotkin has taught them about Marx's "surplus value."

All this would be very ridiculous, if it were not too sad, as the Russian poet Lermontov says. And it is sad indeed. Whenever the proletariat makes an attempt to somewhat ameliorate its economic position, "large-hearted people," vowing they love the proletariat most tenderly, rush in from all points of the compass, and depending on their halting syllogisms, put spokes into the wheel of the movement, do their utmost to prove that the movement is useless. We have had an example of this with regard to the eight-hour day, which the anarchists combated, whenever they could, with a zeal worthy of a better cause. When the proletariat takes no notice of this, and pursues its "immediately economic" aims undisturbed—as it has the fortunate habit of doing—the same "large-hearted people" reappear upon the scene armed with bombs, and provide the government with the desired and sought-for pretext for attacking the proletariat. We have seen this at Paris on 1st May, 1890; we have seen it often during strikes. Fine fellows these "large hearted men"! And to think that among the workers themselves there are men simple enough to consider as their friends, these personages who are, in reality, the most dangerous enemies of their cause!

An anarchist will have nothing to do with "parliamentarism," since it only lulls the proletariat to sleep. He will have none of "reforms," since reforms are but so many compromises with the possessing classes. He wants the revolution, a "full, complete, immediate, and immediately economic" revolution. To attain this end he arms himself with a saucepan full of explosive materials, and throws it amongst the public theater or cafe. He declares this is the "revolution." For our own part it seems to us nothing but "immediate" madness.

It goes without saying that the bourgeois governments, while inveighing against the authors of these attempts, cannot but congratulate themselves upon these tactics. "Society is in danger!" "Caveant consules!" And the police "consuls" become active, and public opinion applauds all the reactionary measures resorted to by ministers in order to "save society."

> "The terrorist saviours of society in uniform, to gain the respect of the philistine masses, must appear with the halo of true sons of 'holy order,' the daughter of Heaven rich in blessings, and to this halo the schoolboy attempts of these terrorists help them. Such a silly fool, lost in his fantastical imaginings, does not even see that he is only a puppet, whose strings are pulled by a cleverer one in the terrorist wings; he does not see that the fear and terror he causes only serve to so deaden all the senses of the philistine crowd, that it shouts approval of every massacre that clears the road for reaction."

Napoleon III already indulged from time to time in an "outrage" in order once again to save society menaced by the enemies of order. The foul admissions of Andrieux, the acts and deeds of the German and Austrian "agents provocateurs," the recent revelations as to the attempt against the Madrid Parliament, etc., prove abundantly that the present governments profit enormously by the tactics of the "companions," and that the work of the terrorists in uniform would be much more difficult if the anarchists were not so eager to help in it.

Thus it is that spies of the vilest kind, like Joseph Peukert, for long years figured as shining lights of anarchism, translating into German the works of foreign anarchists; thus it is that the French bourgeois and priests directly subvention the "companions," and that the law-and-order ministry does everything in its power to throw a veil over these shady machinations. And so, too, in the name of the "immediate revolution," the anarchists become the precious pillars of bourgeois society, inasmuch as they furnish the *raison d'être* for the most immediately reactionary policy.

Thus the reactionary and conservative press has always shown a hardly disguised sympathy for the anarchists, and has regretted that the socialists, conscious of their end and aim, will have nothing to do with them. "They drive them away like poor dogs," pitifully exclaims the Paris *Figaro*, apropos of the expulsion of the anarchists from the Zurich Congress.

An anarchist is a man who—when he is not a police agent—is fated always and everywhere to attain the opposite of that which he attempts to achieve.

"To send working men to a Parliament," said Bordat, before the Lyons tribunal in 1893, "is to act like a mother who would take her daughter to a brothel." Thus it is also in the name of morality that the anarchists repudiate political action. But what is the outcome of their fear of parliamentary corruption? The glorification of theft ("Put money in thy purse," wrote Most in his *Freiheit*, already in 1880), the exploits of the Duvals and Ravachols, who in the name of the "cause" commit the most vulgar and disgusting crimes. The Russian writer, Herzen, relates somewhere how on arriving at some small Italian town, he met only priests and bandits, and was greatly perplexed, being unable to decide which were the priests and which the bandits. And this is the position of every impartial person today; for how are you going to divine where the "companion" ends and the bandit begins? The anarchists themselves are not always sure, as was proved by the controversy caused in their ranks by the Ravachol affair. Thus the better among them, those whose honesty is absolutely unquestionable, constantly fluctuate in their views of the "propaganda of deed."

"Condemn the propaganda of deed?" says Élisée Reclus. "But what is this propaganda except the preaching of well-doing and love of humanity by example? Those who call the 'propaganda of deed' acts of violence prove that they have not understood the meaning of this expression. The anarchist who understands his part, instead of massacring somebody or other, will exclusively strive to bring this person around to his opinions, and to make of him an adept who, in his turn, will make "propaganda of deed" by showing himself good and just to all those whom he may meet."

We will not ask what is left of the anarchist who has divorced himself from the tactics of "deeds."

We only ask the reader to consider the following lines:

"The editor of the *Sempre Avanti* wrote to Élisée Reclus asking him for his true opinion of Ravachol. 'I admire his courage, his goodness of heart, his greatness of soul, the generosity with which he pardons his enemies, or rather his betrayers. I hardly know of any men who have surpassed him in nobleness of conduct. I reserve the question as to how far it is always desirable to push to extremities one's own right, and whether other considerations moved by a spirit of human solidarity ought not to prevail. Still I am nonetheless one of those who recognise in Ravachol a hero of a magnanimity but little common.'"

This does not at all fit in with the declaration quoted above, and it proves irrefutably that citizen Reclus fluctuates, that he does not know exactly where his "companion" ends and the bandit begins. The problem is the more difficult to solve that there are a good many individuals who are at the same time "bandits" and anarchists. Ravochol was no exception. At the house of the anarchists, Ortiz and Chiericotti, recently arrested at Paris, an enormous mass of stolen goods were found. Nor is it only in France that you have the combination of these two apparently different trades. It will suffice to remind the reader of the Austrians Kammerer and Stellmacher.

Kropotkin would have us believe that anarchist morality, a morality free from all obligations or sanction, opposed to all utilitarian calculations, is the same as the natural morality of the people, "the morality from the habit of well doing." The morality of the anarchists is that of persons who look upon all human action from the abstract point of view of the unlimited rights of the individual, and who, in the name of these rights, pass a verdict of "Not guilty" on the most atrocious deeds, the most revoltingly arbitrary acts. "What matter the victims," exclaimed the anarchist poet Laurent Tailhade, on the very evening of Vaillant's outrage, at the banquet of the "Plume" Society, "provided the gesture is beautiful?"

Tailhade is a decadent, who, because he is "blasé" has the courage of his anarchist opinions. In fact the anarchists combat democracy because democracy, according to them, is nothing but the tyranny of "the morality from the habit of well-doing." The morality of the [majority] impose[s] its wishes upon the minority. But if this is so, in the name of what moral principle do the anarchists revolt against the bourgeoisie? Because the bourgeoisie are not a minority? Or because they do not do what they "will" to do?

"Do as thou would'st," proclaim the anarchists. The bourgeoisie "want" to exploit the proletariat, and do it remarkably well. They thus follow the anarchist precept, and the "companions" are very wrong to complain of their conduct. They become altogether ridiculous when they combat the bourgeoisie in the name of their victims. "What matters the death of vague human beings"—continues the Anarchist logician Tailhade—"if thereby the individual affirms himself?" Here we have the true morality of the anarchists; it is also that of the crowned heads. "*Sic volo, sic jubeo!*"

Thus, in the name of the revolution, the anarchists serve the cause of reaction; in the name of morality they approve the most immoral acts; in the name of individual liberty they trample under foot all the rights of their fellows.

And this is why the whole anarchist doctrine founders upon its own logic. If any maniac may, because he "wants" to, kill as many men as he likes, society, composed of an immense number of individuals, may certainly bring him to his senses, not because it is its caprice, but because it is its duty, because such is the *conditio sine qua non* of its existence.

VII. Conclusion

The "father of Anarchy," the "immortal" Proudhon, bitterly mocked at those people for whom the revolution consisted of acts of violence, the exchange of blows, the shedding of blood. The descendants of the "father," the modern anarchists, understand by revolution only this brutally childish method. Everything that is not violence is a betrayal of the cause, a foul compromise with "authority." The sacred bourgeoisie does not know what to do against them. In the domain of theory they are absolutely impotent with regard to the anarchists, who are their own enfants terribles. The bourgeoisie was the first to propagate the theory of laissez faire, of disheveled individualism. Their most eminent philosopher of today, Herbert Spencer, is nothing but a conservative anarchist. The "companions" are active and zealous persons, who carry the bourgeois reasoning to its logical conclusion.

The magistrates of the French bourgeois Republic have condemned Grave to prison, and his book, *Société Mourante et l'Anarchie*, to destruction. The bourgeois men of letters declare this puerile book a profound work, and its author a man of rare intellect.

And not only has the bourgeoisie no theoretical weapons with which to combat the anarchists; they see their young folk enamored of the anarchist doctrine. In this society, satiated and rotten to the marrow of its bones, where all faiths are long since dead, where all sincere opinions appear ridiculous, in this *monde ou l'on s'ennui*, where after having exhausted all forms of enjoyment they no longer know in what new fancy, in what fresh excess to seek novel sensations, there are people who lend a willing ear to the song of the anarchist siren. Among the Paris "companions" there are already not a few men quite *comme il faut*, men about town who, as the French writer, Raoul Allier, says, wear nothing less than patent leather shoes, and put a green carnation in their buttonholes before they go to meetings. Decadent writers and artists are converted to anarchism and propagate its theories in reviews like the *Mercure de France*, *La Plume*, etc. And this is comprehensible enough. One might wonder indeed if anarchism, an essentially bourgeois doctrine, had not found adepts among the French bourgeoisie, the most blasée of all bourgeoisies.

By taking possession of the anarchist doctrine, the decadent, *fin-de-siecle* writers restore to it its true character of bourgeois individualism. If Kropotkin and Reclus speak in the name of the worker, oppressed by the capitalist, *La Plume* and the *Mercure de France* speak in the name of the *individual* who is seeking to shake off all the trammels of society in order that he may at last do freely what he "wants" to. Thus anarchism comes back to its starting point. Stirner said: "Nothing for me goes beyond myself." Laurent Tailhade says: "What matters the death of vague human beings, if thereby the individual affirms himself."

The bourgeoisie no longer knows where to turn. "I who have fought so much for Positivism," moans Émile Zola, "well, yes! after thirty years of this struggle, I feel my convictions are shaken. Religious faith would have prevented such theories from being propagated; but has it not almost disappeared today? Who will give us a new ideal?"

Alas, gentlemen, there is no ideal for walking corpses such as you! You will try everything. You will become Buddhists, Druids, Sars Chaldeans, Occultists, Magi, Theosophists, or Anarchists, whichever you prefer—and yet you will remain what you are now—beings without faith or principle, bags, emptied by history. The ideal of the bourgeois has lived.

For ourselves, Social-Democrats, we have nothing to fear from the anarchist propaganda. The child of the bourgeoisie, anarchism, will never have any serious influence upon the proletariat. If among the anarchists there are workmen who sincerely desire the good of their class, and who sacrifice themselves to what they believe to be the good cause, it is only thanks to a misunderstanding that they find themselves in this camp. They only know the struggle for the emancipation of the proletariat under the form which the anarchists are trying to give it. When more enlightened they will come to us.

Here is an example to prove this. During the trial of the anarchists at Lyons in 1883, the working man Desgranges related how he had become an anarchist, he who had formerly taken part in the political movement, and had even been elected a municipal councilor at Villefranche in November, 1879. "In 1881, in the month of September, when the dyers' strike broke out at Villefranche, I was elected secretary of the strike committee, and it was during this memorable event…that I became convinced of the necessity of suppressing authority, for authority spells despotism. During this strike, when the employers refused to discuss the matter with the workers, what did the prefectural and communal administrations do to settle the dispute? Fifty gendarmes, with sword in hand, were told off to settle the question. That is what is called the pacific means employed by governments. It was then, at the end of this strike, that some working men, myself among the number, understood the necessity of seriously studying economic questions, and, in order to do so, we agreed to meet in the evening to study together. It is hardly necessary to add that this group became anarchist."

That is how the trick is done. A working man, active and intelligent, supports the programme of one or the other bourgeois party. The bourgeois talk about the well-being of the people, the workers, but betray them on the first opportunity. The working man who has believed in the sincerity of these persons is indignant, wants to separate from them, and decides to study seriously "economic questions." An anarchist comes along, and reminding him of the treachery of the bourgeois, and the sabers of the gendarmes, assures him that the political struggle is nothing but bourgeois nonsense, and that in order to emancipate the workers political action must be given up, making the destruction of the state the final aim. The working man who was only beginning to study the situation thinks the "companion" is right, and so he becomes a convinced and devoted anarchist! What would happen, if pursuing his studies of the social question further, he had understood that the "companion" was a pretentious ignoramus, that he talked twaddle, that his "Ideal" is a delusion and a snare, that outside bourgeois politics there is, opposed to these, the political action of the proletariat, which will put an end to the very existence of capitalist society? He would have become a Social-Democrat.

Thus the more widely our ideas become known among the working classes, and they are thus becoming more and more widely known, the less will proletarians be inclined to follow the anarchists. Anarchism, with the exception of its "learned" housebreakers, will more and more transform itself into a kind of bourgeois sport, for the purpose of providing sensations for "individuals" who have indulged too freely in the pleasures of the world, the flesh and the devil.

And when the proletariat are masters of the situation, they will only need to look at the "companions," and even the "finest" of them will be silenced; they will only have to breathe to disperse all the anarchist dust to the winds of heaven.

1895

Marx versus Bakunin
Alan Woods

"For the rest, old Hegel has already said: A party proves itself a victorious party by the fact that it splits and can stand the split." (**Engels to Bebel, 20ᵗʰ June, 1873**)

There have been many splits in the history of the Marxist movement. The enemies of Marxism seize upon this fact as proof of an inherent weakness, an intolerant spirit, excessive centralism, bureaucratic and authoritarian tendencies, and so on. In fact, periodic crises and splits are an inevitable consequence of development. Crises are a fact of human existence: birth is a crisis, as is adolescence, old age and death. Weak individuals will allow a crisis to drag them under. Men and women of stronger character will overcome the crisis and emerge stronger and more confident than before.

It is the same with a revolutionary tendency. The movement must constantly strive to rid itself of sectarian and opportunist tendencies, which partly reflect the pressures of alien classes, partly the inability of a layer of the organisation to advance to a higher stage of development. This was the case in the First International, or International Workingman's Association (IWA), when Marx and Engels were obliged to wage a ferocious struggle against the followers of the anarchist Bakunin.

The document that we recently published in installments, *Fictitious Splits in the International,*[1] is a useful reminder of the differences between Marxism and anarchism. We believe it deserves a careful reading for the lessons it has for Marxists today.

Bakunin

Bakunin's intrigues against the General Council began in 1871, although he was in contact with Marx before that. In 1864 he met Marx in London, from whom he learned of the founding of the International. He promised to cooperate. However, Bakunin held the view that Marx exaggerated the importance of the working class, while he held that the intelligentsia, the students, the *lumpenproletariat*, and the middle classes—representatives of bourgeois democracy—were more likely agents of revolution.

1 http://www.marxist.com/marx-bakunin-fictitious-splits-in-international.htm

For this reason, Bakunin began his activity, not in the workers' movement, but in a bourgeois organisation in Switzerland called The League for Peace and Freedom (*Ligue de la Paix et de la Liberté*). He was actually elected to its central committee. He thought he could take over the League and use it as a vehicle for advancing his anarchist doctrines. But at the League's Berne Congress he failed to make any impact, and split away with an insignificant minority.

It was only at this point, having fallen out with and split from the bourgeois League, that he entered the *Romande* Section of the IWA in Geneva. That was at the end of 1868. Bakunin hit on the idea of forming inside the IWA an anarchist faction *with himself as leader*. For this purpose, he established the International Alliance of Socialist Democracy. His aim was to get control of the IWA and foist his anarchist ideas upon it.

But he had a serious problem: the IWA was led by the General Council in London, where Marx had considerable influence. In order to achieve his aim, therefore, Bakunin had to undermine the General Council and blacken the name of Marx. This he did, with no regards to the democratic rules of the International, by factional intrigues and personal attacks. These intrigues, directed ostensibly against the General Council, were in reality directed against the International itself, the ideas, methods and programme of which Bakunin was fundamentally opposed to.

Bakunin's ideas

Marxism and anarchism are completely opposed and mutually exclusive ideologies. The first is a scientific theory and a revolutionary policy reflecting the class interests of the proletariat. Anarchism is a confused and unscientific doctrine that finds its class base in the petty-bourgeoisie and the lumpenproletariat. This is not the place to deal in detail with the ideas of Bakunin, although we may return to this topic in the future. His programme (insofar as it existed) was a superficial mishmash of ideas taken from Proudhon, Saint-Simon and other utopian socialists. Above all, he preached *abstention from the political movement*—an idea that he also took from Proudhon.

As far as the rejection of political action and organisation is concerned, Marx wrote:

> "*N.B. as to political movement:* The political movement of the working class has as its object, of course, the conquest of political power for the working class, and for this it is naturally necessary that a previous organisation of the working class, itself arising from their economic struggles, should have been developed up to a certain point.

"On the other hand, however, every movement in which the working class comes out as a class against the ruling classes and attempts to force them by pressure from without is a political movement. For instance, the attempt in a particular factory or even a particular industry to force a shorter working day out of the capitalists by strikes, etc., is a purely economic movement. On the other hand the movement to force an eight-hour day, etc., *law* is a *political* movement. And in this way, out of the separate economic movements of the workers there grows up everywhere a *political* movement, that is to say a movement of the *class*, with the object of achieving its interests in a general form, in a form possessing a general social force of compulsion. If these movements presuppose a certain degree of previous organisation, they are themselves equally a means of the development of this organisation.

Where the working class is not yet far enough advanced in its organisation to undertake a decisive campaign against the collective power, i.e., the political power of the ruling classes, it must at any rate be trained for this by continual agitation against and a hostile attitude towards the policy of the ruling classes. Otherwise it will remain a plaything in their hands, as the September revolution in France showed, and as is also proved up to a certain point by the game Messrs. Gladstone & Co. are bringing off in England even up to the present time." (*Marx to Bolte*, 23rd November, 1871, published in *Marx and Engels Correspondence;* Publisher: International Publishers, 1968)

The confused ideas of Bakunin got a certain echo in Italy and Spain, where capitalism was still in an embryonic state and the workers' movement still poorly developed, and to some extent in French Switzerland and Belgium. In countries like Britain and Germany it made little progress. In the ranks of the First International the supporters of Bakunin were a small minority. The prevailing influence in the leadership of the International Workingmen's Association (the General Council, based in London) was that of Marx and Engels.

Anarchism or democracy?

To this very day there are people who repeat the arguments of Bakunin as if they were good coin. In particular, the arguments that Marxism is "authoritarian" and dictatorial, and that a centalised revolutionary organisation crushes the freedom of the individual, stifles all creative thought and prepares the way for totalitarian dictatorship, are frequently repeated by the critics of Marxism, although they were answered long ago by Marx and Engels.

It was Bakunin, not Marx, who engaged in dictatorial Machiavellian politics, intriguing behind the backs of the International in order to discredit its leaders in order to disorganise it to set up a rival organisation. It was Bakunin, not Marx, who associated with the likes of Sergei Nechayev.

Together with the latter he wrote pamphlets on a new social order, to be created "*by concentrating all the means of social existence in the hands of Our Committee, and the proclamation of compulsory physical labour for everyone.*"

In this anti-authoritarian paradise, there would be compulsory residence in communal dormitories, rules for hours of work, feeding of children, etc, on which Marx commented ironically:

> "What a beautiful model of barrack-room communism! Here you have it all: communal eating, communal sleeping, assessors and offices regulating education, production, consumption, in a word, all social activity, and to crown all, *Our Committee*, anonymous and unknown to anyone, as the supreme dictator. This indeed is the purest anti-authoritarianism..."

For Bakunin and his followers, the word "authoritarian" just meant anything they didn't like. But it is an undeniable fact that in certain situations authority is necessary and unavoidable. As Engels says:

> "A revolution is certainly the most authoritarian thing there is; it is the act whereby one part of the population imposes its will upon the other part by means of rifles, bayonets, and cannon—authoritarian means, if such there be at all." (Engels, *On Authority*)[2]

Should the revolutionary party mirror the future society?

Another oft-repeated argument of the anti-authoritarians is that a centalised, disciplined party cannot lead to genuine socialism and must lead to totalitarian dictatorship. How many times have we heard this? How many times have we been told that Stalinism is the inevitable product of Leninist centralism?

Some kind of decision-making structure is necessary at any level of human cooperation or organisation. In any community, I must necessarily sacrifice part of my freedom to others. Even in the future classless society, people will still have to make decisions, which will be the decisions of the majority. And under capitalism, the workers must organise collectively to fight to defend their interests. How is this to be done, unless the minority submits to the will of the majority?

It is a regrettable fact that sometimes people do not agree. What are we to do in such circumstances? History has never produced any better instrument for expressing the popular will than democracy. True, even the most perfect democracy has its limitations, but to date nobody has ever proposed anything more perfect. What is the alternative? "Consensus"? But that only means the law of the lowest common denominator. Or perhaps the solution is that all decisions must be unanimous? That is the most undemocratic method of

2 See this volume, 135-38.

all, since the opposition of just one individual can paralyse the will of the majority: in other words it is the right of veto—the dictatorship of a single individual!

The middle classes are used to individualistic methods and have an individualistic mentality. An assembly of students can debate for hours, days and weeks without ever coming to a conclusion. They have plenty of time and are accustomed to that kind of thing. But a factory mass meeting is an entirely different affair. Before a strike, the workers discuss, debate, listen to different opinions. But at the end of the day, the issue must be decided. It is put to the vote and the majority decides. This is clear and obvious to any worker. And nine times out of ten the minority will voluntarily accept the decision of the majority.

The best example of an anti-authoritarian is a strike breaker, who declares that, no matter what his workmates decide, he or she demands the right to express his or her free individuality—by breaking the strike. We know these arguments in favour of the absolute freedom of the individual, which are proclaimed during every strike by the bourgeois press in defence of the scabs. And we also know how the workers on strike regard the latter and how they see the "the absolute freedom of the individual."

In reality, anarchist organisations (surely a contradiction in terms?) always suffer from the most extreme bureaucracy, because someone has to make decisions. Who are they? In practice, decisions are made "spontaneously" by self-appointed groups that are elected by nobody and responsible to nobody—that is to say, government by cliques. That was the method of the Bakuninists in the IWA. Behind the backs of the membership, they organised an intrigue under the slogan of combating the "authoritarian" General Council.

One might add that the same people who were allegedly waging a struggle for democracy and against authoritarianism, were elected by nobody and responsible to nobody. The General Council was the elected leadership of the International. The Bakuninist Alliance was self-appointed and functioned outside the democratic structures of the International. Its members represented only themselves, although their activities were organised and orchestrated by the man referred to as "Citizen B" (Bakunin), who in reality decided everything.

The International Alliance of Socialist Democracy

Bakunin was an unprincipled adventurer who was constantly scheming and intriguing to boost his own position and prestige. For him, theory was always a secondary consideration: merely a means of his personal self-assertion. There have been many such people in the movement both before and since.

Marx wrote to Friedrich Bolte about Bakunin:

"He—a man devoid of theoretical knowledge—put forward the pretension that this separate body was to represent the scientific propaganda of the International, which was to be made the special function of this second *International within the International.*

"…If he is a non-entity as a theoretician, he is in his element as an intriguer."(*Letter to Friedrich Bolte*, 3ʳᵈ November 1871).

The Alliance was characterised by radical-sounding verbiage. It declared war upon God and the state and demanded that all its members be atheists. Its economic programme was confused and ambiguous. Instead of fighting for the abolition of class society, it demanded the *equality of all classes.* Instead of the expropriation of the means of production, it limited itself to a demand for the *abolition of the right of inheritance.* And in order not to frighten away the middle class and liberal bourgeois, it was careful not to define clearly its class character.

The new organisation approached the General Council with the request that it be taken into the International as a separate organisation, with its own constitution and programme. Bakunin wrote an ingratiating letter to Marx, full of false flattery. He wrote:

"Since taking leave solemnly and publicly from the bourgeoisie at the Berne Congress, I no longer know any other society, any other environment, than the world of the workers. My country is now the International, of which you are one of the most important founders. So you see, my dear friend, that I am your disciple, and proud of my title."

Marx was not impressed. Up to the end of 1868 his attitude toward Bakunin was that of extreme tolerance. He had welcomed Bakunin as a collaborator in 1862. Now he was suspicious of the latter's motives—and he was not wrong. Let us remember that only four years earlier Bakunin had written from Italy promising to work for the International. Not only did he not keep his promise, but he devoted all his energies into promoting a rival bourgeois movement, the League for Peace and Freedom. Only after his efforts to take over that organisation had failed did he turn his attention to the International, which was now obviously growing in strength and influence.

The General Council refused the Alliance's request, and Bakunin resorted to a maneuver. He announced that the Alliance would disband and transform its sections, (which would continue to hold to their own programme) into sections of the International. After these assurances, the General Council agreed to admit the sections of the former Alliance into the IWA.

The Alliance claimed to have dissolved on 6ᵗʰ August, and informed the General Council of this. But a few weeks later it reappeared in the guise of a new "Section of Revolutionary Socialist Propaganda and Action," which declared itself in agreement with the general principles of the International, but reserved itself the right to make full use of the freedom which the statutes and the congresses of the International afforded.

It did not take Marx long to conclude that Bakunin had deceived the General Council. Despite having officially disbanded his society, he maintained its central organisation intact for the purpose of taking over the International. Subsequent events proved that the Alliance continued to exist. It conducted a continuous guerrilla war against the International under the guise of fighting the "authoritarianism" of the General Council. For this purpose Bakunin and his followers did not hesitate to resort to any means, even the basest slanders and the most dishonest intrigues.

How intriguers work

It is not difficult for professional intriguers to influence honest party activists. When dealing with this kind of individual, naive honesty is a definite disadvantage, since honest people cannot recognise an intrigue. They take things at face value and believe what is said to them, since they have no reason to suspect the other person's motives, believing them to be honest party workers themselves.

Bakunin hatched the plan of a secret faction, *L'Alliance Internationale de la Démocratie Socialiste*, which, while formally a branch of the IWA, in reality formed a parallel International Association "with the special mission to elaborate the higher philosophical etc. principles" of the proletarian movement. He "would, by a clever trick, have placed our society under the guidance and supreme initiative of the Russian Bakunin."

Bakunin was a skillful intriguer and soon convinced the veteran German revolutionary and friend of Karl Marx and Engels, Johann Philipp Becker, who lived in Switzerland, to put his name to his programme. Marx wrote with regret: "Brave old Becker, always anxious for action, for something stirring, but of no very critical cast of mind, an enthusiast like Garibaldi, easily led away." (*Marx To Paul and Laura Lafargue*, 15th February 1869)

The way in which they set to business was characteristically dishonest. They sent their new programme, placing Becker's name at the head of the signatures, thus hiding behind the moral authority of a veteran of unquestionable honesty. Then, behind the backs of the General Council, they sent emissaries to Paris, Brussels, etc. (In those days they did not possess the Internet, which would have saved them a lot of time and effort). Only in the last moment did they communicate the documents to the London General Council.

The General Council took action to stop these factional intrigues. On 22nd December, 1868, a unanimous decision of the General Council declared the rules of the Alliance laying down its relations with the International Working Men's Association null and void, and refused the Alliance admittance as a branch of the International Working Men's Association. All the branches of the IWA approved the decision.

Becker was resentful towards Marx for this, but, as Marx wrote to the Lafargues: "with all my personal friendship for Becker I could not allow this first attempt at disorganising our society to succeed." (*Marx to Paul and Laura Lafargue*, 15th February 1869). Bakunin reacted by declaring that the Alliance was "dissolved," when in fact it remained in being as a secret organisation working behind the backs of the International.

The Nechayev affair

An indication of Bakunin's adventurism was his association with the notorious Russian terrorist Nechayev, who was tried for the murder of a young student member of his group in Russia and ended his life in a tsarist prison, having seriously compromised the revolutionary cause. It was partly to divert attention away from this scandal that Bakunin intensified his attacks on Marx and the General Council.

There were profound differences between the ideas advocated by Bakunin and those of Marx. Bakunin utterly rejected the idea of the proletariat seizing power. He denied any form of political struggle insofar as it had to be conducted within bourgeois society, which had to be destroyed. Riazanov sums up the essence of Bakunin's creed:

> "First destroy, and then everything will take care of itself. Destroy—the sooner, the better. It would be sufficient to stir up the revolutionary intelligentsia and the workers embittered through want. The only thing needed would be a group composed of determined people with the demon of revolution in their souls." (D. Riazanov, *Karl Marx and Friedrich Engels*, 185)

This is a completely false conception of the class struggle. The working class can only learn through struggle. Without the day-to-day struggle for advance under capitalism, the socialist revolution would be impossible. The struggle for reforms, higher wages, better conditions, a reduction of working hours, etc. creates more favourable conditions for the class organisation of the proletariat. At a certain historical stage, the economic struggles of the working class necessarily become political, as in the fight for democratic rights, freedom of speech and assembly, the right to strike, the right to vote, etc. It is unthinkable that the working class could remain indifferent to such questions.

The slogan of political abstentionism merely means that the working class would remain politically subordinate to the parties of the liberal bourgeoisie, as the example of England already showed clearly. In order to achieve independence from the bourgeoisie in the political sphere, the proletariat must fight for its own independent political party. That was why Marx considered the political struggle and the political organisation of the proletariat for the conquest of political power indispensable. But for the Bakuninists this was a book sealed by seven seals.

As we have seen, Bakunin's adventurism was completely exposed by the Nechayev affair. Nechayev was a young fanatic, a revolutionary adventurer who turned up in Geneva in the spring of 1869, claiming to have escaped from the fortress of St. Peter-Paul. He also claimed to represent an all-powerful committee that would overthrow tsarist Russia. This was a pure invention. He had never been in St. Peter-Paul and the committee never existed.

Nevertheless, Bakunin was impressed by "the young savage," "the young tiger," as he used to call Nechayev. Nechayev was a devoted disciple of Bakunin. But unlike his master, Nechayev was always characterised by an iron consistency. Bakunin had preached that the *lumpenproletariat* were the real carriers of the social revolution. He regarded criminals as desirable elements to be recruited into the revolutionary movement. So it was logical that his loyal disciple Nechayev should conclude that it was necessary to organise a group of lumpens for the purpose of "expropriation" in Switzerland.

In the autumn of 1869 Nechayev returned to Russia with a plan to set up a Bakuninist group there. There is no doubt that he went with Bakunin's full support. He carried with him a written authorization from Bakunin which declared that he was the "accredited representative" of a so-called European Revolutionary Alliance—another invention of Bakunin. He even issued an appeal to the officers of the tsarist army, calling on them to place themselves unconditionally at the disposal of the "committee," although it did not exist.

When a member of Nechayev's group, a student called Ivanov, began to doubt the existence of the secret committee, Nechayev murdered him. This led to numerous arrests, but Nechayev himself managed to avoid arrest. The Nechayev trial opened in St. Petersburg in July 1871, and the whole ghastly affair was publicly exposed. There were over eighty accused, mostly students, Nechayev himself having conveniently escaped to Geneva.

The Nechayev affair did a lot of damage to the movement in Russia and internationally. It affected the IWA because Nechayev let people believe that he was acting in the name of the International, whereas in fact he was an agent of Bakunin. Later, in order to explain away this wretched affair and absolve Bakunin from his personal responsibility for it, it had been claimed that Bakunin fell under the influence of Nechayev who tricked him and used him for his own purposes.

But it was Bakunin who provided him with fake documents that purported to be from the International and were signed by him. It was Bakunin who wrote most, if not all, the proclamations and manifestos of the non-existing "committee," and it was Bakunin who defended Nechayev after he had fled from the scene of his crime, describing the murder of the unfortunate Ivanov as "a political act." Meanwhile, the majority of the students that were put on trial were sentenced to long terms in prison or to a living death in the Siberian mines.

The Basel Congress

It was at Basel that Bakunin first made his appearance, and his faction was well represented there. But as he was still feeling his way, he was cautious about putting forward his real programme. Ironically, the same Bakunin who had always been violently opposed to opportunism, confined himself to demanding the immediate abolition, not of private property, but of *the right of inheritance*.

As usual, Bakunin stood everything on its head. It is not the right of inheritance that is responsible for private property, but the existence of private property that gives rise to the right of inheritance. After the seizure of power, the proletariat will deal with this question, along with many other related secondary issues. But the main task is the expropriation of large-scale private property through the nationalisation of the land, the banks and private monopolies. But this is a political act, and therefore anathema to the anarchists.

To propose the abolition of the right of inheritance in general, apart from its clearly utopian character, leaves out of account the fact that a large part of the middle class, peasants and even a section of the working class would be affected. A workers' state would not expropriate the small property owners, but only large-scale private property. In the meantime, it would be sufficient to impose a heavily graduated tax on wealth and limit the right of inheritance.

For Bakunin, however, these concrete circumstances were irrelevant. His scheme of social revolution was a pure abstraction, outside of time and space. As usual, his empty demagogy only served to sow the maximum confusion. When the question was put to the vote, neither of the resolutions won a sufficient majority, and the whole affair was left in a confused state, which was the inevitable result of the anarchists' "theoretical" interventions. Having made a big mess, Bakunin then forgot about the right of inheritance, and passed onto something else. This was absolutely typical conduct on his part: a) beat the drum loudly on some issue or other; b) cause the maximum confusion; c) move on to some other matter. The disorganising results of this conduct are self-evident.

It is interesting to note that the "authoritarian" structures of the International that Bakunin protested against so vehemently in 1871 and 1872 were introduced to the International *on the motion of Bakunin's supporters, with Bakunin's support.* That was at a time when he was aiming to gain control of the International. Only when this plan failed did Bakunin suddenly discovered the "authoritarian" character of the International's structure and rules. Bakunin always ruled his own faction, the Alliance, with a rod of iron. Certainly, the charge of authoritarianism and dictatorial tendencies can with far greater justice be directed against Bakunin than against Marx.

About this time Wilhelm Liebknecht and August Bebel, after a sharp factional struggle with the Lassallean Schweitzer, had succeeded in establishing a separate party at the Eisenach convention (1869), based on the programme of the International. Bakunin's activity in the League for Peace and Freedom were discussed and rejected by this party congress. The next Congress was supposed to take place in Germany, but it could not be convened. Immediately after the Basel Congress, tensions between France and Prussia were deteriorating fast, and the outbreak of war was imminent.

To the degree that the members of the International became aware of the disorganising conduct of Bakunin and his followers, they reacted against. Marx wrote to Engels on 30th October, 1869:

> "Apropos. The secretary of our French Genevan committee is utterly fed up with being saddled with Bakunin, and complains that he disorganises everything with his "tyranny." In the *Égalite*, Monsieur Bakunin indicates that the German and English workers have no desire for individuality, so accept our *communisme autoritaire*. In opposition to this, Bakunin represents *le collectivisme anarchique*. The anarchism is, however, in his head, which contains only one clear idea—that Bakunin should play first fiddle." (*Marx and Engels Collected Works, Volume 43, 363*)

Bakunin and the Franco-Prussian War

In the middle of all this, stormy events were being prepared. The thunderclouds of war that hung over Europe erupted in the Franco-Prussian War. The defeat of the French armies at Sedan led to the collapse of the Bonapartist regime and to the Paris Commune. France was once more in the throes of revolution. Here the adventurist character of Bakunin was exposed in practice.

During the war Bakunin supported France, fearing that it would become a German colony, "and then instead of living socialism we will have the doctrinaire socialism of the Germans." (James Joll, *The Anarchists*, 90).

When on 19th July, 1870, the war erupted, it took Europe by surprise. A few days after the outbreak of hostilities the General Council published a proclamation written by Marx, which began with a quotation from the Inaugural Address of the International on war: "a foreign policy in pursuit of criminal designs, playing upon national prejudices and squandering in piratical wars the people's blood and treasure."

Marx fiercely denounced Napoleon III, pointing out that whichever side won, the last hour of the Second Empire had struck. This was a prophetic prediction. In about six weeks the regular French army was smashed at Sedan. On 2nd September, Napoleon had already surrendered to the Prussians. Two days later a republic was declared in Paris. But the war continued. It passed into the second phase, in which Prussia was no longer fighting a defensive war against the Empire, but a predatory war against the French people to seize Alsace-Lorraine and plunder France.

On 9th September, 1870, immediately after the proclamation of a Republic in France, the General Council issued its second Manifesto on the war, also written by Marx. It contains one of the most profound analyses in all of Marx's writings. Long before the fall of Sedan, the Prussian general staff declared itself in favour of a policy of conquest. Marx opposed any annexations or indemnities, and prophetically predicted that such a predatory peace would create a state of permanent war in Europe. France would fight to regain what she had lost and would enter into an alliance with tsarist Russia against Germany. This was exactly what happened in 1914.

The Manifesto urged the German workers to demand an honourable peace and the recognition of the French Republic and advised the French workers to keep a watchful eye on the bourgeois republicans and make use of the Republic for the purpose of strengthening their class organisation to fight for their emancipation. However, Marx warned the French workers not to try to take power under present circumstances.

While Marx was trying to restrain the French workers from entering into an untimely battle against overwhelming forces, Bakunin was doing his best to stir them to revolt at all costs. As soon as he heard of a local uprising in Lyons, Bakunin went to that city on 28th September, where he installed himself in the Town Hall. He declared the "administrative and governmental machinery of the State" abolished and the "Revolutionary Federation of the Commune" proclaimed in its place.

Bakunin carried his rejection of authority to the point that he neglected to post guards on the door of the Town Hall, so that when the state finally appeared in the form of the National Guard, it was able to enter the premises without difficulty and arrest everyone inside. Marx wrote about this episode with heavy but justified irony:

"London, 19th October, 1870

"As to Lyons, I have received letters not fit for publication. At first everything went well. Under the pressure of the "International" section, the Republic was proclaimed before Paris had taken that step. A revolutionary government was at once established—*La Commune*—composed partly of workmen belonging to the "International," partly of Radical middle class Republicans. The *octrois* [internal customs dues] were at once abolished, and rightly so. The Bonapartist and Clerical intriguers were intimidated. Energetic means were taken to arm the whole people. The middle class began if not really to sympathize with, at least to quietly undergo, the new order of things. The action of Lyons was at once felt at Marseilles and Toulouse, where the "International" sections are strong.

"But the asses, Bakunin and Cluseret, arrived at Lyons and spoiled everything. Belonging both to the "International," they had, unfortunately, influence enough to mislead our friends. The Hotel de Ville was seized for a short time—a most foolish decree on the abolition *de l'état* [abolition of the state] and similar nonsense were issued. You understand that the very fact of a Russian— represented by the middle class papers as an agent of Bismarck—pretending to impose himself as the leader of a *Comité de Salut de la France* [Committee for the Safety of France] was quite sufficient to turn the balance of public opinion. As to *Cluseret*, he behaved both as a fool and a coward. These two men have left Lyons after their failure.

"At Rouen, as in most industrial towns of France, the sections of the International, following the example of Lyons, have enforced the official admission into the "committees of defence" of the working-class element.

"Still, I must tell you that according to all information I receive from France, the middle class on the whole prefers Prussian conquest to the victory of a Republic with Socialist tendencies." (*Marx and Engels Correspondence*, *Marx to Edward Beesly*)

His attempt to proclaim anarchism having ended in farce, "Citizen B" was compelled to return to Switzerland empty-handed. Now he turned his attention once more to the IWA. Unable to overthrow the bourgeois state, he intensified his efforts to overthrow the General Council, which, on the eve of the Paris Commune, had to take up precious time with Bakunin's constant intrigues.

The Paris Commune

Just as Marx thought, the French republicans immediately showed their cowardice and their readiness to enter into an agreement with Bismarck against the working class, who were prepared to fight against the Prussian forces. The attempt of the French bourgeois to disarm the workers of Paris was the spark that lit the flame of the Paris Commune.

The Commune lasted three months (18th March to 29th May, 1871), but finally succumbed to overwhelming force. A few days after the defeat of the Commune, Marx wrote the famous address we now know as *The Civil War in France*. At a time when the Communards were being systematically maligned by the bourgeois press, Marx defended them. He pointed out that the Paris Commune was the prototype of a future workers' state, a concrete expression of the "dictatorship of the proletariat."

Basing himself on the experience of the Revolution of 1848, Marx had come to the conclusion that the working class, after having seized power, could not simply lay hold of the bourgeois apparatus of the state and use it for its own purposes, but that it would have to demolish this military-bureaucratic machine and erect in its place a new state, a state that would not be a replica of the old state of the oppressor class, but a workers' state, democratically run by the working class, a transitional state dedicated to its own eventual dissolution. The Paris Commune was just such a state.

Bakunin and his followers arrived at diametrically opposite conclusions. Their opposition to politics and the state became even more insistent, advocating the creation of communes in separate towns as soon as possible; with the idea that these communes would inspire other towns to follow their example. But one of the reasons the Commune failed was precisely that it remained isolated in Paris. What was required, as Marx explained, was to march on Versailles, where the counterrevolution was based, and crush the enemy before the enemy crushed the Commune, which was unfortunately what occurred.

Some time later, Garibaldi replied to the Bakuninists that the Paris Commune was defeated because it was not centalised and disciplined enough:

> "You intend, in your paper, to make war upon untruth and slavery. That is a very fine programme, but I believe that the International, in fighting against the principle of authority, makes a mistake and obstructs its own progress. The Paris Commune fell because there was in Paris no authority but only anarchy. Spain and France are suffering from the same evil." (Engels, *Comment upon Giuseppe Garibaldi's letter to Prospero Crescio*, 7th July 1873, MECW, vol. 23, 453.)

After the Commune

The defeat of the Commune inevitably created a very difficult situation for the International, which faced the attacks of enemies on all sides. There were the slanderous attacks by the bourgeois press of all countries. But the General

Council was able to reply to such attacks openly, and for a while they actually served to strengthen the International.

In France, however, the raging counterrevolution meant that for a few years the French workers' movement was paralysed and links with the International were broken. As a consequence of the defeat and the White Terror that followed it, an army of communard refugees flooded into London, virtually the only place in Europe that would receive them. At a time when almost all governments now began to mobilise their forces against the International, it was overwhelmed by the necessity of assisting the many refugees from the Communards, most of whom ended up in London. The collection of the necessary funds to assist them absorbed a lot of the time of Marx and other members of the General Council.

Worse was to come. As so often happens in exile circles following the defeat of a revolution, the French refugees were demoralised and disoriented by events, and bitter factional strife was continually breaking out among them. This affected the General Council, which had co-opted a number of refugees to make up for the loss of contacts in France itself. It was later exposed that a number of French police agents and provocateurs had penetrated the ranks of the French exiles and infiltrated the ranks of the International.

The International was besieged by enemies on all sides. Bakunin launched an attack on Marx and "State communism":

> "We shall fight to the hilt against their false authoritarian theories, against their dictatorial presumption and against their methods of underground intrigues and vainglorious machinations, their introduction of mean personalities, their foul insults and infamous slanders, methods which characterise the political struggles of almost all Germans and which they have unfortunately introduced into the International." (Quoted in Mehring, *Karl Marx*)

Meanwhile, Mazzini published violent attacks on the Commune and on the International in a weekly publication which he published in Lugano, but Garibaldi, who was a genuine revolutionary and a national hero, saw in the International "the rising sun of the future." The German labour movement also suffered the attacks of the state. Bebel and Liebknecht, who had protested against the annexation of Alsace-Lorraine and declared their solidarity with the Paris Commune, were arrested and sentenced to confinement in a fortress. Bismarck came down hard on the German working-class movement and particularly the supporters of the International.

Ultra-leftism and opportunism

Marx was forced to fight on different fronts. On the one hand there were the ultra-left anarchists, but on the other there were all kinds of confused, reformist elements who had joined the International as a means of furthering their trade union activity, but were by no means revolutionaries. These people were frightened by the Paris Commune and the ferocity of the repression that followed. More than one of them deserted the International on one pretext or another.

A typical representative of this trend was the English trade unionist John Hales, who was at the time the General Secretary of the IWA. Hales was a reformist with nationalist prejudices. Marx said that in his dealings with the English reformist workers' leaders he had to be very patient: "mild in manner but bold in content." He must have had the patience of Job!

On reading the minutes of the General Council, one gets a clear impression of what Marx and Engels had to put up with from such people. The English members of the Council displayed a narrow-minded parochial attitude to most questions, indulging in petty quarrels over trivial organisational matters, which often detracted from far more important work.

Needless to say, men like Hales were deeply suspicious of genuine revolutionaries and had an ambivalent attitude to the Paris Commune. They were hostile to Republicanism and inclined to seek accommodation with Liberal elements, as Hales showed in his attitude to the Irish question. He demanded that the Irish members of the IWA should come under the control of the British Federal Council—a demand that was rejected by the General Council with only one vote in favour—that of Hales.

At first sight, it may seem that there could be no common ground between English reformists like Hales and Co. and the Bakuninists. But in politics we can find all sorts of strange bedfellows. The Alliance's demand for autonomy for the national sections found a sympathetic hearing from some of the English. To the degree that Hales felt that his position as General Secretary of the IWA was being threatened, to establish his position he maneuvered the British Federal Council as a counterweight to the General Council.

And that was not all. Bakunin's demand that the workers must abstain from politics also chimed well with the class collaboration politics of the trade union leaders who were stuck firmly to the apron strings of the Liberal Party and had no desire to take the initiative of setting up an independent Labour party. All this was sufficient grounds for the English reformists to make common cause with the Spanish and Italian anarchists—and always against Marx and the General Council.

Barrage of letters

Anarchism is the communism of the petty-bourgeois and the *lumpenproletarian*. In both cases, the central consideration is always the same: extreme individualism, a total rejection of any rules, discipline and centalisation. In the course of the dispute with the Bakuninists, the latter ignored all the democratic structures of the International. They refused to recognise the General Council, although it had been elected by the World Congress and repeatedly reelected.

The Bakuninists were small in numbers, but made a lot of noise. On 28th July, 1871, Engels wrote to Carlo Cafiero:

> "The Bakuninists are a tiny minority within the Association and they are the only ones who have at all times brought about dissension. I am referring mainly to the Swiss, because we had little or nothing to do with the others. We have always allowed them to have their principles and to promote them as they thought best, so long as they renounced all attempts at undermining the Association or imposing their programme on us." (MECW, vol. 44, 183)

The limited resources of the General Council were put under severe strain by the problems that flowed from the defeat of the Commune. The constant attacks by the enemies of the International, the intrigues of the Bakuninists, and need to assist the ever increasing numbers of starving and destitute refugees from France, took up a colossal amount of time. For weeks on end Marx was unable to dedicate any time to *Capital* and other important theoretical work. He wrote in desperation to Kugelmann:

> "Remember, *mon cher*, that if the day had 48 hours, I would still not have finished my day's work for months now.

> "The work for the International is immense, and in addition London is overrun with refugees, whom we have to look after. Moreover, I am overrun by other people—newspaper men and others of every description—who want to see the "monster" with their own eyes.

> "Up till now it has been thought that the emergence of the Christian myths during the Roman Empire was possible only because printing had not yet been invented. Precisely the contrary. The daily press and the telegraph, which in a moment spreads its inventions over the whole earth, fabricate more myths in one day (and the bourgeois cattle believe and propagate them still further), than could have previously been produced in a century." (*Marx to Ludwig Kugelmann*, 27th July 1871, MECW, vol. 44, 176–77)

One way of sabotaging the work of an organisation is by overloading it with tasks that surpass its real ability to cope. The Bakuninists adopted the tactic of bombarding the sections and individual members with a barrage of letters, circulars, etc., defaming Marx and the General Council. Commenting on this tactic, Engels wrote:

"As private correspondents these men are assiduous beyond belief; and if he [were] a member of the Alliance they would certainly have bombarded him with letters and blandishments." (*Engels to Paul Lafargue,* 19th January, 1872, MECW, vol. 44, 301).

Engels fortunately did not live in the age of emails, or he would have had a lot more to complain about.

The Sonvillier circular accused the London Conference of the deadliest of all deadly sins—*authoritarianism*:

"This Conference has... taken resolutions... which tend to turn the International, which is a free federation of autonomous sections, into a hierarchical and authoritarian organisation of disciplined sections placed entirely under the control of a General Council which may, at will, refuse their admission or suspend their activity [!]"

The circular claimed that the very fact that some people were members of the General Council had a "corrupting effect," for "it is absolutely impossible for a person who has power" (!) over his fellows to remain a moral person. The General Council is becoming a "hotbed of intrigue." This is just another way of expressing the common prejudice of backward workers that "all leaders are corrupt." If that were really the case, the outlook for socialism would be very poor indeed.

Yet another complaint of the "anti-authoritarians" is that the same members of the General Council were reelected every year. The same leadership was sitting in the same place (London). The General Council has been "composed for five years running of the same persons, continually reelected." To this complaint Marx gave the obvious answer: "The reelection of the General Council's original membership, at successive Congresses at which England was definitely under-represented, would seem to prove that it has done its duty within the limits of the means at its disposal." (Ibid.)

It is clear that the Congress would only reelect a leadership if it considered that its work was generally satisfactory. The Sixteen, on the contrary, interpreted this only as a proof of the "blind confidence of the Congresses," carried at Basel to the point of "a sort of voluntary abdication in favour of the General Council." In their opinion, the Council's "normal role" should be "that of a simple correspondence and statistical bureau."

No leadership?

The idea that the International should have no guiding centre, and that its leading bodies should only coordinate the work of the national sections, was later put into practice by the Second International, which, as Lenin remarked, was not an International but only a post office. This played a big part in bringing about the national-reformist degeneration of the Second International.

Moreover, this argument is not confined to the International. It equally applies to national and local organisations. The logic of it would be to dissolve the organisation altogether—which suits the anarchist point of view admirably. Unfortunately, the workers are involved in the class struggle and cannot do without strong centalised organisation to fight the bosses. The workers' organisations are very democratic and willing to discuss different opinions as to whether to call a strike or not. But at the end of the day, the issue is put to the vote and the majority decides.

The question is: what is the real character of a revolutionary leadership? Is it to provide political leadership, or merely to act in an administrative (i.e. bureaucratic) character? Is it to organise and centalise the work or merely to pass on information and coordinate the work of the constituent bodies that will function with complete autonomy? Is the revolutionary organisation a school without any definite ideas, which discusses endlessly the views of every comrade in order for an idea to "emerge" of its own accord? Or is it an organisation that is formed on the basis of very definite ideas, theories, and principles that are regularly rediscussed, concretized, and voted on in democratic congresses with elected delegates?

Marx answered the anarchists as follows:

"First, the General Council should be nominally a simple correspondence and statistical bureau. Once it has been relieved of its administrative functions, its correspondence would be concerned only with reproducing the information already published in the Association's newspapers. The correspondence bureau would thus become needless.

"As for statistics, that function is possible only if a strong organisation, and especially, as the original Rules expressly say, a common direction are provided. Since all that smacks very much of "authoritarianism," however, there might perhaps be a bureau, but certainly no statistics. In a word, the General Council would disappear. The federal councils, the local committees, and other "authoritarian" centres, would go by the same token. Only the autonomous sections would remain.

"What, one may ask, will be the purpose of these "autonomous sections," freely federated and happily rid of all superior bodies, "even of the superior body elected and constituted by the workers"?

"Here, it becomes necessary to supplement the circular by the report of the Jura Federal Committee submitted to the Congress of the Sixteen:

"'In order to make the working class the real representative of humanity's new interests, 'its organisation must be' guided by the idea that will triumph. *To evolve* this idea from the needs of our epoch, from mankind's vital aspirations, by a consistent study of the phenomena of social life, *to then carry* this idea to our workers' organisations—such should be our aim," etc. Lastly, there must be created "amid our working population a real revolutionary socialist *school.'*

"Thus, the autonomous workers' sections are in a trice converted into *schools*, of which these gentlemen of the Alliance will be the masters. They "evolve" the idea by "consistent" studies which leave no trace behind. They then "carry this idea to our workers' organisations." To them, the working class is so much raw material, a chaos into which they must breathe their Holy Spirit before it acquires a shape." (*Fictitious Splits in the International, MECW*, vol. 23, 114)

As the elected leadership of the International, the General Council could not allow itself to be bullied and blackmailed by self-appointed individuals and groups. In a letter to Carmelo Palladino, dated 23rd November, 1871, Marx explained his attitude to all this:

"Whatever your fears in regard to the great responsibility the General Council has taken upon itself, that Council will remain ever loyal to the flag entrusted to its care seven years ago by the faith of the working men of the civilised world. It will respect individual opinions, it is prepared to transfer its powers to the hands of its mandators, but as long as it is charged with the supreme direction of the Association, it will see to it that nothing is done to vitiate the character of the movement which has made the International what it now is, and will abide by the resolutions of the Conference until such time as a congress has decided otherwise." (*MECW*, vol. 44, 261–62)

Marx pointed out, the only sin that the General Council was guilty of was—carrying out Congress decisions. The Congress consists of elected delegates who, after participating freely in democratic debate, decide by a majority what ideas and methods the International has to follow. The International elected a leadership composed of the most capable and experienced people to do precisely this. And democracy has always consisted of the fact that the majority decides. The minority has the right to express its views within the organisation, but if you are in a minority you have to accept it, not shout about "authoritarianism."

The problem here—and in general with the "anti-authoritarians"—is that they do not respect the rights of the majority. Their real complaint is that they are a minority, and not the majority. They believe that the tail ought to wag the dog. Marx remarked ironically:

"They seem to think that the mere fact of belonging to the General Council is sufficient to destroy not only a person's *morality*, but also his common sense. How else can we suppose that a majority will transform itself into a minority by voluntary co-options?" (*Fictitious Splits in the International, MECW*, vol. 23, 114)

Factional use of private correspondence

As part of "their "anti-authoritarian" campaign, the Bakuninists did not hesitate to make unscrupulous use of private correspondence for factional purposes, and even demanded that the General Council should debate with them in public. When the Bakuninist papers *Égalité* joined the *Progrès* in inviting the *Travail* (a Paris paper) to denounce the General Council, Marx wrote:

> "The General Council does not know of any article, either in the Rules, or the Regulations, which would oblige it to enter into correspondence or into polemic with the *Égalité* or to provide "replies to questions" from newspapers. The Federal Committee of Geneva alone represents the branches of Romance Switzerland vis-à-vis the General Council. When the Romance Federal Committee addresses requests of reprimands to us through the only legitimate channel, that is to say through its secretary, the General Council will always be ready to reply. But the Romance Federal Committee has no right either to abdicate its functions in favour of the *Égalité* and *Progrès*, or to let these newspapers usurp its functions. *Generally speaking, the General Council's administrative correspondence with national and local committees cannot be published without greatly prejudicing the Association's general interests.* Consequently, if the other organs of the International were to follow the example of the *Progrès* and the *Égalité*, the General Council would be faced with the alternative of either discrediting itself publicly by its silence or violating its obligations by replying publicly." (*Fictitious Splits in the International, MECW*, vol. 23, 90—my emphasis, AW)

This is quite clear: the leadership of the International is not under any obligation to enter into public polemics with anybody. On the contrary, to do so would represent a violation of its obligations. Internal correspondence *cannot be published without greatly prejudicing the Association's general interests.* Such correspondence must be conducted through the normal channels that exist for that purpose. To suggest anything else would be tantamount to proposing the dissolution of the International, eradicating the difference between members and non-members, and abolishing any element of internal democracy, congress decisions, elections, etc. In other words, it would represent the triumph of anarchy over democratic centralism—which is precisely what Bakunin wanted.

The Sonvillier circular complained bitterly that:

"...the [London] Conference aimed a blow at freedom of thought and its expression... in conferring upon the General Council the right to denounce and disavow any publicity organ of the sections or federations that discussed either the principles on which the Association rests, or the respective interests of the sections and federations, or finally the general interests of the Association as a whole (see *L'Égalité* of 21st October)."

What had *L'Égalité* of 21st October published? It had published a resolution in which the Conference "gives warning that henceforth the General Council will be bound to publicly denounce and disavow all newspapers calling themselves organs of the International which, following the precedents of *Progrès* and *Solidarité*, discuss in their columns, before the middle-class public, questions exclusively reserved for the local or federal committees and the General Council, or for the private and administrative sittings of the Federal or General Congresses."

To which Marx replied:

"To appreciate properly the spiteful lamentations of B. Malon, we must bear in mind that this resolution puts an end, once and for all, to the attempts of some journalists who wished to substitute themselves for the main committees of the International and to play therein the role that the journalists' bohemia is playing to the bourgeois world. As a result of one such attempt, the Geneva Federal Committee had seen some members of the Alliance edit *L'Égalité*, the official organ of the Romanish Federation, in a manner completely hostile to the latter." (*Fictitious Splits in the International, MECW*, vol. 23, 104)

Marx and Engels did not regard the party press as an open forum where anyone could air their views in public. On 9th August, 1871, *Der Volksstaat* published a statement by Amand Goegg addressed to the editors of the *Schwäbischer Merkur*, in which he declared himself an advocate of anarchist individualism. On 12th August *Der Volksstaat* published a letter by Bernhard Becker referring to the time of his expulsion from the General Association of German Workers in 1865.

When Engels found out, he was furious and wrote to the German social-democratic leader Wilhelm Liebknecht: "Why bother to rehabilitate that good-for-nothing B. Becker? And allow that jackass Goegg to parade his own idiocies before the public?" (*MECW*, vol. 44, 199). Even the publication of a letter by an undesirable element was considered to be unacceptable. This shows how far Marx and Engels were from the idea of the party press as a free-for-all.

Another issue was the public distribution of private and internal correspondence for factional purposes. On this we can cite Marx's numerous comments on the subject. Marx wrote a letter to Nikolai Danielson, 12th December, 1872, in which he says:

Dear Friend,

From the enclosed you can see the results of the Hague Congress. I read out the letter to Lyubavin to the Commission *d'enquête* on the Alliance in the strictest confidence and without divulging the name of the addressee. Nevertheless, the secret was not kept, firstly because the Commission included Splingard, the Belgian lawyer, among its numbers, and he was in reality no more than an agent of the Alliancists; secondly, because *Zhuhovsky, Guillaume* et Co. had already earlier—as a preventive measure—recounted the story all over the place in their own way and with apologist interpretations. This was how it came about that, in its report to the Congress, the Commission was compelled to pass on the facts relative to Bakunin that were contained in the letter to Lyubavin (of course, I had not revealed his name, but Bakunin's friends had already been informed on that score by Geneva). The question that presents itself now is whether the Commission appointed by the Congress to publish the minutes (of which I am a member) *may make public use* of that letter or not? That is for Lyubavin to decide. However, I may note that—ever since the Congress—the facts have been doing the rounds of the European press, and this was none of our doing. *I found the whole business all the more distasteful since I had reckoned on the strictest discretion and solemnly demanded it.*" (MECW, vol. 44, 455–56, *Marx to Nikolai Danielson*—last sentence my emphasis, AW)

We see here that Marx considered the public use of private and internal party correspondence as something absolutely unacceptable, in fact, distasteful. It amounts to a breach of trust between comrades and an unscrupulous misuse of information. It goes without saying that one does not necessarily speak in the same terms about a subject in a private conversation as one would in a public meeting. If I believe that any chance remark I make in a private communication (either spoken or written) will the next day be broadcast to the four winds, I will be very careful about what I say, and a frank and honest interchange of ideas will be impossible.

This is particularly true in the course of a factional dispute, where tempers can flare up and even the most reasonable comrades may make comments that they may later regret. If one wishes to solve a dispute in the best (i.e. political) way, it is necessary to shrug one's shoulders at such things, which constitute the small change of politics, trivial details that represent nothing serious. But if one wishes, not to solve a dispute, but to inflame it, to poison the atmosphere, increase tension, create personal clashes and carry matters to the point of a split, then the correct tactic is to spread all kinds of gossip, reveal in public what has been said (or written) to you in private, and violate every norm of comradely behaviour.

When Engels discovered that the Italian Bakuninists had got hold of a letter he had written to a comrade in Italy, and were using it for factional purposes, he was indignant. This is what he wrote:

> "Having rebelled against the whole organisation of the International, and knowing that it will have great difficulty in justifying itself at the Congress next September, the Jura Committee is now looking for letters and mandates from the General Council in order to fabricate false accusations against us. I, like all of us, willingly consent to all letters being read to the Congress, but we do not find it agreeable to learn that the same letters, written for this or that section, have been put at the disposal of these gentlemen." (*Engels to Cesare Bert*, 7th June 1872, *MECW*, vol. 44, 392)

Problems in England

The triumphant reaction in Europe rained blows down on the International. The correspondence of Marx and Engels reflect the increasingly desperate position:

> "In Spain many people have been imprisoned and others are in hiding. In Belgium the government is trying with all its might to give free rein to the law and even more against us. In Germany the followers of Bismarck are even starting to play this game too." (*Engels to Carlo Cafiero*, 16th July 1871, *MECW*, vol. 44, 171)

There were internal problems everywhere, including in England. The war between France and Germany had benefited the English capitalists, who were able to give a part of their enormous profits to a section of the working class. As a sign of the confidence of the English bourgeoisie, several of the old anti-union laws were abolished. The idea of class collaboration began to take firm root among trade union leaders, including some who were members of the General Council.

As the International was becoming more radical, many of the union leaders were becoming increasingly moderate. To tell the truth, the alliance of these reformist union leaders with the revolutionary socialists was never very firm or wholehearted. Now it was put under extreme pressure by the Paris Commune. Some of the trade union leaders were alarmed by the Commune and the ferocious reaction that followed the defeat frightened them even more.

The intensity of the attacks on the International in the bourgeois press made them uneasy. It threatened their good relations with the bourgeois liberals, and they were anxious to put some distance between the General Council and themselves. Marx's address, *The Civil War in France*, was the last straw. Although it had been written by Marx at the request of the General

Council, two English Council members, Lucraft and Odger, disassociated themselves from it and resigned in protest. Engels wrote to Carlo Cafiero on 28th July, 1871:

> "If Mazzini calls our friend Marx a *"man of corrosive…intellect, of domineering temper,"* etc., etc., I can only say that Marx's corrosive *domination* and his jealous nature have kept our Association together for seven years, and that he has done more than anyone else to bring it to its present proud position. As for the break-up of the Association, which is said to have begun already here in England, the fact is that *two* English members of the Council, who had been getting on too close terms with the bourgeoisie, found our address on the civil war too strong and they withdrew. In their place we have four new English members and one Irishman, and we reckon ourselves to be much stronger here in England than we were before the two renegades left." (*MECW*, vol. 44, 186)

The fact is that the trade union leaders were already beginning to seek a rapprochement with the Liberals, in order to win seats in Parliament. Even in 1868 Marx had complained of these "intriguers," naming Odger, who stood for Parliament on several occasions, as one of them. After they split, Marx accused them of having sold themselves to the Liberal Ministry.

This caused a split in the English section of the International. However, not all the English trade union leaders broke away. Applegarth signed the Address of the General Council on *The Civil War in France* and remained a member of the Council to the end. But now there were serious problems with John Hale. He was pushing strongly for the establishment of a special Federal Council to be formed for England. Marx opposed the proposal, fearing, rightly, that it would become a tool in the hands of radical bourgeois members of Parliament.

Conflicts in the American section

Marx placed great hopes in the prospects for the International in the USA, where a young and fresh proletariat was developing rapidly with the growth of industry. But even in the New World there were problems. They were the exact opposite of the problems the IWA faced in Europe, where after the Paris Commune the bourgeois and middle class were ferociously hostile to the International. In America on the contrary, socialism was becoming quite fashionable among the cultured middle classes.

Here the International was seen, not as a threat, but rather as an interesting novelty. It attracted the attention of all sorts of middle class "progressives": liberals, pacifists, feminists, temperance societies and even religious preachers. In New York, Section 12 of the IWA was taken over by a wealthy bourgeois feminist by the name of Victoria Woodhull, who Marx described as "a banker's woman, free-lover, and general humbug [hypocrite]," and Tennessee Claflin, her sister.

Section 9 was founded by her sister and was of the same kind. Woodhull was the first woman, along with her sister, to operate a brokerage firm in Wall Street, and then open a weekly newspaper called modestly *Woodhull and Claflin's Weekly*, advocating among a hodgepodge of demands including sex education, free love, women's suffrage, short skirts, spiritualism, vegetarianism, and licensed prostitution. But its main purpose for the sisters was advertising themselves and their bourgeois-liberal ideas.

Marx referred to Section No. 12 as a group "founded by Woodhull, and almost exclusively consisting of middle-class humbugs and worn-out Yankee swindlers in the reform business." On 30th August, 1871, the journal published "An Appeal of Section No. 12" (to the English-speaking citizens of the United States) signed by W. West, secretary of Section 12. The following excerpts are from this appeal:

> "The object of the International is simply to emancipate the labourer, male and female, by the conquest of political power. (…) It involves, first, the Political Equality and Social Freedom of men and women alike.

> "Political Equality means the personal participation of each in the preparation, administration, and execution of the laws by which all are governed. (…) Social Freedom means absolute immunity from impertinent intrusion in all affairs of exclusively personal concernment, such as religious belief, the sexual relation, habits of dress, etc.

> "The proposition involves, secondly, the establishment of a Universal Government… Of course, the abolition of… even differences of language are embraced in the programme."

These extracts are sufficient to give an accurate idea of the class content and ideas of these people.

Immigrant workers

The most militant, class-conscious and revolutionary sections of the young American proletariat were refugees from Europe: Germans, Poles, Russians, Irish, Jews, etc. Many did not speak English. By contrast, Section 12 was dominated by middle-class English-speaking Americans with political ambitions. Section No. 12 invited the formation of "English-speaking sections" in the United States on the basis of this programme. In practice, this was an attempt by bourgeois careerists to use the name of the International for place hunting and electoral purposes:

"If practicable, for the convenience of political action, there should be a section formed in every primary election district.

"There must ultimately be instituted in every town a municipal committee or council corresponding with the common councils; in every state, a state committee or council corresponding with the state legislature; and in the nation, a national committee or council corresponding with the United States National Congress.

"The work of the International includes nothing less than the institution, within existing forms, of another form of government, which shall supersede them all."

This Appeal led to the formation of "all sorts of middle-class humbug sections, free-lovers, spiritists, spiritist Shakers, etc." It caused a split in the American section, when Section 1 (composed mainly of German-speakers) of the old Council demanded 1) that Section 12 be expelled, and 2) that no section be admitted to membership unless it consisted of at least two-thirds workers.

Marx considered it imperative that the IWA should purge its ranks of these elements. He wrote to Bolte: "Obviously the General Council does not support in America what it combats in Europe. Resolutions I (2) and (3) and IX [I, II, III, and IX—ed.] now give the New York committee legal weapons with which to put an end to all sectarian formations and amateur groups and if necessary to expel them." This was what was done. Five dissidents formed a separate Council on 19th November, 1871, which consisted of English-speaking Americans as well as Frenchmen, and Germans.

On 19th November, 1871 Woodhull's journal protested against Section 1 and declared, among other things:

"The simple truth is that Political Equality and Social Freedom for all alike, of all races, both sexes, and every condition, are necessary precursors of the more radical reforms demanded by the International." (our emphasis)

And:

"The extension of equal citizenship to women, the world over, must precede any general change in the subsisting relations of capital and labour."

Moreover:

"Section 12 would also remonstrate against the vain assumption, running all through the Protest (of Section 1) under review, that the International Working Men's Association is an organisation of the working classes...." (Marx, Notes on the American split, *The General Council of the First International 1871-1872, Minutes*, 324)

In these few lines the bourgeois-liberal character of this trend stands out clearly. Here we have very similar ideas to that of the "trendy lefts" today: feminists, pacifists, ecologists and all the other petty-bourgeois movements that have infiltrated the labour movement in a period when the class struggle was at a low ebb. These elements tend to be highly eloquent and assertive in pushing their particular views. They elbow the workers to one side and seize positions, which they use for their own advantage.

For these people, the struggle for socialism is always subordinate to their particular hobby, in this case, feminism. Although they were very far removed from anarchism, like Bakunin, they were very keen to assert their "autonomy" against the General Council, and their absolute right to "do their own thing." This is very characteristic of middle class tendencies at all times—the assertion of "my" rights as an absolute and inviolable principle as against the rights of the majority. In the pages of Woodhull's journal, 21st October, 1871, Section 12 asserted:

> "The independent right of each section to have, hold, and give expression to its own constructions of said proceedings of the several Congresses, and the Rules and Regulations [!] of said General Council, each section being alone responsible for its own action."

This is how these people understood the role of the proletariat. In Woodhull's journal, 25th November, 1871, we read the following:

> "It is not true that the "common understanding or agreement" of the workingmen of all countries, of itself, standing alone, constitutes the Association... The statement that the emancipation of the working classes can only be conquered by themselves cannot be denied, yet it is true so far as it described the fact that the working classes cannot be emancipated against their will [!]."

This is the authentic voice of the bourgeois socialist, loud and clear!

On 3rd December, 1871, the new Federal Council for North America was formally founded. The very next day it denounced the bourgeois swindlers in a circular to all sections of the International in the United States. It states, among other things:

> "In the Committee [of the old Central Committee] which was to be a defence against all reform swindles, the majority finally consisted of practically forgotten reformers and panacea-mongers....

> "Thus it came about that the people who preached the evangels of free love sat fraternally beside those who wanted to bring to the whole world the blessing of a single common language—land co-operativists, spiritualists, atheists, and deists—each striving to ride his own hobbyhorse. Particularly Section 12,

Woodhull... The first step that has to be taken here to further the movement is to organise and at the same time arouse the revolutionary element to be found in the opposing interests of capitalists and workers...

"The delegates of Sections 1, 4, 5, 7, 8, 11, 16, 21, 23, 24, 25, and others, having seen that all efforts to control this mischief were in vain, decided, after the adjournment of the old Central Council *sine die* (3rd December, 1871), to establish a new one, which would consist of real workers and which would exclude all those who would only confuse the question." (*New Yorker Democrat*, 9th December, 1871)

The break with Section 12

The two rival Councils appealed to the General Council for recognition. This obviously caused some confusion. Various sections, for example, the French Section No. 10 (New York), and several Irish sections, withdrew their delegates from both councils until the General Council made its decision.

The Woodhull journal (West, etc.) lied unashamedly when it asserted that it was sure of the support of the General Council. An article of 2nd December carried the headline: *Section 12 Sustained. The Decision of the General Council.* This was a direct fabrication. On the contrary, the decision of the General Council, 5th November, 1871, sustained the Central Committee against the claims of Section 12, which tried to replace it.

The fate of the International in the United States depended on carrying out a complete break with Woodhull and Co. As soon as the resolutions reached New York, they began to follow their old tactics. First they had discussed the original split in the most notorious New York bourgeois papers. Now they did the same against the General Council (presenting the matter as a conflict between Frenchmen and Germans, between socialism and communism), to the joy of all the enemies of the International.

The middle class elements particularly resented the proposal of the General Council that two-thirds of the members of any section should be made up of workers. Very characteristic were the marginal comments in Woodhull's journal on 15th December, 1871:

"No new test of membership, as that two-thirds or any part of a section shall be wage slaves, as if it were a crime to be free, was required."

The journal dated 4th May, 1872, commented on the resolution of the General Council:

"... In this decree of the General Council its authors presume to recommend that in future no American section be admitted of which two-thirds at least are not wage slaves. Must they be politically slaves also? As well one thing as the other..."

To these complaints of the petty-bourgeois elements, Marx replied: "The intrusion into the International Working Men's Association of bogus reformers, middle-class quacks, and trading politicians is mostly to be feared from that class of citizens who have nothing better to depend upon than the proceeds of wage slavery."

Presidential ambitions

Ignoring the clear repudiation by the General Council, Woodhull and her supporters continued to organise a ceremony of confusion, arguing, without the slightest justification, that the International had accepted her feminist views. In an article signed W. West, in Woodhull's, etc., journal, 2nd March, 1872, one reads:

> "The issue of the "Appeal" of Section 12 to the English-speaking citizens of the United States in August last was a new departure in the history of the International, and has resulted in the recognition by the General Council of Political Equality and Social Freedom of both sexes alike, and of the essential political character of the work before us."

Meanwhile, as the Presidential elections approached, the cloven hoof showed itself—namely, that the International should serve in the election of— Madame Woodhull! She decided to run as the first woman for the United States Presidency in 1872, but it turned out to be a farce. In order to get support for her campaign, she flirted with the bourgeois Liberals. On 2nd March, 1872, under the title, "The Coming Combination Convention," we read the statement:

> "There is a proposition under consideration by the representatives of the various reformatory elements of the country looking to a grand consolidated convention to be held in this city in May next, during Anniversary week... Indeed, if this convention in May acts wisely, who can say that the fragments of the defunct Democratic party will come out from them and take part in the proposed convention... Every body of radical [mind] everywhere in the United States should, as soon as the call is made public, take immediate steps to be represented in it."

The Appeal was headed by the signature: Victoria C. Woodhull, followed by Theodore H. Banks (one of the founders of the Counter Council) and R. W. Hume. In this Appeal: the convention will consider "nominations for President and Vice-President of the United States." Specially invited were:

> "Labour, land, peace, and temperance reformers, and Internationals and Women Suffrages—including all the various suffrage associations—as well as all others

who believe the time has come when the principles of eternal justice and human equality should be carried into our halls of legislation."

The whole affair was the laughing stock of New York and United States. Section 2 of the IWA stated:

"Recognising the principle of women's right to vote, in view of the insinuations of Citizeness Woodhull, at the meeting in Apollo Hall, leading the public to believe that the International supports her candidacy.

Declares:

That for the present the International cannot and should not be taken in tow by any American political party; for none of them represents the workers' aspirations; none of them has for its objective the economic emancipation of the workers.

Section 2 had thought:

That our sole objective ought to be, for the present, the organisation and the solidarity of the working class in America."

Under the title "Internationals, watch out!", the same issue of *Socialiste* states, among other things:

"The International is not, and cannot be, persecuted in America; the politicians, far from aiming at its destruction, think only of using it as a lever and supporting point for the triumph of their personal views. Should the International let itself be dragged into this path, it would cease to be the Association of Workers and become a ring of politicians.

"For a long time now, there have been cries of alarm; but the convention in Apollo Hall, nominating, in the name of the International, Madame Woodhull as candidate for the Presidency, should henceforth open the eyes of the less perceptive. Internationals of America, watch out!"

Ms. Woodhull tried to use her money to buy herself an International. But it proved to be too expensive. The bourgeois policies advocated by Section 12 were sufficient grounds for the expulsion of the Woodhull group and its supporters from the First International. The Hague Congress ratified the expulsion of these middle class interlopers and recognised the new, proletarian Council.

The London Conference

The congress in Basel in 1869 had decided that the next congress should take place in Paris, and was now (1871) due, but under conditions of ferocious state repression, the General Council decided to hold a closed conference in London, similar to the one which had taken place in 1865. Under the general conditions of reaction, the Conference had to have a secret character. Marx wrote to the Russian Utin on 27th July, 1871:

> "Last Tuesday the General Council resolved that there would not be a *Congress* this year (in view of extraordinary circumstances) but that, as in 1865, there should be a private *conference* in London to which different sections would be invited to send their delegates. The convocation of this Conference *must not be published in the press*. Its meetings will not be public ones. The Conference will be required to concern itself, not with theoretical questions, but exclusively with questions of *organisation*." (*Marx to Nikolai Utin, MECW*, vol. 44, 178.)

The London conference took place from 17th to 23rd September with only 23 delegates present, including six from Belgium, two from Switzerland and one from Spain. Thirteen members of the General Council were also present, but six of them had only a consultative vote.

It approved a resolution that the emancipation of the working class could be achieved only by constituting itself into a special political party against the bourgeois parties. The conference also declared that the German workers had fulfilled their proletarian duty during the Franco-Prussian War. And it rejected all responsibility for the so-called Nechayev affair. The resolution adopted on the question of the political struggle represented a total defeat for the Bakuninists, as we see from the concluding paragraphs:

> "In presence of an unbridled reaction which violently crushes every effort at emancipation on the part of the working men, and pretends to maintain by brute force the distinction of classes and the political domination of the propertied classes resulting from it;...

> "That this constitution of the working class into a political party is indispensable in order to insure the triumph of the Social Revolution and its ultimate end—the abolition of classes;

> "That the combination of forces which the working class has already effected by its economical struggles ought at the same time to serve as a lever for its struggles against the political powers of landlords and capitalists—

> The Conference recalls to the members of the International:

> "That in the militant state of the working class, its economical movement and its political action are indissolubly united." (*The General Council of the First International 1870–1871*—Minutes, 444–45.)

The General Council was convinced that, despite Bakunin's protestations, his secret society continued to exist. The conference adopted a resolution prohibiting any organisation with an independent programme to function within the body of the International.

The conference declared that the question of the Alliance was settled, now that the Geneva section had voluntarily dissolved itself. With regard to the Jura sections, the conference ratified the decision of the General Council, recognising the Federal Council in Geneva as the only representative body for the Latin Swiss members. It advised the workers of the Jura sections to affiliate once again to the Federal Council in Geneva. Alternatively, they should call themselves the Jura Federation.

The conference further declared categorically that the International had nothing to do with the Nechayev affair, and that Nechayev had falsely appropriated and utilized the name of the International. This was directed at Bakunin, who was well known to have been connected with Nechayev for a long time. Finally, the Conference left it to the discretion of the General Council to decide the time and place of the next congress or conference.

Marx regarded the results of the Conference as positive. He wrote to Jenny Marx on 23rd September, 1871, with a tone of palpable relief: "The conference is at last coming to an end today. It was hard work. Morning and evening sessions, commission sessions in between, hearing of witnesses, reports to be drawn up and so forth. But more was done than at all the previous Congresses put together, because there was no audience in front of which to stage rhetorical comedies." (*Marx to Jenny Marx*, MECW, vol. 44, 220)

Attacks on the General Council

The London Conference brought the conflict with the Bakuninists to a head. For years the General Council had to fight against this conspiracy. Unable to prove what was going on behind the backs of the members of the International, Marx and Engels had to put up with the campaign of insults and attacks for almost a year. At last, by means of Conference resolutions I, II, III, IX, XVI, and XVII, it delivered its long prepared blow.

The Bakuninists now declared open war against the General Council. They accused it of rigging the conference and of forcing upon the International the dogma of the necessity of organising the proletariat into a special party for the purpose of winning political power. The Bakuninists accused Marx and his followers as opportunists who were hindering the social revolution. They demanded another Congress where this question would be definitely settled.

In a barrage of circulars and letters, the Bakuninists publicly abused Marx in the most foul and disgusting language. In this furious campaign to discredit

Marx and the General Council, they did not hesitate to accuse Marx of being an agent of Bismarck. They were even prepared to make use of anti-Semitism.

Bakunin felt threatened by Resolution XIV, and made strenuous efforts to get a protest started against the Conference decision. For this purpose he made use of some demoralised elements among the French political refugees in Geneva and London. Playing unscrupulously on the anti-German sentiments of the French, Bakunin compared Marx to Bismarck. He put out the slogan that the Geneva Council was dominated by *Pan-Germanism*.

Bakunin used national prejudice without scruples. He argued that all Germans held authoritarian views, and repeatedly compared Marx to Bismarck. He also repeatedly accused Marx of advocating a universal dictatorship, and a socialism "decreed from the top down." This accusation had not the slightest basis in fact. All his life Marx insisted that "the emancipation of the working classes can only be the work of the working classes themselves." But as the hack journalists say: why let the facts spoil a good story? Lies and slanders are the stock-in-trade of all intriguers. And if a lie is repeated with sufficient insistence, some people are sure to believe it.

In slandering Marx, Bakunin did not even stop at racist and anti-Semitic smears, which he raised on more than one occasion. For example, he wrote in 1872:

> "Proudhon understood and felt liberty much better than Marx; Proudhon, when he was not dealing with doctrine and metaphysics, had the true instinct of the revolutionary—he worshipped Satan and proclaimed anarchy. It is possible that Marx might theoretically reach an even more rational system of liberty than that of Proudhon—but he lacks Proudhon's instinct. As a German and a Jew he is authoritarian from head to foot. Hence come the two systems: the anarchist system of Proudhon broadened and developed by us and freed from all its metaphysical, idealist and doctrinaire baggage, accepting matter and social economy as the basis of all development in science and history. And the system of Marx, head of the German school of authoritarian communism." (James Joll, *The Anarchists*, 90)

Marx refers to all this as "the intrigues of this bunch of scoundrels," a description that, as we see, was fully justified.

Bakunin had a base in Italy and the French region of Switzerland. His main base was among the skilled watchmakers of the Jura region of Switzerland who were beginning to suffer from the competition of the developing industries.

The London Conference had given the General Council authority to disown all alleged organs of the International which, like the *Progrès* and the *Solidarité* in the Jura, discussed internal questions of the International in public. The Bakuninists changed the name of *Solidarité* to *La Révolution*

Sociale, which immediately began a ferocious attack on the General Council of the International, which it described as the "German Committee led by a brain à la Bismarck."

This was a scandalous attempt to play on the anti-German prejudices of the French. Marx wrote to an American friend: "It refers to the unpardonable fact that I was born a German and that I do in fact exercise a decisive intellectual influence on the General Council. *Nota bene:* the German element in the General Council is numerically two-thirds weaker than the English and the French. The crime is, therefore, that the English and French elements are dominated (!) in matters of theory by the German element and find this dominance, i.e., German science, useful and even indispensable." (Marx, *Letter to Bolte*)

The Bakuninists then tried the trick of changing their name. On 20th October the new Section for Revolutionary Socialist Propaganda and Action appeared in Geneva and approached the General Council with a request for affiliation. After the General Council had consulted the Federal Council in Geneva, the request was rejected. In the end the Bakuninists set themselves up as the Jura Federation. Marx wrote to the Belgian César de Paepe on 24th November, 1871:

> "On the other hand, there will be the Jura Federation in Switzerland (in other words the men of the Alliance who hide behind this name), Naples, possibly Spain, part of Belgium and certain groups of French refugees (who, by the by, to judge by the correspondence we have had from France, would not appear to exert any serious influence there), and these will form the opposing camp. Such a split, in itself no great danger, would be highly inopportune at a time when we must march shoulder to shoulder against the common foe. Our adversaries harbor no illusions whatever about their weakness, but they count on acquiring much moral support from the accession of the Belgian Federal Council." (*MECW*, vol. 44, 264)

The Jura sections organised a congress on 12th November in Sonvillier, although only 9 out of 22 sections were represented, by only 16 delegates. However, to make up for their small numbers, they made more noise than ever. They expressed resentment at the fact that the London Conference had forced a name on them, but for tactical reasons they decided to call themselves in the future the Jura Federation.

In Switzerland many members of the International supported the London Conference. On 21st–22nd December, Marx's daughter Jenny wrote to Kugelmann as follows:

> "In Geneva, that hotbed of *intrigants*, a congress representing thirty sections of the International has declared itself for the General Council, has passed

a resolution to the effect that the separatist factions cannot henceforth be considered to form parts of the International, their acts having clearly shown that their object is to disorganise the Association; that these sections, who, under another name, are only a fraction of the old Alliance faction, by continuing to sow dissentions, are opposed to the interests of the Federation. This resolution was voted unanimously in an assembly of 500 members. The Bakuninists who had come all the way from Neuchatel to be present would have been seriously ill-used, had it not been for the men whom they style "des Bismarckians" Outine, Perret, etc., who rescued them and begged the assembly to allow them to speak. (Outine of course was well aware that the best means of killing them altogether was to allow them to make their speeches.)" (*Documents of the First International,* 530, notes)

However, in revenge, the Sonvillier congress sent out a circular to all the Federations of the International attacking the validity of the London Conference and appealing against its decisions to a general congress to be called as quickly as possible. They began to spread the rumor that the International was in a mortal crisis and on a downward path. In their view, the IWA had been formed as "a tremendous protest against any kind of authority," and that every section had been guaranteed complete independence. They argued that the General Council was only an executive organ, but now the members had come to place a blind confidence in it. As a result, the Basel Congress had given the General Council authority to accept, reject or dissolve sections, pending the approval of the next congress.

What the author of the circular (Guillaume) did not mention was that this decision had been adopted after Bakunin had spoken enthusiastically in its favour, and that Guillaume had been in complete agreement with it. The reason was quite simple: the Bakuninists, who were strongly represented at Basel, believed that the General Council was going to be moved to Geneva, and they could control it. It is usually the case that the "anti-authoritarian" tendency is only against authority when they are in a minority. When they are in the majority, they are invariably despots and bullies.

"Anti-authoritarianism"

The Congress of Sixteen proceeded to "reorganise" the International by attacking the Conference and the General Council in a "Circular to All Federations of the International Working Men's Association." The Sonvillier circular used demagogic arguments to "prove" the dictatorial nature of the General Council, which had consisted of the same men and met in the same place for five years. This was cited as proof that the General Council now regarded itself as the (Bismarckian) "brains" of the International. Why were the ideas of the General Council regarded as the official theory of the

International? Why were they considered to be the only ones permissible? Why did the General Council regard the different opinions of other groups and individuals as heresy?

A stifling orthodoxy had developed in the International and in the members of the General Council, they argued, which prevented creative thinking and oppressed the free spirits of everybody else. The omnipotence of the General Council necessarily had a corrupting effect. It was impossible that a man like Marx who held such power could retain a moral character. This was a recipe for tyranny, and so on and so forth.

The decisions taken at Basel were bad enough, they said. But now the London Conference had taken further steps to transform the International from a free association of independent sections into an authoritarian and hierarchical organisation in the hands of the General Council. It had decided that the General Council should have power to determine the time and place of the next congress, or of a conference to replace it. Thus the General Council had the power to replace the congresses with secret conferences.

They demanded that the powers of the General Council be reduced to those of a simple bureau for correspondence and the collection of statistics, and dictatorship and centalisation be replaced by a free association of independent groups "without any directing authority, even if set up by voluntary agreement."

The General Council was to be no more than a "simple statistical and corresponding bureau." The International must be the very image of the future communist society:

> "The future society should be nothing but a universalization of the organisation which the International will establish for itself. We must therefore try to bring this organisation as close as possible to our ideal [...] The International, embryo of the future human society, must henceforth be the faithful image of our principles of liberty and federation, and must reject any principle leading to authoritarianism, to dictatorship."

This whole line of argument (which is still repeated today, even by people who think they are Marxists) is false from start to finish. The revolutionary party is a necessary tool for overthrowing capitalism. Must a tool resemble what it produces? In order to make a chair, a saw is required. But a saw that resembled a chair would never produce a chair or anything else.

This is not only nonsense but dangerous nonsense, and particularly so at the time we are considering, when, following the defeat of the Commune, the International was under attack from the bourgeois state, its members in many countries facing arrest and imprisonment or deportation.

As Marx remarked: "The Paris Communards would not have failed if they had understood that the Commune was 'the embryo of the future human society' and had cast away all discipline and all arms—that is, the things which must disappear when there are no more wars!" (*MECW*, vol. 23, 115)

The real attitude of the "anti-authoritarians" was shown by the following incident. When the IWA representative, the Russian Utin, went to Zurich, he was attacked and beaten by eight men, who would have killed him, except that four German students happened to appear and saved him. It appears that this attack was organised by Slav supporters of Bakunin, whose activities were to be investigated by Utin. This kind of conduct was not only considered acceptable by Bakunin. He actively encouraged it, as we see in the case of Nechayev.

The Jura circular did not achieve its aim. The demand for the calling of a congress met with no support. Only in Belgium was it decided to call for a change in the Statutes of the International, to turn it into an association of independent federations and make the General Council "a Centre for Correspondence and Information."

The Sonvillier circular provided welcome ammunition to the enemies of the International and was widely publicized by the bourgeois press, which, particularly since the fall of the Paris Commune, had been assiduously spreading lies about the sinister power of the General Council. These fairy stories were now confirmed from within the ranks of the International. The *Bulletin Jurassien*, which now took the place of the *Révolution Sociale,* reprinted the articles of approval of the bourgeois newspapers.

It was the noisy campaign of slander and disinformation initiated by the Sonvillier circular that caused the General Council to issue an answer to it, also in the form of a circular, entitled *Fictitious Splits in the International* (*Les prétendues Scissions dans l'Internationale*). In this circular the General Council answered all the lies and distortions of the Bakuninists.

The London conference's acknowledgement that the German workers had done their proletarian duty during the Franco-Prussian War, this was used as an excuse for the accusation of "Pan-Germanism," which was said to dominate the General Council.

These ridiculous accusations were brought forward in order to undermine the centalisation of the International, which, in practice, would have meant its complete dissolution. Particularly in the prevailing conditions of counterrevolution, state repression and the systematic infiltration of workers' organisations by police spies, centalisation was the only possibility of saving the organisation, as Marx explained:

"It [the Alliance] proclaims anarchy in the ranks of the proletariat as the infallible means of breaking the powerful concentration of political and social forces in the hands of the exploiters. Under this pretext and at a moment when the old world is seeking to destroy the International it demands that the latter should replace its organisation by anarchy."

But such considerations made no difference to the anarchists, whose unprincipled and baseless attacks on the International leadership from within served to reinforce the attacks of the bourgeois state from without. Marx systematically exposed the machinations of the intriguers, and in particular Bakunin.

The Hague Congress

This Congress was convened in September 1872. For the first time Marx was present in person, but Bakunin stayed away, probably because he knew he would be heavily defeated. The resolution of the London Conference on political action was ratified. There was one small addition which was copied verbatim from the Inaugural Address of the International. It reads:

"Since the owners of land and capital are always using their political privileges to protect and perpetuate their economic monopolies and to enslave labour, the great duty of the proletariat is to conquer the political power."

On the 5th March, 1872, the General Council had announced the calling of the annual congress for the beginning of September. In a letter to Kugelmann on 29th July, Marx wrote: "The international congress (Hague, opens on 2nd September) will be a matter of life or death for the International and before I withdraw[3] I want at least to protect it from the forces of dissolution."

Part of Marx's plan to protect the International from the destructive activities of the Bakuninists was the proposal to move the General Council from London, where it was becoming increasingly bogged down in rows and conflicts, to New York. The Bakuninists were not represented on the General Council, but they had succeeded in causing such confusion among the German, English and French members that the Council was obliged to form a special subcommittee to deal with the constant disputes.

The Hague congress met from 2nd to 7th September. There were 61 delegates, and Marx had a certain majority. With the exception of Lafargue, all five Spanish delegates were Bakuninists, as also were the eight Belgian and the four Dutch representatives. But the Italian Bakuninists sent no representatives to the congress, since their Rimini conference in August had

---

3 Marx and Engels had both decided not to stand for reelection to the General Council—ed.

broken off all relations with the General Council. The Jura Federation sent Guillaume and Schwitzguébel.

The rows began immediately, with the preliminary examination of the mandates, which lasted three days, so that the actual business of the congress began only on the fourth day with the reading of the report of the General Council, which was drawn up by Marx. The report detailed all the acts of repression against the International, the bloody suppression of the Paris Commune, the terrorism of the English government against the Irish sections. It also reported on the steady progress made by the International in Holland, Denmark, Portugal, Ireland and Scotland, and its growth in the United States, Australia, New Zealand and Buenos Aires. The report was adopted with acclaim.

It is interesting to note the attitude of Marx and Engels to the question of imperative mandates: that is, the practice of mandating delegates to vote in a particular way. This is an essentially undemocratic practice, which prevents delegates from arriving at their own conclusion as a result of participating in a debate and listening to the arguments of all sides. Engels wrote on the subject:

> "We shall only note that if all electors gave their delegates imperative mandates concerning all points on the agenda, meetings and debates of the delegates would be superfluous. It would be sufficient to send the mandates to a central counting office which would count up the votes and announce the results. This would be much cheaper." (Engels, *Imperative mandates at the Hague Congress*, 17ᵗʰ September 1872, *MECW*, vol. 23, 277)

Nowadays, when it has become fashionable in certain quarters to revive anarchist theories on organisation, using the pretext of modern technology and particularly the Internet, these lines have a great relevance. If all that is required is the click of a mouse; congresses, conferences, debates and so on, are quite unnecessary. They can be replaced by emails. How Engels would have enjoyed that idea!

There followed the discussion on the General Council. Lafargue explained that the daily struggle of the working class against capitalism could not be conducted effectively without a central leadership. Opposing this, Guillaume denied the necessity for a General Council except as a central office for correspondence and statistics and without any authority. The International was not the property of one clever man, and so on and so forth.

The discussion ended on the fifth day of the congress in a closed session. In a long speech Marx demanded that the previous powers of the General Council should not only be maintained, but increased. It should be given the right to suspend, not only individual sections, but whole federations, under certain conditions, pending the decisions of the next congress. It had neither police nor soldiers at its disposal, but it could not permit its moral power to decay. Rather than degrade it to a letter-box it would be better to abolish the General Council altogether. Marx's viewpoint was carried with 36 votes against 6, with 15 not voting.

Engels then moved that the General Council should be moved from London to New York for at least a year. The proposal caused consternation, particularly from the French delegates, who succeeded in getting a separate vote first on whether the seat of the General Council should be moved at all, and secondly whether it should be moved to New York. In the end, the motion that the seat of the General Council should be moved was carried with a small majority. Twelve members of the new General Council were then elected and given the right to co-opt seven other members.

In the same session the discussion on political action was opened. Vaillant brought in a resolution in the spirit of the decision of the London conference, declaring that the working class must constitute itself its own political party independent of, and in opposition to, all bourgeois political parties. He pointed to the lessons of the Paris Commune, which had collapsed for the lack of a political programme. Guillaume, on the other hand, wanted to have nothing to do with this. The anarchists wanted to destroy political power, not to conquer it.

The Blanquists Ranvier, Vaillant and the others left the congress in protest at the decision to remove the General Council to New York. Serge took the chair in place of Ranvier and Vaillant's proposal was then adopted with 35 against 6 votes, and 8 votes not cast. Some of the delegates had already left for home, but most of them had left written declarations in favour of the resolution.

The last hours of the last day of the congress were taken up with the report on Bakunin and the Alliance. The problem had been hanging round the neck of the International like a heavy millstone. It is one thing to engage in internal discussions about political differences, something that can be highly educational, but it is another thing to be involved in the kind of constant wrangles with intriguers whose aim is not to fight for ideas but to confuse, disorient and disrupt because they cannot convince the majority.

Such a phenomenon does not educate or raise the level, but spreads demoralisation. Marx already pointed to the destructive effects the Bakuninists were having in Switzerland, when he wrote *Fictitious Splits in the International* that "the Geneva Federal Committee […] was exhausted after its two years of struggle against the sectarian sections." (*MECW*, vol. 23, 93) It was not the only case.

A committee of five declared with four votes against one (a Belgian) that it considered that a secret Alliance had existed with statutes directly contrary to the statutes of the International, although there was not sufficient evidence to prove that the Alliance still existed.

Secondly, it was proved by a draft of the statutes and by letters of Bakunin that he had attempted to form a secret society within the International with statutes differing fundamentally from the statutes of the International. Thirdly, Bakunin had adopted fraudulent practices in order to obtain possession of the property of others, and either he or his agents had used intimidation. On these grounds the majority of the committee then demanded the expulsion of Bakunin, Guillaume and a number of their supporters from the International.

This was accepted. The Congress had ample reasons for expelling Bakunin on purely political grounds. But there is one final point to make: in addition to the above-mentioned grounds Bakunin was expelled also for a "personal reason."

This "personal reason" refers to matters related to the Nechayev affair. While in Switzerland, Nechayev had been involved in an act of blatant blackmail. In order to earn some money, Bakunin had promised to undertake the translation of *Das Kapital* for a Russian publisher, who paid him an advance of three hundred rubles. The translation was never done, but Bakunin agreed that Nechayev should arrange to release him from his contract. Nechayev then wrote a letter to Lyubavin, the publisher's agent in Switzerland, threatening him with "the vengeance of the People's Justice" (i.e., death) if he continued to bother Bakunin.

Marx alludes to this in a letter to Nikolai Danielson, dated 15th August, 1872:

"Bakunin has worked secretly since years to undermine the International and has now been pushed by us so far as to throw away the mask and *secede openly* with the foolish people led by him—the same man who was the manager in the Nechayev affair. Now this Bakunin was once charged with the Russian translation of my book [Volume I of *Capital*], received the money for it in advance, and instead of giving work, sent or had sent to Lubanin (I think) who transacted for the publisher with him the affair, a most infamous and compromising letter. It would be of the highest utility for me, *if this letter was sent me* immediately. As this is a mere *commercial* affair and as in the use to be made of the letter no names will be used, I hope you will procure me that letter. But no time is to be lost. If it is sent, it ought to be sent at once as I shall leave London for the Haag Congress at the end of this month." (*MECW*, vol. 44, 422)

The Hague Congress settled this question once and for all.

The expulsion of Bakunin

Bakunin and his chief lieutenant Guillaume were finally expelled at the Hague Congress. Engels wrote:

"These expulsions constitute an open declaration of war by the International to the "Alliance" and the whole of Mr. Bakunin's sect. Like every other shade of proletarian socialism Bakunin's sect was admitted in the International on the general condition of maintaining peace and observing the Rules and the Congress resolutions. Instead of doing so, this sect led by dogmatic members of the bourgeoisie having more ambition than ability tried to impose its own narrow-minded programme on the whole of the International, violated the Rules and the Congress resolutions and finally declared them to be authoritarian trash which no true revolutionary need be bound by.

"The almost incomprehensible patience with which the General Council put up with the intrigues and calumny of the small band of mischief-makers was rewarded only with the reproach of dictatorial behaviour. Now at last the Congress has spoken out, and clearly enough at that. Just as clear will be the language of the documents concerning the Alliance and Mr. Bakunin's doings in general which the Commission will publish in accordance with the Congress decision. Then people will see what villainies the International was to be misused for." (Engels, *On the Hague Congress of the International*, 17th September, 1872, MECW, vol. 23, 268–69)

Guillaume had already refused to appear before the committee set up to investigate the activities of the Alliance. When he was called upon by the chairman to defend himself, but declared that he would make no attempt to defend himself as he was unwilling to take part in a "farce." The attack, he declared, was not directed against individuals, but against the federalist (i.e., anarchist) tendency as a whole. The supporters of this tendency had already drawn up a statement, which was then read to the congress. It was signed by five Belgian, four Spanish and two Jura delegates and also by an American and a Dutch delegate.

Engels later described the scene at the Congress:

"The debate on this question was heated. The members of the "Alliance" did all they could to draw out the matter, for at midnight the lease of the hall expired and the Congress had to be closed. The behaviour of the members of the Alliance could not but dispel all doubt as to the existence and the ultimate aim of their conspiracy. Finally the majority succeeded in having the two main accused who were present—Guillaume and Schwitzguébel—take the floor; immediately after their defence the voting took place. Bakunin and Guillaume were expelled from the International, Schwitzguébel escaped this fate, owing to his personal

popularity, by a small majority; then it was decided to amnesty the others."
(Ibid., 268)

Engels, who spoke in the debate, said:

> "The good faith of the General Council and of the whole International,
> to whom the correspondence had been submitted, was betrayed in a most
> disgraceful manner. Having once committed such a deception, these men were
> no longer held back by any scruples from their machinations to subordinate the
> international, or, if this were unsuccessful, to disorganise it." (Engels, *Report on
> the Alliance of Socialist Democracy presented in the name of the General Council to
> the Congress at the Hague*, late August 1872, *MECW*, vol. 23, 231)

Seeing that they were in a minority, as usual the Bakuninists resorted to a
maneuver. Allegedly in order to avoid a split in the International, they declared
that they were willing to maintain "administrative relations" with the General
Council, but rejected any interference on its part in the internal affairs of
the Federations. The signatories of the Bakuninist resolution appealed to all
federations and to all sections to prepare themselves for the next congress
in order to carry the principle of free association (*autonomie fédérative*) to
victory.

However, the congress was not prepared to be sidetracked by such tricks
and sophistry. It voted to expel Bakunin immediately with 27 against 7 votes,
8 votes not being cast. Then Guillaume was expelled with 25 against 9 votes,
and 9 votes not being cast. The other expulsion proposals of the committee
were rejected, but it was instructed to publish its material on the Alliance.

After the expulsion of Bakunin and Guillaume, the Alliance, which
had control of the Association in Spain and Italy, unleashed a campaign
of vilification against Marx and the General Council everywhere. It joined
forces with all the disreputable elements and attempting to force a split into
two camps. Marx was undismayed. He wrote *to Nikolai Danielson*:

> "However, its ultimate defeat is assured. Indeed, the Alliance is only helping us
> to *purge* the Association of the unsavory or feeble-minded elements who have
> pushed their way in here and there." (*Marx to Nikolai Danielson*, 12th December,
> 1872, *MECW*, Volume 44, 455)

After the Hague Congress

Crises and splits put people to the test. The result can have a demoralising
effect on the weaker elements and people who are not theoretically prepared.
This was no exception. Writing on 8th May, 1873, to Sorge, Engels declared:

"Although the Germans have their own squabbles with the Lassalleans, they were very disappointed with the Hague congress where they expected to find perfect harmony and fraternity in contrast to their own wrangling, and they have become very disinterested."

The split also had a demoralising effect on the French émigrés, who were already disoriented by the defeat of the Commune. Writing again to Sorge on 12th September, 1874, Engels declared:

"The French emigrants are completely at sixes and sevens. They have quarrelled amongst themselves and with everyone else for purely personal reasons, mostly in connection with money, and we shall soon be completely rid of them ... The irregular life during the war, the Commune and in exile has demoralised them frightfully, and only hard times can save a demoralised Frenchman." (*Engels to Friechrich Adolph Sorge in Hoboken, MECW*, vol. 45, 40)

In Italy, the Bakuninists were strong and the Marxists were a small minority. Engels wrote:

"I hope that the outcome of the Hague Congress will make our Italian "autonomous" friends think. They ought to know that wherever there is an organisation, some autonomy is sacrificed for the sake of unity of action. If they do not realise that the International is a society organised for struggle, and not for fine theories, I am very sorry, but one thing is certain: the great International will leave Italy to act on its own until it agrees to accept the conditions common to all." (Engels, *Letters from London—More about the Hague Congress*, 5th October, 1872, *MECW*, vol. 23, 283.)

The wavering elements naturally raised the banner of *unity at all costs*. But the loud demands for unity were answered in advance by the Bakuninists, who in their Rimini Conference, held at the beginning of August 1872, publicly announced that they had split from the International and formed a separate organisation. By so doing they had placed themselves outside the ranks of the IWA, as Engels pointed out:

"The *Bakuninists* have now finally placed themselves outside the International. A conference (ostensibly of the International, in reality of the Italian Bakuninists) has been held in *Rimini*. Of the 21 sections represented, only *one*, that from Naples, really belonged to the International. The other 20, in order not to endanger their "autonomy," had deliberately *neglected to take all the measures* on which the Administrative Regulations of the International make admission conditional; they had neither written to the General Council requesting admission, nor sent their subscriptions. And these 21 "International" sections decided unanimously in Rimini on 6th August:

'The Conference solemnly declares to all workers of the world that the Italian Federation of the International Working Men's Association severs all solidarity with the General Council in London, proclaiming instead, all the louder, its economic solidarity with all workers, and urges all sections that do not share the authoritarian principles of the General Council *to send* their representatives on 2nd September, 1872, *not to The Hague, but to Neuchâtel in Switzerland* in order to open the general anti-authoritarian Congress there on the same day.'" (Engels, *On the Rimini Conference*, 24th August, 1872, *MECW*, vol. 23, 216)

Engels always spoke with the greatest contempt of the unity-mongers, who went around shouting at the top of their voice that the split was a disaster, that unity must be restored at any price, and all the rest of it. In a letter to Bebel written on 20th June, 1873, he wrote:

"One must not allow oneself to be misled by the cry for "unity." Those who have this word most often on their lips are those who sow the most dissension, just as at present the Jura Bakuninists in Switzerland, who have provoked all the splits, scream for nothing so much as for unity. Those unity fanatics are either the people of limited intelligence who want to stir everything up together into one nondescript brew, which, the moment it is left to settle, throws up the differences again in much more acute opposition because they are now all together in one pot (you have a fine example of this in Germany with the people who preach the reconciliation of the workers and the petty-bourgeoisie) or else they are people who consciously or unconsciously (like Mühlberger, for instance) want to adulterate the movement. For this reason the greatest sectarians and the biggest brawlers and rogues are at certain moments the loudest shouters for unity. Nobody in our lifetime has given us more trouble and been more treacherous than the unity shouters." (*Engels to August Bebel, MECW*, vol. 44, 512)

The Blanquists split

The subsequent proposal that the permanent residence of the General Council be transferred to New York was dictated in part by purely practical considerations. Given the prevailing wave of counterrevolution, the International lost its base not only in France and Germany, but also in England. But the proposal was bound to meet with vigorous resistance from the German, French and English leaders, and the resistance to it after the Hague Congress was ferocious and embittered.

The immediate effect was that the Blanquists walked out of the International. They were furious at the decision to move the Council to New York because they had hoped to get control of it. They split from the International as a result. The proposal of Marx and Engels to move the General Council to New York had been taken in order to prevent the Blanquists from using the Council to promote their adventurist tactics. But by splitting from the International they consigned themselves to oblivion.

On the two chief questions at issue, the question of political activity and the question of strict centalisation, the Blanquists were in agreement with Marx, but their political adventurism and advocacy of revolutionary coups made them an even greater danger than the reformists in the prevailing conditions of European reaction. It was presumed that the transfer of the International would be a temporary move, to be reversed when conditions permitted. However, as it turned out, the Hague Congress was the last of any significance in the history of the International.

Eccarius, Jung and Hales

It frequently happens in politics, as in other aspects of life, that the most trivial personal considerations (jealousy, ambition, spite, etc.) can play a disproportionate role in shaping events. Of course, in the revolutionary movement, such factors play the role of a catalyst for far more deep-seated political differences, which are not immediately obvious, but become clearer *ex post facto*. To use the celebrated expression of Hegel, necessity expresses itself through accident.

This was the case with Eccarius and Jung, two members of the General Council who had been Marx's most loyal comrades for years. But in May, 1872, a definite breach occurred between Marx and Eccarius. The immediate cause was quite trivial. Eccarius announced that he was leaving his position as General Secretary of the International, as he was unable to live on his weekly salary of fifteen shillings.

Unfortunately, he was replaced by the Englishman John Hales and Eccarius unjustly blamed Marx for this. On the other hand, Marx was annoyed by the fact that Eccarius published information about the internal affairs of the International in the bourgeois press in return for payment, in particular information concerning the private conference of the International in London.

To give an indication of the problems Marx and Engels had to put up with from Eccarius on the General Council, the following extract from the meeting of 11th May, 1872, will suffice. When questioned about his making public the internal affairs of the General Council, Eccarius refused to show the incriminating correspondence, taking refuge behind legalistic arguments:

"Citizen Eccarius said he was in the same position as Hales; he kept no copies and should decline to answer; he should stand on the principle of English law, which was that those who prosecute should prove. [...]

"Citizen Marx considered Hales had been guilty of grave indiscretion, as he had compromised the Council.

"Citizen Engels agreed with the remarks of Citizen Marx. With respect to the defence of Citizen Eccarius, the Council has nothing to do with British law. It had a right to know: had Eccarius written the letter he was charged with writing? Yes or no?

"Citizen Eccarius thought when the charge was made the proofs would be forthcoming, but instead of the proofs being produced he was asked to acknowledge his guilt. He should refuse to give any answer until the letter was in his hand. It had all along been assumed that he had been guilty of criminal correspondence, and he should let those who made the charge prove it.

"Citizen Marx said he said nothing about criminal correspondence, but he did say it was a crime if Eccarius wrote the letter which had the damaging character— of destroying the influence of the Council.

"With regard to the demand that the charge should be proved, he would point out that this was not an ordinary tribunal where there was a defendant and a prosecutor. It was a question of the conservation of the influence of the Council. [...]

"Citizen Engels said that the sentimentality of the previous sitting, when it was said it was cruel to let charges hang over a man's head etc., only made the cry for delay more comical." (*Documents of the First International*, vol. 5, 191–92)

It is not the last time we have heard the demand that, in dealing with disciplinary cases, the International must follow the strict procedures of bourgeois law—an argument, which, as we see from the above, was indignantly rejected by Marx and Engels, who also had no time for appeals to sentimentality, hurt feelings and so on. The overriding consideration was to defend the revolutionary organisation. By releasing internal information and spreading gossip, Eccarius had damaged the influence of the General Council, and Marx considered this to be a crime.

For his part, Jung was jealous of Marx's closeness to Engels, with whom he was in daily contact since he moved to London from Manchester. Jung and Eccarius felt offended by this and complained that "the General," as Engels was nicknamed in the circle, had *an abrupt military tone*. Whenever he took the chair at the meetings of the General Council, there was usually a row, they said.

It is fairly typical of mediocre individuals to make such complaints about the "*tone*" of a discussion, and the alleged "arrogance" of people more able than themselves. Trotsky pointed out that it was unworthy of a revolutionary to take offense because he or she has suffered a "flip on the nose." In revolutionary politics what is important is not form but content, not *the tone* with which something is said but *what* is said.

Sometimes, however, such secondary considerations can give rise to friction and enmities that can later be filled with a political content. That was the case with Jung and Eccarius. They were not necessarily bad people, but they had a limited political understanding and allowed their personal feelings and hurt pride to cloud their political judgment. With Hales things were very different. When he was elected General Secretary, a sharp personal conflict arose between him and Eccarius. On the part of the latter it was mainly a question of jealous resentment. But Hales was an opportunist and a reformist to the marrow of his bones and he had always distrusted the revolutionary ideas of Marx.

The London conference decided to set up an English Federation, and it held its first congress in Nottingham on 21st and 22nd July. This was Hales' opportunity to build a counterweight to the General Council and cancel out the influence of Marx. He proposed to the 21 delegates who were present that the Federation should establish contact with the other Federations not through the General Council, but directly, and that at the coming congress of the International the new Federation should support a change in the Statutes of the International with a view to reducing the authority of the General Council.

This was music to the ears of the Bakuninists, fitting in well with their slogan of the "endangered autonomy of the Federations." In fact, the English trade unionists had absolutely nothing in common with the ideas of the Bakuninists, being inclined to towards English Liberalism. But none of this mattered. They were all agreed on one thing: implacable opposition to Marx and the "authoritarian" General Council. In this way an unholy alliance was formed between Hales, Eccarius and Jung.

Although, as we have seen, the reformist Hales had nothing in common with the ideas of the anarchists, he had secretly entered into close relations with the Jura Federation at the Hague. This unprincipled bloc was based on the well-known idea: "the enemy of my enemy is my friend." For these people, any weapon or ally was useful if it gave one a stick to beat Marx and the General Council!

On 6th November, 1874, writing in the name of the English Federal Council, Hales declared that the "hypocrisy of the old General Council" had now been exposed. Previous to this, on 18th September, Hales moved a vote of censure against Marx in the British Federal Council, using as an excuse Marx's comments at the Hague concerning the corrupt nature of some English working-class leaders. The vote of censure was adopted. Hales then gave notice that he intended to present a resolution for the expulsion of Marx from the International, while another member gave notice for a resolution rejecting the decisions of the Hague congress.

The theory of "two rival bureaucracies"

Hales developed an original and peculiar theory: Marx and Bakunin were really... the same. According to Hales, Marx had attempted to organise a secret society within the International on the pretext of destroying another secret society which it had invented to suit its aims. It was only a matter of one authoritarian bureaucracy fighting against another authoritarian bureaucracy to get control of the International!

At the same time, however, Hales pointed out that the English were not in agreement with the Jura Federation politically. They (the English) were convinced of the usefulness of political action. Here he spoke the unvarnished truth, since the English trade union leaders were trying to get into parliament, and for this purpose they needed the help of the Liberals. However, they were quite prepared to grant complete autonomy to all other federations as demanded by the different conditions in the various countries—and the different interests of the leaders.

Politics knows strange bedfellows. Although Hales and Eccarius had previously entertained a violent dislike for each other, they now became the most zealous allies, and Jung finally became one of the most violent opponents of Marx and Engels. In the cases of both Eccarius and Jung, they permitted their political judgment to be clouded by personal jealousies and resentments. As Lenin once remarked, spite in politics always plays the most destructive role.

In the past, Eccarius and Jung had become known to the whole International as the most faithful defenders of the opinions of Marx. Now they did a 180-degree somersault and appealed for support for the Jura Federation against the "intolerance" of the Hague decision and the "dictatorial tendencies" of Marx and Engels. However, the two men met with vigorous resistance in the English sections, and in particular the Irish. Even in the Federal Council they encountered opposition. So, as befits such committed advocates of democracy and toleration, they carried out a coup d'état in the English branch of the International. They issued an appeal to all sections and all members, declaring that the British Federal Council was so divided against itself that further cooperation was impossible. They demanded the calling of a congress to reverse the decisions taken at the Hague.

The minority immediately replied to these maneuvers with a counter-appeal, probably written by Engels, which condemned the proposed congress as illegal. Nevertheless, the congress took place on 26th January, 1873. Hales delivered violent attacks on the old General Council and on the Hague

Congress, and was actively supported by Jung and Eccarius. The congress unanimously condemned the Hague decisions and refused to recognise the new General Council in New York, and declared itself in favour of a new international congress. Hales intrigued quite openly against the General Council and in August he was removed from his post. But the split in the British Federation was by now an accomplished fact.

The end of the International

The history of the First International really ends with the Hague congress. The leading figure of the new General Council in New York was Sorge, who was well acquainted with American conditions and a loyal supporter of Marx. But still the moving of the new General Council to New York failed to save the IWA. The movement in America lacked the experience and material means to prosper there.

The sixth congress of the International was called by the General Council in New York for 8th September in Geneva. But its only purpose was to sign the death certificate of the International. The Bakuninists organised their counter-congress in Geneva on 1st September. It was attended by two English delegates—the old arch-enemies Hales and Eccarius, five delegates each from Belgium, France and Spain, four delegates from Italy, one delegate from Holland and six delegates from the Jura.

Marx frankly admitted that the congress had been "a fiasco" and advised the General Council not to emphasise the formal organisational side of the International for the moment, but, if possible, to keep the centre point in New York going, to prevent it from falling into the hands of adventurers and others who might compromise the cause. Events would assure the recreation of the International on a higher level in the future. History was to prove Marx correct.

In 1876 the General Council in New York published the notice that the First International had ceased to exist. For ten years the International had dominated one part of European history. But now it faced an uncertain future because of objective difficulties and internal problems. In 1874, Engels wrote, "A general defeat of the working-class movement such as was suffered in the period from 1849 to 1864 will be necessary before a new international, an alliance of all proletarian parties in all countries, along the lines of the old one can come into being. At present the proletarian world is too big and too diffuse."

Unlike its successors, the Second (Socialist) and Third (Communist) Internationals, the First International was never a mass organisation. Moreover, in its beginnings it was politically confused, being made up of all kinds of different elements: English reformist trade unionists, French Proudhonists, followers of Mazzini, the Italian nationalist, Blanquists, Bakuninists and others. But thanks to the patient and tireless work of Marx and Engels, the ideas of scientific socialism eventually triumphed.

In the building of a genuine International, the importance of ideas is as fundamental as are strong foundations in the building of a house. The International Workingman's Association was the first real attempt to establish an international organisation of the working class. It was the equivalent of laying down the foundations of a house. If a house is to withstand the battering of the elements, it must have strong foundations.

The great merit of Marx's work in the IWA was that it established a firm theoretical base for the movement, without which the future development of the International would have been impossible. The First International laid the basis for the creation of the mass social-democratic workers' parties in Germany, Switzerland, Denmark, Portugal, Italy, Belgium, Holland and North America. It had established the theoretical foundations for the future development of socialism on a world scale.

An important role in this was the fierce ideological battle with other trends, especially Bakuninist anarchism. In the end, the combination of an extremely unfavourable objective situation following the defeat of the Paris Commune and the destructive factional intrigues of the Bakuninists undermined the International. Marx and Engels transferred the centre to New York, partly to prevent it from falling into the hands of the Bakuninists and other intriguers, but partly because they hoped that the workers' movement in North America would come to the rescue.

In the end, these hopes did not materialize, and they were compelled to recognise that the IWA had played out its historical role. The International, as an organised force, ceased to exist. But the tradition of the International lived on. *It survived as an idea and a programme, to reemerge about a decade later on a higher level.* The emergence of mass workers' parties and trade unions towards the end of the nineteenth century provided the basis for the founding of a new International—the Second International.

In July 1889 the International Socialist Congress opened its doors in Paris, attended by delegates from 20 countries. They founded the new Socialist International and declared May Day an international working-class holiday. And they adopted the principles of the International Workingmen's Association founded a quarter of a century before. The International, like the phoenix of ancient legend, had risen from the ashes to spread its mighty wings.

London, 9th March 2010

On Authority

Frederick Engels

Anumber of Socialists have latterly launched a regular crusade against what they call the *principle of authority*. It suffices to tell them that this or that act is *authoritarian* for it to be condemned. This summary mode of procedure is being abused to such an extent that it has become necessary to look into the matter somewhat more closely.

Authority, in the sense in which the word is used here, means: the imposition of the will of another upon ours; on the other hand, authority presupposes subordination. Now, since these two words sound bad, and the relationship which they represent is disagreeable to the subordinated party, the question is to ascertain whether there is any way of dispensing with it, whether—given the conditions of present-day society—we could not create another social system, in which this authority would be given no scope any longer, and would consequently have to disappear.

On examining the economic, industrial and agricultural conditions which form the basis of present-day bourgeois society, we find that they tend more and more to replace isolated action by combined action of individuals. Modern industry, with its big factories and mills, where hundreds of workers supervise complicated machines driven by steam, has superseded the small workshops of the separate producers; the carriages and wagons of the highways have become substituted by railway trains, just as the small schooners and sailing feluccas have been by steamboats. Even agriculture falls increasingly under the dominion of the machine and of steam, which slowly but relentlessly put in the place of the small proprietors big capitalists, who with the aid of hired workers cultivate vast stretches of land.

Everywhere combined action, the complication of processes dependent upon each other, displaces independent action by individuals. But whoever mentions combined action speaks of organisation; now, is it possible to have organisation without authority?

Supposing a social revolution dethroned the capitalists, who now exercise their authority over the production and circulation of wealth. Supposing, to adopt entirely the point of view of the anti-authoritarians, that the land and the instruments of labour had become the collective property of the workers who use them. Will authority have disappeared, or will it only have changed its form? Let us see.

Let us take by way of example a cotton spinning mill. The cotton must pass through at least six successive operations before it is reduced to the state of thread, and these operations take place for the most part in different rooms. Furthermore, keeping the machines going requires an engineer to look after the steam engine, mechanics to make the current repairs, and many other labourers whose business it is to transfer the products from one room to another, and so forth. All these workers, men, women and children, are obliged to begin and finish their work at the hours fixed by the authority of the steam, which cares nothing for individual autonomy. The workers must, therefore, first come to an understanding on the hours of work; and these hours, once they are fixed, must be observed by all, without any exception. Thereafter particular questions arise in each room and at every moment concerning the mode of production, distribution of material, etc., which must be settled by decision of a delegate placed at the head of each branch of labour or, if possible, by a majority vote, the will of the single individual will always have to subordinate itself, which means that questions are settled in an authoritarian way. The automatic machinery of the big factory is much more despotic than the small capitalists who employ workers ever have been. At least with regard to the hours of work one may write upon the portals of these factories: *Lasciate ogni autonomia, voi che entrate!* [Leave, ye that enter in, all autonomy behind!]

If man, by dint of his knowledge and inventive genius, has subdued the forces of nature, the latter avenge themselves upon him by subjecting him, in so far as he employs them, to a veritable despotism independent of all social organisation. Wanting to abolish authority in large-scale industry is tantamount to wanting to abolish industry itself, to destroy the power loom in order to return to the spinning wheel.

Let us take another example—the railway. Here too the cooperation of an infinite number of individuals is absolutely necessary, and this cooperation must be practiced during precisely fixed hours so that no accidents may happen. Here, too, the first condition of the job is a dominant will that settles all subordinate questions, whether this will is represented by a single delegate or a committee charged with the execution of the resolutions of the majority of persons interested. In either case there is a very pronounced authority. Moreover, what would happen to the first train dispatched if the authority of the railway employees over the Hon. passengers were abolished?

But the necessity of authority, and of imperious authority at that, will nowhere be found more evident than on board a ship on the high seas. There, in time of danger, the lives of all depend on the instantaneous and absolute obedience of all to the will of one.

When I submitted arguments like these to the most rabid anti-authoritarians, the only answer they were able to give me was the following: Yes, that's true, but there it is not the case of authority which we confer on our delegates, *but of a commission entrusted!* These gentlemen think that when they have changed the names of things they have changed the things themselves. This is how these profound thinkers mock at the whole world.

We have thus seen that, on the one hand, a certain authority, no matter how delegated, and, on the other hand, a certain subordination, are things which, independently of all social organisation, are imposed upon us together with the material conditions under which we produce and make products circulate.

We have seen, besides, that the material conditions of production and circulation inevitably develop with large-scale industry and large-scale agriculture, and increasingly tend to enlarge the scope of this authority. Hence it is absurd to speak of the principle of authority as being absolutely evil, and of the principle of autonomy as being absolutely good. Authority and autonomy are relative things whose spheres vary with the various phases of the development of society. If the autonomists confined themselves to saying that the social organisation of the future would restrict authority solely to the limits within which the conditions of production render it inevitable, we could understand each other; but they are blind to all facts that make the thing necessary and they passionately fight the world.

Why do the anti-authoritarians not confine themselves to crying out against political authority, the state? All socialists are agreed that the political state, and with it political authority, will disappear as a result of the coming social revolution, that is, that public functions will lose their political character and will be transformed into the simple administrative functions of watching over the true interests of society. But the anti-authoritarians demand that the political state be abolished at one stroke, even before the social conditions that gave birth to it have been destroyed. They demand that the first act of the social revolution shall be the abolition of authority. Have these gentlemen ever seen a revolution? A revolution is certainly the most authoritarian thing there is; it is the act whereby one part of the population imposes its will upon the other part by means of rifles, bayonets and cannon—authoritarian means, if such there be at all; and if the victorious party does not want to have fought in vain, it must maintain this rule by means of the terror which its arms inspire in the reactionists. Would the Paris Commune have lasted a single day if it had not made use of this authority of the armed people against the bourgeois? Should we not, on the contrary, reproach it for not having used it freely enough?

Therefore, either one of two things: either the anti-authoritarians don't know what they're talking about, in which case they are creating nothing but confusion; or they do know, and in that case they are betraying the movement of the proletariat. In either case they serve the reaction.

1872

Anarchism and Socialism
V I Lenin

Theses:

1. Anarchism, in the course of the 35 to 40 years (Bakunin and the *International*, 1866–) of its existence (and with Stirner included, in the course of many more years) has produced nothing but general platitudes against *exploitation*.

- These phrases have been current for more than 2,000 years. What is missing is (α) an understanding of the *causes* of exploitation; (β) an understanding of the *development* of society, which leads to socialism; (γ) an understanding of the *class struggle* as the creative force for the realisation of socialism.

2. An understanding of the *causes* of exploitation. *Private* property as the basis of *commodity* economy. Social property in the means of production. In anarchism—nil.

- Anarchism is bourgeois *individualism* in reverse. Individualism as the basis of the entire anarchist world outlook.
- Defence of petty property and *petty economy* on the land.
- *Keine Majorität.*[1]
- Negation of the unifying and organising power of the authority.

3. Failure to understand the development of society—the role of large-scale production—the development of capitalism into socialism.

- (Anarchism is a product of *despair*. The psychology of the unsettled intellectual or the vagabond and not of the proletarian.)

4. Failure to understand the *class* struggle of the proletariat.

- Absurd negation of politics in bourgeois society.
- Failure to understand the role of the organisation and the education of the workers.
- Panaceas consisting of one-sided, disconnected means.

5. What has anarchism, at one time dominant in the Romance countries, contributed in recent European history?

- No doctrine, revolutionary teaching, or theory.
- Fragmentation of the working-class movement.

---

1 No majority (i.e., the anarchists' non-acceptance of the submission by the minority to the majority).—*Ed.*

– Complete fiasco in the experiments of the revolutionary movement (Proudhonism, 1871; Bakuninism, 1873).
– Subordination of the working class to *bourgeois* politics in the guise of negation of politics.

1901

Michael Albert and Parecon

Josh Lucker

In the United States, and throughout the more advanced countries of the West, the numbers for youth unemployment are approaching "third world" levels. Public education is being slashed across the country, as state governments reckon with massive deficits, transferred from the private sector through immense bailouts of the banks. 1.5 million children in the US are homeless. To put it bluntly, the future for young people in America is bleak. In these conditions, millions of youth are beginning to question whether capitalism has anything to offer.

But what is the alternative? Unlike the rest of the industrialised world, the US has no mass labour party and no continuity in its "left tradition." There is not and has never been a truly mass Socialist or Communist Party. Western expansion, the Palmer Raids, the New Deal, World War II, McCarthyism, the crimes of Stalinism, the extended post-war economic boom, and the collapse of the Soviet Union have all, in their turn, played a role in cutting across the development of a serious left in this country.

Given the absence of a traditional left party of any considerable size, even one that is reformist in nature, working class youth in the US are drawn either into the "liberal wing" of the Democratic Party—one of the two bosses' parties—or are further radicalised, often becoming anarchists by default.

Many American leftists begin their political lives as anarchists of some form or another. I know this was true for myself. Youthful anarchists vary widely in seriousness, often graduating from a simple rejection of the "status quo" to a more serious study and analysis of problems and solutions, of history and philosophy.

For those who are more serious and seeking a more thorough understanding of anarchist theory, a few names tend to dominate the field of anarchist intellectuals. Noam Chomsky is the name that everyone knows, even if they don't know that he is an anarchist. But perhaps even more influential than Chomsky, in terms of constructing anarchist ideology, is Michael Albert, co-founder of Z-Magazine, the Z-Net website, and South End Press. Albert's ideas, which he calls "Parecon" (Participatory Economics), have become a sort of theoretical basis for an entire school of "libertarian socialists," or anarchists.

With the explosion of the Occupy movement onto the scene in late 2011, young people have once again taken to the streets. The Occupy phenomenon, which at this stage is still experimenting with different ideas, is to a large extent a youth movement. Many Occupiers claim to be "above" to politics. However, many understand that we cannot be indifferent to politics, that we must seek a political explanation and solution to the crisis. As a result, many young people are gravitating toward Marxist ideas, while others are attracted to various anarchist trends.

Albert's Parecon represents perhaps the most serious and well-known attempt to offer a worked-out alternative to capitalism amongst the anarchist left. As Marxists, we take the discussion of what sort of society should replace capitalism very seriously, and thank Michael Albert for raising the idea of a society after capitalism amongst thousands of workers and students. However, does Michael Albert's Parecon offer a viable way forward? From the Marxist perspective, Parecon leaves quite a bit to be desired, and is in large part a repackaging of old ideas in a shiny new package.

It is in some ways complex, in others rather simple; but we feel that it is certainly worth our time to study, because of the influence that it has garnered amongst a layer of some of the most forward-thinking and critical anarchist youth. Elements of Parecon may appear rather peculiar to someone unfamiliar with it. In fact, many of the peculiarities of Parecon flow from a desire to avoid the rise of a so-called "coordinator class," which in turn is a fear that flows from Albert's analysis of the events surrounding the Bolshevik Revolution in 1917 and its aftermath. This is a central, and often unstated undercurrent in all of Albert's writings. Therefore, before we get into Parecon itself, we think it would useful to first to deal with the question of the Soviet Union, and with Albert's "coordinator class."

The Russian Revolution

For many people, when you bring up the question of socialism, the immediate question is: "Well, what about Russia?" The ability to answer the question "What happened in the Soviet Union?" is critical for revolutionaries. To not take the question seriously or to consider it an irrelevance that we can ignore would doom us. This is why it is essential for Marxists to study *both the victory and* the degeneration of the revolution. We must therefore study Stalinism, in order to explain this phenomenon to people with natural questions about the process that took place in Russia following the revolution, but also in order to work to prevent similar processes in the future.

For Marxists, the October Revolution of 1917 represented the most important event in human history. For the first time ever, with the exception of the brief but heroic episode of the Paris Commune, the working class laid hold of the reins of state power, threw aside capitalist property relations, and began the process of socialist transformation. The revolution represented a huge victory for the working class, as the factories passed into their hands; for the peasants, as the land passed into theirs; for women, who saw full legal equality for the first time in Russia; for national and ethnic minorities, particularly Jews, who had suffered greatly under the Great Russian chauvinism of the autocratic tsarist regime.

The revolutionary uprising itself, in the capital of Petrograd, was virtually bloodless. In fact, more people died in the filming of Sergei Eisenstein's film about the Russian Revolution, *October*, than died in the insurrection itself. However, this relatively peaceful moment was to pass shortly, as history would teach us to expect. As Leon Trotsky explained: "…no ruling class has ever voluntarily and peacefully abdicated. In questions of life and death, arguments based on reason have never replaced the arguments of force. This may be sad, but it is so. It is not we that have made this world. We can do nothing but take it as it is."[1]

Twenty-one foreign armies including the United States invaded the fledgling Soviet state, as the Bolshevik Party, led by Vladimir Lenin and alongside Trotsky, struggled to establish the peace they had promised to the Russian masses. Because although the Bolsheviks pulled Russia out of the World War I, peace was not to be had in the near term, as the invading forces bolstered the homegrown forces of counterrevolution. Russia erupted into full-blown civil war, with revolutionary Reds clashing with counterrevolutionary Whites for control of Russia's future.

Meanwhile, the revolutionary movement was spreading beyond Russia's borders, beginning with uprisings in Germany in 1918–19, the brief soviet republic in Hungary in 1919, the revolutionary strike wave in Italy, also in 1919, and so on. This was precisely as the Bolsheviks had predicted. Russia was an underdeveloped, semi-feudal economy, incapable of building socialism alone, as to do so requires building upon the foundations of the most advanced capitalism. However, capitalism was to break at its "weakest link." It was never Lenin and Trotsky's idea that the Bolsheviks could somehow build socialism in Russia alone, but rather, that a revolution in Russia would subsequently spark off successful revolutions in European countries with more advanced capitalist economies, which could then in turn lift Russia out of backwardness and lay the basis for socialist development.

1 Trotsky, Leon. "In Defence of October," 1932 speech in Copenhagen, http://www.marxists.org/archive/trotsky/1932/11/oct.htm

However, despite the initial optimism, all of these revolutions were defeated, not because of any failure in the theory of international revolution, but due to the failures and inadequacies of the revolutionary leadership in each country respectively. The Soviet Union, still suffering from civil war at home, and now from the failures of revolutionary movements abroad, was becoming more and more isolated. At the time of the revolution, Russia was a virtually illiterate, overwhelmingly peasant country despite having a strong working class in a few industrial centres. Under these conditions, "all the old filthy business," to use Marx's words, began to revive, as want became generalised and the struggle for even basic necessities was intensified.[2] Far from building upon the highest technology and productivity yet reached by world capitalism, the Soviet Union inherited a ruined and extremely backward economy. The material basis for building socialism is simple: having more than enough to go around for everyone. But where breadlines exist, police exist to police the breadlines.

Under these conditions of isolation and destitution, the rise of a bureaucratic caste was in effect inevitable. In the final analysis, that is exactly what Stalinism represents: a bureaucratic caste that rises out of and grafts itself onto the workers' state, skimming the cream off the top of social production, reserving it for itself, and using force to defend its power and privileges.

The result is a deformed, or in the case of Russia, a degenerated workers' state. The economic basis of society, i.e., the property forms, remain those of socialism: capitalist private property of the means of production is abolished, and is brought under centalised state control to be administered collectively. However, instead of a regime of workers' democracy administering the economy and the state, political power is usurped by a bureaucratic caste.

This is not a phenomenon unique to post-capitalist societies, as this form of political usurpation, in which the state elevates itself above society and rules somewhat independently, balancing between the various classes, can be seen in different forms throughout history: Caesarism in ancient Rome; the absolute monarchs of the feudal age; the rule of Napoleon Bonaparte in France; and the fascist and military dictatorships of the twentieth century. In the case of Stalinism, Marxists refer to this phenomenon as "proletarian Bonapartism." This is because the economic base of the regime is "proletarian," while the political superstructure is "Bonapartist."

The "coordinator class"

Despite the many problems it confronted, the early Soviet Union was the most democratic society humanity has yet seen. The system of workers' democracy

---

2   Karl Marx, *The German Ideology*, in *The Marx-Engels Reader* (New York: Norton, Second Edition, 1978), 161.

which existed under Lenin in the early 1920s had absolutely nothing in common with the monstrous totalitarian bureaucracy that coalesced around Stalin in the 1930s. In order to consolidate his power, Stalin was forced to liquidate the entire Bolshevik Central Committee as it had existed in 1917. Michael Albert, however, sees continuity between Lenin and Stalinism. Moreover, he believes that the legacy of Lenin and Trotsky is not the legacy of the working class, but rather of a new class, which he calls the "coordinator class." Specifically, what is the "coordinator class," according to Albert?

> "[The] "coordinator class" [is] composed of those who receive a wage for their labours but who, unlike workers, do jobs that have considerable influence over their own and other people's economic situations and who retain their more empowering jobs largely due to monopolizing certain skills and knowledge. And we can note that the class of workers such as assemblers, waiters, truckers, and janitors, and the class of coordinators such as managers, doctors, lawyers, and engineers, regard one another with opposed interests. And that each also opposes capitalists, though in different ways."[3]

Albert, in turn, views the victory of the October Revolution as the conspiratorial seizure of power by this class to rule in its own interests:

> "[U]nder certain historical conditions, if they manage to eliminate private ownership, they can run the economy without capitalists above them and with workers still below them.
>
> "The still sceptical Marxist might then ask, "Under what circumstances would they all unite against both workers below and capitalists above? Surely you can't mean they would do that.
>
> "My reply is that yes, to adopt such a stance publicly would be suicidal, of course. Rather, what this class's foremost elements would do if they wanted to usher in a new economy in their own interests is wage a class war against capital by identifying capitalism's many horrors to appeal to all those who suffer capitalism's indignities and impoverishment. In the course of the ensuing anti-capitalist struggles, however, the coordinator class, seeking its own domination and not just an end to capital's rule, would monopolize control over institutions into its own hands, elevate its own culture and values, and impose its rule on more grass roots movements and new institutions, all as a kind of reflex of itself image and its image of others. In this way the coordinator class would wind up dominating the new society, not only theoretically as I have just described, but, as has actually occurred in historical practice, in all countries where Leninists have taken power.[4]

---

3   Michael Albert, *Parecon: Life After Capitalism* (New York: Verso, 2004), 26.
4   Michael Albert, *Realising Hope: Life Beyond Capitalism* (New York: Zed Books, 2006), 152–53.

"That is, instead of having a capitalist ruling class, in centrally planned economies we see a coordinator class of planners and managers inexorably becoming the ruling class."[5]

Albert insists of "coordinators" that:

"They aren't workers with a slight difference to most other workers. They aren't capitalists with a slight difference from most other capitalists. Nor are they some kind of amalgam of the two, or the bottom stratum of capitalists merging into the top stratum of workers, thereby occupying what some might call a contradictory position. Instead this group has its own well defined position, its own clear definition, and, as a result, its own views and interests."[6]

We therefore need to ask ourselves two questions: 1) Do the "coordinators" Albert is referring to represent a unique "class" position in society? 2) Was the October Revolution in 1917 the seizure of power by this layer, whether or not they constitute a unique class?

Marxists do not use the word "class" in the loose way that it is used in standard, everyday American English. When most people talk about "class," they are referring to income level or some other variable. Americans have, at least until very recently, viewed class not as a collective identity, but rather as a series of gradations.

This view is part and parcel of the "American Dream" mythology, which promotes the belief that anyone can make it in America, that we are all potential millionaires in waiting, and that "we are all 'middle class.'" This outlook was bolstered by the prosperity afforded by the post-war economic boom. However, the material basis for this view has been under attack since the mid-1970s. The mass appeal of the "We are the 99%" and the "99% vs the 1%" slogans and ideas put forward by the Occupy movement, testify to the beginning of the end of the belief in the "American Dream."

The fact is that class is not a series of gradations, and we are not "all middle class." For Marxists, class has a very precise, scientific meaning. It is not determined by income level, but by *relations to the production process*, and ultimately, by the *question of ownership*. I am a worker, not because I make x amount of money in wages, but because, as I do not own any private property in the form of capital, a large portfolio of stocks and bonds, or vast tracts of commercial, agricultural, and other rental properties, I am forced to sell what I do have—my ability to work—to a capitalist, in exchange for wages.

By the same token, Warren Buffet is a capitalist, not because he made x billion dollars last year, but because, through his ownership of capital and

5   Albert, *Parecon*, 50.
6   Albert, *Realising Hope*, 151.

what we call the "means of production," he employs wage labour, which he, through the labour process, exploits to make a profit.

The workers do not form a monolithic, homogeneous class. There is a wide range of incomes among those who must sell their labour power for a wage, and a correspondingly wide range of ideological world views. But whether they make minimum wage, or $100,000 per year, they remain part of the working class due to their relation to the means of production. It is above all ownership of those means, or the lack thereof, that determines whether an individual is part of the working class or the capitalist class.

Between these two great classes—the working class (the proletariat) and the capitalist class (the bourgeoisie)—there is also what Marxists call the "middle class," or the petty-bourgeoisie. This class bears no resemblance to the "middle class" envisioned in the "American Dream" ideology of the two-car garage and the white picket fence in suburbia. The petty-bourgeoisie stands between the working class and the capitalist class, both materially and ideologically. They are the small business owners, the doctors or lawyers with their own practice, the small farmers, etc. These are not big capitalists, in the sense that, while they may own some capital and exploit workers, they are forced to work themselves; i.e., they do not make enough simply by virtue of their ownership of the means of production to survive. More and more, capitalism tends to drive members of this class into the working class. As Marx put it in the *Manifesto*:

> "The bourgeoisie has stripped of its halo every occupation hitherto honoured and looked up to with reverent awe. It has converted the physician, the lawyer, the priest, the poet, the man of science, into its paid wage-labourers.[7]

> "The lower strata of the middle class—the small tradespeople, shopkeepers, and retired tradesmen generally, the handicraftsmen and peasants—all these sink gradually into the proletariat, partly because their diminutive capital does not suffice for the scale on which modern industry is carried on, and is swamped in the competition with the large capitalists, partly because their specialized skill is rendered worthless by new methods of production. Thus the proletariat is recruited from all classes of the population."[8]

This class is extremely unstable, as they stand at the precipice, with a cliff on either side. Depending on which statistics are to be believed, 50–90% of small businesses fail *within the first year*. Less than 1% of Americans (just 2.2 million out of a population of 310 million) are farmers, and more small farmers are driven out of farming by big agribusiness and corporate farming every day. Descending into the ranks of the working class is far more likely

7   Karl Marx, *Manifesto of the Communist Party*, in *Four Marxist Classics* (St. Paul: Wellred, 2008), 5.
8   Ibid., 10.

for a member of the petty-bourgeoisie than ascending into the ranks of the capitalist class.

While Albert insists that his "coordinator class" is not synonymous with the Marxist definition of the "petty-bourgeoisie," nonetheless, a large number of the professions that he associates with "coordinatorism" fit neatly into this class category, while those that do not, are simply higher-paid workers, with perhaps a college education or a specialized skillset. But they are hardly a well-defined layer with a unique relation to the means production, thereby representing the class interests and aspirations of a new and previously undiscovered class.

And yet, for Albert, "coordinators," such as doctors, university professors, small businesspeople, and shop floor foremen, do indeed form a single, independent class, not bound by property ownership or lack thereof. Furthermore, Albert argues that this class can seize and wield political power. According to Albert, failure to recognise this is Marxism's great weakness:

> "Marxism's fatal weakness in this regard is that it ignores the possibility that factors other than ownership can produce classes, and that its overlooking additional possibilities compromises many core insights of the Marxist framework."[9]

Albert argues that Marxism "only asserts, and never really proves, or even argues, that we should see property relations as the only cause of class difference."[10] This is simply not true; and is, ironically, merely asserted by Albert, rather than proven. In fact, Marx and Engels both wrote extensively on the subject, not simply "asserting," but explaining in great detail why relations to production should be used as the defining feature of class identification. As Marx explains in Volume III of *Capital*:

> "The specific economic form in which unpaid surplus-labour is pumped out of the direct producers determines the relationship of rulers and ruled, as it grows directly out of production itself and, in turn, reacts upon it as a determining element. Upon this, however, is founded the entire formation of the economic community which grows up out of the production relations themselves; thereby simultaneously its specific political form. It is always the direct relationship of the owners of the conditions of production to the direct producers—a relation always naturally corresponding to a definite stage in the development of the methods of labour and thereby its social productivity—which reveals the innermost secret, the hidden basis of the entire social structure, and with it the political form of the relation of sovereignty and dependence, in short the corresponding specific form of the state."[11]

9   Albert, *Realising Hope*, 151.

10   Ibid.

11   Karl Marx, *Capital, Volume III* (London: Penguin Classics, 1991), 927. (also: http://www.marxists.org/archive/marx/works/1894-c3/ch47.htm)

Further, class is merely a particular form of the social division of labour. As Marx described elsewhere:

> "Insofar as millions of families live under economic conditions of existence that divide their mode of life, their interest and their culture from those of the other classes, and put them in hostile contrast to the latter, they form a class. Insofar as there is merely a local interconnection among these small peasants, and the identity of their interests begets no unity, no national union and no political organisation, they do not form a class. They are consequently incapable of enforcing their class interest in their own name, whether through a parliament or through a convention."[12]

For Marxists, a social layer simply working in similar conditions, e.g., conditions of "empowering work," does not alone constitute this social layer into a class. For example, Marx is above referring to the French peasants of 1851. He continues:

> "The small peasants form a vast mass, the members of which live in similar conditions, but without entering into manifold relations with one another. Their mode of production isolates them from one another, instead of bringing them into mutual intercourse."[13]

This is the opposite of the position of the working class, which finds itself thrust into social conditions that not only encourage, but necessitate a collective mindset. In contradistinction to the position of the working class, both the middle class, as Marxists understand the term, and to an even greater extent Albert's "coordinators," are isolated one from another by their relationship to the means of production. This isolated, parochial view is what has, as Marx described above, condemned the peasantry and middle class to eternally *follow* one or another of the two great classes in society, as their own class position prevents them from playing any sort of independent role in social transformation. This is as true of the peasant revolts of the Middle Ages, as it was with the peasantry in Russia in 1917.

In the same way, the middle class in modern society wavers between supporting the working class and the capitalist class, tending to tilt in the direction of whichever class appears to have the upper hand at a given moment. In cases where the petty-bourgeoisie movement has developed more broadly, they have invariably been manipulated cynically from above, resulting in the rise of fascism. Far from achieving any real degree of "independence", they ultimately they became nothing more than a battering ram against the working class, for the preservation and continuation of capitalism.

---

12   Karl Marx, *Eighteenth Brumaire of Louis Bonaparte*, in *The Marx-Engels Reader*, 608.
13   Ibid.

Did Albert's "coordinatorist" layer come to power in 1917? Absolutely not. Let's begin with Lenin, who is often presented as an "elitist" by anarchist writers, including Albert. These writers quote by rote the same line from Lenin's early work *What is to be Done?*:

> "We have said that *there could not have been* Social-Democratic consciousness among the workers. It would have to be brought to them from without. The history of all countries shows that the working class, exclusively by its own effort, is able to develop only trade union consciousness, i.e., the conviction that it is necessary to combine in unions, fight the employers, and strive to compel the government to pass necessary labour legislation, etc."[14]

What those who use isolated quotations as a replacement for genuine argumentation fail to recognise, is that this quotation comes from a very specific debate against the "economist" trend within the Russian Social-Democratic Labour Party (RSDLP). This was a trend that rejected the political struggle, and preferred to focus exclusively on "economic" or trade union demands. In stating the above, Lenin was restating a position held by Karl Kautsky, at that time a key leader of the German Social-Democratic Party. In making his case against economism, Lenin later admitted that he had exaggerated in the heat of the debate:

> "We all now know that the "economists" have gone to one extreme. To straighten matters out somebody had to pull in the other direction—and that is what I have done."[15]

Here is Lenin several years later, clarifying his position:

> "The working class is instinctively, spontaneously Social-Democratic, and more than ten years of work put in by Social-Democracy has done a great deal to transform this spontaneity into consciousness."[16]

Was Lenin's goal the construction of a party of intellectuals or "coordinators" to seize power in their own interests? Replying once again to those who misunderstood his argument against the economists, Lenin seems to answer Michael Albert himself:

> "[Some say that I take] no account whatever of the fact that the workers, too, have a share in the formation of an ideology. Is that so? Have I not said time

---

14   V.I. Lenin, *Collected Works* (hereafter *LCW*), Volume 5 (Moscow: Progress, Fifth Printing, 1977), 375.
15   Lenin, "Second Congress of the RSDLP" in *LCW* 6, 489. (also: http://www.marxists.org/archive/lenin/works/1903/2ndcong/14.htm)
16   V.I. Lenin, "The Reorganisation of the Party," part I, in LCW 10, 32. (also: http://www.marxists.org/archive/lenin/works/1905/reorg/i.htm)

and again that the shortage of fully class-conscious workers, worker-leaders, and worker-revolutionaries is, in fact, the greatest deficiency in our movement? Have I not said there that the training of such worker-revolutionaries must be our immediate task?"[17]

Further, Lenin on multiple occasions sought to reduce the ratio of intellectuals to workers in the RSDLP and later the Bolshevik Party:

"At the Third Congress of the Party I suggested that there be about eight workers to every two intellectuals in the Party committees. How obsolete that suggestion seems today!

"Now we must wish for the new Party organisations to have one Social-Democratic intellectual to several hundred Social-Democratic workers.[18]

"Only the broadening of the Party by enlisting *proletarian* elements can, in conjunction with open mass activity, eradicate all the residue of the circle spirit which has been inherited from the past and is unsuited to our present tasks."[19]

Wouldn't a party of, by, and for the "coordinators" want to maintain strict control of the entry of "*proletarian* elements" into the party? We shall see below that Lenin and Trotsky were also in favour of the working class entering the sphere of management and administration, of both society and of the economy, despite Albert's claims to the contrary. This also runs counter to the "coordinatorist" theory.

The degeneration of the revolution happened for a number of very specific historical reasons, which we discussed above, not least of which was the isolation of the revolution. The process was accelerated by the Civil War, as the best, most self-sacrificing and class-conscious workers often were the first to give their lives in the war to defend the revolution.

It is true that Stalin, particularly after his creation of the "Cult of Lenin," used the anti-Marxist idea of an elite guard of intellectuals, separate from, and above the masses, as a useful ideological bulwark against challenges from the working class and the Old Bolsheviks to his leadership. However, this had absolutely nothing in common with the regime that existed during Lenin's lifetime, and which Trotsky and hundreds of thousands of others died defending against Stalin's gangsters.

Stalin based his rise in the party upon the isolationist aspirations of the war-weary, small-proprietor *kulaks* in the countryside, and the layer of

---

17 Lenin, "Second Congress of the RSDLP", 489.
18 V.I. Lenin, "The Reorganisation of the Party," part II, in *LCW* 10, 36n. (also: http://www.marxists. org/archive/lenin/works/1905/reorg/ii.htm)
19 V. I. Lenin, "Preface to the Collection *Twelve Years*" in *LCW* 13, 105. (also: http://www.marxists. org/archive/lenin/works/1907/sep/pref1907.htm)

careerist bureaucrats who had flooded the party once victory in the Civil War appeared assured, as well as the more backward elements of the working class, also beaten down and tired from years of civil war. The bureaucratic layer around Stalin, whose interests he personified, did not constitute a class in the scientific, Marxist sense of the word, as their power did not derive from direct ownership of any property. Rather, they formed a bureaucratic caste, encrusted on the top of Soviet society, ruling pragmatically in their own narrow interests, not the interests of the Soviet or world working class.

Even from the early days of the Soviet state, there were "bureaucratic deformations," as Lenin was always clear to point out. But to argue that Lenin, on the one hand, and Stalin on the other, both ruled Russia as representatives of a "coordinator class" seems a monstrous distortion of reality.

We have dealt elsewhere in this volume with the issues raised in the suppression of the Kronstadt mutiny, and the actions of the anarchist Makhno.[20] We believe we have shown that Leninism bears no resemblance to Stalinism, and that Leninism is not a movement of, by, and for "coordinators," and that these layers do not constitute a unique class in society, with unified interests and a unique relation to production.

On the (mis)use of quotations

Before we get to the ideas of Parecon itself, we have to deal one final time with Albert's usage of quotations. On ancient maps, the phrases *"hic sunt dracones"* ("Here be dragons") or *"hic sunt leones"* ("Here be lions") denoted undiscovered or dangerous territory, not to be traversed by the unskilled or unwary traveler. Similarly, in nearly every one of his books, Michael Albert marks out Lenin and Trotsky's work as "dangerous territory," not to be seriously studied, by using a relatively small number of "scary" quotations that he claims "prove" their wickedness and utter contempt for democracy and workers' control.

A similar method is employed by other anarchist writers, as well as right-wing enemies of Marxism. The quotations used usually vary little between texts, and the same short quotations, lacking context, and secondhand misquotations, appear in one book or article after another, so we need to deal with a few of them in detail.

First, we need to say a few words about the usage of quotations in political texts. Karl Marx, Frederick Engels, Vladimir Lenin, Leon Trotsky, Rosa Luxemburg, Ted Grant, and other great Marxist writers are not religious figures. The works they have written are not religious texts, and the things that they have said are not "red-lettered." Finding a quotation from one of them that may be slightly off-putting, or even wholly incorrect, does not

---

20 See this volume, 265-96.

discredit the body of their work, any more than would finding a new, as-yet-unexplained fossil invalidate the entire theory of evolution, as some creationists believe.

There are those so-called Marxists, who refer to some of the above writers in an almost religious manner, with the expectation that finding the "right quote" from the "right writer" will "prove" an argument. Such a method is alien to Marxism and to serious social science. Quotations can certainly shed light on and supplement an argument, as often someone has previously said or written something that can clarify an argument in a far more eloquent or concise manner than the writer can manage on his or her own. It is also true that there is a certain political authority that comes with the arguments made by the leaders of a movement, both past and present, just as there are within scientific fields. But while this authority may or may not be earned, it cannot in and of itself decisively "prove" an argument, whether in the realm of revolutionary theory or in other scientific fields.

"Man is a lazy animal"

To begin with, let's take a look at a few quotations that Albert lifts from *Terrorism and Communism*, Trotsky's 1918 book in defence of the use of revolutionary terror against the counterrevolutionary White Armies during the Russian Civil War. One of Albert's favourite quotations is the following, which he quotes as follows in his book *What is to be Undone?*:

> "It is a general rule that man will try to get out of work. Man is a lazy animal."[21]

Albert elaborates further his interpretation of this quotation in *Looking Forward: Participatory Economics for the Twenty First Century*:

> "As to why Trotsky championed "one-man management" in the factory we need look no further than his cynical view of human nature: "It is a general rule that man will try to get out of work. Man is a lazy animal." Naturally comrades at the centre of society must sometimes coerce "lazy animals" for their own good."[22]

In the second book, Albert provides no citation, so it is impossible to know which edition of *Terrorism and Communism* he is using. However, in *What is to be Undone?*, Albert references a second-hand citation of "Trotsky in Cohn-Bendit" in his endnotes. This is, of course, a reference to Cohn-Bendit's *Obsolete Communism*. Why Albert did not see fit to source the original text is hard to understand. The entire paragraph from which the quotation by Trotsky is extracted is as follows:

21   Michael Albert, *What is to be Undone?* (Boston: Porter Sargent, 1974), 110.
22   Michael Albert, *Looking Forward: Participatory Economics for the Twenty First Century* (Cambridge: South End Press, 1991), 7.

"As a general rule, man strives to avoid labour. Love for work is not at all an inborn characteristic: it is created by economic pressure and social education. One may even say that man is a fairly lazy animal. It is on this quality, in reality, that is founded to a considerable extent all human progress; because if man did not strive to expend his energy economically, did not seek to receive the largest possible quantity of products in return for a small quantity of energy, there would have been no technical development or social culture. It would appear, then, from this point of view that human laziness is a progressive force. Old Antonio Labriola, the Italian Marxist, even used to picture the man of the future as a "happy and lazy genius." We must not, however, draw the conclusion from this that the party and the trade unions must propagate this quality in their agitation as a moral duty. No, no. We have sufficient of it as it is. The problem before the social organisation is just to bring "laziness" within a definite framework, to discipline it, and to pull mankind together with the help of methods and measures invented by mankind itself."[23]

He goes on to add:

"The whole of human history is the history of the organisation and education of collective man for labour, with the object of attaining a higher level of productivity. Man, as I have already permitted myself to point out, is lazy; that is, he instinctively strives to receive the largest possible quantity of products for the least possible expenditure of energy. Without such a striving, there would have been no economic development. The growth of civilisation is measured by the productivity of human labour, and each new form of social relations must pass through a test on such lines."[24]

Several things stand out when reading the full quotations, in their original context. It is hard to miss the dishonest way in which Trotsky is presented by Albert and others. First, one will notice that Albert, or if we are to be fair, Cohn-Bendit, has removed the middle of the quotation ("Love for work is not at all an inborn characteristic: it is created by economic pressure and social education.") without the use of ellipses. This removes Trotsky's own elabortion of what it is he means. Also, the more moderate, "One may even say that man is a fairly lazy animal," in Trotsky has been replaced by Cohn-Bendit with the much more harshly worded, "Man is a lazy animal." These initial objections may appear at first glance to be mere questions of semantics, but they speak to the honesty of the method used by Trotsky's detractors.

Taken as a whole, the quotations from Trotsky present an analysis which is hard to deny, i.e., that "laziness", or put another way, our desire to do as little work as possible while still achieving as much as possible out of this

---

23   Leon Trotsky, *Terrorism and Communism: A Reply to Karl Kautsky* (London: New Park, 1975), 144–45.
24   Ibid., 155.

work, forms the basis for our desire to increase the productivity of our labour, and thus, ultimately, all of human technological development. Does Albert deny this? Does he prefer that humanity do more labour and get less out of this labour? Of course, we are a tool-making, labouring animal, but our labouring nature exists in a dialectical interrelationship with our natural inclination toward "laziness", which in turn plays an undeniably progressive historical role.

However, Trotsky's further point, that it does not follow that laziness should therefore be encouraged, as it requires no encouragement, is equally valid. What was necessary, in order to win the Civil War against the armies of counterrevolution, and to develop the Russian economy out of absolute backwardness, was to bring laziness "within a definite framework".

"One-man management"

This brings us to the next quotation Albert attempts to use against Trotsky, concerning "one-man management". It again comes from the period of the Civil War, which stretched the young Soviet state to its limits, as the Soviet workers and peasants fought off 21 invading armies, the vicious counterrevolutionary White Armies, and starvation in the cities across the country.

> "Corroborating our implication that militarisation of political and economic life was no hated necessity, but a well thought-out, believed-in universal policy Trotsky said:

> "'I consider that if the Civil War had not plundered our economic organs of all that was strongest, most independent, most endowed with initiative, we should undoubtedly have entered the path of one-man management much sooner and much less painfully.'"[25]

Once again, Albert quotes a second-hand source, this time Maurice Brenton's *The Bolsheviks and Workers' Control*. In another work, Albert uses the same quotation, with no citation, and draws this conclusion:

> "In other words, Trotsky didn't reluctantly accede to coordinator structures out of necessities compelled by the Civil War, as apologists maintain, but because he preferred them."[26]

Trotsky does indeed write this, in *Terrorism and Communism*, but he *makes clear that this is not to be elevated to a principle for all time*. Not more than a few paragraphs down from the above quote, Trotsky adds:

25   Albert, *What is to be Undone?*, 111.
26   Albert, *Looking Forward*, 7.

"Variants and combinations are possible here. Where the worker can manage alone, let us put him in charge of the factory and give him an expert as an assistant. Where there is a good expert, let us put him in charge and give him as assistants two or three of the workers. Finally, where a "board" has in practice shown its capacity for work, let us preserve it. This is the sole serious attitude to take up, and only in such a way shall we reach the correct organisation of production."[27]

So much for Albert's "universal policy." The above actually presents a very flexible approach to how labour should be more efficiently organised so as to defend the revolution against the counterrevolution, both domestic and foreign. What Trotsky is saying is that, in those scenarios where management by a board of workers has shown itself to work in practice, then this should be maintained ("let us preserve it"). The attentive reader will also note that Trotsky proposes that if a worker can run things, the expert acts as an assistant, but if an expert is needed to manage, then two or three workers should be there to assist (or rather, to keep the expert in line). If Trotsky "preferred" one-man management as some sort of "universal policy," then why would he concede to preserving boards of workers where these were functioning well?

This, however, also misses Trotsky's main point concerning "one-man management." Given the conditions of backwardness and the isolation of the revolution in Russia, one-man management in effect became an inevitability. Were it not for the chaos caused by the Civil War, the transition would have occurred far more smoothly—and probably more quickly. Trotsky actually explains this quite clearly in the lines preceding the above quotation:

"The necessity of making use of technical knowledge and methods accumulated in the past, the necessity of attracting experts and of making use of them on a wide scale, in such a way that our technique should go not backwards but forwards—all this was understood and recognised by us, not only from the very beginning of the revolution, but even long before October."[28]

Nowhere does Trotsky elevate one-man management to an eternal principle, even less to a "preference." In fact, while arguing against the idea that one-person management of this or that factory inherently represents an attack upon the "independence of the working class," Trotsky states:

"The independence of the workers is determined and measured not by whether three workers or one are placed at the head of a factory, but by factors and phenomena of a much more profound character—the construction of the economic organs with the active assistance of the trade unions; the building up of all Soviet organs by means of the Soviet congresses, representing tens

27   Trotsky, *Terrorism and Communism*, 172–73.
28   Ibid., 170–71.

of millions of workers; *the attraction into the work of administration, or control of administration, of those who are administered*. It is in such things that the independence of the working class can be expressed." (our emphasis)[29]

Thus, the bringing of the working class into the field of the administration of their own affairs was, in fact, a task which Lenin and Trotsky had set for the fledgling Soviet state from the beginning. In point of fact, Trotsky considers it the means by which "the independence of the workers is determined and measured."

Trotsky made this point even clearer in his *Transitional Programme*:

"Within the framework of this plan, the workers would demand resumption, as public utilities, of work in private businesses closed as a result of the crisis. Workers' control in such case: would be replaced by *direct workers' management*.

"The working out of even the most elementary economic plan—from the point of view of the exploited, not the exploiters— is impossible without workers' control, that is, without the penetration of the workers' eye into all open and concealed springs of capitalist economy. Committees representing individual business enterprises should meet at conference to choose corresponding committees of trusts, whole branches of industry, economic regions and finally, of national industry as a whole. Thus, workers' control becomes a *school for planned economy*. On the basis of the experience of control, the proletariat will prepare itself for direct management of nationalised industry when the hour for that eventuality strikes." (our emphasis) [30]

And what happens after nationalisation? Does Trotsky become an advocate of "one-man management" in the case of a workers' or left-leaning party coming to power and nationalising the key levers of industry?

"...nationalisation and workers' control do not exclude each other at all. Even if the government were an extremely left one and full of the best intentions, we would stand for the control of workers over industry and circulation; we do not want a bureaucratic management of nationalised industry; we demand *direct participation of the workers themselves in control and administration through shop committees, trade unions, etc.* Only in this way can we lay the supporting bases for proletarian dictatorship in economy." (our emphasis)[31]

This hardly sounds like someone committed to a "coordinator structure." Lenin expressed similar ideas on the question of workers' management:

---

29   Ibid., 169–70.

30   Leon Trotsky, *The Transitional Programme*, in *Four Marxist Classics*, 185.

31   Leon Trotsky, "Revisionism and Planning: The Revolutionary Struggle against Labour Fakers" in *Writings of Leon Trotsky [1933–34]* (New York: Pathfinder, 2011), 63. (also: http://www.marxists.org/archive/trotsky/1934/01/planning.htm)

"[E]xpropriation alone, as a legal or political act, does not settle the matter by a long chalk, because it is necessary to depose the landowners and capitalists in actual fact, *to replace their management of the factories and estates by a different management, workers' management, in actual fact.* There can be no equality between the exploiters—who for many generations have been better off because of their education, conditions of wealthy life, and habits—and the exploited, the majority of whom even in the most advanced and most democratic bourgeois republics are downtrodden, backward, ignorant, intimidated and disunited. For a long time after the revolution the exploiters inevitably continue to retain a number of great practical advantages: they still have money (since it is impossible to abolish money all at once); some movable property—often fairly considerable; they still have various connections, habits of organisation and management; knowledge of all the "secrets" (customs, methods, means and possibilities) of management; superior education; close connections with the higher technical personnel (who live and think like the bourgeoisie); incomparably greater experience in the art of war (this is very important), and so on and so forth."[32]

And again in *The State and Revolution*:

"Given these *economic* preconditions, it is quite possible, after the overthrow of the capitalists and the bureaucrats, to proceed immediately, overnight, to replace them in the *control* over production and distribution, in the work of *keeping account* of labour and products, by the armed workers, by the whole of the armed population."[33]

These quotations could be reproduced *ad nauseum*, as there are far more statements from Lenin and Trotsky about the need for workers' management and participation than there are small snippets, taken out of context, which "prove" their alleged diabolic plots to run roughshod over the workers. In fact, during a debate with a member of the British SWP, Albert essentially admitted his bias:

"I will admit that perhaps I have a fetish or a bias with dumping on Lenin and Trotsky, maybe I do, that causes me to miss the complexity that gives them excuses or makes their behaviour contextually reasonable."

Moments later, Albert in fact recanted this confessional, but were we to simply leave the above quotation without further comment, you would never know, which proves our point. In short, out-of-context quotations are not a serious means of argumentation.

---

32   V.I. Lenin, *The Proletarian Revolution and the Renegade Kautsky* (Peking: Foreign Language Press, 1975), 33–34.
33   V.I. Lenin, *The State and Revolution*, in *Four Marxist Classics*, 156.

Vision and utopianism

Albert makes a big deal out of the need for "vision" and accuses the Left in general of a great deficiency in this regard. His favourite way of phrasing this is to say that leftists usually put forward a list of grievances without formulating an alternative, so that the audience, at best, is left with the impression that things are horrible, but that there is no better alternative. Albert compares this to trying to create a "movement against ageing," which most people, despite its obviously negative consequences, view as an inevitability.

It is true that "the Left" often does end up "complaining" more than offering solutions, particularly if we include within this "left," liberals and reformists, who genuinely believe that the only minimal improvements can be made, and are achievable only within the confines of the existing system. However, Albert goes further. He ascribes this failure to "Marxism's general taboo against 'utopian' speculation."[34] Albert's solution? Nothing more, and nothing less than utopian speculation!

Is it true, as Albert claims, that Marxism offers no vision of what a future society may look like? Absolutely not! However, for Marxists, this discussion is based on analyzing historical experience and concrete possibilities. Marxists, for example, study the Paris Commune, the Russian Revolution, the degeneration of the Revolution into Stalinist counterrevolution, the Spanish Civil War, the German Revolution, etc., not simply for historical interest, but because there are lessons to learn from the successes and failures of these revolutions. We have to learn from concrete historical experience. One of the things that history teaches us is that no detailed "blueprint" of what a future society is going to look like is needed for a revolution to be successful. More importantly, since the concrete conditions under which socialism will be built will depend on the actual course of and timing of the revolution, no such predetermined plan could ever be implemented as its designers intended.

Profound social transformations—revolutions—are the product of massive discontent against the status quo, brought about by objective conditions, by the contradictions built up within the very foundations of society; not something that springs ready-made from the minds of great thinkers. During normal periods this discontent lies dormant, but under certain conditions, explodes toward the surface, much like lava from a volcano. Even the social forms, such as workers' councils (*soviets*, in Russian), which become instrumental in revolutionary events, are typically not produced first in the minds of theorists, but rather are thrown up during the course of struggle itself. Neither the Bolsheviks, the Mensheviks, the anarchists, nor any

34 Albert, *Realising Hope*, 154.

other revolutionary grouping in Russia theorized about even the possibility of *soviets* before they became a reality during the 1905 Revolution, an eternal testament to the independent creativity of the working class in struggle.

While some "vision" is critical, an overly detailed vision of the future is bound to come into conflict with the realities and complexities of the living struggle between the classes. Often, despite the best intentions of the designers of overarching visions of the future, the end result looks nothing like they intended. For example, in France, Robespierre sought the "Rule of Reason"; In England, Cromwell sought the "Kingdom of Heaven"; in Cuba, Fidel Castro viewed Abraham Lincoln and the US as a primary inspiration, and so on. The end result in each of these cases was dictated not solely by the "vision" of this or that individual, but by historical conditions and their limitations: the relative level of development of society, the world situation, the isolation of a revolution, etc. This is not to say that ideas and leadership do not matter (they obviously do!), but ideas are materially constrained. As Marx famously put it:

> "Men make their own history, but they do not make it just as they please; they do not make it under circumstances chosen by themselves, but under circumstances directly found, given and transmitted from the past. The tradition of all dead generations weighs like a nightmare on the brains of the living."[35]

The attempt to formulate, by way of abstract thought, the workings of a future socialist society, was one of the primary failings of the utopian socialists of the nineteenth century, who wrote detailed "visions" of what such a future society would look like (e.g., Edward Bellamy in the US), or created experimental communities to put their vision into practice (e.g. the Owenites in Britain).

While Bellamy's novel *Looking Backward* was wildly influential, inspiring the likes of Eugene Debs for example, his utopian vision of an evolution towards the end of private property through the goodwill of the capitalist class contained no resemblance to the reality of the world in which he lived— or to that of the world we live in today. Furthermore, on what are we to base either our criticism or agreement with these utopian schemes beyond engaging in mere abstract speculation, such as, "That wouldn't work," "That might work," etc.?

To their credit, the utopian experiments of Robert Owen and the Owenites in Britain and the Bellamy Societies in the US took things a step further. Not happy with simply speculating about the future, some decided to put their "vision" into practice with the formation of "ideal" communities. However, all of these experiments, even if some were successful in the short term, operated within the confines of a capitalist marketplace hostile to them,

---

35   Marx, *Eighteenth Brumaire*, 595.

and were destined for failure in the end. Nonetheless, early utopian socialism, which Engels provides a brief history of in his pamphlet *Socialism: Utopian and Scientific*, showed by heroic example the realistic potential of the goals of socialism.

However, while recognising the historic contribution of utopian thought to the cause of socialism, is it therefore incumbent upon us to "look backward" to pre-Marxist socialism for our ideas? Not at all. As stated above, Marxism looks first to material conditions and to an analysis of history for answers to the questions of what a future society will look like.

Based on historical precedent, we can say, that when the working class enters struggle, it tends to throw up organs for its own rule, what we call *soviets* or workers' councils. These form the basis for a new state, a more democratic and participatory workers' state. Such an embryonic state stands in opposition to the existing capitalist state, bringing about a situation of "dual power."

We can also say that the economy of a socialist society must be rationally planned, rather than operating according to the anarchy of the capitalist marketplace. This would allow for the maximum utilization of society's resources. Further, drawing on the lessons of Stalinism, we can also say that the plan must also be democratic, implemented and controlled by the workers themselves. We will deal with planning in much more detail later, as it figures hugely in Albert's system.

These and other lessons are not drawn from thin air, but are the product of a thorough study of past revolutionary experience. Similarly the points in the programme of the Workers International League are not drawn from abstract desires or "vision," but from the objective necessities of the movement of the working class. We base it on the direction of the movement and of society, ultimately raising the sights of the workers towards what must be our ultimate goal: the socialist transformation of society.

In the beginning were the values

How does Albert, by contrast, arrive at the ideas of participatory economics? Rather than beginning from an analysis of the real, material world, Albert begins from "first principles," i.e. like a prophet, he begins with "vision":

> "When examining and evaluating economic systems, there are four main questions about values we must address:
>
> 1 Equity: How much should people get and why?
>
> 2 Self-management: What kind of say over their conditions should people have?
>
> 3 Diversity: Should paths to fulfilment be diversified or narrowed?

    4 Solidarity: Should people cooperate or compete?

"Our first step in envisioning a new economy is to address these four areas of concern."[36]

Albert adds, further on, a fifth value—efficiency:

"Of course, in addition to solidarity, diversity, equity, and participatory self-management, there is one more evaluative norm we must keep in mind. It will not do, for example, to have economic institutions that promote all our economic values but do not get the economic job done. It will not do, that is, to have an economy that does not meet expressed needs, or that does so to a limited degree though delivering fewer or less desirable outputs than would have been possible with more efficient operations."[37]

Albert has determined that these five are the best values for us to use to "envision" a new economy, or to stand in judgment of existing ones:

"[H]aving these five values—solidarity, diversity, equity, and participatory self-management, plus meeting expressed needs without waste—gets us a long way toward being able to judge economies. If an economy obstructs one or more of these values, to that degree, we do not like it. On the other hand, if an economy furthers these preferred values, that's very good, though we must still look further to see if there are any offsetting problems."[38]

Why these values? Because these are the values Albert himself has chosen, though he admits they may come into contradiction with others' values:

"[T]hough these values mean to be encompassing and critically important so that not furthering them is a damning criticism, there are many other values—such as privacy, personal freedom, artistic fulfilment, or even something specific like the right to employ others for personal gain—which might (or might not) also merit attention. And we can imagine that our favoured values could come into conflict with one or more of these other values in certain contexts... in which case someone could argue that one of our values should be somewhat sacrificed to attain conflicting desirable ends."[39]

Having discovered the five ideal means of evaluating economies, Albert's next step is to establish institutions, in ideal form, which further those values. For Albert and the followers of Parecon, these values are: workers' and consumers' councils; remuneration for effort and sacrifice; balanced job complexes; and participatory planning. These institutions form the foundations of Parecon.

36   Albert, *Parecon*, 28.
37   Ibid., 42.
38   Ibid.
39   Ibid.

Workers' and consumers' councils

The first institution, workers' and consumers' councils, requires little explanation, as these are intended to be democratic bodies for the rule of society by the working class. They also have the virtue, along with the planning component of Albert's system, of being the only institutions within Parecon based on anything that has ever actually existed on a mass scale in the material world.

That being said, in a country like the United States, as well as in much of the industrialised world, most consumers are also workers and *all* workers are also consumers, so the division between the two is artificial. Allowing undue influence to "consumers" is not only confusing, but even dangerous from a class perspective, as "consumers" do not represent a definite class within society; for example, Bill Gates is also a consumer. What should interest us are councils that reflect the will of the majority of society (i.e., the workers).

Albert's nested system of consumer councils would make an individual family unit the lowest level of a "consumers' council"; which would in turn belong to a "neighbourhood consumption council"; which would belong to "a federation of neighbourhood councils the size of a city ward or a rural county," and so on.[40] Aside from the obvious complications flowing from participating in a small decision-making body with members of one's immediate family, it is hypothetically possible that a future society could organise itself in this way.

But it is far more likely that production will be planned through workers' councils (by those actually doing the producing), with input on consumption needs, priorities, and targets coming from the broader community (i.e., workers as consumers). By linking up workers', neighbourhood, and other councils that may be formed to ensure maximum participation of all those affected by decisions taken, and utilizing the latest technology, a genuinely democratic and participatory economy could organised. Albert's artificial division of society into "workers" and "consumers" makes little theoretical or practical sense.

The critical component is not the particular form of organisation of the workers' councils, but their very existence. Even more important is that the rule of the working class is exercised through such councils. In other words, *which class rules society is of more immediate importance than the specific means by which they rule.* And to rule society, the workers must hold the reins of political power in their hands. More on that later.

Within Albert's books on Parecon, he goes into considerable detail as to how he believes these councils need to work, i.e., how often they should meet, how they should take decisions, on what and whom their decisions should be binding, etc. But frankly, these are not questions of critical importance.

40   Ibid., 93.

While a certain amount of speculation is fine, it is very different to assert that a particular method, untested on a mass scale, is superior to other methods, both tested and untested. History itself will provide the definite answer to the question "how will the working class organise itself in a new society?"

After its conquest of power, the working class will undoubtedly try out various forms and methods of efficiently organising itself: within the workplace, the family, the community, etc. Some will work, some will not, but as Marxists, we have absolute confidence, based on historical experience, in the creativity of the working class, and its ability to come up with appropriate and perhaps as-of-yet un-thought of solutions. Far more important at present is the question of how the workers will achieve political and economic power in the first place.

Remuneration and labour productivity

The next "institution" Albert deals with is "remuneration for effort and sacrifice." According to Albert, Marxism gets the question of remuneration wrong by rewarding for output, rather than effort and sacrifice. But is this the final word Marxism has to say on remuneration, or payment for work? In contrast to Parecon, which Albert presents as a finished, fully-worked-out system, Marxism postulates a transitional evolution from the workers' state of socialism into a classless, stateless communism.

Initially, we must deal with a new society "not as it has *developed* on its own foundations, but, on the contrary, just as it *emerges* from capitalist society, which is thus in every respect, economically, morally and intellectually, still stamped with the birthmarks of the old society from whose womb it emerges."[41] What does this mean? Marx explains:

> "Accordingly, the individual producer receives back from society—after the deductions have been made—exactly what he gives to it. What he has given to it is his individual quantum of labour... He receives a certificate from society that he has furnished such and such an amount of labour (after deducting his labour for the common funds), and with this certificate he draws from the social stock of means of consumption as much as costs the same amount of labour. The same amount of labour which he has given to society in one form he receives back in another."[42]

For Marx, does this mean that those unable to work, for example, the injured or elderly, are left to fend for themselves? Clearly not! These are included in the "deductions" Marx refers to:

41   Karl Marx, *Critique of the Gotha Programme in The Marx-Engels Reader*, 529.
42   Ibid., 529–30.

"Before this is divided among the individuals, there has to be deducted again from it:

"*First, the general costs of administration not belonging to production.*

"This part will from the outset, be very considerably restricted in comparison with present-day society and it diminishes in proportion as the new society develops.

"*Secondly, that which is intended for the common satisfaction of needs,* such as schools, health services, etc.

"From the outset this part grows considerably in comparison with present-day society and it grows in proportion as the new society develops.

"*Thirdly, funds for those unable to work,* etc., in short, for what is included under so-called official poor relief today."[43]

For Albert, however, this payment for productivity is completely unacceptable:

"Luck in external circumstance and in the genetic lottery are no better basis for remuneration than luck in the property inheritance lottery... If a person has the fine fortune to have genes that give her an advantage for producing things of merit, or if she is lucky as regards her field of work, there is no reason on top of this good luck to provide her with an exorbitant income as well."[44]

Marx, however, recognised this problem long before Albert. In his *Critique of the Gotha Programme*, Marx observed:

"In spite of this advance, this *equal right* is still constantly stigmatized by a bourgeois limitation. The right of the producers is *proportional* to the labour they supply; the equality consists in the fact that measurement is made with an *equal standard*, labour."

"But one man is superior to another physically or mentally and so supplies more labour in the same time, or can labour for a longer time; and labour, to serve as a measure, must be defined by its duration or intensity, otherwise it ceases to be a standard of measurement. This *equal* right is an unequal right for unequal labour. It recognises no class differences, because everyone is only a worker like everyone else; but it tacitly recognises unequal individual endowment and thus productive capacity as natural privileges. *It is therefore, a right of inequality, in its content, like every right.*"[45]

---

43   Ibid., 529.
44   Albert, *Parecon*, 35.
45   Marx, *Critique of the Gotha Programme*, 530.

In other words, as long as we are in a transitional society from capitalism, through socialism, to communism, elements of the old inequality, of bourgeois right, will inevitably remain. For Albert, a means around this problem must be "envisioned":

> "To achieve this goal we would have to assess each job's characteristics for the effort or sacrifice per hour expended at an average level of exertion, plus have some means of oversight to keep track of which workers are expending effort at levels above or below average."[46]

How would this be done in practice?

> "The precise methodology for doing this need not be the same from workplace to workplace… Here is a general approach, however, that many workplaces might opt for. Imagine each worker receives a kind of "evaluation report" from their workplace that determines their income to be used for consumption expenditures. This evaluation report would indicate hours worked at a balanced job complex [We'll discuss these shortly. –JL] and intensity of work, yielding an "effort rating" in the form of a percentage multiplier… The system could be a highly precise numeric rating system where people are graded to two decimal places above or below average, for example. Or it might simply read "superior," "average," or "below average," with the designation meaning average income, or a tenth above or a tenth below (that having been agreed in the workplace to be the only variation permitted)."[47]

This is an extremely complex arrangement, and the above, presented in his book, *Parecon*, intended for popular consumption, is his most "basic" explanation. This attempt to get around remuneration for productivity is complex precisely because it attempts to fit a square peg into a round hole, i.e., it attempts to overcome the inevitable defects of bourgeois right before the material capabilities to do so exist. "Right can never be higher than the economic structure of society and its cultural development conditioned thereby."[48]

Emerging from the womb of capitalism, socialist society will not only be limited by the relative productive capacity of that society, but also by the ideology of capitalism, the moral and intellectual stamp Marx refers to, which will remain on the minds of millions for some time after the overthrow of capitalist property relations. With this will come certain expectations, among them, the expectation of payment for work done. Some adjustment may be made on the basis of "duration or intensity," particularly relative to capitalist society where the most onerous jobs are often the worst paid. Nonetheless,

46   Albert, *Parecon*, 115.
47   Ibid., 115–16.
48   Marx, *Critique of the Gotha Programme*, 530.

labour time and the productivity of that labour will for a time, perhaps quite a long time, need to be the primary determinants of remuneration, even after the revolution.

In reality, this is the realisation of the right to the fruits of one's individual labour that capitalism has always claimed to provide. Capitalism, however, is incapable of genuinely implementing remuneration for productivity, because allocation of wealth under this system is based on ownership of private property, greatly stacking outcomes in favour of those owning productive property, rather than those involved in productive labour.

Is "bourgeois right," however, Marx's final word on the matter? No; he continues:

> "In a higher phase of communist society, after the enslaving subordination of the individual to the division of labour, and therewith also the antithesis between mental and physical labour, has vanished; after labour has become not only a means of life but life's prime want; after the productive forces have also increased with the all-round development of the individual, and all the springs of cooperative wealth flow more abundantly—only then can the narrow horizon of bourgeois right be crossed in its entirety and society inscribe on its banner: From each according to his ability, to each according to his needs!"[49]

But for Albert, Marx's "From each according to his ability, to each according to his needs" is:

> "…not only utopian in being unattainable; even if we could attain it, it would curtail needed information transfer and thereby obscure rather than reveal the relative preferences people have for different economic choices."[50]

Albert says elsewhere of remuneration based on needs that, "it expresses a value beyond equity or justice that we aspire to and implement when possible or desirable… such as in cases of illness, catastrophe, incapacity, and so on."[51]

Beyond being pessimistic about the future potential for an economy of super-abundance, and by extension, genuine communism, i.e., classlessness and statelessness, Albert gets Marx's own prescription wrong. Not only do Marx, Engels, Lenin, Trotsky, and their modern adherents *not* argue that allocating based on productivity, i.e., bourgeois right, is an end in itself, we also do not argue that one must achieve fully-developed communism in order to begin to see beyond the limitations of bourgeois right. As Marx said, bourgeois right is only overcome "in its entirety" by society's ascension to the higher phase of communism.

49   Ibid., 531.
50   Albert, *Realising Hope*, 154.
51   Albert, *Parecon*, 37–38.

A society's ability to even begin the process of overcoming bourgeois right, i.e., its enslavement to the norms of bourgeois society in the realm of allocation of the means of consumption, is relative to its level of development. For example, in Russia, following the October Revolution, even beginning to overcome the limitations of bourgeois right was absolutely unthinkable in a country without even a developed capitalist economy. By contrast, the advanced capitalist economies of the twenty-first century offer tremendous potential, unimaginable to the Russians in 1917. This is not to say that bourgeois right will be overcome, even in the advanced countries, immediately following their successful revolutions. However, we would begin this process on a far higher level, on the basis of the tremendous productive capacity built up (and currently being squandered) by capitalism in these societies.

This being said, in the last analysis, the ability to overcome the limitations of bourgeois right is not dependent upon a complex system of weighting the onerousness of one's work or the relative effort one does in the process of work, but rather upon the successful conquest of power by the working class in every country around the world, and the raising of the productivity of labour to the point where production for need becomes a reality for every human on earth.

"Balanced job complexes" and the division of labour

Parecon's most complex institution is the "balanced job complex." What is a balanced job complex?

> "Each job involves many tasks. Of course each job should be suited to the talents, capacities, and energies of the person doing it. But in a parecon each job must also contain a mix of tasks and responsibilities such that the overall quality of life and especially the overall empowerment effects of work are comparable for all."[52]

Albert is quick to point out:

> "Those who assemble cars today need not assemble computers tomorrow, much less every imaginable product. Nor should everyone who works in a hospital perform brain surgery as well as every other hospital function. The aim is not to eliminate divisions of labour, but to ensure that over some reasonable time frame people should have responsibility for some sensible sequence of tasks for which they are adequately trained and such that no one enjoys consistent advantages in terms of the empowerment effects of their work."[53]

And how is *this* to be achieved?

---

52   Albert, *Realising Hope*, 13.
53   Albert, *Parecon*, 104.

"[W]e can imagine someone listing all possible tasks to be done in a workplace. We can then imagine someone giving each task a rank of 1 to 20, with higher being more empowering and lower being more deadening and stultifying. So in this experiment we have hundreds or perhaps even thousands of stripped-down tasks from which we create actual jobs. No single task is enough to constitute a whole job. Some jobs may take only a few tasks, some many… Instead of combing a bunch of 6s into a 6 job, and a bunch of 18ths into an 18 job [as is done under what Albert calls a "corporate division of labour"—JL], every job is now a combination of tasks of varied levels such that each job in the workplace has the same average grade."[54]

We can certainly "imagine" any number of things; but it is also easy to "imagine" this becoming a bureaucratic mess! Further, Albert envisions a scenario where:

"…delegates of workers from different councils and industries develop a flexible rating process to balance across workplaces. As one plausible solution, there could be "job complex committees" both within each workplace and for the economy as a whole. The internal committees would be responsible for proposing ways to combine tasks and assign work times to achieve balanced work complexes within workplaces. The economy-wide committees arrange positions for workers in less desirable and less empowering primary workplaces some time in more desirable and more empowering environments, and vice versa."[55]

This complex arrangement of balanced job complexes is obviously meant to overcome the division of labour and more specifically, the potential domination of society by Albert's "coordinator class":

"If some workers have consistently greater information and responsibility on their jobs, they will dominate workplace decisions and in that sense become a ruling "coordinator class," even though they operate in democratic councils and have no special ownership of the workplace."[56]

We dealt earlier with the question of the so-called coordinators, i.e., whether they constitute a "class" and whether it is possible for them to become the rulers of a post-capitalist society, so we will not go into that question further here. Suffice it to say in connection with this question that the "coordinators" cannot become a ruling class simply by means of not cleaning bedpans or toilets. But are Marxists, who according to Albert, represent "coordinatorist" interests, unconcerned with the division of labour?

The division of labour moves from the sphere of kinship to encompass individuals performing different functions within the economy with the

54   Ibid., 105–6.
55   Ibid., 109.
56   Ibid, 103.

advent of class society. The division of labour then proceeds over time from its humble origins towards greater and greater complexity. Capitalism sees this division of labour reach new heights, both within national economies and between nations. However, more and more, the division of labour in society, particularly at its most extreme, between "thinkers" and "doers," has become an absolute fetter to human development. As Alan Woods and Ted Grant describe in their book on Marxism and modern science, *Reason in Revolt*:

> "The total divorce between theory and practice in present day society has become harmful in the extreme... It is time to reexamine the whole system of education, and the class system of society upon which it rests. It is time to reconsider the validity of dividing humanity into the *"thinkers"* and *"doers,"* not from the standpoint of some abstract moral justice, but simply because it has now become a hindrance to the development of culture and society. The future development of humanity cannot be based on the old rigid divisions. New complex technology demands an educated workforce capable of a creative approach to work. That can never be achieved in a society split down the middle by class apartheid."[57]

We have already seen that, for Marx, communism is only possible "after the enslaving subordination of the individual to the division of labour" becomes a thing of the past. But Lenin also famously remarked that one of the preconditions for healthy socialist development was a progressive rotation of tasks, so as to prevent the development of bureaucracy:

> "We are not utopians. We know that an unskilled labourer or a cook cannot immediately get on with the job of state administration. In this we agree with the Cadets, with Breshkovskaya, and with Tsereteli.[58] We differ, however, from these citizens in that we demand an immediate break with the prejudiced view that only the rich, or officials chosen from rich families, are capable of *administering* the state, of performing the ordinary, everyday work of administration. We demand that *training* in the work of state administration be conducted by class-conscious workers and soldiers and that this training be begun at once, i.e., that a *beginning* be made at once in training all the working people, all the poor, for this work."[59]

Trotsky, in *Terrorism and Communism*, proposed as concrete measures to be applied *in practice* that:

---

57   Alan Woods and Ted Grant, *Reason in Revolt: Dialectical Philosophy and Modern Science, Volume II* (New York: Algora, 2003), 218.

58   In revolutionary Russia, the Cadet Party (Constitutional Democrats) represented bourgeois liberalism.

59   Lenin, "Can the Bolsheviks Retain State Power?" in LSW 26, 113.

"The trade unions must organise scientific and technical educational work on the widest possible scale, so that every worker in his own branch of industry should find the impulses for theoretical work of the brain, while the latter should again return him to labour, perfecting it and making him more productive."[60]

This is the only serious approach to take towards the question of the division of labour. Trotsky explains how to concretely, not merely in abstract formulae, *begin the process* of throwing the division of labour into the dustbin of history. Only by means of a raising of the cultural level of the working class as a whole, is overcoming the division of labour possible.

In short, Marxists are in favour of a rotation of tasks, and we are also in favour of this being done in a rational and reasonable manner. How exactly this general principle is applied, we leave to the inventive minds of the working class. Michael Albert would be welcome to put forward his rather complex proposal. However, we would only caution Albert and his supporters that no complicated scheme, no matter how well-imagined in advance, can alone prevent the rise of a bureaucracy. Only an engaged, active, armed, and educated working class, basing itself on ever-increasing material wealth for all, can serve as a curb against the encrustation of a bureaucracy on the workers' state.

For a democratically planned economy

Often, when we explain the need for a plan of production, very reasonable questions are raised about the Soviet Union, and the bureaucratic and authoritarian planning process which dominated that country and the rest of the "Eastern Bloc." That the plan in the USSR had huge advantages over the anarchy of the capitalist market should not be overlooked. In terms of raw industrial output, a centalised plan of production allowed Russia to go from a backward, semi-feudal economy to a world economic power and the first in space within the span of two generations. However, this plan was horribly hampered by an unelected and unaccountable bureaucracy, which sought to preserve itself and its power, rather than work in the interests of the working class as a whole. The inefficiencies of bureaucratic planning from above without the direct input of the producers and consumers ultimately acted as a brake upon development once the economy of the Soviet Union reached a certain level of complexity. In fact, democracy and participation are simply more efficient.

In a capitalist economy, the primary "check" on the economy, that is to say, what is and what is not produced, is the anarchy of the profit-driven market and supply and demand. This is an extremely imperfect check, as

60 Trotsky, *Terrorism and Communism*, 158.

witnessed by capitalism's colossal waste and regular crises of overproduction. But it is the only means by which some sort of quality control is maintained in a capitalist economy. For example, if a factory owner produces one hundred more left shoes than right shoes, they will be guaranteed to have one hundred left shoes that they cannot sell. Thus, under capitalism, there is an economic incentive to eliminate such inefficiencies, or go out of business.

However, in a planned economy, the "blind" laws of supply and demand are removed from the equation, or at any rate, are greatly reduced in inverse proportion to the growth of the planning principle. So while the Soviet plan showed its superiority in an absolute sense in the production of ever-greater quantities of iron, steel, miles of railroad, etc., inefficiencies nonetheless clearly expressed themselves once more complicated consumer goods, particularly technological items of increasing complexity, entered the market in the 1970s. The only real check on the quality of such items would have been the democratic participation of the working class in the planning and producing process. As Trotsky explained:

> "If a universal mind existed, of the kind that projected itself into the scientific fancy of Laplace—a mind that could register simultaneously all the processes of nature and society, that could measure the dynamics of their motion, that could forecast the results of their interreactions—such a mind, of course, could a priori draw up a faultless and exhaustive economic plan, beginning with the number of acres of wheat down to the last button for a vest. The bureaucracy often imagines that just such a mind is at its disposal; that is why it so easily frees itself from the control of the market and of Soviet democracy."[61]

Democracy, therefore, is necessary, not simply desirable. Or, as Trotsky put it, "socialism needs democracy like the human body needs oxygen." In this spirit, all serious proposals for an alternative to the bureaucratic planning of Stalinism should be welcomed by revolutionaries. Michael Albert describes his ideal planning process in *Parecon*:

> "The participants in participatory planning are the workers' councils and federations, the consumers' councils and federations, and various Iteration Facilitation Boards (IFBs). Conceptually, the planning procedure is quite simple. An IFB announces what we call "indicative prices" for all goods, resources, categories of labour, and capital. Consumers' councils and federations respond with consumption proposals taking the indicative prices of final goods and services as estimates of the social cost of providing them. Workers councils and federations respond with production proposals listing the outputs they would make available and the inputs they would need to produce them, again,

---

61   Trotsky, "The Soviet Economy in Danger" in *Writings of Leon Trotsky [1932]* (New York: Pathfinder, 1973), 273–74. (also: http://www.marxists.org/archive/trotsky/1932/10/sovecon.htm)

taking the indicative prices as estimates of the social benefits of outputs and true opportunity costs of inputs. An IFB then calculates the excess demand or supply for each good and adjusts the indicative price for the good up, or down, in light of the excess demand or supply, and in accord with socially agreed algorithms. Using the new indicative prices, consumers and workers councils and federations revise and resubmit their proposals."[62]

He goes into exhaustive detail into the ins and outs of the process, but the above sufficiently sums up the planning side of Participatory Economics. According to Albert, this setup allows for participation in the planning process, while eliminating the need for "central planners," which are to be replaced by his "Iteration Facilitation Boards." The "indicative prices" established by the IFBs at the various stages of the process encourage "consumers [to] reassess their requests in light of the new prices and most often 'shift' their requests for goods in excess towards goods whose indicative prices have fallen," and place those workers' councils whose input-output calculations were out of balance "under pressure to increase either their efficiency or effort, or to explain why the quantitative indicators are misleading in their particular case."[63] Thus, "indicative prices" are used as a directive category by the IFBs in order to encourage certain economic activities and discourage others, of course, all based on "socially agreed algorithms." This, at least, is Albert's "vision" for a future plan.

It should be noted that directive price setting was also used by Stalinist bureaucrats in order to manipulate the Soviet economy, as Trotsky explained in *The Revolution Betrayed*:

> "...the obedient professors managed to create an entire theory according to which the Soviet price, in contrast to the market price, has an exclusively planning or directive character. That is, it is not an economic, but an administrative category, and thus serves the better for the redistribution of the people's income in the interests of socialism... Experience has managed to say its decisive word on this subject. "Directive" prices were less impressive in real life than in the books of scholars. On one and the same commodity, prices of different categories were established. In the broad cracks between these categories, all kinds of speculation, favouritism, parasitism, and other vices found room, and this rather as the rule than the exception."[64]

More importantly, what is left out of the Albert's explanation above is just how such a unified plan is to be reached and agreed upon. This could be because the answer is slightly embarrassing to a plan that claims to have "no

---

62   Albert, *Parecon*, 154.
63   Ibid., 131–32.
64   Leon Trotsky, *The Revolution Betrayed* (Mineola, NY: Dover, 2004), 57–58.

centre or top."[65] In Albert's scheme, while initially the IFBs are simply to act as pricing agencies, when one reaches the "fifth iteration of our hypothetical procedure… facilitation boards would extrapolate from the previous iterations to provide five different final plans that could be reached by the iterative process," i.e. the IFBs would present proposals to be voted upon, albeit proposals that are the product of a thorough democratic discussion.[66]

The fact that workplace and community councils have input into its development does not preclude the need for central coordination of the plan, if only in the form of working out unified proposals—as even Albert seems to recognise. But the need for coordination does not preclude the possibility, or rather the need, for democracy in the development of an efficient and optimized plan in a modern, complex, industrial economy. These two components, democracy, and centalisation—i.e., democratic participation in the planning process by the workers, who themselves are also consumers, and central coordination of the plan nationally and ultimately internationally, in order to optimize its efficiency—are not in opposition to each other, but rather form a dialectical whole. A complex planned economy would need both.

When Albert counterposes in language "participatory planning" to "central planning" and defines the latter as undemocratic and authoritarian by nature, he clarifies nothing. Of course, we would agree that a socialist economic plan must be democratic and participatory. But it must also balance this with centralisation, so as to have one unified plan of production across the whole economy, rather than many "plans" operating in opposition and competition with one another, as in a capitalist economy, where planning occurs *within* individual enterprises, but chaos reigns across the economy as a whole.

Albert, on the other hand, proposes "no centre or top" to the process. This is fine if what he means is that there should be no unaccountable, bureaucratic layer exercising undue influence on the plan. But it is also critical that the planning process to produce a single plan of production, rather than multiple plans from various councils or federation planning boards in competition with one another. This implies some level of centralisation.[67]

Once again, the details of how we will organise a planned economy in the future, on an efficient and democratic basis, will be worked out in the course of the socialist transformation itself. As Trotsky put it:

> "The art of socialist planning does not drop from heaven nor is it presented full-blown into one's hands with the conquest of power. This art may be mastered

65   Albert, *Parecon*, 128.
66   Ibid., 138.
67   Ibid., 128.

only by struggle, step by step, not by a few but by millions, as a component part of the new economy and culture."[68]

One can envision any number of possible ways by which the plan could be coordinated at a central point from various inputs, e.g., elected representatives, accountable experts, Parecon's iteration process, and at a certain stage, even artificial intelligence. But the critical component, *vis-à-vis* efficiency, is the democratic participation of "not a few but millions" in its construction, the potential for which is virtually boundless in a modern, high-tech economy.

To simply compare the potentials existing in Russia in 1921 with those of the United States in 2012, as Albert so often does, is a great mistake. As Trotsky explained, the difference between the relative levels of development of the two countries was vast, even in 1934:

> "Actually American *soviets* will be as different from the Russian soviets as the United States of President Roosevelt differs from the Russian Empire of Czar Nicholas II.[69]…Your soviet government will simply abolish all trade secrets, will combine all the findings of these researches for individual profit and will transform them into a scientific system of economic planning. In this your government will be helped by the existence of a large class of cultured and critical consumers. By combining the nationalised key industries, your private businesses and democratic consumer cooperation, you will quickly develop a highly flexible system for serving the needs of your population."[70]

Today this is true one thousand times over. Imagine the power of the Internet, smart phones, interactive television, etc., applied to developing a plan of production, not from above, but through the direct input of the working majority using the most modern technology. The potential for the development of a bureaucracy—or a caste of "coordinators," to use Albert's language—which would exercise power over the workers in a Soviet America, would be effectively nil.

Do we look forward or backward?

Questions are no doubt forming in the reader's mind. For example: "So what exactly is 'anarchistic' about Parecon?" After all, we saw earlier that Albert's views concerning "remuneration based on need" betray an implicit pessimism about the achievability of super-abundance, and by implication, write off the possibility of genuine communism and statelessness. It is clear that Albert sees Parecon, not as a temporary apparatus intended to wither away, but rather as a

68   Trotsky, "The Soviet Economy in Danger", 260. (also: http://www.marxists.org/archive/trotsky/1932/10/sovecon.htm)
69   Leon Trotsky, "If America Should Go Communist" in *Writings of Leon Trotsky: [1934–35]* (New York: Pathfinder, 2011), 129.
70   Ibid., 133–34.

permanent fixture, i.e., the ideal society, or at least his current approximation of it. It is also surprising to find out that the anarchist "ideal society" of Parecon comes complete with a "police function," and that Albert's view on policing is that "like flying planes or doing surgery, [it] involves special skills and knowledge."

What is the state if not armed bodies of men and women: the police, army, courts, prisons, etc.? In our opinion, despite claims by some of its adherents, Pareconism does not truly represent a form of "anarchist economics," whatever that might mean, but rather, as is so often the case with ideas that claim to be entirely new and fresh, Parecon is simply a repackaging of old ideas. In this case, Albert has concocted a mix of academic, pseudo-Marxist lingo, with pre-Marxist, nineteenth -century utopianism and modern reformism.

We do not doubt that those who today support the ideas of Participatory Economics, or other forms of anarchist thought, genuinely want to change society for the better. However, we believe that they will eventually come, through the bitter test of experience, to Marxist ideas. Many honest radicalised youth, regardless of their current ideological proclivities, will fight alongside the revolutionary workers to the end. We welcome these comrades in struggle. But we also encourage them to not simply take what Michael Albert or Noam Chomsky *say* about Marx, Engels, Lenin, or Trotsky as the final word on Marxism, but to *actually study* the words and ideas of these revolutionaries for themselves. Many people are more than a bit surprised to find out that Marxism is not at all what it has been made out to be by the mainstream media and by the most popular anarchist authors. Many even find that they have been "unconscious Marxists" all along.

In the Workers International League, we believe that the working class needs to look forward to the living struggle, rather than backwards to abstract, sectarian schemas. If you would like to learn more about the WIL and these ideas, visit us at www.socialistappeal.org.

June 2012

Section Two

Marxist and Anarchist Tactics

Why Marxists Oppose Individual Terrorism

Leon Trotsky

Our class enemies are in the habit of complaining about our terrorism. What they mean by this is rather unclear. They would like to label all the activities of the proletariat directed against the class enemy's interests as terrorism. The strike, in their eyes, is the principal method of terrorism. The threat of a strike, the organisation of strike pickets, an economic boycott of a slave-driving boss, a moral boycott of a traitor from our own ranks—all this and much more they call terrorism. If terrorism is understood in this way as any action inspiring fear in, or doing harm to, the enemy, then of course the entire class struggle is nothing but terrorism. And the only question remaining is whether the bourgeois politicians have the right to pour out their flood of moral indignation about proletarian terrorism when their entire state apparatus with its laws, police and army is nothing but an apparatus for capitalist terror!

However, it must be said that when they reproach us with terrorism, they are trying—although not always consciously—to give the word a narrower, less indirect meaning. The damaging of machines by workers, for example, is terrorism in this strict sense of the word. The killing of an employer, a threat to set fire to a factory or a death threat to its owner, an assassination attempt, with revolver in hand, against a government minister—all these are terrorist acts in the full and authentic sense. However, anyone who has an idea of the true nature of international Social Democracy ought to know that it has always opposed this kind of terrorism and does so in the most irreconcilable way.

Why?

"Terrorizing" with the threat of a strike, or actually conducting a strike is something only industrial workers can do. The social significance of a strike depends directly upon first, the size of the enterprise or the branch of industry that it affects, and second, the degree to which the workers taking part in it are organised, disciplined, and ready for action. This is just as true of a political strike as it is for an economic one. It continues to be the method of struggle that flows directly from the productive role of the proletariat in modern society.

Belittles the role of the masses

In order to develop, the capitalist system needs a parliamentary superstructure. But because it cannot confine the modern proletariat to a political ghetto, it must sooner or later allow the workers to participate in parliament. In elections, the mass character of the proletariat and its level of political development—quantities which, again, are determined by its social role, i.e. above all, its productive role—find their expression.

As in a strike, so in elections the method, aim, and result of the struggle always depend on the social role and strength of the proletariat as a class. Only the workers can conduct a strike. Artisans ruined by the factory, peasants whose water the factory is poisoning, or lumpen proletarians in search of plunder can smash machines, set fire to a factory, or murder its owner.

Only the conscious and organised working class can send a strong representation into the halls of parliament to look out for proletarian interests. However, in order to murder a prominent official you need not have the organised masses behind you. The recipe for explosives is accessible to all, and a Browning can be obtained anywhere. In the first case, there is a social struggle, whose methods and means flow necessarily from the nature of the prevailing social order; and in the second, a purely mechanical reaction identical anywhere—in China as in France—very striking in its outward form (murder, explosions and so forth) but absolutely harmless as far as the social system goes.

A strike, even of modest size, has social consequences: strengthening of the workers' self-confidence, growth of the trade union, and not infrequently even an improvement in productive technology. The murder of a factory owner produces effects of a police nature only, or a change of proprietors devoid of any social significance. Whether a terrorist attempt, even a "successful" one throws the ruling class into confusion depends on the concrete political circumstances. In any case the confusion can only be short-lived; the capitalist state does not base itself on government ministers and cannot be eliminated with them. The classes it serves will always find new people; the mechanism remains intact and continues to function.

But the disarray introduced into the ranks of the working masses themselves by a terrorist attempt is much deeper. If it is enough to arm oneself with a pistol in order to achieve one's goal, why the efforts of the class struggle? If a thimbleful of gunpowder and a little chunk of lead is enough to shoot the enemy through the neck, what need is there for a class organisation? If it makes sense to terrify highly placed personages with the roar of explosions, where is the need for the party? Why meetings, mass agitation and elections if one can so easily take aim at the ministerial bench from the gallery of parliament?

In our eyes, individual terror is inadmissible precisely because it belittles the role of the masses in their own consciousness, reconciles them to their powerlessness, and turns their eyes and hopes towards a great avenger and liberator who some day will come and accomplish his mission. The anarchist prophets of the "propaganda of the deed" can argue all they want about the elevating and stimulating influence of terrorist acts on the masses. Theoretical considerations and political experience prove otherwise. The more "effective" the terrorist acts, the greater their impact, the more they reduce the interest of the masses in self-organisation and self-education. But the smoke from the confusion clears away, the panic disappears, the successor of the murdered minister makes his appearance, life again settles into the old rut, the wheel of capitalist exploitation turns as before; only the police repression grows more savage and brazen. And as a result, in place of the kindled hopes and artificially aroused excitement comes disillusionment and apathy.

The efforts of reaction to put an end to strikes and to the mass workers' movement in general have always, everywhere, ended in failure. Capitalist society needs an active, mobile and intelligent proletariat; it cannot, therefore, bind the proletariat hand and foot for very long. On the other hand, the anarchist "propaganda of the deed" has shown every time that the state is much richer in the means of physical destruction and mechanical repression than are the terrorist groups.

If that is so, where does it leave the revolution? Is it rendered impossible by this state of affairs? Not at all. For the revolution is not a simple aggregate of mechanical means. The revolution can arise only out of the sharpening of the class struggle, and it can find a guarantee of victory only in the social functions of the proletariat. The mass political strike, the armed insurrection, the conquest of state power—all this is determined by the degree to which production has been developed, the alignment of class forces, the proletariat's social weight, and finally, by the social composition of the army, since the armed forces are the factor that in time of revolution determines the fate of state power.

Social Democracy is realistic enough not to try to avoid the revolution that is developing out of the existing historical conditions; on the contrary, it is moving to meet the revolution with eyes wide open. But—contrary to the anarchists and in direct struggle against them—Social Democracy rejects all methods and means that have as their goal to artificially force the development of society and to substitute chemical preparations for the insufficient revolutionary strength of the proletariat.

Before it is elevated to the level of a method of political struggle, terrorism makes its appearance in the form of individual acts of revenge. So it was in Russia, the classic land of terrorism. The flogging of political prisoners impelled Vera Zasulich to give expression to the general feeling of indignation by an assassination attempt on General Trepov. Her example was imitated in the circles of the revolutionary intelligentsia, who lacked any mass support. What began as an act of unthinking revenge was developed into an entire system in 1879–81. The outbreaks of anarchist assassination in Western Europe and North America always come after some atrocity committed by the government—the shooting of strikers or executions of political opponents. The most important psychological source of terrorism is always the feeling of revenge in search of an outlet.

There is no need to belabour the point that Social Democracy has nothing in common with those bought-and-paid-for moralists who, in response to any terrorist act, make solemn declarations about the "absolute value" of human life. These are the same people who, on other occasions, in the name of other absolute values—for example, the nation's honour or the monarch's prestige—are ready to shove millions of people into the hell of war. Today their national hero is the minister who gives the sacred right of private property; and tomorrow, when the desperate hand of the unemployed workers is clenched into a fist or picks upon a weapon, they will start in with all sorts of nonsense about the inadmissibility of violence in any form.

Whatever the eunuchs and pharisees of morality may say, the feeling of revenge has its rights. It does the working class the greatest moral credit that it does not look with vacant indifference upon what is going on in this best of all possible worlds. Not to extinguish the proletariat's unfulfilled feeling of revenge, but on the contrary to stir it up again and again, to deepen it, and to direct it against the real causes of all injustice and human baseness—that is the task of the Social Democracy.

If we oppose terrorist acts, it is only because individual revenge does not satisfy us. The account we have to settle with the capitalist system is too great to be presented to some functionary called a minister. To learn to see all the crimes against humanity, all the indignities to which the human body and spirit are subjected, as the twisted outgrowths and expressions of the existing social system, in order to direct all our energies into a collective struggle against this system—that is the direction in which the burning desire for revenge can find its highest moral satisfaction.

November 1911

Marxism and Direct Action

Phil Mitchinson

T he recent anti-capitalist demonstrations have brought together many different groups protesting against the destruction of the environment, racism, the exploitation of the third world, and also many ordinary young people protesting at the state of things in general. They have certainly shattered the myth that everyone is happy and that the capitalist system is accepted as the only possible form of society.

All around us we see the misery this system causes. Famine, war, unemployment, homelessness and despair; these are the violent acts that the system perpetrates against millions every day. Witnessing and experiencing this destruction and chaos, young people everywhere are driven to protest.

However, the idea of getting involved in a political organisation is a turn-off for many, who understandably want to do something, and do something now. In reality, the attempt to juxtapose organisation, discussion, and debate with "direct action" is pure sophistry. The ideas of Marxism are not the subject of academic study, they are precisely a guide to action. We are all in favour of action, but it must be clearly thought out, with definite aims and objectives, if it is to succeed. Otherwise we end up with directionless action. Furthermore, without political organisation, who decides what action is to be taken, when and where?

There can be no greater direct action than the seizing of control over our own lives by the vast majority of society. In that act lies the essence of revolution. Not just an aimless "direct action" but mass, democratic and conscious action, the struggle not just against capitalism, but for a new form of society, socialism.

The most recent demonstration, on May Day, was used by the bosses' mouthpieces in the press to whip up their usual hysterical garbage. They made great play of the graffiti on the cenotaph and the daubing of Churchill's statue. However, their party was somewhat spoiled by the news that the culprit was not some "yob," but a former Royal Marine, now studying at Anglia University in Cambridge. Appearing before magistrates, he made a speech condemning imperialism and Churchill's anti-Semitism. It had an impact on the magistrate, who demonstrated his own class position by mocking the young ex-soldier because of his dependence on a student loan: "you see, you can't survive without capitalism," he said.

It also appears that an Eton schoolboy participated in the smashing of a McDonalds window. This is not an accident. It is a symptom of the impasse of society that not only working class and middle class youth, but even these privileged layers rebel.

So, what comes next? The organisers of the demo tell us this was not a protest in order to secure changes, reforms apparently are a waste of time. No, simply by participating in what they call the "carnival" we become better people, and eventually more and more people will participate, until a critical mass is reached and we all ignore capitalism, don't pay our bills, until they go away. What an infantile flight of fancy! The genuine intentions of those protesting is not open to question. However, the way to hell is paved with many such good intentions. Are we really to believe that while we all "place ourselves outside of capitalism," the bosses will do nothing to defend their system? This ostrich-like tactic of burying our heads in the sand until they go away is not serious. Nor is it action. In reality, it is irresponsible, indirect inaction.

"Self-organisations"

Anarchist organisations have always hidden behind a facade of "self-organisation." They claim to have no leaders, no policy, etc. Yet who decides? If there was no leadership and no policy then there could be no action of any kind. The recent demonstrations have been highly organised and coordinated on an international scale. Good, so it should be. However, without organisation and democracy no one, except a clique at the top, has any say in why, where and when. Such a movement will never bring international capital trembling to its knees.

One of the best known anarchist groups in Britain, Reclaim the Streets, gave the game away in their spoof Mayday publication, *Maybe*. Incidentally, who wrote these articles, who decided what went in and what didn't, who edited it, where did the money come from? Our intention here is not to accuse them of dodgy financing—simply to point out that this "no leaders" stuff is a self-organised myth.

On page 20 they announce, "Reclaim the Streets is non-hierarchical, spontaneous and self-organised. We have no leaders, no committee, no board of directors, no spokespeople. There is no centalised unit for decision making, strategic planning and production of ideology. There is no membership and no formalized commitment. There is no master plan and no predefined agenda."

There are two problems here. Firstly who is "we," who made the above statement, and who decided it? Secondly, if it were true, it would not be something of which to be proud. Whether you like it or not, there is no way the capitalist system will ever be overthrown by such a haphazard and slipshod method. There is no theory, no coherent analysis of society, no alternative programme. To brag of a lack of direction, a lack of purpose and a lack of coherence, in the face of such a highly organised and brutal enemy as international capital, is surely the height of irresponsibility.

In reality the leaders of these movements are not devoid of ideology, they are anarchists. Anarchism is not simply a term of abuse, it comes from the Greek word *anarchos* meaning "without government." To anarchists, the state—the institutions of government, the army, police, courts, etc.—is the root cause of all that is wrong in the world. It must be destroyed and replaced, not with any new form of government, but the immediate introduction of a stateless society.

This opposition to the state and authority leads to a rejection of participation in any form of parliamentary activity, belonging to a political party, or fighting for any reforms; that is, political change through the state.

Of course, Marxism is opposed to the brutal domination of the capitalist state, too. Marx saw a future society without a state, but instead, "an association in which the free development of each is the condition for the free development of all." That is, a self-governing people. The question, however, is how can this be achieved?

Since anarchism sees in the state the root of all problems, it therefore believes these problems will be resolved by the destruction of the state. Marxism, meanwhile, sees the division of society into classes—a minority who own the means of producing wealth, and the majority of us whose labour is the source of that wealth—as the crux of the matter. It is this class division of society which gives rise to the state—because the minority need a special force to maintain their rule over the majority—which has evolved over thousands of years into the complicated structures we see today.

Abolition of the state

The modern capitalist state can wear many guises: monarchy, republic, dictatorship; but in the end its purpose remains the same, to maintain the minority rule of the capitalist class. Marxism's goal, therefore, is not simply to abolish the state, but to put an end to class society.

The state was born with the split of society into classes to defend private property. So long as there are classes there will be a state. So, how can class society be ended?

Not by its denial, but only by the victory of one of the contending classes. Triumph for capitalism spells ruin for millions. As Marx once explained, the choice before us is not socialism or the status quo, but socialism or barbarism. The capitalists' constant striving for profits will drive ever more millions into poverty and hunger. Their striving to control markets and raw materials will lead to endless war and destruction.

The victory of the working class can only mean the destruction of the capitalist state. Will the capitalists take defeat like sporting ladies and gentlemen, retiring quietly to the pavilion? No, all history suggests that they would not. The workers would need to create a new state, for the first time to defend the rule of the majority over the minority.

Lenin, in his masterpiece *The State and Revolution* argues, "The proletariat needs the state only temporarily. We do not at all disagree with the anarchists on the question of the abolition of the state as the aim. We maintain that, to achieve this aim, we must temporarily make use of the instruments resources and methods of state power against the exploiters."[1]

Similarly, Trotsky in *Stalinism and Bolshevism* explains, "Marxists are wholly in agreement with the anarchists in regard to the final goal: the liquidation of the state. Marxists are 'stateist' only to the extent that one cannot achieve the liquidation of the state simply by ignoring it."[2]

From the very beginning this would be like no previous state machine. From day one it would be in effect a semi-state. The task of all previous revolutions was to seize state power. From the experience of the Paris Commune of 1871, Marx and Engels concluded that it would not be possible for the workers to simply use the old state apparatus; they would instead have to replace it with an entirely new one, to serve the interests of the majority and lay the basis for a socialist society.

To ensure that the workers maintain control over this state, Lenin argued for the election of all officials, who should be held accountable and subject to recall, and paid no more than the wage of a skilled worker. All bureaucratic tasks should be rotated. There should be no special armed force standing apart from the people, and, we would add, all political parties except fascists should be allowed to organise.

The task of this state would be to develop the economy to eradicate want. Less need, means less need to govern society, less need for a state. Class society and the state will begin to wither away as the government of people, the rule

1 *Four Marxist Classics* (St. Paul: Wellred, 2008), 124–25.
2 *Writings of Leon Trotsky [1936–37]* (New York: Pathfinder, 2010), 540.

of one class over another, is replaced by the administration of things, the planned use of resources to meet society's needs

Anarchism's utopian calls to abolish the state overnight demonstrates neither the understanding of what the state is, nor the programme of action necessary to achieve the goal it sets itself.

As a modern philosophy, anarchism developed in the nineteenth century alongside the explosive growth of capitalism and its state machine. It represented a rebellion by a section of the petty-bourgeoisie at the loss of their position in society, driven to the wall by the growth of monopoly.

Their case was argued by Mikhail Bakunin and his supporters in the First International. At an anarchist conference in 1872, they argued, "The aspirations of the proletariat can have no other aim than the creation of an absolutely free economic organisation and federation based on work and equality and wholly independent of any political government, and such an organisation can only come into being through the spontaneous action of the proletariat itself...no political organisation can be anything but the organisation of rule in the interests of a class and to the detriment of the masses...the proletariat, should it seize power, would become a ruling, and exploiting, class..."

Conquest of power

Although this sounds radical enough, it nonetheless amounts to a recipe for inaction and disaster. As Trotsky explained, "To renounce the conquest of power is voluntarily to leave the power with those who wield it, the exploiters. The essence of every revolution consisted and consists in putting a new class in power, thus enabling it to realise its own programme in life. It is impossible to wage war and to reject victory. It is impossible to lead the masses towards insurrection without preparing for the conquest of power."

Anarchists see in the degeneration of the Soviet Union into a totalitarian dictatorship proof that Bakunin was right. In reality, only Leon Trotsky and Marxism have been able to explain the causes of that degeneration, finding its roots not in men's heads or personalities, but in the real life conditions of civil war, armies of foreign intervention, and the defeat of revolution in Europe. The position of anarchism only serves to endorse the bourgeois slander that Stalinism was inherent in Bolshevism.

In its early days, this modern anarchism found a certain support among the workers. However, through the course of struggle, workers learned the need for organisation in the shape of the trade unions, and also for political organisation, which led to the building of the mass workers parties. Bakunin and co. denounced participation in parliament, or the fight for reforms, as a betrayal of the revolution; they "rejected all political action not having as its immediate and direct objective the triumph of the workers over capitalism, and as a consequence, the abolition of the state."

Marxism fights for the conquest of political power by the working class and the building of a socialist society, under which the state will wither away. Until then should workers refrain from political activity? Should they reject all reforms that might improve their existence? Nothing would please Blair or the bosses more. Of course not; we must advocate the struggle for every gain, no matter how minor, and use any and every field open to us. Only the dilettante can reject better wages or a health care system. Precisely through these struggles, and the struggles to transform the workers organisations, the unions and the parties, we learn and become more powerful and bring closer the day when it will be possible to transform society for good.

Reforms under capitalism

Marxists fight for every reform, while at the same time explaining that while capitalism continues none of these advances are safe. Only socialism can really solve the problems of society.

Our modern day anarchists, Reclaim the Streets and others, have no support in Britain amongst the organised workers. Some radicalised youth, however, are attracted to their "direct action" stance. There is a vacuum left by the absence of a mass Labour youth organisation which, fighting for a socialist programme, could attract these young workers and students. With no lead being given by the tops of the unions, and Labour in government attacking young people, that vacuum can be temporarily and partly filled by groups like Reclaim the Streets.

What action do they propose though? In their press statement (2/5/00) they explain, "We were not protesting. Under the shadow of an irrelevant parliament we were planting the seeds of a society where ordinary people are in control of their land, their resources, their food and their decision making. The garden symbolized an urge to be self-reliant rather than dependent on capitalism."

The fact that parliament appears powerless to prevent job losses or the destruction of the environment only demonstrates that it serves the interests of capitalism. However, under pressure from below, it is possible to introduce reforms through parliament that are in the interests of ordinary people. It is no use declaring parliament to be irrelevant, and turning your back on it when the majority do not agree, and still look to government to make their lives better. This is the mirror image of the sects' attitude to the Labour Party. Any and every avenue which can be used to improve our lives must be used.

"Self-reliance"

In any case this "self-reliance" is no alternative. Self-reliance won't get electricity into your house, educate your children, or treat you when you are ill. We have the resources to cater for all of society's needs; the only problem is that we do not own them. Individualism (self-reliance) cannot be an alternative to socialism, where all the resources of society are at all of our disposal, and equally we all contribute what we can to society.

Guerrilla gardening, and its related varieties that have sprung up in various places, is nothing more than an offshoot of the old utopian idea of changing society by example. The roots of this scheme lie in idealist philosophy. Philosophical idealism refers to the notion that people's actions are a consequence of their thoughts, that ideas and not our conditions of life determine our outlook. When, through a long process of accumulation, we change people's minds, then they will live differently, capitalism will simply be redundant. The capitalist class themselves will presumably sit idly by and watch their system fall apart.

While believing in a revolutionary struggle to overthrow capitalism, anarchists argue that it must be replaced by...nothing. Yet with no central apparatus, no organisation, how would the trains run on time, how could organ transplants be organised, how could the world's resources be channeled into permanently overcoming famine?

In their paper, *Maybe*, Reclaim the Streets tell us, "The radical social movements that are increasingly coming together don't want to seize power but to dissolve it. They are dreaming up many autonomous alternative forms of social organisation, forms that are directly linked to the specific needs of locality. What might be an alternative to capitalism for people living currently in a housing estate in Croydon is completely different to what might be suitable for the inhabitants of the slums of Delhi."

It cannot be of no concern to us what form a new society will take in different countries or even different regions. The economic power we have created over centuries can and must be used in a planned, rational way to eradicate hunger, disease and illiteracy. It must be used in the interests of the whole of society. That can only be achieved by the democratic planning of society, where the power at our fingertips could be used with due respect for the future of the planet, the conservation of its resources, our own working conditions, and living standards. Whether we like it or not, growing a few carrots on empty plots of land will not eradicate hunger and famine.

We have the power to do just that, but only if we combine new technology, industry and the talents and active participation of millions.

The economic power we have created can be compared to the destructive force of lightning, untamed and anarchic under the market, yet, organised into cables and wires, electricity transforms our lives. Industry is not the enemy, nor are machines. The state is, but it is a symptom, not the disease. It is capitalism and its ownership of the economy, its stewardship of society that we have to replace.

The task of our time is to combine the strength and experience of the working class and its mighty organisations with the power and energy of the youth internationally, on the basis of a clear understanding of what capitalism is, what the state is, and a programme for changing society. That requires a combination of theory and action. In that combination lies the strength of Marxism.

If you want to fight against capitalism, do so fully armed with a socialist programme and perspective. Join with us in the struggle for the socialist transformation of the planet.

4th May 2000

Section Three

Anarcho-Syndicalism

A Necessary Discussion with Our Syndicalist Comrades

Leon Trotsky

[This article was written in reply to Comrade Louzon, just after the Fourth World Congress of the Communist International. At that time, more attention was being devoted to the struggle against the socialist right, against the last batch of dissidents, Verfeuil, Frossard, etc. In this struggle our efforts were, and remain, united with the efforts of the syndicalists, and I preferred to postpone the publication of this article. We are firmly convinced that our excellent understanding with the revolutionary syndicalists will never die. It was a great day for us when our old friend Monatte entered the Communist Party. The revolution needs people of this kind. But it would be wrong to pay for this rapprochement *with a confusion of ideas. In recent months, the Communist Party of France has been purified and consolidated; hence we can enter into a tranquil and friendly discussion with our syndicalist comrades, alongside whom we will have much work to do and many battles to fight. - Note by Trotsky]*

In a series of articles and personal explanations, Comrade Louzon put forward views on the fundamental question of the relations between party and trade union which differ radically from the opinions of the Communist International and from Marxism. French comrades whose opinion I am accustomed to respect, speak with great esteem of Comrade Louzon and his devotion to the proletariat. It is all the more necessary, therefore, to correct the errors made by him in such an important question. Comrade Louzon defends the complete and unqualified independence of the trade unions. Against what? Obviously against certain attacks. Whose? Against attacks ascribed to the party. Trade union autonomy, an indisputable necessity, is endowed with a certain absolute and almost mystical significance by Louzon. And our comrade here appeals, quite wrongly, to Marx.

The trade unions, says Louzon, represent the "working class as a whole." The party, however, is only a party. The working class as a whole cannot be subordinated to the party. There is not even room for equality between them.

"The working class has its aim in itself" The party, however, can only either serve the working class or be subordinated to it. Thus the party cannot "annex" the working class. The mutual representation of the Communist International and the Red International of Labour Unions, which existed until the last Moscow congresses, signify, according to Louzon, the actual equalisation of party and class. This mutual representation has now been abolished. The party thereby resumes its role of servant again. Comrade Louzon approves of this. According to him, this was also the standpoint of Marx. The end of the mutual representation of the political and trade union internationals in each other is, to Louzon, the rejection of the errors of Lassalle (!) and of the Social Democrats (!) and a return to the principles of Marxism.

This is the essence of an article which appeared in *La Vie Ouvrière* of 15th December. The most astonishing thing in this and other similar articles is that the writer is obviously, consciously and determinedly, shutting his eyes to what is actually going on in France. One might think that the article had been written from the star Sirius. How else is it possible to understand the assertion that the trade unions represent the "working class as a whole"? Of what country is Louzon talking? If he means France, the trade unions there, so far as we are informed, do not unfortunately, include even half of the working class. The criminal maneuvers of the reformist trade unionists, supported on the left by some few anarchists, have split the French trade union organisation. Neither of the two trade union confederations embraces more than 300,000 workers. Neither singly nor together are they entitled to identify themselves with the whole of the French proletariat of which they form only a modest part. Moreover, each trade union organisation pursues a different policy. The reformist trade union confederation [Confédération Générale du Travail (CGT)] works in cooperation with the bourgeoisie; the Unitary General Confederation of Labour [Confédération Générale du Travail Unitaire (CGTU)] is, fortunately, revolutionary. In the latter organisation, Louzon represents but one tendency. What then does he mean by the assertion that the working class, which he obviously regards as synonymous with the trade union organisation, bears its own aim in itself? With whose help, and how, does the French working class express this aim? With the help of Jouhaux's organisation? Certainly not. With the help of the CGTU? The CGTU has already rendered great services. But unfortunately it is not yet the whole working class. Finally, to mention everything, it was not so long ago that the CGTU was led by the anarcho-syndicalists of the "Pact." At the present time its leaders are syndicalist communists. In which of these two periods has the CGTU best represented the interests of the working class? Who is to judge? If we now attempt, with the aid of the international experience of our party, to answer this question, then, in Louzon's opinion, we commit a mortal sin, for we then demand that the party judge what policy is most beneficial to the working class. That is, we place the party above the working class. But if we were to turn to the working class as a whole, we would unfortunately find it divided, impotent, and mute. The different parts of the class organised into different confederations, even different trade unions in the same confederation, and even different groups in the same trade union, would all give us different replies. But the overwhelming majority of the proletariat, standing outside both trade union confederations, would, at the present time, give us no reply at all.

There is no country in which the trade union organisation embraces the whole working class. But in some countries it at least comprises a very large section of the workers. This is, however, not the case in France. If, as Louzon believes, the party must not "annex" the working class (what is this term actually supposed to mean?), then for what reason does Comrade Louzon accord this right to syndicalism? He may reply: "Our trade union organisation is still weak. But we do not doubt its future and its final victory." To this we should reply: "Certainly; we too share this conviction. But we have just as little doubt that the party too will win the unqualified confidence of the great majority of the working class." Neither for the party nor for the trade unions is it a question of "annexing' the proletariat—it is wrong for Louzon to employ the terminology customarily used by our opponents in their fight against the revolution—it is a question of winning the confidence of the working class. And it is only possible to do this with correct tactics, tested by experience. Where and by whom are these tactics consciously, carefully, and critically prepared? Who suggests them to the working class? Certainly they do not fall from heaven. And the working class as a whole, as a "thing in itself," does not teach us these tactics either. It seems to us that Comrade Louzon has not faced this question.

"The proletariat has its aim within itself." If we strip this sentence of its mystical trappings, its obvious meaning is that the historical tasks of the proletariat are determined by its social position as a class and by its role in production, in society, and in the state. This is beyond dispute. But this truth does not help us answer the question with which we are concerned, namely: how is the proletariat to arrive at subjective insight into the historical task posed by its objective position? Were the proletariat as a whole capable of grasping its historical task immediately, it would need neither party nor trade union. Revolution would be born simultaneously with the proletariat. But in actuality the process by which the proletariat gains an insight into its historic mission is very long and painful, and full of internal contradictions.

It is only in the course of long struggles, severe trials, many vacillations, and extensive experience, that insight as to the right ways and methods dawns upon the minds of the best elements of the working class, the vanguard of the masses. This applies equally to party and trade union. The trade union also begins as a small group of active workers and grows gradually as its experience enables it to gain the confidence of the masses. But while the revolutionary organisations are struggling to gain influence in the working class, the bourgeois ideologists counterpose the "working class as a whole" not only against the party of the working class but against its trade unions, which these ideologists accuse of wanting to "annex" the working class. *Le Temps* writes this whenever there is a strike. In other words, the bourgeois ideologists counterpose the working class as object to the working class as conscious subject. For it is only through its class-conscious minority that the working class gradually becomes a factor in history. We thus see that the criticism leveled by Comrade Louzon against the "unwarranted claims" of the party applies equally well to the "unwarranted claims" of the trade unions. Above all in France, for French syndicalism—we must repeat this—was and is, in its organisation and theory, likewise a party. This is also why it arrived, during its classic period (1905–7), at the theory of the "active minority," and not at the theory of the "collective proletariat." For what else is an active minority, held together by the unity of their ideas, if not a party? And on the other hand, would not a trade union mass organisation, not containing a class-conscious active minority, be a purely formal and meaningless organisation?

The fact that French syndicalism was a party was fully confirmed by the split which took place as soon as divergences in political viewpoints appeared in its ranks. But the party of revolutionary syndicalism fears the aversion felt by the French working class for parties as such. Therefore it has not assumed the name of party and has remained incomplete as regards organisation. It is a party that attempted to have its members blend into the trade union membership, or at least take cover behind the trade unions. The actual subordination of the trade unions to certain tendencies, factions, and even cliques of syndicalism is thus explained. This is also the explanation of the "Pact," which is a Masonic caricature of a party within the bosom of the trade union organisation. And vice versa: the Communist International has most determinedly combated the split in the trade union movement in France, that is, its actual conversion into syndicalist parties. The main consideration of the Communist International has been the historical task of the working class as a whole, and the enormous independent significance of the trade union organisation for solving the tasks of the proletariat. In this respect the Communist International has from its very inception defended the real and living independence of the trade unions, in the spirit of Marxism.

Revolutionary syndicalism, which was in France in many respects the precursor of present-day communism, has acknowledged the theory of the active minority, that is, of the party, but without openly becoming a party. It has thereby prevented the trade unions from becoming if not an organisation of the whole working class (which is not possible in a capitalist system), at least of its broad masses. The Communists are not afraid of the word "party," for their party has nothing in common, and will have nothing in common, with the other parties. Their party is not one of the political parties of the bourgeois system; it is the active, class-conscious minority of the proletariat, its revolutionary vanguard. Hence the Communists have no reason, either in their ideology or their organisation, to hide themselves behind the trade unions. They do not misuse the trade unions for machinations behind the scenes. They do not split the trade unions when they are a minority in them. They do not in any way disturb the independent development of the trade unions, and they support trade union struggles with all their strength. But at the same time the Communist Party reserves the right of expressing its opinion on all questions in the working-class movement including the trade union question, to criticise trade union tactics, and to make definite proposals to the trade unions, which, on their part are at liberty to accept or reject these proposals. The party strives to win the confidence of the working class, above all, of that section organised in the trade unions.

What is the meaning of the quotations from Marx adduced by Comrade Louzon? It is a fact that Marx wrote in 1868 that the workers' party would emerge from the trade union. When writing this he was thinking mainly of Britain, at that time the sole developed capitalist country already possessing extensive labour organisations. Half a century has passed since then. Historical experience has in general confirmed Marx's prophecies insofar as Britain is concerned. The British Labour Party has actually been built up on the foundation of the trade unions. But does Comrade Louzon really think that the British Labour Party, as it is today, led by Henderson and Clynes, can be looked upon as representative of the interests of the proletariat as a whole? Most decidedly not. The Labour Party in Great Britain betrays the cause of the proletariat just as the trade union bureaucracy betrays it, although in Britain the trade unions come closer to comprising the working class as a whole than anywhere else. On the other hand, we cannot doubt but that our Communist influence will grow in this British Labour Party which emerged from the trade unions, and that this will contribute to render more acute the struggle between the masses and leaders within the trade unions until the treacherous bureaucrats are ultimately driven forth and the Labour Party is completely transformed and regenerated. And we, like Comrade Louzon, belong to an International which includes the little British Communist Party, but which combats the Second International supported by the British Labour Party that had its origin in the trade unions.

In Russia—and in the law of capitalist development Russia is just the antipode of Great Britain—the Communist Party, the former social-democratic party, is older than the trade unions, and created the trade unions. Today, the trade unions and the workers' state in Russia are completely under the influence of the Communist Party, which by no means had its origin in the trade unions but which, on the contrary, created and trained them. Will Comrade Louzon contend that Russia has evolved in contradiction to Marxism? Is it not simpler to say that Marx's judgment on the origin of the party in the trade union has been proved by experience to have been correct for Britain, and even there not 100 percent correct, but that Marx never had the least intention of laying down what he himself once scornfully designated as a "supra-historical law"? All the other countries of Europe, including France, stand between Great Britain and Russia on this question. In some countries the trade unions are older than the party, in others the contrary has been the case; but nowhere, except in Britain and partially in Belgium, has the party of the proletariat emerged from the trade unions. In any case, no Communist party has developed organically out of the trade unions. But are we to deduce from this that the entire Communist International is of illegitimate birth?

When the British trade unions alternately supported the Conservatives and the Liberals and represented to a certain extent a labour appendage to these parties, when the political organisation of the German workers was nothing more than a left wing of the democratic party, when the followers of Lassalle and Eisenach were quarrelling among themselves—Marx demanded the independence of the trade unions from all parties. This formula was dictated by the desire to counterpose the labour organisations to all bourgeois parties, and to prevent their being too closely bound up with socialist sects. But Comrade Louzon may perhaps remember that it was Marx who founded the First International as well, the object of which was to guide the labour movement in all countries, in every respect, and to render it fruitful. This was in 1864 and the International created by Marx was a party. Marx refused to wait until the international party of the working class formed itself in some way out of the trade unions. He did his utmost to strengthen, within the trade unions, the influence of the ideas of scientific socialism—ideas first expressed in 1847 in the Communist Manifesto. When Marx demanded for the trade unions complete independence from all existing parties and sects, that is, from all the bourgeois and petty-bourgeois parties and sects, he did this in order to make it easier for scientific socialism to gain dominance in the trade unions. Marx never saw in the party of scientific socialism one of the existing political parties (parliamentary, democratic, etc.). For Marx the International was the class-conscious working class, represented at that time by a still very small vanguard.

If Comrade Louzon were consistent in his trade union metaphysic and in his interpretation of Marx, he would say, "Let us renounce the Communist Party and wait till this party arises out of the trade unions." That kind of logic would be fatal, not only for the party but for the union. Actually, the present French trade unions can only regain their unity and win decisive influence over the masses if their best elements are constituted in the class-conscious revolutionary vanguard of the proletariat, that is, in a Communist Party. Marx gave no final answer to the question of the relations between party and trade unions, and indeed he could not do so. For these relations are dependent on the varying circumstances in each separate case. Whether the party and the trade union confederation are mutually represented on their central committees, or whether they form joint committees of action as needed, is a question of no decisive importance. The forms of organisation may alter, but the fundamental role of the party remains constant. The party, if it be worthy of the name, includes the whole vanguard of the working class and uses its ideological influence for rendering every branch of the labour movement fruitful, especially the trade union movement. But if the trade unions are worthy of their name, they include an ever growing mass of workers, many backward elements among them. But they can only fulfill their task when consciously guided on firmly established principles. And they can only have this leadership when their best elements are united in the party of proletarian revolution.

The recent purification of the Communist Party of France, which rid itself on the one hand of whining petty-bourgeois, of drawing-room heroes, of political Hamlets and sickening careerists, and on the other hand actuated the rapprochement of Communists and revolutionary syndicalists, implies a great stride towards the creation of suitable relations between trade union organisations and the political organisation, which in turn means a great advance for the revolution.

23rd March 1923

The Anarcho-Syndicalist Prejudices Again!

Leon Trotsky

Comrade Louzon's latest article contains even more errors than his earlier articles, though this time his main line of argument takes an entirely different turn.

In his earlier articles, Comrade Louzon's starting points were abstractions which assumed that the trade unions represented the "working class as a whole!" In my reply I put the question: "Where does Comrade Louzon write his articles—in France or on Sirius?" In his latest article Comrade Louzon deserts the shaky foundation of universal laws and attempts to stand upon the national ground of French syndicalism. Yes, he says, the French trade unions are not actually the working class as a whole, but only the active minority of the working class. That is, Comrade Louzon acknowledges that the trade unions form a sort of revolutionary party. But this syndicalist party is distinguished by being purely proletarian in its constituents; here lies its tremendous advantage over the Communist Party. And it has still another advantage: the syndicalist party categorically rejects the bourgeois state institutions; it does not "recognise" democracy, and thus takes no part in the parliamentary struggles.

Comrade Louzon never tires of repeating that we are dealing with the peculiarities of French development and with these only. Beginning with a broad generalisation, in the course of which he transformed Marx into a syndicalist, Louzon now sets Britain, Russia, and Germany apart. He does not reply to our question on why he himself belongs to the Communist International, in company with the small British Communist Party, and not to the Second International, in company with the British trade unions and the British Labour Party which is supported by them. Louzon began with a supra-historical law for all countries, and closes by claiming an exceptional law for France. In this new form Louzon's theory bears a purely national character. More than this, its essential character excludes the possibility of an International: How can common tactics be spoken of unless there are common fundamental premises? It is certainly very difficult to understand why Comrade Louzon belongs to the Communist International. It is no less difficult to understand why he belongs to the French Communist Party, since there exists another party possessing all the advantages of the Communist and none of its drawbacks.

But though Comrade Louzon leaves international ground for the sake of national, he systematically ignores that "national" question put to him in our former article: What about the role played by the CGT during the war? The role played by Jouhaux was by no means less treacherous and despicable than that played by Renaudel. The sole difference consisted in the fact that the social patriotic party arranged its views and actions in accordance with a certain system, while the trade union patriots acted purely empirically and veiled their actions in wretched and stupid improvisations. It may be said that as regards patriotic betrayal, the Socialist Party, with its definite character, surpassed the semi-definite syndicalist party. At bottom, Jouhaux was at one with Renaudel.

And how is it today? Does Louzon desire the union of the two confederations? We desire it. The International deems it necessary. We should not be alarmed even if the union were to give Jouhaux the majority. Naturally we would not say—as does Comrade Louzon —that syndicalism, although headed by Jouhaux, Dumoulin, Merrheim and their like, is the purest form of proletarian organisation, that it embodies "the working class as a whole," etc., etc.—for such a phrase would be a travesty of the facts. But we should consider the formation of a larger trade union organisation, that is, the concentration of greater proletarian masses, forming a wider battlefield for the struggle for the ideas and tactics of communism, to be a greater gain for the cause of revolution. But for this the first necessity is that the ideas and tactics of communism do not remain in midair, but are organised in the form of a party. With regard to Comrade Louzon, he does not pursue his thoughts to the end, but his logical conclusion would be the substitution of the party by a trade union organisation of the "active minority." The inevitable result of this would be a substitute party and substitute trade union, for those trade unions required by Comrade Louzon are too indefinite for the role of a party, and too small for the role of a trade union.

Comrade Louzon's arguments to the effect that the trade unions do not want to soil their fingers by contact with the organs of bourgeois democracy, already form a weak echo of anarchism. It may be assumed that the majority of the workers organised in the CGTU will vote at the elections for the Communist Party (at least we hope that Comrade Louzon, as a member of the Communist Party, will call upon them to do so), while the majority of the members of the yellow confederation will vote for the Blum-Renaudel party. The trade union, as a form of organisation, is not adapted for parliamentary struggle, but the workers organised in the trade unions will nevertheless have their deputies. It is simply a case of division of labour on the same class foundation. Or is it perchance a matter of indifference to the French worker what happens in parliament? The workers do not think so. The trade unions have frequently reacted to the legislative work of parliament and will continue to do so in the future. And if there are, at the same time, Communist deputies in parliament itself, who work hand in hand with the revolutionary trade unions against the deeds of violence and blows of imperialist "democracy," this is naturally a plus and not a minus. French "tradition" says that deputies are traitors. But the Communist Party has been called into being for the express purpose of doing away with all tradition. Should any deputy think of retreating from the class line, he will be thrown out of the party. Our French party has learned how to do this, and all distrust in it is completely unfounded.

But Louzon complains that the party contains many petty-bourgeois intellectuals. This is so. But the Fourth Congress of the Communist International recognised and adopted resolutions on this, and the resolutions have not been without effect. Further work is required to establish the proletarian character of the party. But we shall not attain this end with the self-contradictory trade union metaphysics of Comrade Louzon, but rather by means of systematic party work in the sphere of the trade unions, and in every other sphere of proletarian struggle. There is already a considerable number of workers in the Central Committee of our French party. This is mirrored in the whole party. The same tendency is at work, in accordance with the resolutions passed by the Fourth Congress, in the parliamentary and municipal elections. By this the party will win the confidence of the revolutionary proletariat. And this means that the party will less and less lack really competent and active proletarians to occupy the most important and responsible revolutionary posts. I greatly fear that Comrade Louzon's views may exercise a retarding influence on this profound progressive evolution of the vanguard of the French working class. But I have no doubt that Communism will succeed in overcoming this obstacle, like all others.

Moscow, 8th May 1923

Communism and Syndicalism

Leon Trotsky

The trade union question is one of the most important for the labour movement and, consequently, for the Opposition. Without a precise position on the trade union question, the Opposition will be unable to win real influence in the working class. That is why I believe it necessary to submit here, for discussion, a few considerations on the trade union question.

1. The Communist Party is the fundamental weapon of revolutionary action of the proletariat, the combat organisation of its vanguard, that must raise itself to the role of leader of the working class in all the spheres of its struggle without exception, and consequently, in the trade union field.

2. Those who, in principle, counterpose trade union autonomy to the leadership of the Communist Party, counterpose thereby—whether they want to or not—the most backward proletarian section to the vanguard of the working class, the struggle for immediate demands to the struggle for the complete liberation of the workers, reformism to communism, opportunism to revolutionary Marxism.

3. Prewar French syndicalism, at the epoch of its rise and expansion, by fighting for trade union autonomy actually fought for its independence from the bourgeois government and its parties, among them that of reformist-parliamentary socialism. This was a struggle against opportunism—for a revolutionary road.

Revolutionary syndicalism did not, in this connection, make a fetish of the autonomy of the mass organisations. On the contrary, it understood and preached the leading role of the revolutionary minority in relation to the mass organisations, which reflect the working class with all its contradictions, its backwardness, and its weaknesses.

4. The theory of the active minority was, in essence, an incomplete theory of a proletarian party. In all its practice, revolutionary syndicalism was an embryo of a revolutionary party as against opportunism, that is, it was a remarkable draft outline of revolutionary communism.

5. The weakness of anarcho-syndicalism, even in its classic period, was the absence of a correct theoretical foundation, and, as a result, a wrong understanding of the nature of the state and its role in the class struggle; an incomplete, not fully developed and, consequently, a wrong conception of the role of the revolutionary minority, that is, the party. Thence the mistakes in tactics, such as the fetishism of the general strike, the ignoring of the connection between the uprising and the seizure of power, etc.

6. After the war, French syndicalism found not only its refutation but also its development and its completion in communism. Attempts to revive revolutionary syndicalism now would be to try and turn back history. For the labour movement, such attempts can have only reactionary significance.

7. The epigones of syndicalism transform (in words) the independence of the trade union organisation from the bourgeoisie and the reformist socialists into *independence in general*, into *absolute* independence from all parties, the Communist included.

If, in the period of expansion, syndicalism considered itself a vanguard and fought for the leading role of the vanguard minority among the backward masses, the epigones of syndicalism now fight against the identical wishes of the Communist vanguard, attempting, even though without success, to base themselves upon the lack of development and the prejudices of the more backward sections of the working class.

8. Independence from the influence of the bourgeoisie cannot be a passive state. It can express itself only by political acts, that is, by the struggle against the bourgeoisie. This struggle must be inspired by a distinct programme which requires organisation and tactics for its application. It is the union of programme, organisation, and tactics that constitutes the party. In this way, the real independence of the proletariat from the bourgeois government cannot be realised unless the proletariat conducts its struggle under the leadership of a revolutionary and not an opportunist party.

9. The epigones of syndicalism would have one believe that the trade unions are sufficient by themselves. Theoretically, this means nothing, but in practice it means the dissolution of the revolutionary vanguard into the backward masses, that is, the trade unions.

The larger the mass the trade unions embrace, the better they are able to fulfill their mission. A proletarian party, on the contrary, merits its name only if it is ideologically homogeneous, bound by unity of action and organisation. To represent the trade unions as self-sufficient because the proletariat has already attained its "majority," is to flatter the proletariat, is to picture it other than it is and can be under capitalism, which keeps enormous masses of workers in ignorance and backwardness, leaving only the vanguard of the proletariat the possibility of breaking through all the difficulties and arriving at a clear comprehension of the tasks of its class as a whole.

10. The real, practical and not the metaphysical autonomy of trade union organisation is not in the least disturbed nor is it diminished by the struggle of the Communist Party for influence. Every member of the trade union has the right to vote as he thinks necessary and to elect the one who seems to him most worthy. Communists possess this right in the same way as others.

The conquest of the majority by the Communists in the directing organs takes place quite in accordance with the principles of autonomy, that is, the self-administration of the trade unions. On the other hand, no trade union statute can prevent or prohibit the party from electing the general secretary of the Confederation of Labour to its central committee, for here we are entirely in the domain of the autonomy of the party.

11. In the trade unions, the Communists, of course, submit to the discipline of the party, no matter what posts they occupy. This does not exclude but presupposes their submission to trade union discipline. In other words, the party does not impose upon them any line of conduct that contradicts the state of mind or the opinions of the majority of the members of trade unions. In entirely exceptional cases, when the party considers impossible the submission of its members to some reactionary decision of the trade union, it points out openly to its members the consequences that flow from it, that is, removals from the trade union posts, expulsions, and so forth.

With juridical formulas in these questions—and autonomy is a purely juridical formula—one can get nowhere. The question must be posed in its essence, that is, on the plane of trade union policy. A correct policy must be counterposed to a wrong policy.

12. The character of the party's leadership, its methods and its forms, can differ profoundly in accordance with the general conditions of a given country or with the period of its development.

In capitalist countries, where the Communist Party does not possess any means of coercion, it is obvious that it can give leadership only by Communists being in the trade unions as rank-and-file members or functionaries. The number of Communists in leading posts of the trade unions is only one of the means of measuring the role of the party in the trade unions. The most important measurement is the percentage of rank-and-file Communists in relation to the whole unionized mass. But the principal criterion is the general influence of the party on the working class, which is measured by the circulation of the Communist press, the attendance at meetings of the party, the number of votes at elections and, what is especially important, the number of working men and women who respond actively to the party's appeals to struggle.

13. It is clear that the influence of the Communist Party in general, including the trade unions, will grow, the more revolutionary the situation becomes.

These conditions permit an appreciation of the degree and the form of the true, real, and not the metaphysical autonomy of the trade unions. In times of "peace," when the most militant forms of trade union action are isolated economic strikes, the direct role of the party in trade union action falls back to second place. As a general rule, the party does not make a decision on every isolated strike. It helps the trade union to decide the question of knowing if the strike is opportune, by means of its political and economic information and by its advice. It *serves* the strike with its agitation, etc. First place in the strike belongs, of course to the trade union.

The situation changes radically when the movement rises to the general strike and still more to the direct struggle for power. In these conditions, the leading role of the party becomes entirely direct, open, and immediate. The trade unions—naturally not those that pass over to the other side of the barricades—become the organisational apparatus of the party which, in the presence of the whole class, stands forth as the leader of the revolution, bearing the full responsibility.

In the field extending between the partial economic strike and the revolutionary class insurrection are placed all the possible forms of reciprocal relations between the party and the trade unions, the varying degrees of direct and immediate leadership, etc. But under all conditions, the party seeks to win general leadership by relying upon the real autonomy of the trade unions which, as organisations—it goes without saying—are not "submitted" to it.

14. Facts show that politically "independent" unions do not exist anywhere. There never have been any. Experience and theory say that there never will be any. In the United States, the trade unions are directly bound by their apparatus to the general staffs of industry and the bourgeois parties. In Britain the trade unions, which in the past mainly supported the Liberals, now constitute the material basis of the Labour Party. In Germany, the trade unions march under the banner of the Social Democracy. In the Soviet republic, their leadership belongs to the Bolsheviks. In France, one of the trade union organisations follows the Socialists, the other the Communists. In Finland, the trade unions were divided only a little while ago, one going towards the social democracy, the other towards communism. That is how it is everywhere.

The theoreticians of the "independence" of the trade union movement have not taken the trouble up to now to think of this question: why their slogan not only does not approach its realisation in practice anywhere, but why, on the contrary, the dependence of the trade unions upon the leadership of a party becomes everywhere, without exception, more and more evident and open. Yet, this corresponds entirely to the character of the imperialist epoch, which bares all class relations and which, even within the proletariat, accentuates the contradictions between its aristocracy and its most exploited sections.

15. The consummate expression of outdated syndicalism is the so-called Syndicalist League. By all its traits, it comes forward as a political organisation which seeks to subordinate the trade union movement to its influence. In fact the League recruits its members not in accordance with the trade union principle, but in accordance with the principle of political groupings; it has its platform, if not its programme, and it defends it in its publications; it has its own internal discipline within the trade union movement. In the congresses of the confederations, its partisans act as a political faction in the same way as the Communist faction. If we are not to lose ourselves in words, the tendency of the Syndicalist League reduces itself to a struggle to liberate the two confederations from the leadership of the Socialists and Communists and to unite them under the direction of the Monatte group.

The League does not act openly in the name of the right and the necessity for the advanced minority to fight to extend its influence over the most backward masses; it presents itself masked by what it calls trade union "independence." From this point of view, the League approaches the [practice of the] Socialist Party, which also realises its leadership under cover of the phrase "independence of the trade union movement." The Communist Party, on the contrary, says openly to the working class: Here is my programme, my tactics and my policy, which I propose to the trade unions.

The proletariat must never believe anything blindly. It must judge by its work. But the workers should have a double and triple distrust toward those pretenders to leadership who act incognito, under a mask, who make the proletariat believe that it has no need of leadership in general.

16. The right of a political party to fight to win the trade unions to its influence must not be denied, but this question must be posed: In the name of what programme and what tactics is this organisation fighting? From this point of view, the Syndicalist League does not give the necessary guarantees. Its programme is extremely amorphous, as are its tactics. In its political evaluations it acts only from event to event. Acknowledging the proletarian revolution and even the dictatorship of the proletariat, it ignores the party and fights against Communist leadership, without which the proletarian revolution would always risk remaining an empty phrase.

17. The ideology of trade union independence has nothing in common with the ideas and sentiments of the proletariat as a class. If the party, by its direction, is capable of assuring a correct, clear-sighted, and firm policy in the

trade unions, not a single worker will have the idea of rebelling against the leadership of the party. The historical experience of the Bolsheviks has proved that.

This also holds good for France, where the Communists received 1,200,000 votes in the elections while the *Confédération Générale du Travail Unitaire* (the central organisation of the Red trade unions) has only a fourth or a third of this number. It is clear that the abstract slogan of independence can under no condition come from the masses. Trade union bureaucracy is quite another thing. It not only sees professional competition in the party bureaucracy, but it even tends to make itself independent of control by the vanguard of the proletariat. The slogan of independence is, by its very basis, a bureaucratic and not a class slogan.

18. After the fetish of "independence" the Syndicalist League also transforms the question of *trade union unity* into a fetish.

It goes without saying that the maintenance of the unity of the trade union organisations has enormous advantages, from the point of view of the daily tasks of the proletariat as well as from the point of view of the struggle of the Communist Party to extend its influence over the masses. But the facts prove that since the first successes of the revolutionary wing in the trade unions, the opportunists have set themselves deliberately on the road of split. Peaceful relations with the bourgeoisie are dearer to them than the unity of the proletariat. That is the indubitable summary of the post-war experiences.

We Communists are in every way interested in proving to the workers that the responsibility for the splitting of the trade union organisations falls wholly upon the Social Democracy. But it does not at all follow that the hollow formula of unity is more important for us than the revolutionary tasks of the working class.

19. Eight years have passed since the trade union split in France. During this time, the two organisations linked themselves definitely with the two mortally hostile political parties. Under these conditions, to think of being able to unify the trade union movement by the simple preaching of unity would be to nurture illusions. To declare that without the preliminary unification of the two trade union organisations not only the proletarian revolution but even a serious class struggle is impossible, means to make the future of the revolution depend upon the corrupted clique of trade union reformists.

In fact, the future of the revolution depends not upon the fusion of the two trade union apparatuses, but upon the unification of the majority of the working class around revolutionary slogans and revolutionary methods of struggle. At present the unification of the working class is only possible by fighting against the class collaborationists (coalitionists) who are found not only in political parties but also in the trade unions.

20. The real road to the revolutionary unity of the proletariat lies in the development, the correction, the enlargement, and the consolidation of the revolutionary CGTU and in the weakening of the reformist CGT.

It is not excluded but, on the contrary, very likely that at the time of its revolution, the French proletariat will enter the struggle with two confederations: behind one will be found the masses and behind the other, the aristocracy of labour and the bureaucracy.

21. The new trade union opposition obviously does not want to enter on the road of syndicalism. At the same time, it breaks with the party—not with a certain leadership, but with the party in general. This means quite simply that ideologically it definitely disarms itself and falls back to the positions of craft or trade unionism.

22. The trade union opposition as a whole is very variegated. But it is characterised by some common features which do not bring it closer to the Left Communist Opposition but, on the contrary, alienate it and oppose it.

The trade union opposition does not fight against the thoughtless acts and wrong methods of the Communist leadership, but against the influence of Communism over the working class.

The trade union opposition does not fight against the ultra-leftist evaluation of the given situation and the tempo of its development but acts, in reality, counter to revolutionary perspectives in general.

The trade union opposition does not fight against caricatured methods of anti-militarism but puts forward a pacifist orientation. In other words, the trade union opposition is manifestly developing in the reformist spirit.

23. It is entirely wrong to affirm that in these recent years—contrary to what has happened in Germany, Czechoslovakia, and other countries—there has not been constituted in France a right-wing grouping in the revolutionary camp. The main point is that, forsaking the revolutionary policy of Communism, the Right Opposition in France, in conformity with the traditions of the French labour movement, has assumed a trade union character, concealing in this way its political physiognomy. At bottom, the majority of the trade union opposition represents the right wing, just as the Brandler group in Germany, the Czech trade unionists who, after the split, have taken a clearly reformist position, etc.

24. One may seek to object that all the preceding considerations would be correct only on condition that the Communist Party has a correct policy. But this objection is unfounded. The question of the relationships between the party, which represents the proletariat as it should be, and the trade unions, which represent the proletariat as it is, is the most fundamental question of revolutionary Marxism. It would be veritable suicide to spurn the only possible principled reply to this question solely because the Communist

Party, under the influence of objective and subjective reasons of which we have spoken more than once, is now conducting a false policy towards the trade unions, as well as in other fields. A correct policy must be counterposed to a wrong policy. Towards this end, the Left Opposition has been constituted as a faction. If it is considered that the French Communist Party in its entirety is in a wholly irremediable or hopeless state—which we absolutely do not think—another party must be counterposed to it. But the question of the relation of the party to the class does not change one iota by this fact.

The Left Opposition considers that to influence the trade union movement, to help it find its correct orientation, to permeate it with correct slogans, is impossible except through the Communist Party (or a faction for the moment) which, besides its other attributes, is the central ideological laboratory of the working class.

25. The correctly understood task of the Communist Party does not consist solely of gaining influence over the trade unions, such as they are, but in winning, through the trade unions, an influence over the majority of the working class. This is possible only if the methods employed by the party in the trade unions correspond to the nature and the tasks of the latter. The struggle for influence of the party in the trade unions finds its objective verification in the fact that they do or do not thrive, and in the fact that the number of their members increases, as well as in their relations with the broadest masses. If the party buys its influence in the trade unions only at the price of a narrowing down and a factionalizing of the latter—converting them into auxiliaries of the party for momentary aims and preventing them from becoming genuine mass organisations—the relations between the party and the class are wrong. It is not necessary for us to dwell here on the causes for such a situation. We have done it more than once and we do it every day. The changeability of the official Communist policy reflects its adventurist tendency to make itself master of the working class in the briefest time, by means of stage-play, inventions, superficial agitation, etc.

The way out of this situation does not, however, lie in counterposing the trade unions to the party (or to the faction) but in the irreconcilable struggle to change the whole policy of the party as well as that of the trade unions.

26. The Left Opposition must place the questions of the trade union movement in indissoluble connection with the questions of the political struggle of the proletariat. It must give a concrete analysis of the present stage of development of the French labour movement. It must give an evaluation, quantitative as well as qualitative, of the present strike movement and its perspectives in relation to the perspectives of the economic development of France. It is needless to say that it completely rejects the perspective of capitalist stabilization and pacifism for decades. It proceeds from an

estimation of our epoch as a revolutionary one. It springs from the necessity of a timely preparation of the vanguard proletariat in face of the abrupt turns which are not only probable but inevitable. The firmer and more implacable is its action against the supposedly revolutionary ranting of the centrist bureaucracy, against political hysteria which does not take conditions into account which confuses today with yesterday or with tomorrow, the more firmly and resolutely must it set itself against the elements of the right that take up its criticism and conceal themselves under it in order to introduce their tendencies into revolutionary Marxism.

27. A new definition of boundaries? New polemics? New splits? That will be the lament of the good but tired souls who would like to transform the Opposition into a calm retreat where one can tranquilly rest from the great tasks, while preserving intact the name of revolutionist "of the left." No! we say to them, to these tired souls: we are certainly not travelling the same road. Truth has never yet been the sum of small errors. A revolutionary organisation has never yet been composed of small conservative groups, seeking primarily to distinguish themselves from each other. There are epochs when the revolutionary tendency is reduced to a small minority in the labour movement. But these epochs demand not arrangements between the small groups with mutual hiding of sins but on the contrary, a doubly implacable struggle for a correct perspective and an education of the cadres in the spirit of genuine Marxism. Victory is possible only in this way.

28. So far as the author of these lines is personally concerned, he must admit that the notion he had of the Monatte group when he was deported from the Soviet Union proved to be too optimistic and, by that fact false. For many years, the author did not have the possibility of following the activity of this group. He judged it from old memories. The divergences showed themselves in fact not only profounder but even more acute than one might have supposed. The events of recent times have proved beyond a doubt that without a clear and precise ideological demarcation from the line of syndicalism, the Communist Opposition in France will not go forward. The theses proposed represent by themselves the first step on the road of this demarcation, which is the prelude to the successful struggle against the revolutionary jabbering and the opportunist essence of Cachin, Monmousseau, and company.

14th October 1929

The Errors in Principle of Syndicalism

Leon Trotsky

To serve in the discussion with Monatte and his friends

W hen I arrived in France in October 1914, I found the French Socialist and trade union movement in a state of the deepest chauvinist demoralisation. In the search for revolutionaries, with candle in hand, I made the acquaintance of Monatte and Rosmer. They had not succumbed to chauvinism. It was thus that our friendship began. Monatte considered himself an anarcho-syndicalist; despite that, he was immeasurably closer to me than the French Guesdists, who were playing a pitiful and shameful role. At that time, the Cachins were making themselves familiar with the servants' entrance to the ministries of the Third Republic and the Allied embassies. In 1915, Monatte left the central committee of the CGT, slamming the door behind him. His departure from the trade union centre was in essence nothing but a split. At that time, however, Monatte believed—and rightly so—that the fundamental historical tasks of the proletariat stood above unity with chauvinists and lackeys of imperialism. It was in this that Monatte was loyal to the best traditions of revolutionary syndicalism.

Monatte was one of the first friends of the October Revolution. True, unlike Rosmer, he had held aloof for a long time. That was well in keeping with the character of Monatte, as I was later convinced, of standing aside, of waiting, of criticising. At times this is absolutely unavoidable. But as a basic line of conduct it becomes a kind of sectarianism that has a close affinity to Proudhonism, but nothing in common with Marxism.

When the Socialist Party of France became the Communist Party, I frequently had occasion to discuss with Lenin the onerous heritage the International had received in the person of leaders like Cachin, Frossard and other heroes of the League of the Rights of Man, of the Freemasons, of parliamentarians, careerists, and babblers. One of these conversations—if I am not mistaken I have already published it in the press—follows:

225

"It would be good," Lenin said to me, "to drive out all these weathercocks, and to draw into the party the revolutionary syndicalists, the militant workers, people who are really devoted to the cause of the working class. And Monatte?"

"Monatte would of course be ten times better than Cachin and those like him," I replied. "But Monatte not only continues to reject parliamentarism but to this day he has not grasped the significance of the party."

Lenin was astonished: "Impossible! Has not grasped the significance of the party after the October Revolution? That's a very disturbing symptom."

I carried on a correspondence with Monatte in which I invited him to Moscow. He was evasive. True to his nature, he preferred in this case, too, to stand aside and wait. And besides, the Communist Party did not suit him. In that he was right. But instead of helping to transform it, he waited. At the Fourth Congress we succeeded in taking the first step towards cleansing the Communist Party of France of Freemasons, pacifists, and office-seekers. Monatte entered the party. But it is not necessary to emphasise the fact that this did not mean to us that he had adopted the Marxian viewpoint; not at all. On 23rd March, 1923, I wrote in *Pravda*: "The entrance of our old friend Monatte into the Communist Party was a great day for us. The revolution needs men of this kind. But it would be wrong to pay for a *rapprochement* with a confusion of ideas." In this article, I criticised the scholasticism of Louzon on the relations among the class, the trade unions, and the party. In particular, I explained that prewar syndicalism had been an embryo of the Communist Party, that this embryo had since become a child, and that, if this child was suffering from measles and rickets, it was necessary to nourish and cure it, but that it would be absurd to imagine that it could be made to return to its mother's womb. I may perhaps be permitted to say in this regard that the arguments of my 1923 article, in caricature, serve to this day as the main weapons against Monatte in the hands of Monmousseau and other anti-Trotskyist warriors.

Monatte joined the party; but he hardly had time to turn about and accustom himself to a house far vaster than his little shop on the *Quai de Jemmapes* when the *coup d'état* in the International burst upon him: Lenin was taken ill; the campaign against "Trotskyism" and the Zinovievist "Bolshevization" began. Monatte could not submit to the careerists who, by leaning on the general staff of the epigones at Moscow and disposing of unlimited resources, carried on by means of intrigue and slander. Monatte was expelled from the party. This episode, important but still only an episode, was of decisive moment in the political development of Monatte. He decided that his brief experience in the party had fully confirmed his anarcho-syndicalist prejudices against the party in general. Monatte then began insistently to retrace his steps towards abandoned positions. He began to seek again the *Amiens Charter*. To do all that, he had to turn his face to the past. The experiences of the war, of the Russian Revolution, and of the world trade union movement were lost upon him, leaving hardly a trace. Once again Monatte stood aside and waited. What for? A new Amiens Congress. During the last few years I was unfortunately unable to follow the retrogressive evolution of Monatte: the Russian Opposition lived in a blockaded circle.

Out of the whole treasure of the theory and practice of the world struggle of the proletariat, Monatte has extracted but two ideas: *trade union autonomy* and *trade union unity*. He has elevated these two pure principles above sinful reality. It is on trade union autonomy and trade union unity that he has based his newspaper and his Syndicalist League. Unfortunately, these two ideas are hollow and each of them resembles the hole in a ring. Whether the ring be made of iron, silver or gold, Monatte does not care in the least. The ring, you see, always hampers the trade unions' activity. Monatte is interested only in the hole of autonomy.

No less empty is the other sacred principle: *unity*. In its name, Monatte even stood out against the rupture of the Anglo-Russian Committee, even though the General Council of the British trade unions had betrayed the general strike. The fact that Stalin, Bukharin, Cachin, Monmousseau and others supported the bloc with the strikebreakers until the latter kicked them out, does not in the least reduce Monatte's mistake. After my arrival abroad, I made an attempt to explain to the readers of the *Révolution prolétarienne* (magazine published in the 1930s) the criminal character of this bloc, the consequences of which are still being felt by the workers' movement. Monatte did not want to publish my article. And how could it have been otherwise, since I had made an assault upon the sacred trade union unity, which solves all questions and reconciles all contradictions?

When strikers encounter a group of strikebreakers in their path, they throw them out of their midst without sparing blows. If the strikebreakers are union men, they throw them out immediately, without worrying about the sacred principle of trade union unity. Monatte surely has no objections to this. But the matter is entirely different when it is a question of the trade union bureaucracy and its leaders. The General Council is not composed of starving and backward strikebreakers; no, they are well-fed and experienced traitors, who found it necessary at a given moment to stand at the head of the general strike in order to decapitate it all the more quickly and surely. They worked hand in hand with the government, the bosses, and the church. It would seem that the leaders of the Russian trade unions, who were in a political bloc with the General Council, should have immediately, openly, and relentlessly broken with it at that very moment, in full view of the masses deceived and betrayed by it. But Monatte rises up fiercely: it is forbidden to disturb trade union unity. In an astonishing manner, he forgets that he himself upset this unity in 1915 by leaving the chauvinist General Council of the *Confédération Générale du Travail*.

It must be said outright: between the Monatte of 1915 and the Monatte of 1929, there is an abyss. To Monatte it seems that he is remaining entirely faithful to himself. Formally, this is true, up to a certain point. Monatte repeats a few old formulas, but he ignores entirely the experiences of the last fifteen years, richer in lessons than all the preceding history of humanity. In the attempt to return to his former positions, Monatte fails to notice that they disappeared a long time ago. No matter what question is raised, Monatte looks backward. This may be seen most clearly in the question of the party and the state.

Some time ago, Monatte accused me of underrating the "dangers" of state power (*Révolution Prolétarienne*, No.79, 1st May 1929). This reproach is not a new one; it has its origin in the struggle of Bakunin against Marx and it shows a false, contradictory, and essentially non-proletarian conception of the state.

With the exception of one country, state power throughout the world is in the hands of the bourgeoisie. *It is in this, and only in this, that, from the point of view of the proletariat, the danger of state power lies.* The proletariat's historical task is to wrest this most powerful instrument of oppression from the hands of the bourgeoisie. The Communists do not deny the difficulties, the dangers that are connected with the dictatorship of the proletariat. But can this lessen by one iota the necessity to seize power? If the whole proletariat were carried by an irresistible force to the conquest of power, or if it had already conquered it, one could, strictly speaking, understand this or that warning of the syndicalists. Lenin, as is known, warned in his testament against the abuse of revolutionary power. The struggle against the distortions of the dictatorship of the proletariat has been conducted by the Opposition since its inception and without the need of borrowing from the arsenal of anarchism.

But in the bourgeois countries, the misfortune lies in the fact that the overwhelming majority of the proletariat does not understand as it should the dangers of the *bourgeois* state. By the manner in which they treat the question, the syndicalists, unwittingly of course, contribute to the passive conciliation of the workers with the capitalist state. When the syndicalists keep drumming into the workers, who are oppressed by the bourgeois state, their warnings about the dangers of a proletarian state, they play a purely reactionary role. The bourgeois will readily repeat to the workers: "Do not touch the state because it is a snare full of dangers to you." The Communist will say to the workers: "The difficulties and dangers with which the proletariat is confronted the day after the conquest of power—we will learn to overcome them on the basis of experience. But at the present time, the most menacing dangers lie in the fact that our class enemy holds the reins of power in its hands and directs it against us."

In contemporary society, there are only two classes capable of holding power in their hands: the capitalist bourgeoisie and the revolutionary proletariat. The petty-bourgeoisie long ago lost the economic possibility of directing the destinies of modern society. Now and then, in fits of desperation, it rises for the conquest of power, even with arms in hand, as has happened in Italy, in Poland and other countries.

But the fascist insurrections only end in this result: the new power becomes the instrument of finance capital under an even more naked and brutal form. That is why the most representative ideologists of the petty-bourgeoisie are afraid of state power as such. The petty-bourgeoisie fears power when it is in the hands of the big bourgeoisie, because the latter strangles and ruins it. The petty-bourgeoisie also fears power when it is in the hands of the proletariat, for the latter undermines all the conditions of its habitual existence. Finally, it fears power when it falls into its own hands because it must inevitably pass out of its impotent hands into those of finance capital or the proletariat. The anarchists do not see the revolutionary problems of state power, its historical role, and see only the "dangers" of state power. The anti-state anarchists are consequently the most logical and, for that reason, the most hopeless representatives of the petty-bourgeoisie in its historical blind alley.

Yes, the dangers of state power exist under the regime of the dictatorship of the proletariat as well, but the substance of these dangers consists of the fact that power can actually return to the hands of the bourgeoisie. The best known and most obvious state danger is *bureaucratism*. But what is its essence? If the enlightened workers' bureaucracy could lead society to socialism, that is, to the liquidation of the state, we would be reconciled to such a bureaucracy. But it has an entirely opposite character: by separating itself from the proletariat, by raising itself above it, the bureaucracy falls under the influence of the petty-bourgeois classes and can by that very fact facilitate the return of power into the hands of the bourgeoisie. In other words, the state dangers for the workers under the dictatorship of the proletariat are, in the final analysis, nothing but the danger of restoring the power to the bourgeoisie.

The question of the *source* of this bureaucratic danger is no less important. It would be radically wrong to think, to imagine, that bureaucratism rises exclusively from the fact of the conquest of power by the proletariat. No, that is not the case. In the capitalist states, the most monstrous forms of bureaucratism are to be observed precisely in the trade unions. It is enough to look at the United States, Britain and Germany. Amsterdam is the most powerful international organisation of the trade union bureaucracy. It is thanks to it that the whole structure of capitalism now stands upright, above all in Europe and especially in Britain. If there were not a bureaucracy of the trade unions, then the police, the army, the courts, the lords, the monarchy would appear before the proletarian masses as nothing but pitiful and ridiculous playthings. The bureaucracy of the trade unions is the backbone of British imperialism. It is by means of this bureaucracy that the bourgeoisie exists, not only in the metropolis, but in India, in Egypt, and in the other colonies. One would have to be completely blind to say to the British workers: "Be on guard against the conquest of power and always remember that your trade unions are the antidote to the dangers of the state." The Marxist will say to the British workers: "The trade union bureaucracy is the chief instrument for your oppression by the bourgeois state. Power must be wrested from the hands of the bourgeoisie, and for that its principal agent, the trade union bureaucracy, must be overthrown." Parenthetically, it is especially for this reason that the bloc of Stalin with the strikebreakers was so criminal.

From the example of Britain, one sees very clearly how absurd it is to counterpose, as if it were a question of two different principles, the trade union organisation and the state organisation. In Britain, more than anywhere else, the state rests upon the back of the working class, which constitutes the overwhelming majority of the population of the country. The mechanism is such that the bureaucracy is based *directly* on the workers, and the state indirectly, *through the intermediary* of the trade union bureaucracy.

Up to now, we have not mentioned the Labour Party, which in Britain, the classic country of trade unions, is only a political transposition of the same trade union bureaucracy. The same leaders guide the trade unions, betray the general strike, lead the electoral campaign and later on sit in the ministries. The Labour Party and the trade unions—these are not two principles, they are only a technical division of labour. Together they are the fundamental support of the domination of the British bourgeoisie. The latter cannot be overthrown without overthrowing the Labourite bureaucracy. And that cannot be attained by counterposing the trade union as such to the state as such, but only by the active opposition of the Communist Party to the Labourite bureaucracy in all fields of social life: in the trade unions, in strikes, in the electoral campaign, in parliament, and in power.

The principal task of a genuine party of the proletariat consists of putting itself at the head of the working masses, organised in trade unions and unorganised, to wrest power from the bourgeoisie and to strike a deathblow to the "dangers of statism."

Constantinople, 21st October 1929

Monatte Crosses the Rubicon

Leon Trotsky

It is now ridiculous and out of place to speak of joint action with the Syndicalist League or the Committee for the Independence of Trade Unionism. Monatte has crossed the Rubicon. He has lined up with Dumoulin against communism, against the October Revolution, against the proletarian revolution in general. For Dumoulin belongs to the camp of the especially dangerous and perfidious enemies of the proletarian revolution. He has demonstrated this in action, in the most repugnant manner. For a long time he has prowled around the left wing only to rally at the decisive moment to Jouhaux, that is, to the most servile and most corrupt agent of capital. The task of the honest revolutionist, above all in France, where unpunished betrayals are innumerable, consists of reminding the workers of the experiences of the past, of tempering the youth in intransigence, of recounting tirelessly the history of the betrayal of the Second International and of French syndicalism, of unmasking the shameful role played not only by Jouhaux and Company, but above all by the French syndicalists of the "left," like Merrheim and Dumoulin. Whoever does not carry out this elementary task towards the new generation deprives himself forever of the right to revolutionary confidence. Can one, for instance, preserve a shadow of esteem for the toothless French anarchists when they again play up as an "anti-militarist" the old buffoon Sébastien Faure who trafficked with pacifist phrases in peacetime and flung himself into the arms of Malvy, that is, of the French *Bourse* [stock exchange—Ed.], at the beginning of the war? Whoever seeks to drape these facts in the toga of oblivion, who grants amnesty to political traitors, can only be considered by us an incorrigible enemy.

Monatte has crossed the Rubicon. From the uncertain ally, he has become first the hesitant foe in order to become, later on, the direct enemy. We must say this to the workers clearly, aloud, and unsparingly.

To simple people, and also to some knaves who put on a simple air, our judgment may appear exaggerated and "unjust." For Monatte is uniting with Dumoulin *solely* for the re-establishment of the unity of the "trade union"

233

movement! Solely! The trade unions, you see, are not a party nor a "sect." The trade unions, you see, must embrace the whole working class, all its tendencies; one can therefore work in the trade union field by Dumoulin's side without taking responsibility either for his past or for his future. Reflections of this sort constitute a chain of those cheap sophisms with which the French syndicalists and Socialists love to juggle when they want to cover up a somewhat odorous job.

If there existed in France united trade unions, the revolutionaries would obviously not have left the organisation because of the presence of traitors, turncoats, and licensed agents of imperialism. The revolutionaries would not have taken upon themselves the initiative for the split. But in joining or in remaining in these trade unions, they would have directed all their efforts *to unmasking the traitors before the masses as traitors*, in order to discredit them on the basis of the experience of the masses, to isolate them, to deprive them of the confidence they enjoy, and in the end, to help the masses run them out. That alone can justify the participation of revolutionaries in the reformist trade unions.

But Monatte does not at all work side by side with Dumoulin within the trade unions, as the Bolsheviks frequently had to with the Mensheviks, while conducting a systematic struggle against them. No, *Monatte has united with Dumoulin as an ally* on a common platform, creating with him a political faction or a "sect" expressing itself in the language of French syndicalism in order later on to lead a political crusade for the conquest of the trade union movement. Monatte does not fight against the traitors on the trade union field; on the contrary, he has associated himself with Dumoulin and takes him under his wing, presenting himself to the masses as Dumoulin's tutor. Monatte says to the workers that one can go hand in hand with Dumoulin against the Communists, against the Red International of Labour Unions, against the October Revolution, and consequently, against the proletarian revolution in general. This is the unvarnished truth which we must speak aloud to the workers.

When we once defined Monatte as a *centrist slipping towards the right*, Chambelland sought to transform this entirely correct scientific definition into a *feuilleton* joke and even to throw the centrist designation back at us, just as a soccer player returns the ball by hitting it with his head. Alas, the head sometimes suffers for it! Yes, Monatte was a centrist, and in his centrism were contained all the elements of his manifest opportunism of today.

Apropos of the execution of the Indochinese revolutionaries in the spring of this year, Monatte developed the following plan of action, in an indirect manner:

"I do not understand why, in such circumstances, the parties and organisations disposing of the necessary means do not send deputies and journalists to investigate on the very spot. Out of the dozen deputies of the Communist Party, and out of the hundred of the Socialist Party, could they not select an investigation commission which would be charged with the elements of a campaign capable of making the colonialists retreat and of saving the condemned?" (*Révolution Prolétarienne*, No.104.)

With the imperious reproaches of a school monitor, Monatte gave the Communists and the Social Democrats advice on the manner of fighting against the "colonialists." The social-patriots and the Communists, for him, were six months ago people of *the same camp*, who had only to follow Monatte's advice in order to carry out a correct policy.

For Monatte there did not even exist the question of knowing in what way the social-patriots can fight against the "colonialists" when they are the partisans and the practical executors of the colonial policy. For can colonies, that is, nations, tribes, races, be governed without shooting down the rebels, the revolutionaries who seek to liberate themselves from the repulsive colonial yoke? Zyromsky and his ilk are not opposed to presenting upon every propitious occasion a drawing-room protest against colonial "bestiality"; but that does not prevent them from belonging to the social-colonialist party which harnessed the French proletariat to a chauvinistic course during the war, one of whose principal aims was to preserve and extend the colonies to the profit of the French bourgeoisie. Monatte has forgotten all this. He reasoned as if there had not been, after this, great revolutionary events in a number of Western and Eastern countries, as if different tendencies had not been revised in action and made clear by experience. Six months ago, Monatte pretended to start all over again. And during this time, history again made game of him. MacDonald, the coreligionist of the French syndicalists, to whom Louzon recently gave some incomparable advice, sends to India not liberating commissions of investigation but armed forces, and comes to grips with the Hindus in a more repulsive manner than would any Curzon. And all the scoundrels of British trade unionism approve this butcher's work. Is this by chance?

Instead of turning away, under the influence of the new lesson, from hypocritical "neutrality" and "independence," Monatte, on the contrary, has taken a new step, this time a decisive one, into the arms of the French MacDonalds and Thomases. We have nothing more to discuss with Monatte.

The bloc of the "independent" syndicalists with the avowed agents of the bourgeoisie has great symptomatic significance. In the eyes of philistines, things seem as though the representatives of both camps had taken a step towards each other in the name of unity, of the cessation of the fratricidal struggle, and other sweet phrases. There can be nothing more disgusting, more false, than this phraseology. In reality the meaning of the bloc is entirely different.

In the various circles of the labour bureaucracy and also in part in circles of the workers themselves, Monatte represents those elements who sought to approach the revolution but who lost hope in it through the experience of the last ten or twelve years. Don't you see that it develops by such complicated and perplexing roads that it leads to internal conflicts, to ever new splits, and after a step forward it takes a half step and sometimes a full step backward? The years of bourgeois stabilization, the years of the ebbing of the revolutionary tide, have heaped up despair, fatigue, and opportunist moods in a certain part of the working class. All these sentiments have only now matured in the Monatte group and have driven it to pass definitively from one camp to the other. On the way, Monatte met with Louis Sellier, who had his own reasons for turning his back, covered with municipal honours, to the revolution. Monatte and Sellier have quit together. To their meeting, there came no less a one than Dumoulin. This means that at the moment when Monatte shifted from left to right, Dumoulin judged it opportune to shift from right to left. How is this to be explained? It is because Monatte, as an empiricist— and centrists are always empiricists, otherwise they would not be centrists—has expressed his sentiments on the stabilization period at a moment when this period *has begun to be transformed into another, much less tranquil and much less stable.*

The world crisis has taken on gigantic dimensions and for the moment it is becoming deeper. Nobody can predict where it will stop or what political consequences it will bring in its train. The situation in Germany is extremely strained. The German elections produced acute elements of disturbance, not only in internal relations but also in international relations, showing again on what foundation the edifice of Versailles rests. The economic crisis has inundated the frontiers of France, and we already see there, after a long interlude, the beginnings of unemployment. During the years of relative prosperity, the French workers suffered from the policy of the CGT bureaucracy. During the years of crisis, they can remind it of its betrayals and its crimes. Jouhaux cannot but be uneasy. He necessarily requires a left wing, perhaps more necessarily than Blum. What purpose then does Dumoulin serve? Obviously it must not be thought that everything is arranged like the notes of a piano and has been formulated in a conversation. That is not necessary. All these people know each other, they know what they are capable of and especially the limits to which one of them can go to the left, with impunity for himself and his bosses. (The fact that the CGT bureaucracy preserves a watchful and critical attitude towards Dumoulin, sometimes even with a nuance of hostility, in no way invalidates what is said above. The reformists must take their measures of precaution and keep an eye upon Dumoulin so that he does not let himself get carried away by the work with which the reformists have charged him and go beyond the limits marked out.)

Dumoulin takes his place in the line of march as the left wing of Jouhaux at the very moment when Monatte, who has shifted constantly to the right, has decided to cross the Rubicon. Dumoulin must re-establish his reputation at least a little—with the aid of Monatte and at his expense. Jouhaux can have no objection when his own Dumoulin compromises Monatte. In this way, everything is in order: Monatte has broken with the left camp at the moment when the CGT bureaucracy has felt the necessity of covering up its uncovered left flank.

We are analyzing personal shifts not for Monatte, who was once our friend, and certainly not for Dumoulin, whom we long ago judged as an irreconcilable enemy. What interests us is the symptomatic significance of these personal regroupments, which reflect far more profound processes in the working masses themselves.

This radicalisation which the clamorers proclaimed two years ago is indisputably approaching today. The economic crisis has arrived in France—after a delay, it is true; it is not impossible that it will unfold in a mild manner compared with Germany. Experience alone can establish this. But it is indisputable that the balanced state of passivity in which the French working class existed in the years of the so-called "radicalisation" will give way in a very brief time to a growing activity and a spirit of militancy. It is towards this new period that the revolutionaries must turn.

On the threshold of the new period, Monatte gathers up the fatigued, the disillusioned, the exhausted, and makes them pass into the camp of Jouhaux. So much the worse for Monatte, so much the better for the revolution!

The period opening up before us will not be a period of growing, false neutrality of the trade unions but rather, on the contrary, a period of the reinforcement of the Communist positions in the labour movement. Great tasks present themselves to the Left Opposition. Sure of the successes awaiting it, what must it do to gain them? Nothing but *remain faithful to itself*. But on this point, next time.

Prinkipo, 15th December 1930

The Mistakes of Rightist Elements of the Communist League on the Trade Union Question

Leon Trotsky

Some preliminary remarks

1. If the theoretical structure of the political economy of Marxism rests entirely upon the conception of *value* as materialized labour, the revolutionary policy of Marxism rests upon the conception of the *party* as the vanguard of the proletariat.

Whatever may be the social sources and political causes of opportunistic mistakes and deviations, they are always reduced ideologically to an erroneous understanding of the revolutionary party, of its relation to other proletarian organisations and to the class as a whole.

2. The conception of the party as the proletarian vanguard presupposes its full and unconditional independence from all other organisations. The various agreements (blocs, coalitions, compromises) with other organisations, unavoidable in the course of the class struggle, are permissible only on the condition that the party always turns its own face towards the class, always marches under its own banner, acts in its own name, and clearly explains to the masses the aims and limits within which it concludes the given agreement.

3. At the basis of all the oscillations and all the errors of the Comintern leadership, we find the wrong understanding of the nature of the party and its tasks. The Stalinist theory of a "two-class party" contradicts the ABC of Marxism. The fact that the official Communist International has tolerated this theory for a number of years, and to this day has not yet condemned it with the necessary firmness, is the most unmistakable sign of the falsity of its official doctrine.

4. The fundamental crime of the centrist bureaucracy in the USSR is its false position regarding the party. The Stalinist faction seeks to include administratively in the ranks of the party the whole working class. The party ceases to be the vanguard, that is, the voluntary selection of the most

advanced, the most conscious, the most devoted, and the most active workers. The party is fused with the class as it is and loses its power of resistance to the bureaucratic apparatus. On the other hand, the Brandlerites and the other hangers-on of the centrist bureaucracy justify the Stalinist party regime by the philistine reference to the "lack of culture" of the Russian proletariat, thus identifying the party and the class, that is, liquidating the party in theory as Stalin liquidates it in practice.

5. The basis of the disastrous policy of the Comintern in China was the renunciation of the independence of the party. Practical agreements with the Kuomintang were unavoidable in a certain period. The entrance of the Communist Party into the Kuomintang was a fatal error. The development of this mistake was transformed into one of the greatest crimes in history. The Chinese Communist Party was created only in order to transfer its authority to the Kuomintang. From the vanguard of the proletariat, it was transformed into the tail of the bourgeoisie.

6. The disastrous experiment with the Anglo-Russian Committee was based entirely upon trampling underfoot the independence of the British Communist Party. In order that the Soviet trade unions might maintain the bloc with the strikebreakers of the General Council (allegedly in the state interests of the USSR!), the British Communist Party had to be deprived of all independence. This was obtained by the actual dissolution of the party into the so-called Minority Movement, that is, the leftist opposition inside the trade unions.

7. The experience of the Anglo-Russian Committee was unfortunately the least understood and grasped even in the Left Opposition groups. The demands for a break with the strikebreakers appeared even to some within our ranks as sectarianism. Especially with Monatte, the original sin which led him into the arms of Dumoulin was most clearly manifested in the question of the Anglo-Russian Committee. Yet, this question has a gigantic importance: without a clear understanding of what happened in England in 1925–26, neither Communism as a whole nor the Left Opposition in particular will be able to make its way to a broad road.

8. Stalin, Bukharin, Zinoviev—in this question they were all in solidarity, at least initially—sought to replace the weak British Communist Party by a "broader current," which had at its head, to be sure, not members of the party, but "friends," almost-Communists, at any rate fine fellows and good acquaintances. The fine fellows, the "solid leaders," did not, of course, want to submit themselves to the leadership of a small, weak Communist Party. That was their full right; the party cannot force anybody to submit himself to it. The agreements between the Communists and the "lefts" (Purcell, Hicks, Cook) on the basis of the partial tasks of the trade union movement were, of

course, quite possible and in certain cases essential. But on one condition: the Communist Party had to preserve its complete independence, even within the trade unions, act in its own name in all the questions of principle, criticise its "left" allies whenever necessary, and in this way win the confidence of the masses step by step.

This only possible road, however, appeared too long and uncertain to the bureaucrats of the CI. They considered that by means of personal influence upon Purcell, Hicks, Cook and the others (conversations behind the scenes, correspondence, banquets, friendly backslapping, gentle exhortations), they would gradually and imperceptibly draw the leftist opposition ("the broad current") into the bed of the Communist International. To guarantee such a success with greater security, the dear friends (Purcell, Hicks and Cook) were not to be vexed or exasperated or displeased by petty chicanery, by inopportune criticism, by sectarian intransigence, and so forth. But since one of the tasks of the Communist Party consists precisely of upsetting the peace of and alarming all centrists and semi-centrists, a radical measure had to be resorted to by actually subordinating the CP to the Minority Movement. On the trade union field appeared only the leaders of this movement. The British Communist Party had practically ceased to exist for the masses.

9. What did the Russian Left Opposition demand in this question? In the first place, to re-establish the complete independence of the British Communist Party in relation to the trade unions. We affirmed that it is only under the influence of the independent slogans of the party and of its open criticism that the Minority Movement could take form, appreciate its tasks more precisely, change its leaders, fortify itself in the trade unions while consolidating the position of communism.

What did Stalin, Bukharin, Lozovsky and company reply to our criticism? "You want to push the British Communist Party onto the road of sectarianism. You want to drive Purcell, Hicks and Cook into the enemy's camp. You want to break with the Minority Movement."

What did the Left Opposition rejoin? "If Purcell and Hicks break with us, not because we demand of them that they transform themselves immediately into Communists—nobody demands that! —but because we ourselves want to remain Communists, this means that Purcell and company are not friends but masked enemies. The quicker they show their real nature, the better for the masses. We do not at all want to break with the Minority Movement. On the contrary, we must give the greatest attention to this movement. The smallest step forward with the masses or with a part of the masses is worth more than a dozen abstract programmes of circles of intellectuals, but the attention devoted to the masses has nothing in common with capitulation before their temporary leaders and semi-leaders. The masses need a correct orientation and correct slogans. This excludes all theoretical conciliation and all protection of confusionists who exploit the backwardness of the masses."

10. What were the results of the British experiment of Stalin? The Minority Movement, embracing almost a million workers, seemed very promising, but it bore the germs of destruction within itself. The masses knew as the leaders of the movement only Purcell, Hicks, and Cook, whom, moreover, Moscow vouched for. These "left" friends, in the first serious test, shamefully betrayed the proletariat. The revolutionary workers were thrown into confusion, sank into apathy, and naturally extended their disappointment to the CP itself, which had only been the passive part of this whole mechanism of betrayal and perfidy. The Minority Movement was reduced to zero; the Communist Party returned to the existence of a negligible sect. In this way, thanks to a radically false conception of the party, the greatest movement of the English proletariat which led to the general strike, not only did not shake the apparatus of the reactionary bureaucracy, but on the contrary, reinforced it and compromised communism in Great Britain for a long time.

11. One of the psychological sources of opportunism is a superficial impatience, a lack of confidence in the gradual growth of the party's influence, the desire to win the masses by organisational maneuvers or personal diplomacy. Out of this springs the policy of combinations behind the scenes, the policy of silence, of hushing up, of self-renunciation, of adaptation to the ideas and slogans of others; and finally, the complete passage to the positions of opportunism. The subordination of the CP to the Kuomintang in China, the creation of workers' and peasants' parties in India, the subordination of the British party to the Minority Movement, etc., etc.—in all these phenomena we see the same method of bureaucratic combinationism which commences with a superficial revolutionary impatience and finishes with opportunist treason.[1]

That is precisely why we have constantly insisted in these last few years upon the enormous educational importance of examples of the Comintern's strategy cited above. They should be studied and checked all over again at each fresh experience, not only in order to condemn the historical mistakes and crimes after the fact, but to learn to discern similar errors in a new situation at their very inception and consequently while they can still be corrected.

---

1 The leading comrades in the United States inform us that in the American league certain comrades—to be sure, only individual ones (in the literal sense of the word)—speak for the bloc with the Lovestoneites in the name of "mass work." It is hard to imagine a more ridiculous, a more inept, a more sterile project than this. Do these people know at least a little of the history of the Bolshevik Party? Have they read the works of Lenin? Do they know the correspondence of Marx and Engels? Or has all the history of the revolutionary movement passed them by without leaving a trace? Fortunately, the overwhelming majority of the American league has nothing in common with such ideas. – *L. T.*

12. It must be said directly: the mistakes of some French Oppositionists, members of the League, on the trade union question reveal striking traits of resemblance with the lamentable British experiment. Only, the scale of the errors in France is as yet much smaller, and they have not developed on the basis of a mass movement. This permits certain comrades to overlook these mistakes or to underestimate their importance in principle. Nevertheless, should the League similarly permit its trade union work to be carried on in the future by the methods formulated by the majority of the old leadership, the ideas and the banner of the Left Opposition would be compromised in France for a long time to come.

It would have been criminal to close one's eyes to this. Since there has been no success in rectifying these errors in their initial stage by means of private advice and warnings, then there only remains to name these errors and their authors openly in order to rectify the policy through collective efforts.

13. Beginning with April 1930, the League, in effect, gave up independent work in the trade unions for the benefit of the Unitary Opposition which, on its part, strives to have its own platform, its leadership, its policy. Within these limits we have a striking analogy with the experiment of the Minority Movement in England. It must, however, be said that in the French circumstances there are certain features which, from the very beginning, render this experiment still more dangerous. In England, the Minority Movement as a whole was *more to the left* than the official leadership of the trade unions.

Can this be said of the Unitary Opposition? No. In the ranks of the latter there are elements who are obviously tending towards the Right Opposition, that is, towards reformism. Their specific weight is not as yet clear to us.

The principal force of the Unitary Opposition is the Teachers' Federation. In France, the teachers have always played a serious role in socialism, in syndicalism, and in Communism. Among the teachers, we shall no doubt find many friends. Nevertheless, the federation as a whole is not a proletarian federation. Because of its social composition, the Teachers' Federation can furnish very good agitators, journalists, and individual revolutionaries, but it cannot become the basis of a trade union movement. All its documents bespeak an insufficient clarity of political thought. The Marseilles congress of the federation demonstrated that its members oscillate in a triangle between the official course, the Left Opposition, and the Right Opposition. We would render the worst service to the members of the federation, as well as to the whole proletarian movement, if we were to cover up their mistakes, their vacillations, their lack of precision. Unfortunately, up to a few days ago this was the policy of the editorial board of *La Verité*—a policy of silence—and this was not by chance.

14. Then you want to break with the Unitary Opposition? Whoever poses the question this way says by this alone that the Communists, as *Communists*, cannot participate in the work of the Unitary Opposition. But if this were the case, it would signify quite simply that the Unitary Opposition is an organisation of the masked enemies of Communism. Happily, this is not so. The UO as a whole is neither a communist nor an anti-communist organisation, because it is *heterogeneous*. We are obliged to take this heterogeneity into account in our practical activity. We can and must display the greatest attention towards groups and even towards individuals who are developing towards Marxism. But all this on one condition: that when we appear before the workers in the trade unions, we act in the name of the Communist League without admitting any censorship of our acts except the control of the League itself (or the whole party after the re-establishment of the unity of the Communist ranks).

15. In the ranks of the Unitary Opposition there are indisputably elements who sympathize strongly with the Left Opposition without being members of the League; they must be brought together under our banner. There are indefinite elements who strive with all their strength to remain in this position, transforming it into a "platform." With these elements, we can have tactical agreements on a definite basis, preserving full freedom of mutual criticism. Finally, in the ranks of the UO there are also, indisputably, alien elements, who strayed there accidentally, or who penetrated it as recruiting agents of reformism. They make use of obscurity in order to bring about the UO's decomposition. The sooner they are unmasked and eliminated, the better it will be for the cause.

16. But aren't we for collaboration with all workers in the trade unions, regardless of their political and philosophical views? Certainly, but the UO is not a trade union organisation; it is a political faction having as its task to influence the trade union movement. Let us leave it to Monatte and his friends the POP-ists to act under a mask. Revolutionaries act openly before the workers. In the UO we can work only with those who go side by side with us, in the same direction, even though not to the end of our road.

17. Certain comrades insist above all that the Communists must fight for their influence on the trade unions by means of ideas and not by mechanical means. This thought, which may seem incontestable, is frequently converted into an empty commonplace. The centrist bureaucracy also declares quite frequently, and quite sincerely, that its task is to influence by ideas and not to exercise a mechanical pressure.

The whole question, in the last analysis, is reduced to the political and economic orientation, to the slogans and the programme of action. If the orientation is right, if the slogans correspond to the needs of the moment, then the masses in the trade unions experience no "constraint." On the contrary, if the orientation is wrong, if the policy of revolutionary ascent is proclaimed at the moment of political ebb, and conversely, then the mass inevitably takes this as a mechanical pressure upon it. The question consequently is reduced to whether the theoretical premises of the Left Opposition are sufficiently serious and profound, if its cadres are sufficiently educated to evaluate the situation correctly and to advance the corresponding slogans. All this must be tested in practice. It is therefore all the more impermissible for us to pass over in silence or to underestimate the sins and the mistakes of our temporary allies as well as of ourselves.

18. Certain members of the League, incredible as it may seem, protest against the intention of somebody or other to subordinate the UO to the League.

Without realising it, they base themselves on the same wretched argument that Monatte uses against communism as a whole. In practice, it means that some comrades working in the trade unions want full independence from the League for *themselves*; they think that by their maneuvers, admonitions, and their personal tact they will achieve results that the League cannot attain by collective work. Other comrades, who would like a similar independence for themselves in the press, welcome these tendencies. The question arises: Why did these comrades join the League if they have no confidence in it?

19. How do matters really stand in regard to the "subordination" of the Unitary Opposition? The very question is false. Only its own members are subordinated to the League. As long as the majority of the Unitary Opposition is not in the League, it is a question only of persuasion, compromise, or bloc, but certainly not subordination. In fact the opponents of the so-called subordination of the Unitary Opposition to the League are demanding the effective subordination of the League to the UO. This was precisely the situation until today. In its trade union work, i.e., in its most important work, the League is subordinated to the Unitary Opposition, for whose benefit it has renounced all independence. Marxists cannot and must not tolerate such a policy—not even for one more day.

20. Certain leading comrades, who obstinately conducted a policy of capitulation up to yesterday, declare today that they are "completely in agreement" on the necessity of transforming the UO into a bloc. In reality, they want to content themselves with a change of name. The quicker they "agree" with the Marxist criticism, the more they conduct, in actuality, a struggle for everything to remain as before. They simply want to utilize the phraseology of the Marxist criticism in order to cover up the old policy. These methods are not new, but time does not render them more attractive. A revolutionary organisation would be corrupted for a long time, if not forever,

by the poison of duplicity and falsehood if it permitted an opportunist policy to mask itself with revolutionary phraseology. Let us firmly hope that the League will not permit this.

Prinkipo, 4th January 1931

The Communist International to the IWW

Grigory Zinoviev

An appeal of the Executive Commitee of the Third International at Moscow

Comrades *and fellow workers!*—The Executive Committee of the Communist International in session at Moscow, the heart of the Russian Revolution, greets the revolutionary American proletariat in the ranks of the Industrial Workers of the World.

Capitalism, ruined by the World War, unable any longer to contain within itself the tremendous forces it has created, is breaking down.

The hour of the working class has struck. The social revolution has begun, and here, on the Russian plain, the first vanguard battle is being fought.

History does not ask whether we like it or not, whether the workers are ready or not. Here is the opportunity. Take it—and the world will belong to the workers; leave it—there may not be another for generations.

Now is no time to talk of "building the new society within the shell of the old." *The old society is cracking its shell. The workers must establish the dictatorship of the proletariat, which alone can build the new society.*

An article in *The One Big Union Monthly*, your official organ, asks: "Why should we follow the Bolsheviks?" According to the writer, all that the Bolshevik Revolution in Russia has done is "to give the Russian people the vote."

That is, of course, untrue. The Bolshevik Revolution has taken the factories, mills, mines, land and financial institutions out of the hands of the capitalists and transferred them to the *whole working class.*

We understand, and share with you, your disgust for the principles and tactics of the "yellow" Socialist politicians, who, all over the world, have discredited the very name of socialism. Our aim is the same as yours—a commonwealth without state, without government, without classes, in which the workers shall administer the means of production and distribution for the common benefit of all.

We address this letter to you, fellow workers of the IWW, in recognition of your long and heroic service in the class war, of which you have borne the brunt in your own country, so that you may clearly understand our Communist principles and programme.

We appeal to you, as revolutionists, to rally to the Communist International, born in the dawn of the world social revolution.

We call you to take the place to which your courage and revolutionary experience entitles you, in the front ranks of the proletarian Red Army, fighting under the banner of Communism.

Communism and the IWW

The American capitalist class is revealing itself in its true colours.

The constantly rising cost of living, the growing unemployment, the savage repression of all efforts of the workers to better their condition, the deportation and imprisonment of "Bolsheviks," the series of anti-strike laws, "criminal syndicalist" laws, "red flag" laws, and laws against propaganda advocating the "forcible overthrow of government and the unlawful destruction of property"—all these measures can have but one meaning for every intelligent worker.

Industrial slavery is as old as capitalism itself, and before that there were other forms of slavery for the workers.

But now the capitalists of the world—the American capitalists as well as those of France, Italy, England, Germany, etc.—are planning to reduce the workers once for all to absolute and hopeless serfdom.

Either this, or the dictatorship of the working class—there is no other alternative. And the workers must choose *now*.

Capitalism is making desperate efforts to reconstruct its shattered world. The workers must seize by force the power of the state and reconstruct society in their own interests.

The coming slave state

Before the American Civil War the negro slaves of the South were bound to the land. The industrial capitalists of the North, who needed a floating population to operate their factories, declared slavery to be an outrage, and abolished it by force. Now the industrial capitalists are attempting to bind the workers to the factories.

In every country during the World War it was practically forbidden for the workers to strike, or even to stop work. You will remember the "Work, or Fight" laws in your own country.

And now that the war is over, what has happened? The cost of living has gone up and up, while the capitalists have actually tried to reduce wages.

And when the workers, faced by starvation, are forced to strike, the whole power of the state is mobilised to drive them back to the machines. When the railway shop men walked out the United States Marshal of California threatened to bring in Federal troops to force them to work. When the Railroad Brotherhoods demanded higher wages or the rationalization of the railways, the President of the United States menaced them with the full-armed power of the government. When the United Mine Workers laid down their tools, thousands of soldiers occupied the mines, and the court issued the most sweeping injunction in history, forbidding the union leaders from sending out the strike order or in any way assisting in conducting the strike, and forcibly [halting] the payment of strike benefits. And, finally, the Attorney General of the United States declared officially that the government would not permit strikes in "industries necessary to the community."

Judge Gary, head of the Steel Trust, can refuse the demand of the President of the United States to meet a committee of his steelworkers, but when the workers dare to go on a strike for a living wage and the elementary right to join a union, they are called Bolsheviks and shot down in the streets by the Pennsylvania Cossacks.

And you, fellow workers of the IWW, with your bitter memories of Everett, of Tulsa, of Wheatland, of Centralia, in which your comrades were butchered, with your thousands in prison—you who nevertheless must do the "dirty work" in the harvest fields, on the docks, in the forests—you must see plainly the process by which the capitalists, by means of their weapon, the state, are trying to inaugurate the slave society.

Everywhere the capitalists cry: "More production! More production!" In other words, the workers must do more work for less wages, so that their blood and sweat may be turned into gold to pay the war debts of the ruined capitalist world.

In order to accomplish this the workers must no longer have the right to leave their jobs; they must be forbidden to organise so that they may be able to wring concessions from the bosses, or profit by capitalist competition. At all costs the labour movement must be halted and broken.

To save the old system of exploitation the capitalists must unite and chain the workers to the machines of industry.

Or the social revolution

Will the capitalists be able to do this?

They will, unless the workers declare war on the whole capitalist system, overthrow the capitalist governments and set up a government of the working class, which shall destroy the institution of capitalist private property and make all wealth the property of all the workers in common.

This is what the Russian workers have done, and this is the *only way* for the workers of other countries to free themselves from industrial slavery, and to make over the world so that the worker shall get *all he produces*, and nobody shall be able to make money out of the labour of other men.

But unless the workers of other countries rise against their own capitalists the Russian Revolution cannot last. The capitalists of the entire world, realising the danger of the example of Soviet Russia, have united to crush it. The Allies have quickly forgotten their hatred for Germany and have invited the German capitalists to join them in the common cause.

And the workers of other countries are beginning to understand. In Italy, Germany, France and England the tide of revolution is rising. In America, too, even the Conservative members of the A.F. of L. are realising that strikes for higher wages and better conditions don't mean anything, because the cost of living is always higher and higher. They have proposed all sorts of remedies, reforms, such as the Plumb Plan, nationalisation of mines, etc. They have founded a so-called "Labour Party," which works for municipal and government ownership of industry, more democratic electoral machinery, etc.

But these reforms wouldn't solve the problem, even if they could be achieved. *So long as the capitalist system exists some men will be making money out of the labour of others. All reforms of the present system of society simply fool the worker into believing that he isn't being robbed as much as he was before.*

The social revolution has begun, and the first battle is on in Russia. It will not wait for the workers to experiment with reforms. The capitalists have already destroyed the Hungarian Soviet Republic. If they can dominate and break the labour movement in other countries, then will follow the industrial slave state.

Before it is too late the class-conscious workers of the world must prepare to meet the shock of the capitalist assault, to attack and destroy capitalism and root it out of the world.

The capitalist state

The war and its aftermath have revealed with startling clearness the real function of the capitalist state—with its legislatures, courts of justice, police, armies and bureaucrats.

The state is used to defend and strengthen the power of the capitalists and to oppress the workers. This is particularly true in the United States, whose constitution was framed by the great merchants, speculators and land owners, with the deliberate purpose of protecting their class interests against the majority of the people.

At the present time the government of the United States is openly acting as the weapon of the capitalists against the workers.

The IWW should realise this more clearly than any other body of workers, for it has been savagely persecuted by the government—its leaders imprisoned, its papers suppressed, its members deported, jailed on false charges, refused bail, tortured, its headquarters closed and its propaganda made illegal in many states.

Any worker can see this fact with his own eyes. All the people vote for governors, mayors, judges and sheriffs, but in time of strike the governor calls in the militia to protect the scabs, the mayor orders the police to beat up and arrest pickets, the judge imprisons the workers for "rioting," or "disturbing the peace," and the sheriff hires *thugs as deputies*, to break the strike.

Capitalist society altogether presents a solid front against the worker. The priest tells the worker to be contented; the press curses him for a "Bolshevik"; the policeman arrests him; the court sentences him to jail; the sheriff seizes his furniture for debt; and the poorhouse takes his wife and children.

In order to destroy capitalism the workers must first wrest the state power out of the hands of the capitalist class. They must not only *seize* this power, but *abolish the old capitalist state apparatus entirely*.

For the experience of revolutions has shown that the workers cannot take hold of the state machine and use it for their own purposes—such as the Yellow Socialist politicians propose to do. The capitalist state is built to serve capitalism, and that is all it can do, no matter who is running it.

And in place of the capitalist state the workers must build their own *workers' state*, the dictatorship of the proletariat.

The dictatorship of the proletariat

Many members of the IWW do not agree with this. They are against "the state in general." They propose to overthrow the capitalist state and to establish in its place immediately the industrial commonwealth.

The Communists are also opposed to the "State." They also wish to abolish it—to substitute for the government of men the administration of things.

But unfortunately this cannot be done immediately. The destruction of the capitalist state does not mean that capitalism automatically and immediately disappears. The capitalists still have arms, which must be taken away from them; they are still supported by hordes of loyal bureaucrats, managers, superintendents, foremen and trained men of all sorts, who will sabotage industry—and these must be persuaded or compelled to serve the working class; they still have army officers who can betray the revolution, preachers who can raise superstitious fears against it, teachers and orators who can misrepresent it to the ignorant thugs [who] can be hired to discredit it by evil behaviour, newspaper editors who can deceive the people with floods

[of] lies, and "yellow" Socialists and labour fakers [who] prefer capitalist "democracy" to the revolution. All these people must be sternly repressed.

To break down the capitalist state, to crush capitalist resistance and disarm the capitalist class, to confiscate capitalist property and turn it over to the *whole working class in common*—for all these tasks a government is necessary—a state, the dictatorship of the proletariat, in which the workers, through their soviets, can uproot the capitalist system with an iron hand.

This is exactly what exists in Soviet Russia today.

But this dictatorship of the proletariat is only temporary. We Communists also want to abolish the state. The state can only exist as long as there is class struggle. The function of the proletarian dictatorship is to abolish the capitalist class as a class; in fact, to do away with all class divisions of every kind. And when this condition is reached, then the *proletarian dictatorship automatically disappears*—to make way for an industrial administrative body, which will be something like the General Executive Board of the IWW

In a recent leaflet Mary Marcy argues that although the IWW does not theoretically recognise the necessity for the dictatorship of the proletariat, it will be forced to do so *in fact* at the time of the revolution, in order to suppress the capitalist counterrevolution.

This is true, but unless the IWW acknowledges beforehand the necessity of the workers' state, and prepares for it, there will be confusion and weakness at a time when firmness and swift action are imperative.

The workers' state

What will be the form of the workers' state?

We have before us the example of the Russian Soviet Republic, whose structure, in view of the conflicting reports printed in other countries, it may be useful to describe briefly here.

The unit of government is the local Soviet, or Council, of Workers', Red Army and Peasants' Deputies.

The city Workers' Soviet is made up as follows:

- Each factory elects one delegate for a certain number of workers, and each local union elects delegates. These delegates are elected according to political parties—or, if the workers wish it, as individual candidates.

- The Red Army delegates are chosen by military units.

- For the peasants, each village has its local Soviet, which sends delegates to the township Soviet, which in turn elects to the county Soviet, and this to the provincial Soviet.

- Nobody who employs labour for profit can vote.

- Every six months the city and provincial Soviets elect delegates to the All-Russia Congress of Soviets, which is the supreme governing body of the country. This Congress decides upon the policies which are to govern the country for six months and then elects a Central Executive Committee of two hundred, which is to carry out these policies. The Congress also elects the Cabinet, the Council of People's Commissars, who are heads of government departments— or People's Commissariats.

- The People's Commissars can be recalled at any time by the Central Executive Committee. The members of all Soviets can be recalled very easily, and at any time, by their constituents.

These Soviets are not only *legislative* bodies, but also *executive* organs. Unlike your Congress, they do not make the laws and leave them to the president to carry out, but the members carry out the laws themselves; and there is no Supreme Court to say whether or not these laws are "constitutional."

Between the All-Russia Congresses of Soviets the Central Executive Committee is the *supreme power* in Russia. It meets at least every two months, and in the meanwhile the Council of People's Commissars directs the country, while the members of the Central Executive Committee go to work in the various government departments.

The organisation of production and distribution

In Russia the workers are organised in industrial unions, all the workers in each industry belonging to one union. For example, in a factory making metal products, even the carpenters and painters are members of the Metal Workers' Union. Each factory is a Local Union, and the Shop Committee elected by the workers is its Executive Committee.

The All-Russia Central Executive Committee of the federated unions is elected by the annual Trade Union Convention. A Scale Committee elected by the Convention fixes the wages of all categories of workers, With very few exceptions, all important factories in Russia have been nationalised and are now the property of all the workers in common. The business of the unions is therefore no longer to fight the capitalist, but to *run industry*.

Hand in hand with the unions works the Department of Labour of the Soviet Government, whose chief is the People's Commissar of Labour, elected by the Soviet Congress, with the approval of the unions.

In charge of the economic life of the country is the elected Supreme Council of People's Economy, divided into departments, such as metal department, chemical department, etc., each one headed by experts and workers, appointed with the approval of the Union, by the Supreme Council of People's Economy.

In each factory production is carried on by a committee consisting of three members: a representative of the Shop Committee, a representative of the Central Executive Committee of the Unions, and a representative of the Supreme Council of People's Economy.

Democratic centalisation

The Unions are thus a *branch of the government*—and this government is the *most highly centalised government that exists.*

It is also the most democratic government in history. For all the organs of government are in constant touch with the worker masses and constantly sensitive to their will. Moreover, the local Soviet—all over Russia have complete autonomy to manage their own local affairs, provided they carry out the national policies laid down by the Soviet Congress. Also, the Soviet Government represents *only the workers*, and cannot help but act in the workers' interest.

Many members of the IWW are opposed to centalisation, because they do not think it can be democratic. But where there are great masses of people it is impossible to register the will of individuals; only the will of majorities can be registered, and in Soviet Russia the government is administered only for the common good of the working class.

The private property of the capitalist class, in order to become the *social* property of the workers, cannot be turned over to individuals or groups of individuals. It must become the property of *all in common*, and a centalised authority is necessary to accomplish this change.

The industries, too, which supply the needs of all the people, are not the *concern* only of the workers in each industry, but of *all in common*, and must be administered for the benefit of all. Moreover, modern industry is so complicated and interdependent that in order to operate most economically and with the greatest production it must be subject to one, general scheme and one central management.

The revolution must be defended against the formidable assaults of the combined forces of capitalism. Vast armies must be raised, drilled, equipped and directed. This means centalisation. Soviet Russia has for two years almost alone fought off the attacks of the capitalist world. How could the Red Army, more than two million strong, have been formed without central directing authority?

The capitalist class has a strongly centalised organisation, which permits its full strength to be hurled against the scattered and divided sections of the working class. The war is war. To overthrow capitalism the workers must be a military force, with its general staff —but this general staff elected and controlled by the workers.

In time of strike every worker knows that there must be a strike committee—a centalised organ to conduct the strike, whose orders must be obeyed—although this committee is elected and controlled by the rank and file. *Soviet Russia is on strike against the whole capitalist world. The social revolution is a general strike against the whole capitalist system. The dictatorship of the proletariat is the strike committee of the social revolution.*

Probably the coming proletarian revolutions in America and other countries will develop new forms of organisation. The Bolsheviks do not pretend that they have said the final word in the social revolution. But the experience of two years of workers' government in Russia is naturally of the greatest importance, and should be closely studied by the workers of other countries.

Politics

The word "politics" is to many members of the I.WW. like a red flag to a bull—or a capitalist. Politics, to them, means simply politicians—usually "yellow" Socialist candidates trying to catch votes to elect them to some comfortable office, where they can comfortably forget all about the workers.

These "anti-political" fellow workers oppose the Communists because they call themselves a "political party," and sometimes take part in political campaigns.

This is using the word "politics" in too narrow a sense. One of the principles upon which the IWW was founded is expressed in the saying of Karl Marx: *"Every class struggle is a political struggle."* That is to say, every struggle of the workers against the capitalists is a struggle of the workers for the *political* power—the state power.

This is the sense in which we Communists also use the word "politics."

The "yellow" Socialists believe that they can gradually gain this political power by using the political machinery of the capitalist state to win reforms, and when they have elected a majority of the members of Congress and the Legislatures, and the president, governors, mayors and sheriffs, they can proceed to use the state power to legislate capitalism peacefully out and the industrial commonwealth in.

This leads the "yellow" Socialists to preach all sorts of reforms of the capitalist system, draws to their ranks small capitalists—and political adventurers of all kinds, and finally causes them to make deals and compromises with the capitalist class.

The IWW does not believe in this and *neither do the Communists.*

We Communists do not think that it is possible to capture the state power by using the political machinery of the capitalist state. The state being the particular weapon of the capitalist class, its machinery is naturally constructed so as to defend and strengthen the power of capitalism. Capitalist control of all agencies molding public opinion—press, schools, churches and *labour fakers*, capitalist control of the workers' political conduct through control of their means of living, make it extremely improbable that the workers under the present capitalist "democracy" could ever legally elect a government devoted to their interests.

And at this time, when the capitalist class the world over is launching a desperate campaign of repression against all conscious working-class organisation, it is unthinkable.

But even if it were possible for the workers to win the state power by means of the political machinery, the capitalist state could never be used to introduce the industrial commonwealth. The real source of capitalist power lies in *capitalist ownership and control of the means of production*. The capitalist state exists for the purpose of protecting and extending this ownership and control—it cannot therefore be used to destroy it.

So far the Communists and the IWW are in accord. The capitalist state must be attacked by *direct action*. This, in the correct meaning of the word, is also *political* action, for it has a *political* aim—the seizure of state power.

The IWW proposes to attain this end by the general strike. The Communists go farther. History indicates clearly that the general strike is not enough. The capitalists have arms—and the experience with White Guards in Russia, Finland and Germany proves that they have sufficient organisation and training to use these arms against the workers. Moreover, the capitalists possess stores of food, which enable them to hold out longer than the workers, *always on the verge of actual want*.

The Communists also advocate the general strike, but they add that it must turn into *armed insurrection*. Both the general strike and the insurrection are forms of *political action*.

Revolutionary parliamentarism

If this is so, if the Communists do not believe in capturing state power by means of the ballot box, why do the Communist parties participate in elections, and nominate candidates for office?

The question of whether or not Communists should participate in elections is of secondary importance. Some Communist organisations do, others do not. But those who do act on the political field do so only for propaganda. Political campaigns give an opportunity for revolutionists to speak to the working class, pointing out the class character of the state and *their* class interests as workers. They enable them to show the futility of reforms, to demonstrate the real interests which dominate the capitalist—and "yellow" Socialist—political parties, and to point out why the entire capitalist system must be overthrown.

Communists elected to Congress or the legislatures have as their function to make propaganda; to ceaselessly expose the real nature of the capitalist state, to obstruct the operations of capitalist government and show their class character, to explain the futility of all capitalist reform measures, etc. In the halls of the legislative assembly, against the sounding board of the nation, the Communist can show up capitalist brutality and call the workers to revolt.

Karl Liebknecht showed what a Communist in the Parliament can do. His words, spoken in the German Reichstag, were heard around the world.

Others in Russia, in Sweden (Höglund), and in other countries have done the same things.

The most common objection to electing candidates to capitalist legislatures is that, no matter how good revolutionists they are, they will invariably be corrupted by their environment and will betray the workers.

This belief is born of long experience, chiefly with Socialist politicians and *labour fakers*. But we Communists say that a *really revolutionary party will elect real revolutionists, and will know how to keep them under its control.*

Many members of the IWW are bitterly opposed to making *any* use of legislatures and other government institutions for purposes of propaganda. But the IWW as an organisation has often used them. In the Lawrence Strike of 1912 the IWW made good use *even of Victor Berger, the Socialist Congressman*, who advertised the strike and the IWW on the floor of the House of Representatives. William D. Haywood, Vincent St. John and many other IWW leaders voluntarily testified before the Industrial Relations Commission of the United States Government, using this method to make propaganda for their organisation. But the most striking example of using the political machinery of the state for purposes of propaganda occurred in 1918, when the Federal Court in Chicago was turned into a three-months-long IWW agitation meeting—extremely valuable for us—by the one hundred IWW leaders on trial there.

These are all cases of using the political machinery of the capitalist state to make revolutionary propaganda among the masses. This method of propaganda should be used as circumstances dictate—as should parliamentary action. *No* weapon should be totally condemned.

The special and particular business of the IWW is to train the workers for the seizure and management of industry. The special function of the Communist political party is to train the workers for the capture of political power and the administration of the proletarian dictatorship. All workers should at the same time be of the revolutionary industrial union of their industry, and of the political party which advocates communism.

The social revolution and the future society

The aim of the IWW is "to build the new society within the shell of the old." [This] means, to organise the workers so thoroughly, that at a given time the capitalist system be burst asunder and the industrial commonwealth, fully developed, shall take its place.

Such an act requires the organisation and discipline of the great majority of the workers. Before the war there was reason to believe that this might be feasible—although in the fourteen years of its history the IWW had been able to organise comparatively only a small fraction of the American workers.

But at the present time such a plan is utopian. Capitalism is breaking down, the social revolution is upon us and *history will not wait until the majority of the workers are organised 100 percent according to the plan of the IWW or any other organisation.* There is no longer before us the prospect of normal industrial development which would alone allow the carrying out of such a plan. The war has hurled the peoples of the world into the great cataclysm and they must plan for *immediate action*—not for the working out of schemes which would take years to accomplish.

The new society is not to be built as we thought, within shell of the capitalist system. We cannot wait for that. *The social revolution is here.* And when the workers have overthrown capitalism and have crushed all attempts to re-establish it, then, at their leisure, through their Soviet state, they can build the new society in freedom.

In the face of the social revolution, what is the immediate important work of the Industrial Workers of the World?

They, as the most important organisation based on revolutionary industrial unionism in America, should take the initiative in trying to establish a basis for the uniting in one organisation of all unions which have a class-conscious revolutionary character, of all workers who accept the class struggle, such as the W.I.I.U., the One Big Union and certain insurgent Unions in the A.F. of L. This is no time to quibble about a name, or minor questions of organisation. The essential task is to draw together all workers capable of revolutionary mass action in time of crisis.

They, as revolutionists, should not repel the attempts of the American Communists to come to an agreement with them, for common revolutionary action. The political party and the economic organisation must go forward—shoulder-to-shoulder toward the common goal—the abolition of capitalism by means of the dictatorship of the proletariat and the formation of Soviets and the disappearance of classes and the state.

The Communist International holds out to the IWW the hand of brotherhood.

January 1920

Section Four

Kronstadt and Makhno

The Makhno Anarchists, Kronstadt, and the Position of the Peasants in Post-Revolutionary Russia

A. Kramer

When the October Revolution took place in 1917, Russia was an undeveloped and agrarian country, with peasants comprising 86% of the population. During the February Revolution of 1917 this peasantry, for the first time in Russian history, became actively involved in the political arena, particularly as soldiers' deputies in the soviets.

Of course one must not ignore the great peasant uprisings of the seventeenth and eighteenth centuries, nor the rebellions of 1905. However, it was only during the revolutions of 1917 that the Russian peasantry finally succeeded in securing stable, independent representative stations.

Nevertheless, the February Revolution, having been commandeered by the bourgeoisie through the right-wing socialists, did not solve the problems of the peasantry. The most glaring failure of the Provisional Government in this sphere was its complete inability to solve that question most important to the Russian peasantry: the land question. The peasants responded to the delays and betrayals of the government with spontaneous expropriations of the land. Only the October Revolution, led by the Bolsheviks, recognised the right of the peasants to be masters of the land that they had worked for hundreds of years.

Lenin and his comrades understood that both organising the working-class and defending its interests were to be matters of the highest priority for the Bolshevik Party. But by no means were the Bolsheviks blind towards the needs of the peasants. Unlike the Mensheviks, the Bolsheviks fully understood the significance of the peasantry's militancy during the Revolution of 1905, and recognised that this energy would be a great force in the next revolution. Lenin and Trotsky both had as their aim the union of the workers of the cities and the most revolutionary elements in the villages, which were the agrarian proletariat and the poorest peasants. In the first days of the October Revolution, the Bolsheviks made great strides towards this end with "The Decree on Land," which took the vast territories owned by the landlords and gave them over to the peasantry. The Left Social Revolutionary Party (having split from the collaborationist Social Revolutionary Party) represented the peasant masses, and was invited by the Bolshevik Party to join in the first Soviet government.

Then, beginning in the middle of 1918, the cruel blows of the Civil War drove a wedge between city and country. The peasantry moved in the direction of conservatism. They had gained everything that they wanted out of the revolution and were ready to defend their new property from both the Left and the Right. The undeveloped Russian villages, each operating in the manner of subsistence economy, could survive without cities. The prevailing mood among peasantry was that the cities were good for nothing more than select industrial goods, so long as the prices were low; and that, apart from that, the cities were only a source of trouble—from the bureaucracy, army conscription, taxation and grain levies. This grossly unbalanced outlook was similar to those of later peasant movements in the "Third World," for example that of the Khmer Rouge in Cambodia.

However, whereas the peasant movements of the last several decades have expressed themselves through Maoist or Guevaraist ideas, the Russian peasantry in the period of the Russian Civil War instead adopted anarchist slogans. But this process was gradual. It started with the peasantry's support of the Social Revolutionary Party, which was the party of the Russian populists known as the "Narodniks." This party was petty-bourgeois, and it initially appealed to the peasant communities by advocating a uniquely "Russian Socialism" that emphasised the role of the peasantry—not the working class—as being central to the revolutionary process.

In 1918, the Social Revolutionary Party split into right and left wings, and in the process suffered massive losses of support. The SR Party's role as a leader of the peasantry was slowly replaced by anarchist groupings. Some of these groups were extremely sectarian and anti-Bolshevik, one example being that of the notorious "Nabat" group. This particular group was responsible for organising bloody terrorist actions against the Bolshevik Party Centre in Moscow in 1919. Later, their ideology would be expressed through the Makhno movement.

While the Russian villages had no need to depend upon the cities, the Russian industrial centres depended upon the villages' agricultural products for sustenance and survival. The collapse of the infrastructure which began in 1915 reached a peak in 1918. Numerous crises, including bosses' lock-outs, industrial sabotage, the Civil War, the collapse of transportation, and mass hunger in the cities forced the Bolsheviks to implement the policy of "War Communism." An important feature of this policy was the expropriation of the food surpluses of the villages in order to feed the workers in the cities. This practice was called "*Prodrazverstka*."

The peasantry did not welcome this step. When the representatives of the Soviet government came to the countryside to collect food, they were seen as bandits who were stealing the peasantry's property. Quite often there were cases of these representatives (called "*prodotriadi*") being brutally murdered. Also, there were many cases of *prodzrazverstka* provoking the peasantry to rebellion against the Bolsheviks.

During the Civil War, the petty-bourgeoisie (the peasantry) was pressed from both sides, between the working class and the forces of reaction. Consequently, in some areas the petty-bourgeois peasantry attempted to play an independent role by maneuvering between the Bolsheviks and their counter-revolutionary enemies. Tendencies towards these sorts of actions were especially strong in Siberia and the Ukraine—both areas being less developed economically and industrially, and consequently having a strong and rich peasant class. For a time, these forces allied with the Bolsheviks, as the White Army stood for the restoration of the old landowner system, which was absolutely unacceptable for the mass of the peasantry.

Of all the peasant movements which sought to play the middle ground, the most famous was that led by Makhno in the Ukraine from 1918 to 1921. This military force was a typical peasant army, unchanged from the old Medieval-era structure—possessing both the strengths and weaknesses of that form. Makhno's militia began as a guerrilla force formed when Germany occupied the Ukraine in 1918. These guerrillas excelled in their own sphere of action, but couldn't stand firm against an extended clash with a regular army. While these guerrillas operated in their home areas, they could expect help from locals. But, when fighting away from their home villages, they lived by banditry and as a result lost support from most people.

Makhno led a peasant movement, and so never had a strong base of support in any of the cities. Most of the workers who lived in areas of the Ukraine under Makhno's control sided either with the Bolsheviks or the Mensheviks. The following examples illustrate the attitude that Makhno had towards the working class. When railway and telegraph workers from the Ekaterinoslav-Sinelnikovo line were still suffering after a long period of starvation under Denikin's occupation, they asked Makhno to pay them for their work. He responded with, "We are not like the Bolsheviks to feed you, we don't need the railways; if you need money, take the bread from those who need your railways and telegraphs." In a separate incident, he told the workers of Briansk, "Because the workers do not want to support Makhno's movement and demand pay for the repairs of the armored car, I will take this armored car for free and pay nothing." [1]

With clashes between peasants and landlords on the one hand, and clashes between peasants and workers on the other, Makhno was pressed to institute policies that were far from "libertarian." The real conditions of life for the peasants of the Ukraine from 1919 to 1921 were cruel and repressive. The cities in Makhno's territories were not ruled by Soviets. Instead, they were ruled by mayors drawn from Makhno's military forces. Makhno's movement was severely centalised, with the leadership in the RevCom deciding everything. Makhno even established a police-security organisation (!) led by Leo Zadov (Zinkovsky), a former worker-anarchist who was to become notorious for his brutality. Incidentally, in the early 1920s Zadov returned to the USSR—to join the GPU! He was rewarded for his services with his own execution in 1937. In the Ukraine, we see clearly that the anarchists were committing the same crimes that they accused the Bolsheviks of.

In September of 1920, Ivanov V. (representative of the Southern Front Revolutionary Soviet) visited Makhno. He later wrote this description of Makhno's camp: "The regime is brutal, the discipline is hard as steel, rebels are beaten on the face for any small breach, no elections to the general command staff, all commanders up to company commander are appointed by Makhno and the Anarchist Revolutionary War Council, Revolutionary Military Soviet (*Revvoensovet*) became an irreplaceable, uncontrollable and non-elected institution. Under the revolutionary military council there is a 'special section' that deals with disobediences secretly and without mercy." [2]

In order to acquire supplies and equipment, Makhno would sometimes ally himself with the Red Army. However, he always refused to accept the Red Army's discipline and order. In order to get food, Makhno's forces robbed not only villages under their control but also Red Army convoys. This caused many conflicts. Finally, in 1921, actions like these played a part in the decisive split between Makhno and the Soviet state. It was at this time that Makhno and his anarchist advisors lost support from the peasants as a result of the New Economic Policy of the Bolsheviks, which replaced *prodrazverstka* with a bread tax. After a short period of battles, Makhno's militia was crushed. Nestor Makhno himself escaped to Romania, while the majority of his fighters capitulated and received an amnesty.

The Kronstadt "rebellion" of March 1921 was also an expression of the conflict between the Soviet state and the peasantry. This rebellion was one of many similar rebellions in this period against the Soviet authorities. But

---

1 Jakovlev J. *Machnovshina I Anarchizm*
2 Jakovlev J. op. cit.

Kronstadt stands out amongst them due to its important strategic location and the mythology that was created around it after the event had taken place.

At the end of the 1930s, a group of ex-Trotskyists (Victor Serge, Max Eastman, Souverine, et. al.) criticised Trotsky for his actions as leader of the Red Army during the Kronstadt rebellion. These former Trotskyists championed the events at Kronstadt as a workers' and sailors' rebellion against the "Bolshevik dictatorship," and charged that the crushing of the rebellion constituted the "first step towards Stalinism." Later, anti-Communist ideologues and propagandists would adapt this criticism to serve their own ends.

Trotsky replied in 1938 with a remarkable article entitled *Hue and Cry Over Kronstadt*, in which he analyzed the petty-bourgeois nature of this *putsch manqué* [failed coup—Ed.].[3] It is not necessary to repeat Trotsky's arguments in defence of his actions regarding the Kronstadt mutiny, as anyone who wants to know the truth can find this article easily. Instead, for the purposes of this article it would be more fitting to present some new information from a collection of documents published only in the last few years. This new evidence from the Soviet archives provides us with the definitive proof that the position of Trotsky's critics was based upon false assumptions and incorrect information.

The first myth about Kronstadt is that it was a rebellion of the very same soldiers who were heroes of the October Revolution. While it is true that many of the Kronstadt sailors were anarchists in 1917, they nevertheless loyally served Soviet power. During the Civil War, Kronstadt training camps provided elite and thoroughly revolutionary troops to the fight to maintain Soviet power. However, as more and more of the revolutionary sailors had to be sent to the front lines, green conscripts began to flood in, replacing the revolutionaries. By 1920, the Kronstadt garrison had been swamped with more than 10,000 fresh recruits. That brought the total number of soldiers and sailors at Kronstadt to 18,707. Most of these came from Southern Russia and the Ukraine, areas strongly influenced by Makhno.[4] Only 5000 out of this number took part in the uprising.

These figures prove that the old revolutionary sailors were in a clear minority by 1921. Remarkably, however, the revolutionary sailors still made a bold stand. On 8th March, a number of them published a pamphlet titled "Stop Immediately the Counter-Revolutionary Putsch in the City."[5] On 15th March, the RevCom of Kronstadt ordered the arrest of all of the old sailors

3 See this volume, 273-82

4 Shetinov U. A., *Kronshtadsky miatez i melkoburzuaznie partii*. Kandidatskaia disertazia MGU, Moskva, 1974, pp. 91–98.

5 *Kronshtadskaia tragedia 1921 goda*. Dokumenti v dvuch knigach., Moskva, ROSPEN, 1999, pp. 320–21.

as they refused to "obey orders."[6] This order, however, wasn't carried out fully. On 24th March, a group of old sailors prevented the explosion of the battleship *Petropavlovsk*, arrested officers, and surrendered to the approaching Soviet forces.[7]

The other legend about Kronstadt is that the leaders of the putsch had a revolutionary motive. Some authors have even written that the mutineers died with the slogan of "Long live communism!" on their lips! But this is a lie. The honest facts demolish this myth. General Elvengern, a member of a counterrevolutionary organisation led by Boris Savinikov, revealed his role in the leadership of the rebellion with a report on the events in Petersburg-Kronstadt written in February and March of 1921.

This report was written while he was in Paris: "...from a tactical point of view they [RevCom] declared themselves fanatical supporters of the Soviet power, and said that they only oppose the Communist party dictatorship, with the hope that with such a platform, it would become difficult for the Communists to mobilise Soviet defenders, Soviet units to crush them." [8] The same was written by the cadet G. Zeidler, in a private letter.[9] Pavel Miliukov, possibly the best Russian liberal mind of his day and the leader of the Constitutional Democrats Party (the notorious "Cadets"), summarized these reports in a Paris newspaper with, "Soviet power without Bolsheviks will be temporary."

But what of the ordinary participants of the Kronstadt rebellion? Were these sailors really ready to die for "communism without Bolsheviks"? Sailor Dmitry Urin wrote on 5th March, in a letter to his father in the Herson province of Ukraine, "We dismissed the commune, we have Commune no more, now we have only Soviet power. We in Kronstadt made a resolution to send all the Jews to Palestine, in order not to have in Russia such filth, all sailors shouted: 'Jews Out'..." [10] If anyone had any doubts about the "real revolutionary" content of this letter, this phrase is sufficient to dispel that. It is so stark that it needs no further comment.

From the very beginning of the rebellion, the Communists suffered repression. On 3rd March, 170 Communists in Kronstadt were arrested. [11] Then, on the 15th of March, many old revolutionary sailors were arrested. [12] But it was not only Communists who were repressed. A 17-year-old boy was

6   Ibid, doc. 423, p. 445.
7   Ibid, doc 480, pp. 494–96.
8   Ibid. Vol. 2, doc. 535, p. 61.
9   Ibid, pp. 322–23.
10 Ibid, vol. 1, doc. 58, p. 119.
11 Ibid, vol. 1, p. 15.
12 Ibid, vol. 2, doc. 423, p. 445.

sent to prison for asking why members of the RevCom received better food and bigger portions than ordinary workers. [13]

As Trotsky said, the so-called "Kronstadt Rebellion" was not the first petty-bourgeois anti-Bolshevik movement during the Civil War. It was similar to other movements with slogans such as "Soviets Without Bolsheviks." There were movements of this kind in some factories in the Urals, as well as in the Cossack Armies. From this entire experience, we can see that under the conditions of class warfare—with revolution on one side and counterrevolution on the other—these slogans lead inevitably and invariably to the camp of medieval reaction. No revolution can succeed without a revolutionary party. Ordinary Russian workers and soldiers understood this far better over 80 years ago than many people on the "Left" do now.

Many ordinary, rank-and-file members of anarchist, Menshevik, Social-Revolutionary and other such parties participated in the Soviets alongside the Bolsheviks—not "without" them. There was a huge difference between the ordinary members of those parties and their leaders. Their leadership refused to make any compromise and remained totally anti-Bolshevik. Early in 1920, authorities in some Jewish areas of the Ukraine were recruited from among the Bund's (a Jewish wing of the old Social-Democratic Party) membership. Many anarchists took part in the revolution as well as the Civil War, struggling alongside the Bolsheviks, cooperating with the Soviet power until the rise of Stalinism. Those far-sighted revolutionaries are called traitors by some of today's anarchists. But in the next few years, more information from the Soviet archives and new documents detailing the struggle of the Russian proletariat will continue to dispel more and more of the old slanders. The true legacy of the October Revolution will be clear to everyone.

November 2004

---

13   Ibid., Vol. 2, p. 632.

Hue and Cry Over Kronstadt

Leon Trotsky

A "people's front" of denouncers

The campaign around Kronstadt is being carried on with undiminished vigor in certain circles. One would think that the Kronstadt revolt occurred not seventeen years ago, but only yesterday. Participating in the campaign with equal zeal and under one and the same slogan are Anarchists, Russian Mensheviks, left Social Democrats of the London Bureau, individual blunderers, Miliukov's paper, and, on occasion, the big capitalist press. A "People's Front" of its own kind!

Only yesterday I happened across the following lines in a Mexican weekly which is both reactionary Catholic and "democratic": "Trotsky ordered the shooting of 1,500 (?) Kronstadt sailors, these purest of the pure. His policy when in power differed in no way from the present policy of Stalin." As is known, the left Anarchists draw the same conclusion. When for the first time in the press I briefly answered the questions of Wendelin Thomas, member of the New York Commission of Inquiry, the Russian Mensheviks' paper immediately came to the defence of the Kronstadt sailors and ... of Wendelin Thomas. Miliukov's paper came forward in the same spirit. The Anarchists attacked me with still greater vigor. All these authorities claim that my answer was completely worthless. This unanimity is all the more remarkable since the Anarchists defend, in the symbol of Kronstadt, genuine anti-state communism; the Mensheviks, at the time of the Kronstadt uprising, stood openly for the restoration of capitalism; and Miliukov stands for capitalism even now.

How can the Kronstadt uprising cause such heartburn to Anarchists, Mensheviks, and "liberal" counter-revolutionists, all at the same time? The answer is simple: all these groupings are interested in compromising the only genuinely revolutionary current, which has never repudiated its banner, has not compromised with its enemies, and alone represents the future. It is because of this that among the belated denouncers of my Kronstadt "crime" there are so many *former* revolutionists or *semi*-revolutionists, people who have lost their programme and their principles and who find it necessary to divert attention from the degradation of the Second International or the perfidy of the Spanish Anarchists. As yet, the Stalinists cannot openly join this campaign around Kronstadt but even they, of course, rub their hands with pleasure; for the blows are directed against "Trotskyism," against revolutionary Marxism, against the Fourth International!

Why in particular has this variegated fraternity seized precisely upon Kronstadt? During the years of the revolution we clashed not a few times with the Cossacks, the peasants, even with certain layers of workers (certain groups of workers from the Urals organised a volunteer regiment in the army of Kolchak!). The antagonism between the workers as consumers and the peasants as producers and sellers of bread lay, in the main, at the root of these conflicts. Under the pressure of need and deprivation, the workers themselves were episodically divided into hostile camps, depending upon stronger or weaker ties with the village. The Red Army also found itself under the influence of the countryside. During the years of the civil war it was necessary more than once to disarm discontented regiments. The introduction of the "New Economic Policy" (NEP) attenuated the friction but far from eliminated it. On the contrary, it paved the way for the rebirth of kulaks [wealthy peasants] and led, at the beginning of this decade, to the renewal of civil war in the village. The Kronstadt uprising was only an *episode* in the history of the relations between the proletarian city and the petty-bourgeois village. It is possible to understand this episode only in connection with the general course of the development of the class struggle during the revolution.

Kronstadt differed from a long series of other petty-bourgeois movements and uprisings only by its greater external effect. The problem here involved a maritime fortress under Petrograd itself. During the uprising proclamations were issued and radio broadcasts were made. The Social Revolutionaries and the Anarchists, hurrying from Petrograd, adorned the uprising with "noble" phrases and gestures. All this left traces in print. With the aid of these "documentary" materials (i.e., false labels), it is not hard to construct a legend about Kronstadt, all the more exalted since in 1917 the name Kronstadt was surrounded by a revolutionary halo. Not idly does the Mexican magazine quoted above ironically call the Kronstadt sailors the "purest of the pure."

The play upon the revolutionary authority of Kronstadt is one of the distinguishing features of this truly charlatan campaign. Anarchists, Mensheviks, liberals, reactionaries try to present the matter as if at the beginning of 1921 the Bolsheviks turned their weapons on those very Kronstadt sailors who guaranteed the victory of the October insurrection. Here is the point of departure for all the subsequent falsehoods. Whoever wishes to unravel these lies should first of all read the article by Comrade J.G. Wright in the *New International* (February 1938). My problem is another one: I wish to describe the character of the Kronstadt uprising from a more general point of view.

Social and political groupings in Kronstadt

A revolution is "made" directly by a *minority*. The success of a revolution is possible, however, only where this minority finds more or less support, or at least friendly neutrality, on the part of the majority. The shift in different stages of the revolution, like the transition from revolution to counterrevolution, is directly determined by changing political relations between the minority and the majority, between the vanguard and the class.

Among the Kronstadt sailors there were three political layers: the proletarian revolutionists, some with a serious past and training; the intermediate majority, mainly peasant in origin; and finally, the reactionaries, sons of kulaks, shopkeepers, and priests. In tsarist times, order on battleships and in the fortress could be maintained only so long as the officers, acting through the reactionary sections of the petty officers and sailors, subjected the broad intermediate layer to their influence or terror, thus isolating the revolutionists, mainly the machinists, the gunners, and the electricians, i.e., predominantly the city workers.

The course of the uprising on the battleship *Potemkin* in 1905 was based entirely on the relations among these three layers, i.e., on the struggle between proletarian and petty-bourgeois reactionary extremes for influence upon the more numerous middle peasant layer. Whoever has not understood this problem, which runs through the whole revolutionary movement in the fleet, had best be silent about the problems of the Russian Revolution in general. For it was entirely, and to a great degree still is, a struggle between the proletariat and the bourgeoisie for influence upon the peasantry. During the Soviet period the bourgeoisie has appeared principally in the guise of kulaks (i.e., the top stratum of the petty-bourgeoisie), the "socialist" intelligentsia, and now in the form of the "Communist" bureaucracy. Such is the basic mechanism of the revolution in all its stages. In the fleet it assumed a more centalised, and therefore more dramatic expression.

The political composition of the Kronstadt Soviet reflected the composition of the garrison and the crews. The leadership of the soviets as early as the summer of 1917 belonged to the Bolshevik Party, which rested on the better sections of the sailors and included in its ranks many revolutionists from the underground movement who had been liberated from the hard-labour prisons. But I seem to recall that even in the days of the October insurrection the Bolsheviks constituted less than one-half of the

Kronstadt Soviet. The majority consisted of SRs and Anarchists. There were no Mensheviks at all in Kronstadt. The Menshevik Party hated Kronstadt. The official SRs, incidentally, had no better attitude toward it. The Kronstadt SRs quickly went over into opposition to Kerensky and formed one of the shock brigades of the so-called "left" SRs. They based themselves on the peasant part of the fleet and of the shore garrison. As for the Anarchists, they were the most motley group. Among them were real revolutionists, like Zhuk and Zhelezniakov, but these were the elements most closely linked to the Bolsheviks. Most of the Kronstadt "Anarchists" represented the city petty-bourgeoisie and stood upon a lower revolutionary level than the SRs. The president of the soviet was a non-party man, "sympathetic to the Anarchists," and in essence a peaceful petty clerk who had been formerly subservient to the czarist authorities and was now subservient ... to the revolution. The complete absence of Mensheviks, the "left" character of the SRs, and the Anarchist hue of the petty-bourgeois were due to the sharpness of the revolutionary struggle in the fleet and the dominating influence of the proletarian sections of the sailors.

Changes during the years of civil war

This social and political characterisation of Kronstadt which, if desired, could be substantiated and illustrated by many facts and documents, is already sufficient to illuminate the upheavals which occurred in Kronstadt during the years of the civil war and as a result of which its physiognomy changed beyond recognition. Precisely about this important aspect of the question, the belated accusers say not one word, partly out of ignorance, partly out of malevolence.

Yes, Kronstadt wrote a heroic page in the history of the revolution. But the civil war began a systematic depopulation of Kronstadt and of the whole Baltic fleet. As early as the days of the October uprising, detachments of Kronstadt sailors were being sent to help Moscow. Other detachments were then sent to the Don, to the Ukraine, to requisition bread and organise the local power. It seemed at first as if Kronstadt were inexhaustible. From different fronts I sent dozens of telegrams about the mobilisation of new "reliable" detachments from among the Petersburg workers and the Baltic sailors. But beginning as early as 1918, and in any case not later than 1919, the fronts began to complain that the new contingents of "Kronstadters" were unsatisfactory, exacting, undisciplined, unreliable in battle, and doing more harm than good. After the liquidation of Yudenich (in the winter of 1919), the Baltic fleet and the Kronstadt garrison were denuded of all revolutionary forces. All the elements among them that were of any use at all were thrown against Denikin in the south. If in 1917–18 the Kronstadt sailor stood considerably higher than the average level of the Red Army and formed the framework of its first detachments as well as the framework of the Soviet regime in many districts, those sailors who remained in "peaceful" Kronstadt until the beginning of 1921, not fitting in on any of the fronts of the civil war, stood by this time on a level considerably lower, in general, than the average level of the Red Army, and included a great percentage of completely demoralised elements, wearing showy bell-bottom pants and sporty haircuts.

Demoralisation based on hunger and speculation had in general greatly increased by the end of the civil war. The so-called "sack-carriers" (petty speculators) had become a social blight, threatening to stifle the revolution. Precisely in Kronstadt where the garrison did nothing and had everything it needed, the demoralisation assumed particularly great dimensions. When conditions became very critical in hungry Petrograd the Political Bureau more than once discussed the possibility of securing an "internal loan" from Kronstadt, where a quantity of old provisions still remained. But delegates of the Petrograd workers answered: "You will get nothing from them by kindness. They speculate in cloth, coal, and bread. At present in Kronstadt every kind of riffraff has raised its head." That was the real situation. It was not like the sugar-sweet idealisations after the event.

It must further be added that former sailors from Latvia and Estonia who feared they would be sent to the front and were preparing to cross into their new bourgeois fatherlands, Latvia and Estonia, had joined the Baltic fleet as "volunteers." These elements were in essence hostile to the Soviet authority and displayed this hostility fully in the days of the Kronstadt uprising ... Besides these there were many thousands of Latvian workers, mainly former farm labourers, who showed unexampled heroism on all fronts of the civil war. We must not, therefore, tar the Latvian workers and the "Kronstadters" with the same brush. We must recognise social and political differences.

The social roots of the uprising

The problem of a serious student consists in defining, on the basis of the objective circumstances, the social and political character of the Kronstadt mutiny and its place in the development of the revolution. Without this, "criticism" is reduced to sentimental lamentation of the pacifist kind in the spirit of Alexander Berkman, Emma Goldman, and their latest imitators. These gentlefolk do not have the slightest understanding of the criteria and methods of scientific research. They quote the proclamations of the insurgents like pious preachers quoting Holy Scriptures. They complain, moreover, that I do not take into consideration the "documents," i.e., the gospel of Makhno and the other apostles. To take documents "into consideration" does not mean to take them at their face value. Marx has said that it is impossible to judge either parties or peoples by what they say about themselves. The characteristics of a party are determined considerably more by its social composition, its past, its relation to different classes and strata, than by its oral and written declarations, especially during a critical moment of civil war. If, for example, we began to take as pure gold the innumerable proclamations of Negrín, Companys, Garcia Oliver, and Company, we would have to recognise these gentlemen as fervent friends of socialism. But in reality they are its perfidious enemies.

In 1917–18 the revolutionary workers led the peasant masses, not only of the fleet but of the entire country. The peasants seized and divided the land most often under the leadership of the soldiers and sailors arriving in their home districts. Requisitions of bread had only begun and were mainly from the landlords and kulaks at that. The peasants reconciled themselves to requisitions as a temporary evil. But the civil war dragged on for three years. The city gave practically nothing to the village and took almost everything from it, chiefly for the needs of war. The peasants approved of the "Bolsheviks" but became increasingly hostile to the "Communists." If in the preceding period the workers had led the peasants forward, the peasants now dragged the workers back. Only because of this change in mood could the Whites partially attract the peasants, and even the half-peasants-half-workers, of the Urals to their side. This mood, i.e., hostility to the city, nourished the movement of Makhno, who seized and looted trains marked for the factories, the plants, and the Red Army, tore up railroad tracks, shot Communists, etc. Of course, Makhno called this the Anarchist struggle with the "state." In reality, this was a struggle of the infuriated petty property owner against the proletarian dictatorship. A similar movement arose in a number of other districts, especially in Tambovsky, under the banner of "Social Revolutionaries." Finally, in different parts of the country so-called "Green" peasant detachments were active. They did not want to recognise either the Reds or the Whites and shunned the city parties. The "Greens" sometimes met the Whites and received severe blows from them, but they did not, of course, get any mercy from the Reds. Just as the petty-bourgeoisie is ground economically between the millstones of big capital and the proletariat, so the peasant partisan detachments were pulverized between the Red Army and the White.

Only an entirely superficial person can see in Makhno's bands or in the Kronstadt revolt a struggle between the abstract principles of Anarchism and "state socialism." Actually these movements were convulsions of the peasant petty-bourgeoisie which desired, of course, to liberate itself from capital but which at the same time did not consent to subordinate itself to the dictatorship of the proletariat. The petty-bourgeoisie does not know concretely what it wants, and by virtue of its position cannot know. That is why it so readily covered the confusion of its demands and hopes, now with the Anarchist banner, now with the populist, now simply with the "Green." Counterposing itself to the proletariat, it tried, flying all these banners, to turn the wheel of the revolution backwards.

The counterrevolutionary character of the Kronstadt mutiny

There were, of course, no impassable bulkheads dividing the different social and political layers of Kronstadt. There were still at Kronstadt a certain number of qualified workers and technicians to take care of the machinery. But even they were identified by a method of negative selection as politically unreliable and of little use for the civil war. Some "leaders" of the uprising came from among these elements. However, this completely natural and inevitable circumstance, to which some accusers triumphantly point, does not change by one iota the anti-proletarian character of the revolt. Unless we are to deceive ourselves with pretentious slogans, false labels, etc., we shall see that the Kronstadt uprising was nothing but an armed reaction of the petty-bourgeoisie against the hardships of social revolution and the severity of the proletarian dictatorship.

That was exactly the significance of the Kronstadt slogan, "Soviets without Communists," which was immediately seized upon, not only by the SRs but by the bourgeois liberals as well. As a rather far-sighted representative of capital, Professor Miliukov understood that to free the soviets from the leadership of the Bolsheviks would have meant within a short time to demolish the soviets themselves. The experience of the Russian soviets during the period of Menshevik and SR domination and, even more clearly, the experience of the German and Austrian soviets under the domination of the Social Democrats, proved this. Social Revolutionary-Anarchist soviets could serve only as a bridge from the proletarian dictatorship to capitalist restoration. They could play no other role, regardless of the "ideas" of their participants. The Kronstadt uprising thus had a counter-revolutionary character.

From the class point of view, which—without offense to the honourable eclectics—remains the basic criterion not only for politics but for history, it is extremely important to contrast the behaviour of Kronstadt to that of Petrograd in those critical days. The whole leading stratum of the workers had also been drawn out of Petrograd. Hunger and cold reigned in the deserted capital, perhaps even more fiercely than in Moscow. A heroic and tragic period! All were hungry and irritable. All were dissatisfied. In the factories there was dull discontent. Underground organisers sent by the SRs and the White officers tried to link the military uprising with the movement of the discontented workers.

The Kronstadt paper wrote about barricades in Petrograd, about thousands being killed. The press of the whole world proclaimed the same thing. Actually the precise opposite occurred. The Kronstadt uprising did not attract the Petrograd workers. It repelled them. The stratification proceeded along class lines. The workers immediately felt that the Kronstadt mutineers stood on the opposite side of the barricades—and they supported the Soviet power. The political isolation of Kronstadt was the cause of its internal uncertainty and its military defeat.

The NEP and the Kronstadt uprising

Victor Serge, who, it would seem, is trying to manufacture a sort of synthesis of anarchism, POUMism, and Marxism, has intervened very unfortunately in the polemic about Kronstadt. In his opinion, the introduction of the NEP one year earlier could have averted the Kronstadt uprising. Let us admit that. But advice like this is very easy to give after the event. It is true, as Victor Serge remembers, that I had proposed the transition to the NEP as early as 1920. But I was not at all sure in advance of its success. It was no secret to me that the remedy could prove to be more dangerous than the malady itself. When I met opposition from the leaders of the party, I did not appeal to the ranks, in order to avoid mobilising the petty-bourgeoisie against the workers. The experience of the ensuing twelve months was required to convince the party of the need for the new course. But the remarkable thing is that it was precisely the Anarchists all over the world who looked upon the NEP as ... a betrayal of communism. But now the advocates of the Anarchists denounce us for not having introduced the NEP a year earlier.

In 1921 Lenin more than once openly acknowledged that the party's obstinate defence of the methods of Military Communism had become a great mistake. But does this change matters? Whatever the immediate or remote causes of the Kronstadt rebellion, it was in its very essence a mortal danger to the dictatorship of the proletariat. Simply because it had been guilty of a political error, should the proletarian revolution really have committed suicide to punish itself?

Or perhaps it would have been sufficient to inform the Kronstadt sailors of the NEP decrees to pacify them? Illusion! The insurgents did not have a conscious programme and they could not have had one because of the very nature of the petty-bourgeoisie. They themselves did not clearly understand that what their fathers and brothers needed first of all was free trade. They were discontented and confused but they saw no way out. The more conscious, i.e., the rightist elements, acting behind the scenes, wanted the restoration of the bourgeois regime. But they did not say so out loud. The "left" wing wanted the liquidation of discipline, "free soviets," and better rations. The regime of the NEP could only gradually pacify the peasant, and, after him, the discontented sections of the army and the fleet. But for this time and experience were needed.

Most puerile of all is the argument that there was no uprising, that the sailors had made no threats, that they "only" seized the fortress and the battleships. It would seem that the Bolsheviks marched with bared chests across the ice against the fortress only because of their evil characters, their inclination to provoke conflicts artificially, their hatred of the Kronstadt sailors, or their hatred of the Anarchist doctrine (about which absolutely no one, we may say in passing, bothered in those days). Is this not childish prattle? Bound neither to time nor place, the dilettante critics try (seventeen years later!) to suggest that everything would have ended in general satisfaction if only the revolution had left the insurgent sailors alone. Unfortunately, the world counterrevolution would in no case have left them alone. The logic of the struggle would have given predominance in the fortress to the extremists, that is, to the most counterrevolutionary elements. The need for supplies would have made the fortress directly dependent upon the foreign bourgeoisie and their agents, the White émigrés. All the necessary preparations toward this end were already being made. Under similar circumstances only people like the Spanish Anarchists or POUMists would have waited passively, hoping for a happy outcome. The Bolsheviks, fortunately, belonged to a different school. They considered it their duty to extinguish the fire as soon as it started, thereby reducing to a minimum the number of victims.

The "Kronstadters" without a fortress

In essence, the venerable critics are opponents of the dictatorship of the proletariat and by that token are opponents of the revolution. In this lies the whole secret. It is true that some of them recognise the revolution and the dictatorship—in words. But this does not help matters. They wish for a revolution which will not lead to dictatorship or for a dictatorship which will get along without the use of force. Of course, this would be a very "pleasant" dictatorship. It requires, however, a few trifles: an equal and, moreover, an extremely high, development of the toiling masses. But in such conditions the dictatorship would in general be unnecessary. Some Anarchists, who are really liberal pedagogues, hope that in a hundred or a thousand years the toilers will have attained so high a level of development that coercion will prove unnecessary. Naturally, if capitalism could lead to such a development, there would be no reason for overthrowing capitalism. There would be no need either for violent revolution or for the dictatorship which is an inevitable consequence of revolutionary victory. However, the decaying capitalism of our day leaves little room for humanitarian-pacifist illusions.

The working class, not to speak of the semi-proletarian masses, is not homogeneous, either socially or politically. The class struggle produces a vanguard that absorbs the best elements of the class. A revolution is possible when the vanguard is able to lead the majority of the proletariat. But this does not at all mean that the internal contradictions among the toilers disappear. At the moment of the highest peak of the revolution they are of course attenuated, but only to appear later at a new stage in all their sharpness. Such is the course of the revolution as a whole. Such was the course of Kronstadt. When parlour pinks try to mark out a different route for the October Revolution, after the event, we can only respectfully ask them to show us exactly where and when their great principles were confirmed in practice, at least partially, at least in tendency? Where are the signs that lead us to expect the triumph of these principles in the future? We shall of course never get an answer.

A revolution has its own laws. Long ago we formulated those "lessons of October" which have not only a Russian but an international significance. No one else has even tried to suggest any other "lessons." The Spanish revolution is negative confirmation of the "lessons of October." And the severe critics are silent or equivocal. The Spanish government of the "People's Front" stifles the socialist revolution and shoots revolutionists. The Anarchists participate in this government, or, when they are driven out, continue to support the executioners. And their foreign allies and lawyers occupy themselves meanwhile with a defence ... of the Kronstadt mutiny against the harsh Bolsheviks. A shameful travesty!

The present disputes around Kronstadt revolve around the same class axis as the Kronstadt uprising itself, in which the reactionary sections of the sailors tried to overthrow the proletarian dictatorship. Conscious of their impotence on the arena of present-day revolutionary politics, the petty-bourgeois blunderers and eclectics try to use the old Kronstadt episode for the struggle against the Fourth International, that is, against the party of the proletarian revolution. These latter-day "Kronstadters" will also be crushed— true, without the use of arms since, fortunately, they do not have a fortress.

15th January 1938

Kronstadt: Trotsky Was Right!

A. Kramer

**New material from Soviet archives confirms the Bolsheviks'
position**

For many years the capitalist press, erudite professors, and bourgeois analysts have been going on about the "secrets in the Soviet archives." There was much speculation about the "terrible secrets of the communist regime" that would finally confirm the "evil character" of communism.

After the events that took place in the late 1980s and early 1990s, historians were finally allowed access to the Soviet archives. So one would expect a flow of terribly indicting facts. However the results for the bourgeois historians have been really disappointing. Of course, they did find a large amount of new evidence that confirms the shocking crimes of Stalinism. But we never had any doubt about this. Trotsky and his followers condemned these crimes long before any archives were opened. Trotsky's supporters in Soviet Russia in the 1920s and 1930s had first hand knowledge of these crimes because they were among the first to suffer the consequences of the Stalinist degeneration. Thousands of them died at the hands of Stalin's henchmen.

What the bourgeois historians were hoping for was a mass of evidence that they could use to show that there was no difference between Stalinism and the healthy regime under Lenin and Trotsky in the first period after the revolution. But they met with real problems in trying to find documents that could be used to discredit the leaders of the Russian Revolution—Lenin and Trotsky. The most difficult documents to get to in the past were those concerning the leaders of the Left Opposition. It is now clear to any historian why this was. The archives show that these leaders played a key role in the 1917 revolution and in establishing the Soviet state.

During the last ten years many new interesting sources about critical moments of the Russian Revolution have been published. Among them are two books about the most tragic act of the Russian Revolution—the so-called Kronstadt rebellion.

It is not necessary to describe here all the aspects of this well-known event. At the beginning of March 1921, in one of the most critical periods of the Soviet Republic's existence, in the naval base of Kronstadt near Petrograd, there was an attempt at a military coup against the Soviet government. The critical state that the Soviet Union was passing through in that moment meant that Lenin and Trotsky were forced to deal with the rebels very quickly. After rejecting the government's ultimatum to capitulate, Kronstadt was stormed and captured in the second attack. The rebel leaders escaped to Finland.

At the end of the 1930s a group of former Trotskyists, including Victor Serge, Max Eastman, Boris Souvarine, and some others attacked Trotsky for his behaviour during the rebellion. (In doing this Serge contradicted his own earlier views expressed at the time of the rebellion.) They described the Kronstadt events as a workers' and sailors' rebellion against the "Bolshevik dictatorship," and saw the crushing of the rebels as a "first step towards Stalinism." Later on, this criticism was adopted by other anti-Communist ideologues and propagandists. Trotsky answered these people in 1938 in his article *Hue and Cry Over Kronstadt* where he analyzed the petit-bourgeois nature of this putsch.

There is no need to repeat Trotsky's arguments here, as anyone can read his article.[1] Anyone who wants to know the truth can read Trotsky for themselves. What I intend to do here is to highlight some of the new information published in these recent documents—a collection of material on Kronstadt.

The first book was published under the strange title, *The Unknown Trotsky: the Red Bonaparte* (Krasnov V.G., Moscow, 2000). This attempts to describe the role of Trotsky during the Russian civil war. The second book—*Kronstadt 1921* (Moscow, 2001)—is a collection of documents about the Kronstadt rebellion. It is important to stress that neither of the two books have been written by Bolshevik sympathizers.

The popular image that anti-Bolshevik critics try to portray is that there was widespread sympathy among the then Red Army soldiers towards the rebels. There has been a lot of speculation about the mass of soldiers refusing to take part in the attack for political reasons and also stories of mass desertions among the Red Army soldiers with many of them passing to the side of the Kronstadt rebels. This, however, is a myth.

What really happened was absolutely different. There was one case where one unit moved to the side of those defending Kronstadt. This was during the first unsuccessful attack. It was a battalion from the 561st Red Army regiment. This regiment was recruited among former Makhno, Wrangel and Denikin prisoners. It is a well-known fact that during the civil war in Russia

---

1 See this volume, 273–82.

some peasant units changed sides even several times as a result of military failures.

There was the other case of the 236th and 237th infantry regiment which refused to go attack. Their position was: "We'll not go on the ice," "we'll go to our villages." These peasant units were terrified at the idea of having to attack across the ice this first class fortress defended by battleships. There are other reports about refusals to carry out orders on the part of different units, but in all these cases the causes were such things as the poor quality of food and clothing, the bad quality of the camouflage. No political reasons were given. This is easily understood if we remember how the young Soviet regime inherited a backward economy and, on top of that, had been forced to use its scarce resources to defend itself against the White armies backed by the imperialists who were trying to crush the revolution.

The situation inside Kronstadt also appears different to the myth. There was no solid mass of soldiers, firmly behind the rebellion. Even bourgeois historians such as Krasnov have had to recognise this fact. Inside Kronstadt there were clashes between the old revolutionary sailors and the new recruits who came from peasant and petit-bourgeois families. This fact can be confirmed by the fact that some ships declared their neutrality, while others moved against the rebels.

Here it is worth quoting from some of the statements issued by the crews of a number of ships, among them the minesweepers *Ural*, *Orfei*, and *Pobeditel*: "The men of the White guards that are leading the rebels can do a lot of damage to the Republic, and they may not even hesitate to bomb Petrograd."

The same situation was to be found behind the rebel battle lines. From the 7th Army intelligence report we learn that many rebel sailors and soldiers wanted to move over to the side of the Bolsheviks, but they were terrorized by their commanders.

However, the final nail in the coffin for the anti-Bolshevik mythology built up around Kronstadt comes later. According to documents published in these two books new facts emerge about what happened in the town around Kronstadt. During the attack on Kronstadt, the workers of the town moved against the putschists and liberated the town even before the main forces of the Red Army arrived. So in reality what we had was not a workers' and sailors' rebellion against Bolshevism, but a workers' and sailors' Bolshevik uprising against the "rebels"!

In the proclamations of the Kronstadt sailors we see the words that refer to "the men of the White guards that are leading the rebels." These were not mere words. The real command over the rebels was concentrated not in the Kronstadt Soviet, as some naïve individuals may think, but in the so-called

"Court for the Defence of Kronstadt Fortress." One of its leaders was Rear Admiral S.H. Dmitriev (who was executed after the fortress fell); the other was General A. H. Koslovsky, who escaped to Finland. Both of these senior officers were very far from having any kind of sympathy for socialism, "with Bolsheviks" or "without Bolsheviks."

There is also much talk about S. M. Petrichenko—the sailor and anti-Bolshevik leader. What is really interesting is to note that in 1927 this man was recruited by Stalin's GPU and he was one of Stalin's agents until 1944 when he was arrested by the Finnish authorities. The following year he died in a Finnish concentration camp.

So, the real story is that the Kronstadt workers and sailors actually understood the real nature of these rebels far better than any of the later intellectuals who have tried to build up the myth of Kronstadt. The same can be said of the counterrevolutionary forces that were operating in Kronstadt. The former tsarist prime minister and finance minister, and in emigration the director of the Russian Bank in Paris, Kokovzev, transferred 225 thousand francs to the Kronstadt rebels. The Russian-Asian bank transferred 200 thousand francs. The French prime minister, Briand, during the meeting with the former ambassador of Kerensky's government, Malakov, promised "any necessary help to Kronstadt."

As Trotsky explained, the so-called Kronstadt rebellion was not the first petit-bourgeois, anti-Bolshevik movement to take place during both the Civil War and the Revolution. There were a lot of other movements that were led by people raising the slogan of "Soviets without Bolsheviks," etc. There were such movements in some factories in the Urals and among the Aries Cossacks. But from these experiences we can see clearly that in the conditions of uncompromising class war this kind of slogan can lead straight into the camp of mediaeval reaction and barbarism. There cannot be a revolution without a revolutionary party. And again, the ordinary Russian workers and soldiers of the time understood this very well. They understood it far better than some people today, among them even some people on the left.

The fact is that many ordinary members of the Anarchists, Mensheviks, Social-Revolutionaries and others parties took part in the Soviets with the Bolsheviks, but not without them. There was a huge difference between the ordinary rank-and-file members of these parties and their leaders, who were completely anti-Bolshevik in their feelings. In the early 1920s the local Soviet authorities in some Jewish areas of the Ukraine were totally recruited from members of the Bund. Many Anarchists took part in the Revolution and in the Civil War on the side of the Bolsheviks against the White reaction. They also cooperated with the new power until the rise of Stalinism. To this day, those courageous people are considered by some modern anarchists as "traitors." Some people never learn!

We have nothing to fear from the publication of more material from the Soviet archives. We hope that over the next few years more documents will be found in these archives about the long and glorious struggles of the Russian proletariat. They will surely provide more information on the revolutionary traditions of the Russian workers.

Appendix: Ted Grant on Kronstadt

Before much of the material that has now become available from the Soviet Archives, Ted Grant published his book *Russia: from Revolution to Counterrevolution* (1997). What he wrote about the Kronstadt events is confirmed by what A. Kramer writes in this article. We quote from Part One of the book, pages 86–88:

"A most serious situation arose when the naval garrison at Kronstadt mutinied. Many falsifications have been written about this event, which has been virtually turned into a myth. The purpose, as ever, is to discredit Lenin and Trotsky and show that Bolshevism and Stalinism are the same. Interestingly enough, the hue and cry over Kronstadt unites the bourgeois and social-democratic opponents of October with anarchists and ultra-lefts. But these allegations bear no relation to the truth.

"The first lie is to identify the Kronstadt mutineers of 1921 with the heroic Red sailors of 1917. They had nothing in common. The Kronstadt sailors of 1917 were workers and Bolsheviks. They played a vital role in the October Revolution, together with the workers of nearby Petrograd. But almost the entire Kronstadt garrison volunteered to fight in the ranks of the Red Army during the civil war. They were dispersed to different fronts, from whence most of them never returned. The Kronstadt garrison of 1921 was composed mainly of raw peasant levies from the Black Sea Fleet. A cursory glance at the surnames of the mutineers immediately shows that they were almost all Ukrainians.

"Another lie concerns the role of Trotsky in the Kronstadt episode. Actually, he played no direct role, although as Commissar for War and a member of the Soviet government, he fully accepted political responsibility for this and other actions of the government. The seizure of the Kronstadt fortress by the mutineers placed the Soviet state in extreme danger. They had only just emerged from a bloody civil war. It is true that the negotiations with the garrison were badly handled by the Bolshevik negotiating delegation led by Kalinin, who inflamed an already serious situation. But once the mutineers had seized the most important naval base in Russia, there was no room for compromise.

"The main fear was that Britain and France would use their navies to occupy Kronstadt, using the mutiny as a pretext. This would have placed Petrograd at their mercy, since whoever controlled Kronstadt controlled Petrograd. The only possible outcome was capitalist counterrevolution. That there were actual counterrevolutionary elements among the sailors was shown by the slogan, "Soviets without Bolsheviks." The Bolsheviks were left with only one option. The fortress had to be retaken by force. These events occurred during the 10th Party Congress which interrupted its sessions to allow the delegates to participate in the attack. It is interesting to note that members of the Workers' Opposition, a semi–anarcho-syndicalist tendency present at the Congress, also joined the attacking forces. This nails yet another lie, which attempts to establish a clumsy amalgam between Kronstadt-anarchism-Workers' Opposition—three things that have absolutely nothing in common.

"Victor Serge, who had many sympathies with anarchism, was implacably opposed to the Kronstadt mutineers, as the following passage shows:

"'The popular counterrevolution translated the demand for freely-elected soviets into one for 'soviets without Communists.' If the Bolshevik dictatorship fell, it was only a short step to chaos, and through chaos to a peasant rising, the massacre of the Communists, the return of the émigrés, and in the end, through the sheer force of events, another dictatorship, this time anti-proletarian. Dispatches from Stockholm and Tallinn testified that the émigrés had these very perspectives in mind: dispatches which, incidentally, strengthened the Bolshevik leaders' intention of subduing Kronstadt speedily and at whatever cost. We were not reasoning in the abstract. We knew that in European Russia alone there were at least 50 centres of peasant insurrection. To the south of Moscow, in the region of Tambov, Antonov, the Right Social Revolutionary school teacher, who proclaimed the abolition of the Soviet system and the re-establishment of the Constituent Assembly, had under his command a superbly organised peasant army, numbering several tens of thousands. He had conducted negotiations with the Whites. (Tukhachevsky suppressed this Vendée around the middle of 1921.)'" (Victor Serge, *Memoirs of a Revolutionary 1901–1941*, 128–29.)

1st December 2003

Who Was Makhno and What Did He Stand For?

Vladimir Morozov

To this day, anarchists hold up Makhno as the true champion of the workers and peasants of Russia after the 1917 revolution. This myth ignores the real nature of the Makhnovite army and the social layers that it represented. Because Makhno did not base himself on the working class but on certain layers within the peasantry, he ended up with what amounted to a reactionary position.

Anarchists like to counterpose to the Bolsheviks the example of the peasant Makhno. They claim that, unlike the Bolshevik leaders, he was the real spokesman of the interests of the workers, the advocate of anarcho-communism, in contrast to Lenin's "Party dictatorship." So what was this phenomenon called Makhnovism?

The army of Makhno consisted mainly of peasants. And this fact was directly reflected in its character. The class basis of this movement was the petty-bourgeois peasantry, and this was expressed in the extremely unstable character of its political line, which could just as easily align itself with revolution as with counterrevolution. That was fully revealed at the time of the Civil War in Russia. The peasantry was prone to pass from Red to White and back again, depending on the circumstances.

At the time of the occupation of the Ukraine by the German army, the insurgent forces of Makhno were at war with the invaders and their local Ukrainian puppets, who were pursuing a policy of systematic plunder against the peasants of the Ukraine. After the German interventionists were driven out, the main enemy was the White general Denikin who aspired to bringing about the return of the landowners. At this particular time Makhno had the strongest army in the Ukraine and did good work fighting against the Whites.

His strength was based mainly on the fact that the peasants, defending their own property interests, at this moment had before them a single enemy—Denikin. At this time in the Makhnovite armies, three quarters of the soldiers were made up of poor peasants. And in such a situation Makhno did not have any other alternative but to fight together with the Red Army, since only in this way could he could keep his influence over the Ukrainian peasants.

However, this situation changed with the destruction of Denikin's forces. Once the threat of the return of the big landowners had been removed, the class divisions within the villages came to the fore. The contradiction between the Kulaks (rich peasants) and the poor peasants began to emerge, creating confrontations in the villages. As a result, in the 1920s, Makhno's army swiftly began to lose support. Increasingly, it became a Kulak army.

The Kulaks were above all interested in a free market in grain. Consequently, they now saw the main enemy as the Bolsheviks. The village poor, in contrast, understood that their interests were not represented by Makhno who, whether intentionally or not, was fighting to protect the Kulaks' interests. Makhno declared that there was essentially no difference between mobilisation against the Reds or the Whites.

Likewise, the commitment of the Makhnovites to the principles of "Freedom and Anarchy" is open to serious question. P. Arshinov writes that the maintenance of the insurgent army was assigned to the peasants. However, in Makhno's army only the lower commanders were elected, while all the senior commanders were appointed personally by Makhno himself.

The Makhnovites imposed levies on the captured cities. After the capture of Yekaterinoslav, for instance, they imposed a levy of 50 million rubles. The dictatorial tendencies of the so-called "anarcho-communist" Makhno were revealed by the execution of M. L. Polonsky, the Bolshevik commander of the 13th Crimean regiment. Having accused the latter of trying to poison Makhno, the Makhnovites shot the Bolshevik commander, together with his wife, without any pretence of a trial. When the Yekaterinoslav Communists demanded that Polonsky be tried in public, Makhno, despite all his demagogic rhetoric about freedom and democracy, refused point blank. When the workers of Yekaterinoslav requested the release of the arrested Bolsheviks, Makhno threatened them with execution. In general, the attitude of the workers to Makhno was an extremely negative one.

In the Aleksandrovsk congress of peasants and workers, Makhno launched sharp attacks against the working class, calling workers swine, scoundrels, parasites, henchmen of the bourgeoisie and that the sooner they left the congress the better. By these means, he attempted to ingratiate himself with the great bulk of the army, which consisted of backward peasants, who considered all city-dwellers as their enemies.

As we have pointed out, at the beginning of the 1920s the numbers of Makhnovites began to decline sharply. The external danger posed by Denikin had by now disappeared, as the land which Denikin had returned to the landowners, had once again been transferred to the peasants. Therefore, those who now remained with Makhno were mainly drawn from the Kulaks, who were bitterly opposed to Soviet power. The withdrawal of the poorest peasantry from Makhno's army provoked his anger. In May 1920, after the refusal of the peasants of the village of Rozhdestvensk to join his army, Makhno ordered his men to burn the village down, and opened fire on its inhabitants with machine-guns.

Now Makhno began a reign of open terror against the Party workers and Soviet activists. The threat posed by the White general Wrangel once again provided Makhno with the chance of uniting wider layers of the peasantry under his banner, using the peasants' fear of a return of the landowners. At this difficult moment, Soviet power also needed to reach a truce with the Makhnovites. After the defeat of Wrangel, however, the fate of the Makhnovite armies was decided.

Even the Makhnovites themselves understood the hopelessness of opposition to the Soviet power. Makhno's chief of staff, Belash, recognised that the Makhnovite armies were saved from complete disintegration only by fear of reprisals. Without this, they would have collapsed at once, after the liquidation of Wrangel. The irreversible decline of the Makhnovites begins at this point. Makhno's army now more and more comes to resemble a gang of bandits.

The introduction of the New Economic Policy definitively buried the last hopes of a revival of Makhnovism. And the amnesty declared by the Soviet power deprived Makhno of the majority of his army.

The alleged anarchism of Makhno also raises many questions. This was the case even at that time. His policies eventually compelled some ideological anarchists to criticise him. The well-known anarchist Baron, a member of the secretariat of "Nabat," wrote that: "It is better to disappear in a Soviet prison, than to vegetate in these notorious anarchical conditions." At the all-Ukrainian Conference of "Nabat," the delegates recognised that Makhno had ceased, in fact, to be an anarchist.

The truth is that Makhno was the spokesman of the interests of the prosperous peasantry, and acted accordingly. In order not to lose his influence among this layer, he tailed behind all its meanderings. The Kulaks were mainly interested in "cheap government," in the abolition of taxation and in free trade. Thus, anarchism, with its negation of the state, was the best ideological cover for the creation of a Kulak volunteer army. It is no accident that the Makhnovite movement arose and flourished in the southern Ukrainian region where the Kulaks accounted for 20% of the economy. Outside of this region Makhno never managed to establish a stable base.

Actually, anarchism represents a very reactionary idealistic current. It sets out from the view that it is possible to achieve communism simply through the subjective desire of the population. Despite its revolutionary aura, it inevitably leads to opportunism. Communism is not just a good idea, as the utopian socialists imagined, nor does it arise at will. As Marx explained, socialism must have a material base; it can only arise when the economic conditions have matured for it to come into being. It is absurd to expect to construct socialism on the basis of the peasantry, that is to say, a class of small proprietors, which has no economic future, and is doomed to extinction on the basis of capitalism.

It is impossible to abolish the state just by willing it away, as the anarchists imagine. The state will only wither away when the material conditions that gave rise to it have disappeared. For this reason, a regime of genuine workers' democracy (i.e., the "dictatorship of proletariat", as Marx would put it) is an inevitable stage in the transition from capitalist slavery towards a classless society in which the state and every other manifestation of barbarism will be relegated to the museum of prehistory.

September 30 2009

Section Five

The Spanish Revolution

The Lessons of Spain: The Last Warning

Leon Trotsky

Menshevism and Bolshevism in Spain

The military operation in Ethiopia, in Spain, in the Far East are being studied closely by all military staffs, preparing themselves for the great future war. The battles of the Spanish proletariat, heat lightning flashes of the future world revolution, should be no less attentively studied by the revolutionary staffs: only under this condition will coming events not take us unawares.

Three conceptions fought—with uneven forces—in the so-called republican camp: Menshevism, Bolshevism, and anarchism. So far as the bourgeois republican parties are concerned, they had neither independent ideas nor independent political significance and maintained themselves only on the back of the reformists and Anarchists. Furthermore, it would not be any kind of exaggeration to say that the leaders of Spanish anarcho-syndicalism did everything to repudiate their doctrine and virtually reduce its significance to zero. Actually in the so-called republican camp two doctrines fought: Menshevism and Bolshevism.

In accordance with the viewpoint of the Socialists and Stalinists, i.e., Mensheviks of the first and second mobilisation, the Spanish revolution was to have solved only its "democratic" tasks, for which a single front with the "democratic" bourgeoisie was necessary. From this point of view every attempt of the proletariat to go outside the limits of bourgeois democracy is not only premature but fatal. Moreover, on the order of the day stands not the revolution but the struggle against the insurgent Franco. Fascism is "reaction." Against "reaction" it is necessary to unite all forces of "progress." Menshevism, itself a branch of bourgeois thought, does not have and does not wish to have any understanding of the fact that fascism is not feudal but bourgeois reaction, that one can successfully fight against bourgeois reaction only with the forces and methods of the proletarian revolution.

The Bolshevik point of view, consummately expressed only by the young section of the Fourth International, emanated from the theory of permanent

301

revolution, that is, that even purely democratic problems, like the liquidation of semi-feudal land ownership, cannot be solved without the conquest of power by the proletariat; but this in turn places the socialist revolution on the order of the day. Moreover, the Spanish workers themselves posed practically, from the first stages of the revolution, not only those problems simply democratic but those purely socialist. The demand not to step out of the bounds of bourgeois democracy signifies in actuality not a defence of the democratic revolution but a repudiation of it. Only through an overturn in agrarian relations could the peasantry, the great mass of the population, have been transformed into a powerful bulwark against fascism. But the land owners are tied with indissoluble bonds to the banking-commercial-industrial bourgeoisie and bourgeois intelligentsia dependent on them. Thus the party of the proletariat faced the necessity of a choice between being with the peasant masses or with the liberal bourgeoisie. The inclusion of the peasantry and the liberal bourgeoisie in a common coalition could have been done with but a single aim: to help the bourgeoisie deceive the peasantry and thus isolate the workers. The agrarian revolution could have been accomplished only against the bourgeoisie, hence only through measures of the dictatorship of the proletariat. There does not exist any kind of middle, intermediate regime.

From the viewpoint of theory in Spanish politics, Stalin more than anything astounds one by his complete obliviousness to the alphabet of Leninism. After a lapse of several decades—and what decades!—the Comintern has fully re-established as proper the doctrine of Menshevism. More than that: it has contrived to give to this doctrine a more "consistent" and by that token a more absurd expression. In czarist Russia, on the eve of 1905, the formula of "purely democratic revolution" had behind it in any case immeasurably more arguments than in 1937 in Spain. No wonder that in contemporary Spain "the liberal workers' policy" of Menshevism became a reactionary anti-working class policy of Stalinism. At the same time the doctrine of the Mensheviks, this caricature of Marxism, was transformed into a caricature of itself.

The "theory" of the People's Front

However, it would be naïve to think that at the basis of the politics of the Comintern in Spain there lies a theoretical "mistake." Stalinism rules not through the theory of Marxism, or through any kind of theory in general, but by the empirical interests of the Soviet bureaucracy. In their own circle the Soviet cynics laugh at Dimitrov's "philosophy" of the People's Front. But they have at their disposal for deceiving the masses numerous staffs of preachers of this holy formula, sincere ones and cheats, simpletons and charlatans. Louis Fischer with his ignorance and self-satisfaction, with his provincial reasoning and organic deafness to revolution is the most repulsive representative of this unattractive fraternity. "The union of progressive forces!" The triumph of the idea of the People's Front!" The assault of the Trotskyists on the unity of the anti-fascist ranks!"…Who will believe that the Communist Manifesto was written 90 years ago?

The theoreticians of the People's Front in essence do not go further than the first rule of arithmetic, that is, addition: the total of "Communists," Socialists, Anarchists and liberals is greater than each one separately. Such is all their wisdom. Arithmetic, however, is not sufficient in this problem. Mechanics, at least, is necessary: the law of the parallelogram of forces has validity also in politics. The resultant, as is known, is the shorter the more the component forces diverge from each other. When political allies pull in opposite directions, the resultant can prove equal to zero. A bloc of different political groups of the working class is completely indispensable for the solution of common practical problems. Under certain historical conditions, such a bloc is capable of attracting to itself the oppressed and petty-bourgeois masses whose interests are close to the interests of the proletariat. The general force of such a bloc can prove to be immeasurably stronger than the force of each of its component parts. On the contrary, the political union of the proletariat with the bourgeoisie, whose interests in the present epoch diverge upon basic questions at an angle of 180 degrees, is capable, as a general rule, of only paralysing the revolutionary force of the proletariat.

Civil war, where the force of bare coercion has little validity, demands the spirit of the highest self-denial from its participants. The workers and peasants are capable of assuring victory only if they carry on a struggle for their own liberation. Under these conditions, to subordinate the proletariat to the leadership of the bourgeoisie means beforehand to assure its defeat in the civil war.

These simple truths are least of all the fruit of pure theoretical analysis. On the contrary, they represent the unassailable conclusion of the whole historical experience, beginning, at least, with 1848. The newest history of bourgeois society is filled with the most diverse political combinations for the deception of the toilers. The Spanish experience is but a new tragic link in this chain of crimes and betrayals.

The union with a shadow of the bourgeoisie

Politically most striking is the fact that in the Spanish People's Front there was not in essence a parallelogram of forces: the place of the bourgeoisie was occupied by its shadow. Through the agency of the Stalinists, Socialists, and Anarchists, the Spanish bourgeoisie subordinated the proletariat to itself, not even troubling itself to participate in the People's Front: the overwhelming majority of the exploiters of all political shades openly went over into the camp of Franco. Without any recourse to the theory of "permanent revolution," the Spanish bourgeoisie from the very beginning understood that the revolutionary movement of the masses, no matter what is its initial point, is directed against private property, in land and in the means of production, and that it is utterly impossible to cope with this movement by democratic measures. In the republican camp remained, therefore, only insignificant splinters from the possessing classes, Messrs. Azaña, Companys, and their like—political lawyers of the bourgeoisie but not the bourgeoisie itself. Having placed its stake fully upon a military dictatorship, the possessing classes were able at the same time to make use of their political representatives of yesterday in order to paralyse, disorganise and afterward stifle the socialist movement of the masses upon "republican" territory.

No longer representing in the slightest degree the Spanish bourgeoisie, the left Republicans still less represented the workers and peasants. They represented no one but themselves. However, thanks to their allies—the Socialists, Stalinists, and Anarchists—these political phantoms played the decisive role in the revolution. How? Very simply: in the capacity of incarnating the principle of the "democratic republic," i.e., the inviolability of private property.

The Stalinists in the People's Front

The reasons for the rise of the Spanish People's Front and its inner mechanics are entirely clear. The problem facing the retired leaders of the left wing of the bourgeoisie consisted in stopping the revolution of the masses and thus gaining the lost confidence of the exploiters: "Why do you need Franco if we, the Republicans, can do the same thing?" The interests of Azaña and Companys fully coincided at this central point with the interests of Stalin, who needed to gain the confidence of the French and British bourgeoisie by proving to them in action his ability to preserve "order" against "anarchy." Stalin needed Azaña and Companys as a covering before the workers: Stalin himself, of course, is for socialism, but one should not push aside the republican bourgeoisie! Azaña and Companys needed Stalin as an experienced executioner with the authority of a revolutionist: without this they, an insignificant lot, would never have been capable of attacking the workers. They would not have dared. The traditional reformists of the Second International, long ago thrown off the rails by the course of the class struggle, began to feel a tide of confidence, thanks to the support of Moscow. However, this support was given not to all reformists but only to the more reactionary ones. Caballero represented that face of the Socialist Party which was turned toward the workers' aristocracy. Negrín and Prieto always looked towards the bourgeoisie. Negrín won over

Caballero with the help of Moscow. The left socialists and anarchists, the captives of the People's Front, tried, it is true, to save what could be saved of democracy. But since they did not dare to mobilise the masses against the gendarmes of the People's Front, their efforts at the end were reduced to woeful jeremiads. The Stalinists thus proved to be in alliance with the more rightist, openly bourgeois, wing of the Socialist Party. They directed their repressions against the left: The POUM, the Anarchists, the "left" Socialists, i.e., against the centrist groupings who reflected, though in a remote degree, the pressure of the revolutionary masses.

This political fact, very significant in itself, reveals at the same time the extent of the degeneration of the Comintern during the past years. We once defined Stalinism as bureaucratic centrism, and events gave a series of proofs as to the correctness of this definition. But now it has obviously become obsolete. Already the interests of the Bonapartist bureaucracy will not reconcile with the centrist half-way policy. Searching for reconciliation with the bourgeoisie, the Stalinist clique is capable of entering an alliance only with the more conservative groupings of the international workers' aristocracy. Thus the counterrevolutionary character of Stalinism on an international arena expressed itself definitively.

The counterrevolutionary advantages of Stalinism

We thus closely approach the solution of the enigma of how and why the leadership of the "Communist" Party of Spain, insignificant in numbers and level, proved capable of gathering into its hands all levers of power, in face of the incomparably more powerful organisations of the Socialists and the Anarchists. The usual explanation that the Stalinists merely bartered Soviet weapons for power is extremely superficial. For the supply of arms Moscow received Spanish gold. According to the laws of the capitalist market, this is sufficient. How then did Stalin contrive to get power also into the bargain?

In reply to this we are commonly told: having raised its authority in the eyes of the masses by furnishing military supplies, the Soviet government asked as the condition of its "collaboration" drastic measures against revolutionists and thus removed dangerous opponents from its path. All this is completely indisputable but this is but one, and at that the less important, aspect of the matter. In spite of the "authority" created by the Soviet supplies, the Spanish Communist Party remained a small minority and met with ever-growing hatred on the part of the workers. On the other hand, it is insufficient that Moscow put up conditions; it was necessary that Valencia accept them. In this is the essence of the matter. Not only Zamora, Companys, and Negrín, but Caballero, during his incumbency as premier, all of them more or less readily met the demands of Moscow. Why? Because these gentlemen themselves wished to keep the revolution within bourgeois limits. Not only the Socialists but the Anarchists as well did not seriously oppose the Stalinist programme. They feared a break with the bourgeoisie. They were deathly afraid of every revolutionary onslaught of the workers.

Stalin with his arms and with his counterrevolutionary ultimatum was a saviour for these groups. He guaranteed them, as they hoped, military victory over Franco and at the same time he freed them from responsibility for the course of the revolution. They hastened to put their socialist and anarchist masks into the closet in the hope of making use of them again when Moscow re-established bourgeois democracy for them. As the finishing touch to their comfort, these gentlemen could from now on justify their betrayal to the workers by the necessity for a military agreement with Stalin. Stalin on his part justified his counterrevolutionary politics by the necessity for an agreement with the republican bourgeoisie.

Only from this wider point of view does that angelic toleration which such knights of right and freedom as Azaña, Negrín, Companys, Caballero, García Oliver, and others showed toward the crimes of the GPU become clear to us. If they had no other choice, as they affirm, it was not at all because they could not pay for the airplanes and tanks other than with the heads of the revolutionists and rights of the workers, but because their own "purely democratic," i.e., anti-socialist programme, could not be realised by any other measures except through terror. When the workers and peasants enter on the path of their revolution, i.e., to take possession of the factories, property, drive out the old owners, seize power in the provinces, then the bourgeois counterrevolution—democratic, Stalinist, or Fascist, there is no difference—has no other means to stop this movement except by bloody force, complemented by lies and deceit. The advantage enjoyed by the Stalinist clique on this road consisted in its ability to use at once methods which were not within the capacity of Azaña, Companys, Negrín and their left allies.

Stalin in his own way confirms the correctness of the Theory of Permanent Revolution

Two irreconcilable programmes thus fought on the territory of republican Spain. On the one hand, the programme of saving private property from the proletariat at any cost and—to the extent possible—saving democracy from Franco; on the other hand, the programme abolishing private property through the conquest of power by the proletariat. The first programme expressed the interests of capital through the agency of the workers' aristocracy, the top circles of the petty-bourgeoisie, and especially through the Soviet bureaucracy. The second programme, translated into the language of Marxism, expressed the not fully conscious but powerful tendencies of the revolutionary movement of the masses. Unfortunately for the revolution, between the handful of Bolsheviks and the revolutionary proletariat, stood the counterrevolutionary wall of the People's Front.

The politics of the People's Front was defined, in turn, not at all by the blackmail of Stalin as a supplier of arms. There was, of course, no lack of blackmail. But the reason for the success of this blackmail is lodged in the inner conditions of the revolution itself. The growing onslaught of the masses against the regime of semi-feudal and bourgeois property was, during six whole years, its social background. The need to defend this property by the severest means threw the bourgeoisie into the embrace of Franco. The republican government promised the bourgeoisie to defend property by "democratic" measures but revealed, especially in July 1936, its full bankruptcy. When the situation on the property front became still more threatening than on the military front, the democrats of all colours, including the Anarchists, bowed before Stalin; and he found no other methods in his own arsenal than the methods of Franco.

The baiting of the "Trotskyists," POUMists, revolutionary Anarchists and left Socialists; the filthy slander, false documents, tortures in Stalinist holes, murders in dark alleys—without all this the bourgeois regime, under the republican flag, could not have lasted even two months. The GPU proved to be the master of the situation only because it defended more consistently than the others, i.e., with the greatest baseness and bloodthirstiness, the interests of the bourgeoisie against the proletariat.

In the struggle against the socialist revolution, the "democrat" Kerensky at first sought support in the military dictatorship of Kornilov, then tried to enter Petrograd in the baggage train of the monarchist general Krasnov. On the other hand, the Bolsheviks, in order to bring the democratic revolution to a conclusion, were compelled to overthrow the government of "democratic" charlatans and babblers. Through this they incidentally put an end to every kind of attempt at military (or "fascist") dictatorship.

The Spanish revolution again demonstrates that it is impossible to defend democracy against the revolutionary masses other than by the methods of fascist reaction. And vice versa, it is impossible to lead the actual struggle against fascism other than by methods of the proletarian revolution. Stalin waged war against "Trotskyism" (proletarian revolution), destroying democracy by the Bonapartist measures of the GPU. By this again, and definitively, is overthrown the old Menshevik theory, adopted by the Comintern, which divides the democratic and socialist revolutions into two independent historical chapters, separated in time from each other. The work of the Moscow executioners confirms, in its own way, the correctness of the theory of permanent revolution.

The role of the anarchists

The anarchists had no independent position of any kind in the Spanish revolution. They did no more than waver between Bolshevism and Menshevism. More precisely: the anarchist workers instinctively tried to go on the Bolshevik road (July 1936, the May days 1937) while their leaders, on the contrary, with all their might drove the masses into the camp of the People's Front, i.e., the bourgeois regime.

The Anarchists revealed a fatal lack of understanding of the laws of the revolution and its problems when they tried to limit themselves to their own trade unions, permeated with the routine of peaceful times, ignoring what went on outside of the bounds of the trade unions, in the masses, in the political parties, and in the apparatus of the government. Were the Anarchists revolutionists, they would first of all have called for the creation of Soviets, uniting the representatives of all the workers of the city and the country, including the more oppressed strata who had never joined a trade union. The revolutionary workers would naturally occupy the dominating position in these Soviets. The Stalinists would prove to be an insignificant minority. The proletariat would convince itself of its own invincible strength. The apparatus of the bourgeois state would be suspended in the air. One strong blow would be needed to pulverize this apparatus. The Socialist revolution would have received a powerful impetus. The French proletariat would not for long have permitted Léon Blum to block the proletarian revolution beyond the Pyrenees. Neither could the Moscow bureaucracy permit itself such a luxury. The most difficult questions would prove soluble of themselves.

Instead of this, the anarcho-syndicalists, attempting to hide themselves from "politics" in the trade unions, proved to be, to the great surprise of the whole world and themselves, the fifth wheel in the cart of bourgeois democracy. But not for long: no one needs a fifth wheel. After García Oliver and Co. helped Stalin and his collaborators to take the power away from the workers, the Anarchists themselves were driven out of the government of the People's Front. Even then they found nothing better to do than to run behind the chariot of the victor and assure him of their devotion. The fear of the petty-bourgeois before the big bourgeois, of the petty bureaucrat before the big bureaucrat, they covered up by lachrymose speeches about the holiness of the united front (between the victims and the executioners) and about the inadmissibility of every kind of dictatorship, including their own. "But we could have taken power in July 1936...." "But we could have taken power in May 1937...." The anarchists begged Negrín-Stalin to recognise and reward their treachery to the revolution. A disgusting picture!

This self-justification alone: "We did not capture power not because we could not but because we did not wish to, because we are against every kind of dictatorship," and the like, contains in itself an irrevocable condemnation of anarchism as a fully anti-revolutionary doctrine. To renounce the conquest of power means voluntarily to leave the power with those who have it, i.e. the exploiters. The essence of every revolution consisted and consists in the fact that it puts a new class in power and thus gives it the opportunity to realise its own programme. It is impossible to lead the masses towards insurrection without preparing for the conquest of power. No one could have hindered the Anarchists after the conquest of power from establishing such a regime as they consider necessary, if, of course, their programme is realisable. But the Anarchist leaders themselves lost belief in this. They hid from power not because they are against "every kind of dictatorship"—in actuality, grumbling and whining, they supported and support the dictatorship of Negrín-Stalin— but because they completely lost their principles and courage, if in general they had ever possessed them. They were afraid of Stalin. They were afraid of Negrín. They were afraid of France and England. More than anything did these phrasemongers fear the revolutionary masses.

The renunciation of conquest of power throws every workers' organisation into the mire of reformism and turns it into a plaything of the bourgeoisie: it cannot be otherwise in view of the class structure of society. To oppose the aim: the conquest of power, the anarchists could not in the end fail to be against the means: the revolution. The leaders of the CNT and FAI helped the bourgeoisie not only to hold on to the shadow of power in July 1936, but to re-establish bit by bit what it had lost at one stroke. In May 1937, they sabotaged the uprising of the workers and by that token saved the dictatorship of the bourgeoisie. Thus anarchism, which wished to be anti- political, proved in reality to be anti-revolutionary, and in the more critical moments—counterrevolutionary.

The Anarchist theoreticians, who after the great test of 1931–37, repeat the old reactionary nonsense about Kronstadt and affirm: "Stalinism is the inevitable result of Marxism and Bolshevism," simply demonstrate by this that they are forever dead for the revolution. You say that Marxism is in itself depraved and Stalinism is its legitimate progeny? But why do we, revolutionary Marxists, find ourselves in mortal combat with Stalinism throughout the world? Why does the Stalinist gang see in Trotskyism its chief enemy? Why does every approach to our view or to our methods of action (Durruti, Andrés Nin, Landau, and others) compel the gangsters of Stalinism to resort to bloody reprisals? Why, on the other hand, were the leaders of Spanish anarchism, during the time of the Moscow and Madrid crimes of the GPU, ministers under Caballero-Negrín, i.e., servants of the bourgeoisie and Stalin? Why, even now, under the pretext of fighting fascism, do the

Anarchists remain voluntary captives of Stalin-Negrín, i.e., of the executioners of the revolution, who have demonstrated their incapacity to fight fascism?

The lawyers of anarchism, hiding behind Kronstadt and Makhno, will deceive nobody. In the Kronstadt episode and in the struggle with Makhno we defended the proletarian revolution from the peasant counterrevolution. The Spanish Anarchists defended and defend bourgeois counterrevolution from the proletarian revolution. No kind of sophism will erase from history the fact that anarchism and Stalinism in the Spanish revolution were on one side of the barricades, and the working masses with the revolutionary Marxists—on the other. Such is the truth which will forever remain in the consciousness of the proletariat!

The role of the POUM

Not much better is the record of the POUM. Theoretically it tried, it is true, to base itself on the formula of the permanent revolution (that is why the Stalinists called the POUMists Trotskyists).

But a revolution is not satisfied with theoretical avowals. Instead of mobilising the masses against the reformist leaders, including the Anarchists, the POUM tried to convince these gentlemen of the advantage of socialism over capitalism. On such a pitch pipe were tuned all the articles and speeches of the leaders of the POUM. In order not to quarrel with the Anarchist leaders, they did not build up their nuclei, and in general did not conduct any kind of work inside the CNT. Evading sharp conflicts, they did not carry on revolutionary work in the republican army. Instead of this they built "their own" trade unions and "their own" militia which guarded "their own" buildings or occupied "their own" part of the front. Isolating the revolutionary vanguard from the class, the POUM weakened the vanguard and left the class without leadership. Politically, the POUM remained throughout immeasurably nearer to the People's Front, whose left wing it covered, than to Bolshevism. If the POUM nevertheless fell victim to bloody and base repression, it was because the People's Front could not fulfil its mission of stifling the socialist revolution except by cutting off, piece by piece, its own left flank.

Despite its intentions, the POUM proved to be, in the final analysis, the chief obstacle on the road to the creation of a revolutionary party. The platonic or diplomatic defenders of the Fourth International who, like the leader of the Dutch Revolutionary Socialist Party, Sneevliet, demonstratively supported the POUM in its halfway measures, indecisiveness, evasiveness, in a word, in its centrism, took upon themselves the greatest responsibility. Revolution does not tolerate centrism. Revolution exposes and crushes centrism. In passing, it compromises the friends and lawyers of centrism. That is one of the chief lessons of the Spanish revolution.

The problem of arming

The Socialists and Anarchists who tried to justify their capitulation to Stalin by the necessity of paying for the Moscow arms with principles and conscience simply lie and lie unskillfully. Of course, many of them would prefer to disentangle themselves without murders and frame-ups. But every aim demands corresponding means. Beginning with April 1931, i.e., long before the military intervention of Moscow, the Socialists and Anarchists did what they could to throttle the proletarian revolution. Stalin taught them how to carry this work to a conclusion. They became criminal accomplices of Stalin only because they were his political co-thinkers.

If the leaders of the Anarchists had resembled revolutionists at all, they would have answered the first blackmail from Moscow not only by continuing the socialist advance, but by disclosing Stalin's counterrevolutionary conditions before the working class of the world. Thus they would have forced the Moscow bureaucracy to choose openly between socialist revolution and the dictatorship of Franco. The Thermidorean bureaucracy fears and hates revolution. But it also fears to be stifled in a fascist ring. Besides this it depends on the workers. Everything speaks for the fact that Moscow would have been forced to supply arms and, possibly, at a more reasonable price.

But the world is not limited to Stalinist Moscow. During a year and a half of civil war, the Spanish war industry could and should have been strengthened and developed, adapting a series of non-military factories to the purposes of war. This work was not carried out only because Stalin—and equally with him his Spanish allies—feared the initiative of the workers' organisations. A strong military industry would have become a powerful instrument in the hands of the workers. The leaders of the People's Front preferred dependence upon Moscow.

It is precisely on this question that the perfidious role of the "People's Front" was strikingly exposed; it thrust upon the workers' organisations the responsibility for the treacherous agreement of the bourgeoisie with Stalin. So long as the Anarchists were in the minority they could not, of course, immediately hinder the ruling bloc from assuming whatever obligations they pleased toward Moscow and the masters of Moscow: London and Paris. But they could and they should have, without ceasing to be the best fighters on the front, openly kept clear from the betrayals and betrayers; explained the real situation to the masses; mobilised them against the bourgeois government; [and] increased the forces from day to day in order in the end to conquer power and with it the Moscow arms.

And what if Moscow, in the absence of a People's Front, should in general refuse to give arms? And what, we answer to this, if the Soviet Union in general did not exist in the world? Revolutions have been victorious up to this time not at all thanks to great foreign patrons who supplied them with arms. Usually the counterrevolution enjoyed foreign patronage. Must we recall the experience of the intervention of French, English, American, Japanese, and other armies against the Soviets? The proletariat of Russia won over inner reaction and foreign intervention without military support from the outside. Revolutions succeed, in the first place, with the help of a bold social programme which gives to the masses the possibility of seizing weapons that are on their territory, and disorganising the army of the enemy. The Red Army seized French, English and American military provisions and drove the foreign expeditionary corps into the sea. Has this really been forgotten already?

If, at the head of the armed workers and peasants, i.e., at the head of the so-called "republican" Spain, there were revolutionists and not cowardly agents of the bourgeoisie, the problem of arming would in general not have played a paramount role. The army of Franco, including the colonial Riffs and soldiers of Mussolini, are not at all immune to revolutionary contagion. Surrounded from all sides by the fire of the socialist uprising, the soldiers of fascism would have proved to be an insignificant quantity. Not arms and not military "geniuses" were lacking in Madrid and Barcelona; what was lacking was a revolutionary party!

The conditions for victory

The conditions for victory of the masses in a civil war against the army of exploiters in essence are very simple.

1. The fighters of a revolutionary army should clearly be aware of the fact that they are fighting for their full social liberation and not for the re-establishment of the old ("democratic") forms of exploitation.

2. The workers and peasants in the rear of the revolutionary army, as well as in the rear of the enemy, should know and understand the same thing.

3. The propaganda of their own front, as well as on the front of the adversary and in both rears, should be completely permeated with the spirit of social revolution. The slogan: "First victory, then reforms," is the slogan of all oppressors and exploiters beginning with the Biblical kings and ending with Stalin.

4. Those classes and strata who participate in the struggle determine the policy. The revolutionary masses should have a government apparatus directly and immediately expressing their will. Only the soviets of workers', soldiers' and peasants' deputies can act as such an apparatus.

5. The revolutionary army should not only announce but immediately carry out the more pressing measures of social revolution in the provinces won by them: the expropriation of provisions, manufactured articles and other stores on hand and transferring them to the needy; the redivision of lodgings in the interests of the toilers and especially of the families of the fighters; the expropriation of the land and landowners' inventory in the interests of the peasants; the establishment of workers' control and of the soviet power in place of the former bureaucracy.

6. Enemies of the socialist revolution, i.e., exploiting elements and their agents, even when covering themselves with the mask of "democrats," "republicans," "socialists" and "anarchists," should be mercilessly driven out from the army.

7. At the head of each military unit there should stand a commissar possessing the irreproachable authority of a revolutionist and a warrior.

8. In every military unit there should be a tempered nucleus of the more self-sacrificing fighters, recommended by the workers' organisations. The members of this nucleus have but one privilege: to be the first under fire.

9. The commanding corps of necessity includes at first many alien and unreliable elements in its staff. A verification and selection of them should be carried through on the basis of military experience, the recommendations of the commissar, and testimonials from the rank-and-file fighters. Simultaneously there should proceed an intense preparation of commanders drawn from the ranks of the revolutionary workers.

10. The strategy of civil war should unite the rules of military art with the tasks of the social revolution. Not only in the propaganda but in the military operations it is necessary to take into account the social composition of the different military units of the opponent (the bourgeois volunteers, the mobilised peasants, or as with Franco, the colonial slaves), and in choosing an operative line, to

take into consideration the social structure of the corresponding regions of the land (the industrial regions; the peasant regions, revolutionary or reactionary; the regions of the oppressed nationalities, etc.). Briefly: revolutionary policy dominates strategy.

11. The revolutionary government, as the executive committee of the workers and peasants, should be capable of winning full confidence of the army and of the toiling population.

12. The foreign policy should have as its chief aim the awakening of the revolutionary consciousness of the workers, the exploited peasants, and oppressed nationalities of the whole world.

Stalin guaranteed the conditions of defeat

The conditions for victory, as we see, are quite simple. In their aggregate they are called the socialist revolution. There did not exist in Spain even one of these conditions. The basic reason is that there was not a revolutionary party. Stalin tried, it is true, to transfer to the soil of Spain, the outer forms of Bolshevism; the Politburo, commissar, nuclei, the GPU, etc. But he emptied these forms of their social content. He renounced the Bolshevik programme and with it the soviets as the necessary form of the revolutionary initiative of the masses. He placed the techniques of Bolshevism at the service of bourgeois property. In his bureaucratic limitedness he imagined that the "commissars" by themselves could guarantee victory. But the commissars of private property proved capable only of guaranteeing defeat.

The Spanish proletariat displayed first-class military capacities. In its specific gravity in the economy of the country, in its political and cultural level, it stood in the first day of the revolution not lower but higher than the Russian proletariat at the beginning of 1917. On the road to its victory, its own organisations stood as the chief obstacles. The commanding clique of the Stalinists, in accordance with its counterrevolutionary function, consisted of the hired agents, careerists, declassed elements, and, in general, every kind of social refuse. The representatives of other workers' organisations—flabby reformists, anarchist phrasemongers, helpless centrists of the POUM—grumbled, groaned, wavered, maneuvered, but in the end adapted themselves to the Stalinists. As a result of their aggregate work, the camp of social revolution—workers and peasants—proved to be subordinated to the bourgeoisie, more correctly to its shadow, void of individuality, spirit, life. There was no lack of heroism on the part of the masses and courage on the part of individual revolutionists. But the masses were left to themselves and the revolutionists remained disunited, without programme, without plan of action. The "republican" military commanders occupied themselves more with crushing the social revolution than with winning military victories. The soldiers lost confidence in their commanders, the masses—in the government; the peasants stepped aside; the workers got tired; defeat followed defeat; the demoralisation grew. All this was not difficult to foresee from the beginning of the civil war. Taking as its task the rescue of the capitalist regime, the People's Front doomed itself to military defeat. Having turned Bolshevism on its head, Stalin, with full success, played the role of the grave digger of the revolution.

Incidentally, the Spanish experience again demonstrates that Stalin did not understand either the October Revolution or the Civil War. His sluggish provincial thought lagged hopelessly behind the tempestuous course of events in 1917–21. In those of his speeches and articles in 1917 where he expressed his own thought, his later Thermidorean "doctrine" was fully lodged. In this sense, Stalin in Spain in 1937 is the Stalin of the March conference of the Bolsheviks in 1917. But in 1917 he merely feared the revolutionary workers; in 1937 he throttled them. The opportunist became the executioner.

"Civil war in the rear"

"But for victory over the governments of Caballero and Negrín, a civil war would be necessary in the rear of the Republican army!"—the democratic Philistine exclaims with horror. As if in Republican Spain, even without this, no civil war ever existed, and at that the base and most ignominious one, a war of the owners and exploiters against the workers and peasants. This uninterrupted war finds expression in the arrests and murders of revolutionists, the crushing of the mass movement, the disarming of the workers, the arming of the bourgeois police, the abandoning of workers' detachments without arms and without help on the front, finally, in the artificial impeding of the development of the military industry. Each of these acts represents a severe blow to the front, direct military treason, directed by the class interests of the bourgeoisie. However, the "democratic" Philistines— including the Stalinists, Socialists, and Anarchists—regard the civil war of the bourgeoisie against the proletariat, even in the immediate rear of the front, as the natural and inevitable war, having as its task the safeguarding of the unity of the "People's Front." On the other hand, the civil war of the proletariat against the "republican" counterrevolution is, in the eyes of the same Philistines, a criminal, Fascist, Trotskyist war, breaking up…"the unity of the anti-fascist forces." Dozens of Norman Thomases, Major Atlees, Otto Bauers, Zyromskys, Malraux, and petty traders of lies like Duranty and Louis Fischer spread their slavish wisdom along the face of the earth. At the same time the government of the "People's Front" moves from Madrid to Valencia, from Valencia—to Barcelona.

If, as facts bear witness, only the socialist revolution is capable of crushing fascism, then on the other hand a successful uprising of the proletariat is conceivable only when the ruling classes are caught in the grip of the greatest difficulties. However, the democratic Philistines invoke exactly these difficulties as proof of the impermissibility of the proletarian uprising. If the worker waited until the democratic Philistines showed him the hour of his liberation, he would forever remain a slave. To teach the workers to recognise reactionary Philistines under all their masks and to despise them independently of these masks is the first and chief duty of a revolutionist!

The denouement

The dictatorship of the Stalinists over the republican camp is in its essence not long-lived. If the defeats conditioned by the politics of the People's Front will once more launch the Spanish proletariat into a revolutionary assault, this time successfully, the Stalinist clique will be swept aside with an iron broom. If, as is unfortunately more probable, Stalin will succeed in bringing the work of a grave digger of the revolution to its conclusion, he will not even in this case earn thanks. The Spanish bourgeoisie needed him as an executioner, but he is not at all necessary to it as a patron and a tutor. London and Paris on the one hand, and Berlin and Rome on the other, are in its eyes considerably more stable firms than Moscow. It is possible that Stalin himself wants to cover his tracks in Spain before the final catastrophe; he thus hopes to put the responsibility for the defeat on his closest allies. After this, Litvinov will plead with Franco for the re-establishment of diplomatic relations. All this we have seen more than once.

However, even a full military victory of the so-called republican camp over General Franco would not signify the triumph of "democracy." The workers and peasants twice placed the bourgeois republicans and their left agents in power: in April 1931 and in February 1936. Both times the heroes of the People's Front ceded the victory of the people to the more reactionary and more serious representatives of the bourgeoisie. The third victory, gained by the generals of the People's Front, will signify their inevitable agreement with the fascist bourgeoisie on the backs of the workers and peasants. Such a regime will be but a different form of a military dictatorship, perhaps without monarchy and without an openly dominating Catholic Church.

Finally, it is possible that the partial victories of the republicans will be utilized by the "disinterested" Anglo-French intermediaries in order to reconcile the fighting camps. It is not difficult to understand that in the case of this variant the final remnants of the democracy will prove to be stifled in the fraternal embrace of the generals Miaja (Communist!) and Franco (fascist!). Once again: victory will go either to the socialist revolution, or to fascism.

It is not excluded, incidentally, that tragedy will yet at the last moment give place to farce. When the heroes of the People's Front have to desert their last capital they will, before embarking on steamers and airplanes, perhaps announce a series of "socialist" reforms in order to leave a "good memory" with the people. Nothing will help them. The workers of the whole world will remember with hatred and scorn the parties that ruined the heroic revolution.

The tragic experience of Spain is a threatening—perhaps the last warning before still greater events—addressed to all the advanced workers of the world. "Revolutions," according to the words of Marx, "are the locomotives of history." They move faster than the thought of half-revolutionary or quarter-revolutionary parties. Whoever lingers falls under the wheels of the locomotive, whereby—and this is the chief danger—the locomotive itself is also not infrequently wrecked. It is necessary to adapt policy to the basic laws of the revolution, i.e., to the movement of the classes in conflict and not the prejudices and fears of the superficial petty-bourgeois groups who call themselves "people's" and all kinds of other fronts. The line of least resistance proves in a revolution to be the line of greatest disaster. The fear of "isolation" from the bourgeoisie means isolation from the masses. Adaptation to the conservative prejudices of the workers' aristocracy signifies the betrayal of the workers and the revolution. A superfluity of "cautiousness" is the most baneful rashness. Such is the chief lesson of the destruction of the most honest political organisation in Spain, that is, the centrist POUM. The parties and groups of the London Bureau evidently do not wish or are not capable of drawing the necessary conclusions from the last warning of history. By this token they doom themselves to catastrophe.

But then a new generation of revolutionists is now being educated by the lessons of the defeats. It has in action verified the base reputation of the Second International. It has learned how to judge the Anarchists not by their words but by their actions. It is a great inestimable school, paid for with the blood of innumerable fighters! The revolutionary cadres now gather under the banner of the Fourth International. Born amid great defeats, it will lead the toilers to victory.

Coyoacán, Mexico, 17th December 1937

Trotsky's "The Class, the Party, and the Leadership"

Graeme Anfinson

The Spanish Revolution is in many ways a how-to guide for how *not* to take power and implement a revolutionary workers' democracy. Actually, it was studying the Spanish Revolution that convinced me personally that revolutionary Marxism was correct, and that revolutionary anarchism—at least in practice—didn't actually exist.

As we know, the Spanish Revolution failed, and we saw fascist reaction not only gain control of Spain, but ultimately most of Europe. So why did the Spanish Revolution fail? Was this a failure of leadership, or were the workers simply not "mature" enough to carry through a revolution?

In his posthumously published article, "The Class, the Party, and the Leadership,"[1] Russian revolutionary Leon Trotsky answers that question by politically body-slamming the editors of *Que Faire* ("What To Do"), which was a left-leaning bourgeois intellectual paper published in Paris in the late 1930s. It is interesting that Trotsky made sure to write that the paper itself was of no importance, i.e., it wasn't going to do much other than give a few left liberal types a venue to write their muddle to share amongst themselves (we can draw numerous parallels with this today!). However, he found the piece to be of "symptomatic interest." In other words, it was characteristic of the reasons given by those who Trotsky called "pseudo-Marxists" for the failure of the Spanish Revolution.

The beginning of the document starts with a quote from *Que Faire*'s review of a pamphlet entitled *Spain Betrayed*,[2] by Casanova (which was the pen name of a Polish Marxist named Bernstein who was in Spain during the revolution). At first glance, they might appear to be offering an interesting criticism of Casanova's argument that the leadership of the Communist Party in Spain followed the wrong policy. But at root, *Que Faire* argues that the workers simply weren't ready for a revolution, and reject those like Casanova

---

1 An online version may be found here: http://www.marxists.org/archive/trotsky/1940/xx/party.htm
2 An online version may be found here: http://www.marxists.org/history/etol/document/spain2/index.htm

who blame bogeymen like Stalin and inept anarchist leaders in order to explain the workers' failure. The following is taken from *Que Faire*'s criticism of Casanova's analysis (quoted in Trotsky's article):

> "Why was the revolution crushed? "Because," replies the author [Casanova], "the Communist Party conducted a false policy which was unfortunately followed by the revolutionary masses." But why, in the devil's name, did the revolutionary masses who left their former leaders rally to the banner of the Communist Party? "Because there was no genuinely revolutionary party." We are presented with a pure tautology. A false policy of the masses; an immature party either manifests a certain condition of social forces (immaturity of the working class, lack of independence of the peasantry) which must be explained by proceeding from facts, presented among others by Casanova himself; or it is the product of the actions of certain malicious individuals or groups of individuals, actions which do not correspond to the efforts of "sincere individuals" alone capable of saving the revolution. After groping for the first and Marxist road, Casanova takes the second. We are ushered into the domain of pure demonology; the criminal responsible for the defeat is the chief Devil, Stalin, abetted by the anarchists and all the other little devils; the God of revolutionists unfortunately did not send a Lenin or a Trotsky to Spain as He did in Russia in 1917."[3]

Under closer examination, however, we see that *Que Faire*'s criticism is nothing but empty rhetoric. (It is quite ironic they refer to Casanova's central argument as a "tautology"!) Why were the workers not ready for revolution? Because the revolution failed. Why did the revolution fail? Because the workers were not ready for the revolution. In the end, we are left no closer to understanding what happened in Spain than when we started.

Trotsky then masterfully lays out an exposition of a truly dialectical approach to questions such as this. He gives concrete examples of the "immature" workers being correct and their leadership being wrong. Trotsky writes:

> "In July 1936...the Spanish workers repelled the assault of the officers who had prepared their conspiracy under the protection of the Popular Front. The masses improvised militias and created workers' committees, the strongholds of their future dictatorship. The leading organisations of the proletariat, on the other hand, helped the bourgeoisie to destroy these committees, to liquidate the assaults of the workers on private property, and to subordinate the workers' militias to the command of the bourgeoisie, with the POUM moreover participating in the government and assuming direct responsibility for this work of the counterrevolution."[4]

---

3 Trotsky, *The Spanish Revolution (1931–39)* (New York: Pathfinder, 1973), 354–55.
4 Ibid., 356.

Trotsky points out—which I think is extremely important and interesting given this is still a belief held by many anarchists—that the beginning logic of the "the workers aren't ready" argument is that there will *eventually* come a point when the workers will be so ready that they won't need any sort of leadership. They will simply wake up one day and decide to take power. When and how this develops under capitalism is left unsaid. I suppose we can assume it is done mainly by reading periodicals such as *Que Faire?*

Trotsky anticipates the question of "why would the workers subordinate themselves to poor leadership?" and answers it with more concrete examples of the workers not at all being subordinate to their leadership, and in some cases actively fighting against it. He brings up the well-known fact that the CNT leadership actually refused to take power, and then bragged about it on several occasions. This most certainly wasn't the wish of the masses who fought, and often died, for such power. Unfortunately, the Spanish workers were unable, in the middle of a civil war, to produce new leadership that corresponded to the demands of the revolution. Not just the Stalinists and anarchists, but also the POUM.[5]

To fully answer the subordination question, we also need to examine the old myth that "people get the government they deserve." To the social-evolutionist liberals, society moves in a straight line from despotism to "freedom"—by which they mean bourgeois parliamentarism. Trotsky takes this on quite well and I think it is worth quoting at length. He says:

> "The secret is that a people is comprised of hostile classes, and the classes themselves are comprised of different and in part antagonistic layers that fall under different leadership; furthermore every people falls under the influence of other peoples who are likewise comprised of classes. Governments do not express the systematically growing "maturity" of a "people" but are the product of the struggle between different classes and the different layers within one and the same class, and, finally, the action of external forces— alliances, conflicts, wars, and so on. To this should be added that a government, once it has established itself, may endure much longer than the relationship of forces which produced it. It is precisely out of this historical contradiction that revolutions, coups d'état, counterrevolutions, etc., arise."[6]

This same dialectical approach is needed when dealing with leadership. Again from the text:

---

5 POUM—*Partido Obrero de Unificación Marixista* (Workers' Party of Marxist Unification.) A left party formed by fusion in 1935 that vacillated between reformism and revolution. Led by Andrés Nin, a former secretary of the Comintern's Red International of Labour Unions, and a leader of the former Left Opposition forces in Spain.

6 Trotsky, 357–58.

"A leadership is shaped in the process of clashes between the different classes or the friction between the different layers within a given class. Having once arisen, the leadership invariably arises above its class and thereby becomes predisposed to the pressure and influence of other classes. The proletariat may "tolerate" for a long time a leadership that has already suffered a complete inner degeneration but has not as yet had the opportunity to express this degeneration amid great events.

"A great historic shock is necessary to reveal sharply the contradiction between the leadership and the class. The mightiest historical shocks are wars and revolutions. Precisely for this reason the working class is often caught unawares by war and revolution. But even in cases where the old leadership has revealed its internal corruption, the class cannot immediately improvise a new leadership, especially if it has not inherited from the previous period strong revolutionary cadres capable of utilizing the collapse of the old leading party."[7]

In Spain, the working class was able to move far beyond their leadership, yet they were not able to actually replace them.

As we can see by the example of the Russian working class, workers' "maturity" is not unchanging. In the Bolshevik Party at the beginning of 1917, it was basically just Lenin who had a truly revolutionary understanding of the moment. Many of the other Bolsheviks were scattered around and not sure what move to take next. Many even supported Kerensky's Provisional Government. This highlights exactly how important it is to have a revolutionary leadership during revolutionary times. The maturity of workers is relative to the situation and can change rapidly. The same Russian working class that overthrew the tsar also "allowed" a bureaucracy to rise from within its ranks and betray the revolution.

Que Faire goes on to ask why the revolutionary masses, who left their former leaders, now decided to follow the Communist Party. Trotsky points out this is a falsely posed question. They rallied around the Communist Party and its popular front strategy largely because of the authority the Comintern had gained by carrying out the only successful workers' revolution, in Russia. It isn't as simple as the working class going "window shopping" for new leadership. Tradition and loyalty play a large role in the decision. It is only through their experiences that workers move to new leadership, and new revolutionary parties can grow very rapidly given the right circumstance mixed with the right policies.

The leaders of the POUM—as the party to the left not linked to anarchism or Stalinism—refused to reveal the bourgeois nature of the other parties and of the Popular Front. This was the only way to move the

7 Ibid., 358.

POUM and the revolution forward, but they refused to do it. Trotsky noted of the POUM, "It participated in the 'Popular' election bloc; entered the government which liquidated workers' committees; engaged in a struggle to reconstitute this governmental coalition; capitulated time and again to the Anarchist leadership; conducted, in connection with this, a false trade union policy; and took a vacillating and non-revolutionary attitude toward the May 1937 uprising."[8]

This, however, isn't simply a reflection of the Spanish working class; it is a reflection of concrete events and of the dialectical manner in which revolutions unfold and develop. The working class was far more revolutionary than the POUM, which in turn was more revolutionary than the bourgeois leadership they subordinated themselves to. Why did the POUM leadership subordinate itself to the leadership of the bourgeois state? As we can see, the leadership had risen above its class and was subject to pressures of other classes. When the degeneration of the POUM leadership became known, the working class, in the middle of a revolutionary struggle, was unable to replace them before the counterrevolution got the upper hand.

It is clear that the central point the folks at *Que Faire* were trying to make is that the workers simply weren't ready for a revolution. We can see similar arguments today in places like Venezuela, where despite the masses being far more revolutionary than their leaders, many academics have blamed the slow pace of the revolution on the "maturity" level of the workers. We also see shades of this in the United States, as cynical liberals berate workers for being "stupid" and "backwards." The left sects abandon mainstream unions because of their poor leadership, and some question whether developed economies even have workers!

This is why we study things like the Spanish Revolution, as events today take such a similar course. The folks at *Que Faire* liked to think they were Marxists, and they did that by throwing in phrases like "condition of class forces" and "condition of social forces." This, they thought, gave them a material basis for claiming the workers simply weren't ready for a revolution. The same goes for countless organisations today—all more or less ignored by your average person. Trotsky addresses this with extreme clarity by saying, "Naturally, the 'condition of class forces' supplies the foundation for all other political factors; but just as the foundation of a building does not reduce the importance of walls, windows, doors, roofs, so the 'condition of classes' does not invalidate the importance of parties, their strategy, their leadership."[9]

Que Faire and their present-day equivalents won't tell us how we will know when the working class will be "ready" for revolution. Presumably, someday,

8 Ibid., 363.
9 Ibid., 364.

off in the distant future, we will all just wake up and spontaneously decide to take power; a divine rapture of sorts. This theory has been proven to be absolutely ridiculous. We can and must learn from the tragedy of the Spanish Revolution. Far from leaving things to chance or spontaneity, we must work to build a political leadership that can directly confront the bourgeois state when revolutionary situations inevitably arise in the years ahead.

To some, and especially to the anarchists, this may seem a contradiction: to organise the working class for state power. But understanding contradictions is central to achieving, and wielding, power. You cannot merely "ignore" power; we must build a new kind of power, one that represents the interests of the working majority, not an unelected and unaccountable minority. In short, the answer to bad leadership is not no leadership. We must work to build a democratically accountable leadership that can lead our class to victory and end class exploitation once and for all. That's the kind of leadership the world working class needs and deserves.

January 2012

Name Index

Albert, Michael viii, 145–80

Alcalá Zamora, Niceto 305

Allier, Raoul 76

Arshinov, Peter 294

Aveling, Eleanor Marx 17–18

Avrich, Paul 8–9, 11–13

Azaña, Manuel 304, 306

Bakunin, Mikhail viii, xx, 10, 13–14, 47–59, 68–71, 81–97, 101, 103–04, 108, 113–16, 118–27, 130, 132, 141, 195, 228

Banks, Theodore H. 110

Bebel, August 81, 91, 95, 126

Becker, Bernhard 102

Becker, Philipp 87–88

Beesly, Edward 93

Berger, Victor 259

Berkman, Alexander 277

Bismarck, Otto von 93, 95, 104, 114–17

Blanc, Louis 40

Blanqui, Louis Auguste

121, 126–27, 132

Bolte, Friedrich 83, 85–86, 107, 115

Bonaparte, Napolean 148

Brandler, Heinrich 221, 240

Brenton, Maurice 159

Bukharin, Nikolai xxvii, 227, 240–41

Caballero, Francisco Largo 304–06, 309, 315

Cabet, Étienne 40

Cachin, Marcel 223, 225–27

Cafiero, Carlo 97, 104–05

Cannon, James P. xv

Castro, Fidel 164

Chambelland, Colette 234

Chaudey 47

Chomsky, Noam viii, 145, 180

Churchill, Winston 191

Claflin, Tennessee 106

Cohn-Bendit, Daniel Marc and Gabriel 157–58

Companys, Lluís xxii,

278, 304–06

Condorcet, Marquis de 19

Copernicus, Nicolaus 25

Crescio, Prospero 94

Cromwell, Oliver 164

Danielson, Nikolai 103, 122, 124

De Leon, Daniel xiv

Denikin, Anton 9, 267, 276, 286, 293–94

Desgranges, Pierre 77

d'Holbach, Baron 18, 21

Dimitrov, Georgi 302

Dmitriev, S.H. 288

Dühring, Eugen 5–6

Dumoulin (Kunstlinger, Henri) 212, 233–34, 236–37, 240

Durruti, Buenaventura viii, xxiii, 309

Eastman, Max xv, 269, 286

Eccarius, Johann 127–31

Eisenstein, Sergei 147

Engels, Frederick xxviii–xxxi, xxxiii, 5–6, 18, 25, 33, 81, 83–84,

Revolutionary History from Wellred Books

REVOLUTION AND COUNTER-REVOLUTION IN SPAIN
By Felix Morrow

Published 2012
Paperback
Pages: 295
ISBN: 978 1 900007 43 6

Felix Morrow's book, written in the white heat of the struggle, remains a Marxist classic on the Spanish Civil War. The 1930s was a period of revolution and counter-revolution in which Spain was at the very epicentre of events.

GERMANY: FROM REVOLUTION TO COUNTER-REVOLUTION
By Rob Sewell

Published 2014
Paperback
142 Pages
ISBN: 978 1 900 007 51 1

From 1918 to 1933 revolution and counter-revolution followed hot on each others' heels. The barbarity of the Nazis is well-documented. Rob Sewell gives a picture of the less well-known, tumultuous events that preceded Hitler's rise to power.

REVOLUTION UNTIL VICTORY!
By Alan Woods, Jorge Martin and Others

Published 2011
Paperback
252 Pages
ISBN: 978 1 900 007 40 5

The Arab Revolution represents a turning point in world history. The present volume is a selection of articles on the revolutions in Arab countries published on Marxist.com from January to March 2011.

Order online at www.wellredbooks.net
or send orders to PO Box 50525, London E14 6WG, United Kingdom.

Marxist Theory from Wellred Books

THE CLASSICS OF MARXISM VOLUME ONE
MARX, ENGELS, LENIN AND TROTSKY

Published 2013
Paperback
225 Pages
ISBN: 978 1 900 007 49 8

Now for the first time, The Communist Manifesto,
Socialism: Utopian and Scientific, The State and Revolution, and The
Transitional Programare available in a single, compact volume.

ANTI-DÜHRING
BY FREDERICK ENGELS

Published 2011
Paperback
365 Pages
ISBN: 978 1 900 007 39 9

This book was recommended by Lenin as a "text book"
of scientific socialism. The book is a polemic by Frederick
Engels against a German revisionist, Eugen Dühring.

IN DEFENCE OF MARXISM
BY LEON TROTSKY

Publication Date: 2010
Paperback
263 Pages
ISBN: 978 1 900 007 37 5

A product of a sharp polemic within the American Trotskyist movement in
the period 1939-40, this book touches the very fundamentals of Marxism in
Trotsky's series of articles and letters which answer the questions of the dispute.

More Titles from Wellred Books

The History of the Russian Revolution: Volumes 1-3

by Leon Trotsky

Bolshevism: The Road to Revolution

by Alan Woods

Ted Grant Writings: Volumes 1-2

by Ted Grant

Reason in Revolt

by Alan Woods and Ted Grant

Reformism and Revolution

by Alan Woods

Kashmir's Ordeal

by Lal Khan

Dialectics of Nature

by Frederick Engels

Go to www.wellredbooks.net for more!

Wellred Books is the bookshop and publishing house of the International Marxist Tendency.

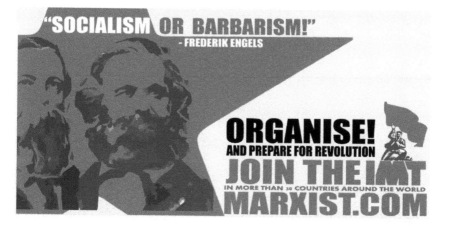

Lightning Source UK Ltd.
Milton Keynes UK
UKHW021028191019
351913UK00011B/233/P